Principles of Contract Law

Fourth Edition

Cavendish
Publishing
Limited

London • Sydney

Principles of Contract Law

Fourth Edition

Professor Richard Stone, LLB, LLM
Inns of Court School of Law

Cavendish
Publishing
Limited

London • Sydney

Fourth edition first published in Great Britain 2000 by Cavendish Publishing Limited, The Glass House, Wharton Street, London WC1X 9PX.

Telephone: +44 (0) 20 7278 8000   Facsimile: +44 (0) 20 7278 8080

E-mail: info@cavendishpublishing.com

Visit our Home Page on http://www.cavendishpublishing.com

This title was previously published under the Lecture Notes series.

© Stone, R   2000
First edition   1994
Second edition 1996
Third edition   1997
Fourth edition 2000

Stone, Richard, 1951–
Principles of contract law – 4th edn (Principles of law series)
1. Contracts – England 2. Contracts – Wales
I. Title II. Contract law
346.4'2'02

ISBN 1 85941 579 2

Printed and bound in Great Britain

PREFACE

Although the law of contract is often studied early in the law student's career, it is not in fact a simple subject. There are complexities in the analysis of the basis of contractual obligations, and in many of the areas which are regarded as fundamental, such as the doctrines of consideration and privity, which create difficulties of understanding for the novice. In addition, there are other areas, such as mistake, where the case law is confusing and inconsistent, or where the relationship between common law and equity (for example, in relation to estoppel), or common law and statute (for example, in relation to exclusion clauses), requires careful analysis. The temptation in writing a book such as this, which is intended as a straightforward readable guide to the English law of contract, is to gloss over these difficulties, or to simplify them out of existence. This is a trap which I have tried to avoid. My object has been, based on nearly 25 years of teaching contract law both to first year LLB students, and to non-law students, to explain the subject in a way which is easy to understand, but which nevertheless gives the student some idea that the 'orthodox' analysis is not necessarily the only possible one, and the subject has depths which (for those who have the opportunity to do so) will repay further study, beyond the demands of the first year examination. The very positive reaction which the first three editions have received from both students and lecturers encourages me to think that I may have achieved some success in this objective.

The main changes in this edition are those of updating. The most significant development has been the coming into force of the Contracts (Rights of Third Parties) Act 1999. This has required the reorganisation and rewriting of a significant proportion of Chapter 5, to take account of this major change to the doctrine of privity. There has also been a considerable number of significant new cases. Among those requiring detailed consideration are *Royal Bank of Scotland v Etridge (No2)* (1997) on undue influence; *Edmonds v Lawson* (2000) dealing with intention and consideration in pupillage contracts; *Stevenson v Rogers* (1999) on the meaning of the phrase 'in the course of business' (casting doubt on the approach taken in *R and B Customs Brokers v UDT* (1998)); *Overseas Medical Supplies Ltd v Orient Transport Services Ltd* (1999) on the factors to be taken into account in assessing 'reasonableness' under UCTA; *Kleinwort Benson Ltd v Lincoln City Council* (1998), holding for the first time that there can be restitution for a mistake of law; and *Attorney General v Blake* (1998), opening up the possibility of damages to prevent unjust enrichment of the defendant, rather than to compensate the claimant.

One change of terminology introduced by the new Civil Procedure Rules in 1999 causes some difficulty. 'Plaintiffs' are now 'claimants'. The convention used here is to use the label which the student or other reader will find if looking up the case in the reports – that is, 'plaintiff' for cases decided under the old procedures and 'claimant' for those under the new. Where the word is used generically, rather than in relation to a particular case, then 'claimant' is used.

The subject areas covered are those of the standard contract syllabus. A chapter on restitution is included. This is a subject of increasing importance, as recognised by its recent inclusion amongst the topics required to be studied for the purposes of professional exemption. The coverage of agency and sale of goods (in Chapters 17 and 18) is more detailed than will be required by many contract courses, but it is hoped that these will be of particular help to those studying contract as part of business studies or accountancy courses.

The law has been stated, as far as possible, as it stood on 1 July 2000.

Richard Stone
Wood Green
July 2000

CONTENTS

Contents

TABLE OF CASES

Table of Cases

Table of Cases

Table of Cases

TABLE OF STATUTES

TABLE OF STATUTORY INSTRUMENTS

TABLE OF ABBREVIATIONS

MA	Misrepresentation Act 1967
MCA	Minors' Contracts Act 1987
LR(FC)A	Law Reform (Frustrated Contracts) Act 1943
SGA	Sale of Goods Act 1979
UCTA	Unfair Contract Terms Act 1977
UTCCR	Unfair Terms in Consumer Contracts Regulations 1999

CHAPTER 1

INTRODUCTION

This chapter deals with some preliminary issues which need discussion before embarking on a detailed consideration of the case law and statutes which make up the English law of contract. These issues are:

- the subject matter of contract law;
- different approaches to analysing contract; and
- the identification of agreements.

1.1 The subject matter of contract law

What is the law of contract about? This is a question to which, perhaps surprisingly, there is no clear, universally accepted answer. Some would argue that the law of contract is simply part of a wider law of 'obligations', which includes tort, and perhaps restitution, and that the boundaries between all three should not be treated as fixed. Others would argue that because there are now so many special rules applying to particular types of contract, such as sale of goods, hire purchase, employment, etc that to talk of a general 'law of contract' is unrealistic. At best one can discuss a law of 'contracts'.

1.1.2 Voluntary transactions

The approach of this book, however, is that there is still a sufficient area of generally applicable principles, which are in practice regarded by the courts as forming a distinct body of law, to justify the attempt to identify a 'law of contract'. Its subject matter is transactions under which people, more or less voluntarily, assume obligations towards each other, in connection with the transfer of property (including money), or the provision of services. The transactions are only 'more or less' voluntary since people have little real choice whether or not to enter into some contracts, for example, contracts to buy food or to obtain work. Even where there is a real choice in this sense, for example, as regards a decision to buy a new CD player, there is likely to be little choice about the terms on which the contract can be made. Large retail organisations are rarely prepared to enter into bargaining with a consumer. Nevertheless, it is only in very rare situations, for example, the compulsory purchase of property by central or local government, that people are forced into a contract which is clearly against their will. Indeed, to the extent that a transaction is not in any way regulated by agreement between the parties, it may be argued that it is not properly categorised as a contract. In *Norweb plc v*

Dixon (1995), for example, the view was taken that a supply of electricity to a consumer which was almost entirely regulated, both as to the creation of the relationship and its terms, by the Electricity Act 1989, could not be regarded as a contract. As a result, money owed by the consumer was not a 'contractual' debt. This decision was followed in *W v Essex CC* (1998) in relation to a fostering agreement which was closely regulated by regulations made under the Children Act 1989. As Stuart-Smith LJ in the Court of Appeal commented:

> If there is a statutory obligation to enter into a form of agreement the terms of which are laid down, at any rate in their most important respects, there is no contract.

We may therefore use the definition at the beginning of this paragraph, in terms of voluntary transactions, as a broad indication of the situations with which we are concerned. The rules of contract law help to determine which transactions will be enforced by the courts and on what terms. They also provide a framework of remedies, when contracts are broken.

Before leaving this point, it is important to remember that, to the extent that there is a 'general law of contract', it applies to all transactions within its scope. That is, the same general rules will apply to the purchase of a packet of sweets from a local newsagent, as to a multi-million pound deal between large international corporations.

1.2   Different approaches to analysing contract

The approach in this book is, for the most part, to analyse the law of contract within its own terms. In other words, the concentration will be on analysing the relevant cases and statutes, examining how contractual principles have developed through them, and critically appraising the end result. This does not mean that all issues of social and political context, or legal history should be ignored, but simply that the focus is on the law as it has emerged through decisions of the courts and legislation. This is sometimes referred to as 'doctrinal analysis', because it concentrates on legal doctrine.

1.2.1   Economic analysis

Other approaches are, of course, possible. Since contract is intimately linked with the commercial world, it is not surprising that attempts have been made to analyse it in terms of economics. Much of this work has originated in the United States (see, for example, Kronman and Posner, *Economics of Contract Law*, 1979, Little Brown). The approach is generally to try to criticise the rules of contract law in terms of their economic efficiency and consequences. To take a simple example, as regards consumer contracts, it may be thought desirable that producers of goods should be strictly liable for the quality of what they sell. If they are to be liable, however, they may need either to introduce strict quality control procedures, or to take out insurance. The costs of either of these two measures will almost certainly be added to the price of the goods. In economic terms, therefore, the cost of greater consumer protection is higher prices. Economic analysis also looks at 'transaction costs' (which may lead to the conclusion that standard form contracts are more economically efficient than those that are individually negotiated), and 'adjudication costs' (which may suggest that it is more economically efficient to have fixed rules of law, rather than leave it to judges to resolve disputes 'on their merits'). To take an example from later in the book, the decision of the House of Lords in the case of *Photo Production v Securicor* (1980) (see 8.4.3 below), upholding a very widely based clause excluding one of the parties from virtually all liability for breach of contract, might be analysed in economic terms as follows. First, it might be said to be based on an assumption that as between two parties, freely negotiating, they will have allocated responsibilities and risks in the most efficient way, and so will have 'maximised wealth'. Secondly, the refusal of the court to interfere in a bargain of this kind may discourage others from litigating, and therefore have the overall beneficial economic effect of reducing transaction costs.

1.2.2 Socio-political analysis

A further way of looking at the law of contract is from a socio-political standpoint. In fact, we all have some political assumptions in the background, even if we are looking at contract cases purely within their own terms. It is, for example, impossible to debate the merits of numerous contract principles without some notion of the value or otherwise of the idea of 'freedom of contract', which is, of course, a political concept. Some writers feel, however, that this political/ideological background, be it capitalist, Marxist, or whatever, should be made explicit. For example, Hugh Collins (*The Law of Contract*, 1st edn, 1986, Weidenfeld and Nicolson, p 1) stated:

> This book identifies the purpose of the law of contract as the channelling and regulation of market transactions according to ideals of social justice.

Another approach is to try to identify the ideologies which underpin the decision of the courts on contract issues. Adams and Brownsword (*Understanding Contract Law*, 2nd edn, 1994, Fontana) identify three competing ideologies which may be found in the cases. These are:

- formalism;
- consumer-welfarism;
- market-individualism.

1.2.3 Formalism

A court may be said to adopt a formalist approach if it feels obliged to follow rules established in earlier cases, even if it does not agree with them, or feels that they do not produce the most satisfactory result on the facts before the court. The case of *Foakes v Beer* (1884) (see 3.10 below) may be said to be an example of this type of approach, at least as far as some members of the House of Lords were concerned, in that they felt bound to follow what was regarded as an established rule that part payment of a debt could never discharge the debtor's liability for the balance, even if the creditor had promised to treat it as so doing.

1.2.4 Consumer-welfarism

'Consumer-welfarism', on the other hand, may operate where a court recognises that individuals may be in a weak position as regards dealings with large organisations, and that the rules of contract need, therefore, to be developed and applied so as to protect them. Examples of this type of approach would be *Carlill v Carbolic Smoke Ball Co* (1893) (see 2.3.5 below), where an advertiser was bound by a promise made to consumers who had relied on the advert; or the pre-1977 exclusion clause cases (see 8.3 below), where the courts devised rules to prevent large organisations from imposing wide clauses exempting them from liability to people who bought their products and services.

1.2.5 Market-individualism

A 'market-individualism' approach, on the other hand, gives freedom of contract the highest priority and leaves the parties to their bargain, even if it appears to operate harshly on one side. In this situation, the court adopts the role simply of 'referee', determining what obligations the parties must be taken to have agreed to, and then applying them to the situation. A case mentioned above in connection with the economic analysis, *Photo Productions v Securicor* (1980), is a good example of the court adopting this approach.

1.2.6 Empirical research

Finally, contract may be approached from the bottom rather than the top. In other words, instead of looking at decisions of the appellate courts, and the rules which they have developed, the focus could be on how contract law operates in people's day-to-day lives. Does the existence of a particular set of contractual rules affect the way in which people behave? Do businesses have contractual principles in mind when they enter into agreements? When things go wrong, to what extent does the law influence the way in which disputes are resolved? There has been surprisingly little research on these issues, but such as there is (for example, the work of Beale and Dugdale ((1975) 2 Brit J Law and Soc 45), and Yates (*Exclusion Clauses*, 2nd edn, 1982, Sweet & Maxwell, pp 16–33), in this country, and Macaulay ((1963) 28 Am Sociological Rev 45) in the United States, suggests that the law of contract is of much less importance to business people than lawyers would like to think. In particular, where parties to a long standing business relationship find themselves in a dispute, the maintenance of their relationship is likely to be a much stronger influence over the way they resolve their differences, than are the strict legal rights between the parties, as determined by the law of contract.

As has been indicated above, the approach taken here is primarily based on looking at legal materials within their own terms. From time to time, however, aspects of one or more of the alternative approaches outlined above, may be referred to, in order to produce a fuller understanding of the way in which the law has developed, or is likely to develop in the future. For that reason, it is worth spending a little time becoming familiar with the basic ideas lying behind them. Since the subject matter of this book is, as we have seen, transactions which are entered into voluntarily, we now need to turn to a preliminary consideration of the concept of 'agreement'.

1.3   The identification of agreements

It is easy to say that the law of contract is based on agreements between two parties. This simple assertion, however, masks a considerable problem in identifying precisely what is meant by an agreement. This may seem easy enough: it is simply a question of identifying a 'meeting of the minds' between the parties at a particular point in time. That, however, is easier said than done. By the time two parties to a contract have arrived in court, they are clearly no longer of one mind. They may dispute whether there was ever an agreement between them at all, or, while accepting that there was an agreement, they may disagree as to its terms. How are such disputes to be resolved? Clearly, the courts cannot discover as a matter of fact what was actually going on in the minds of the parties at the time of the alleged agreement. Nor are they prepared to rely solely on what the parties now say was in their minds at that time (which would be a 'subjective' approach), even if they are very convincing. Instead, the courts adopt what is primarily an 'objective' approach to deciding whether there was an agreement and, if so, what its terms were. This means that they look at what was said and done between the parties from the point of view of the 'reasonable person' and try to decide what they would have thought was going on.

1.3.1   Promisor, promisee and detached objectivity

As has been pointed out by Howarth, however, there are different types of objectivity ((1984) 100 LQR 265). There is 'promisor objectivity' where the court tries to decide what the reasonable promisor would have intended, 'promisee objectivity', where the focus is on what the reasonable person being made a promise would have thought was intended, and 'detached' objectivity which views what has happened through the eyes of an independent third party. In *Smith v Hughes* (1871), for example, where the dispute was over what type of oats the parties were contracting about, the test was said to be whether the party who wishes to deny the contract acted so that 'a reasonable man would believe that he was assenting to the terms proposed by the other party'. In other words, promisee objectivity. As we shall see, however, in subsequent chapters, the courts are not consistent as to which of these types of objectivity they use, changing between one and another as seems most appropriate in a particular case.

1.3.2　State of mind

The objective approach will not be applied, however, if there is clear evidence of a particular state of mind. *The Hannah Blumenthal* (1983), for example, was a case concerning the sale of a ship, where the point at issue was whether the parties had agreed to abandon their dispute. The behaviour of the buyers was such that it would have been reasonable for the sellers to have believed that the action had been dropped. In fact, the sellers had continued to act (by seeking witnesses, etc) in a way which indicated that they did not think the action had been dropped. This evidence of their actual state of mind overrode the conclusion which the court might well have reached by applying a purely objective test. (See, also, the similar case of *The Leonidas D* (1985).)

1.4　The external signs of agreement

The process by which the courts try to decide whether the parties have made an agreement does not necessarily involve looking for actual agreement but rather for the external signs of agreement. They have also come to rely on a number of specific elements, which are regarded as both necessary and sufficient to identify an agreement which is intended to be legally binding. These are:

- offer;

- acceptance;

- consideration.

These three factors, together with an overarching requirement that the court is satisfied that there was an intention to create legal relations, form the basis for the identification of contracts in English law. The next three chapters explore these concepts in detail.

INTRODUCTION

The subject matter of contact law

It may be argued that there is no general law of contract, but that the rules relating to contract are simply part of a more general law of obligations, or are made up of a variable law of 'contracts'.

In so far as there is a general law of contract, it is concerned with transactions under which people, more or less voluntarily, assume obligations towards each other, in connection with the transfer of property, or the provision of services.

The general law of contract applies the same rules to all transactions, no matter how large or small.

Different approaches to analysing contract

There are different approaches to analysing contract:

- Doctrinal – analyses the principles derived from appeal court cases, and statutes.

- Economic analysis – considers the rules of contract law in terms of their economic efficiency and consequences.

- Socio-political analysis – looks at the ideologies underlying contract, for example, capitalist, marxist, etc.

  Adams and Brownsword identify formalism, consumer-welfarism, and market-individualism as three such ideologies used by English courts.

- Empirical research – looks at what actually happens when people make contracts.

The identification of agreements

English law uses an 'objective approach' to identifying agreements – but note that there are different types of objectivity (for example, promisor objectivity, promisee objectivity, or detached objectivity).

Evidence of a party's state of mind at a particular time may, however, override an objective approach (for example, *The Hannah Blumenthal* (1983)).

The external signs, of agreement, are what the courts look for, in particular, 'offer and acceptance' and 'consideration'.

CHAPTER 2

OFFER AND ACCEPTANCE

2.1   Introduction

As has been explained in Chapter 1, the English courts in trying to decide whether two parties have reached a legally binding agreement, look for certain external signs of such agreement. The first two, which inevitably have to be considered together, are 'offer' and 'acceptance'.

2.2   Lack of formality

It is important to note first that, in most cases, English law requires no particular formality in order for a contract to come into existence. In other words, the contract does not have to be put into writing, or signed, nor does any particular form of words have to be used. A purely verbal exchange can result in a binding contract. Many students, on first encountering this aspect of contract law, raise the question of how you establish the existence of an agreement, or what it contains, if nothing has been written down. Doesn't it simply become a question of one person's word against another? Not necessarily. In some cases, a person's actions may be used as an indicator of their intentions. Suppose, for example, it is alleged that X has verbally agreed to sell certain goods to Y, but that X denies that any such agreement was made. Evidence that X had put the goods on one side, and labelled them with Y's name would suggest that he did in fact intend to sell them to Y, and would therefore be strong (though not conclusive) evidence that the alleged verbal agreement had been made. In other situations, however, it may be that the court has no such evidence to go on. It may well then be a case of one person's word against the other's. We should avoid getting side-tracked into this issue, however, because to do so is to forget that the primary function of a court in most cases of dispute is to decide what actually happened between the parties, even though there is no documentary evidence. This is true of the criminal law, where the determination of issues of fact in serious cases will be entrusted to the jury, and in tort cases, such as those arising out of road accidents, where a judge will have to decide who did what to whom, and whether they were acting negligently at the time. It is the same in contract. If there is a purely verbal agreement about which there is a dispute, the parties, and any witnesses, will have to give evidence as to their version of events, and the court will have to decide whom it believes. These issues are, however, more properly the province of the law of evidence and procedure, and do not involve substantive issues of contract law, which are our main concern.

2.2.1 Written agreements

There are, however, some important types of contract where writing is required. Just two will be mentioned here. First, by virtue of s 2(1) of the Law of Property (Miscellaneous Provisions) Act 1989, all contracts involving the sale, or other disposal, of an interest in land, must be in writing, and signed by the parties. The need for writing in relation to contracts concerning land is of long standing in English law, though prior to 1989 the requirement was only that the contract should be *evidenced* in writing, and signed by the person against whom it was to be enforced (s 40 of the Law of Property Act 1925). Although in practice the vast majority of such contracts were put into written form, this formulation left open the possibility of a verbal contract being evidenced by, for example, a letter signed by the relevant party. The 1989 amendment of this rule means that the agreement itself must be in writing and signed by both parties. The justification for the stricter rules which apply in relation to this type of contract is that contracts involving land are likely to be both complicated and valuable. Many commercial contracts, however, are also complex and valuable, yet there is no requirement of a written agreement (though in practice there is likely to be one). The second type of contract where there is a requirement of a certain degree of formality arises under the Consumer Credit Act 1974, which requires that contracts of hire purchase, and other credit transactions, should be in writing and signed. This is a protective provision, designed to make sure that the individual consumer has written evidence of the agreement, and has the opportunity to see all its terms. A similar protective procedure operates in relation to contracts of employment, though here the requirement is simply that the employee should receive a written statement of terms and conditions within a certain period of starting the job, rather than that the agreement itself should be in writing (s 1 of the Employment Rights Act 1996).

These types of contract are exceptions, however. In most cases, a verbal offer and acceptance will suffice.

2.3 Offer

An offer may be defined as an indication by one person that he or she is prepared to contract with one or more others, on certain terms, which are fixed, or capable of being fixed, at the time the offer is made. Thus, the statement 'I will sell you 5,000 widgets for £1,000' is an offer, as is the statement 'I will buy from you 5,000 shares in X Ltd, at their closing price on the London Stock Exchange next Friday'. In the former case, the terms are fixed by the offer itself, in the latter they are capable of becoming fixed on Friday, according to the price of the shares at the close of business on the Stock Exchange. Once there is an indication of willingness to contract of this type, all that is then required from the other person is a simple assent to the terms suggested, and a contract will be formed. As we shall see, the 'indication' referred to above may take a number of forms – for example, the spoken word, a letter, a fax message, a radio signal or a newspaper advertisement. As long as it communicates to the potential acceptor or acceptors the basis on which the offeror is prepared to contract, then that is enough. It is not necessary for the offer itself to set out all the terms of the contract. The parties may have been negotiating over a period of time, and the offer may simply refer to terms appearing in earlier communications. That is quite acceptable, provided that it is clear what the terms are.

2.3.1 Distinction from 'invitation to treat'

Distinction should be made between an offer and an 'invitation to treat'. Sometimes a person will wish simply to open negotiations, rather than make an offer which will lead immediately to a contract on acceptance. If I wish to sell my car, for example, I may enquire if you are interested in buying it. This is clearly not an offer. Even if I indicate a price at which I am willing to sell, this may simply be an attempt to discover your interest, rather than committing me to particular terms. The courts refer to such a preliminary communication as an 'invitation to treat' or, even more archaically, as an 'invitation to chaffer'. The distinction between an offer and an invitation to treat is an important one, but is not always easy to draw. Even where the parties appear to have reached agreement on the terms on which they are prepared to contract, the courts may decide that the language they have used is more appropriate to an invitation to treat than an offer.

This was the view taken in *Gibson v Manchester City Council* (1979). Mr Gibson was a tenant of a house owned by Manchester City Council. The Council, which was at the time under the control of Conservative Party members, decided that it wished to give its tenants the opportunity to purchase the houses which they were renting. Mr Gibson wished to take advantage of this opportunity, and started negotiations with the Council. He received a letter which indicated a price, and which stated 'The Corporation may be prepared to sell the house to you' at that price. It also instructed Mr Gibson, if he wished to make 'a formal application', to complete a form and return it. This Mr Gibson did. At this point, local elections took place, and control of the Council changed from the Conservative Party to the Labour Party. The new Labour Council immediately reversed the policy of the sale of council houses, and refused to proceed with the sale to Mr Gibson. Despite the fact that all terms appeared to have been agreed between the parties, the House of Lords held that there was no contract. The language of the Council's letter to Mr Gibson was not sufficiently definite to amount to an offer. It was simply an invitation to treat. Mr Gibson had made an offer to buy, but that had not been accepted.

The narrowness of the distinction being drawn can be seen by comparing this case with *Storer v Manchester City Council* (1974), where on very similar facts a contract was held to exist, as Mr Storer had signed and returned a document entitled 'Agreement for Sale'. This document was deemed to be sufficiently definite to amount to an offer which Mr Storer had accepted. As regards the state of mind of the parties in the two cases, however, it is arguable that there was little difference. In both, each party had indicated a willingness to enter into the transaction, and there was agreement on the price. The fact that the courts focus on the external signs, rather than the underlying agreement, however, led to the result being different in the two cases.

2.3.2 Self-service displays

Another area of difficulty arises in relation to the display of goods in a shop window, or on the shelves of a supermarket, or other shop where customers serve themselves. We commonly talk of such a situation as one in which the shop has the goods 'on offer'. This is especially true of attractive bargains which may be labelled 'special offer'. Are these 'offers' for the purpose of the law of contract? The issue has been addressed in a number of criminal cases where the offence in question was based on there being a 'sale' or an 'offer for sale'. These cases are taken to establish the position under the law of contract, even though they were decided in a criminal law context. The Court of Appeal has recently suggested that it is not appropriate to use contractual principles in defining the behaviour which constitutes a criminal offence, in this case relating to an offer to supply drugs: *R v Karamnit Singh Dhillon* (2000). This does not, however, affect the contractual rules deriving from older criminal cases where this was done. The first to consider is *Pharmaceutical Society of Great Britain v Boots Cash Chemists* (1953).

Section 18(1) of the Pharmacy and Poisons Act 1933 made it an offence to sell certain medicines unless 'the sale is effected by, or under the supervision of, a registered pharmacist'. Boots introduced a system under which some of these medicines were made available to customers on a self-service basis. There was no supervision until the customer went to the cashier. At this point, a registered pharmacist would supervise the transaction, and could intervene, if necessary. The Pharmaceutical Society claimed that this was an offence under s 18, because, it was argued, the sale was complete when the customer took an article from the shelves and put it into his or her basket. The Court of Appeal disagreed, and held that the sale was made at the cash desk, where the customer made an offer to buy, which could be accepted or rejected by the cashier. The reason for this decision was that it is clearly unacceptable to say that the contract is complete as soon as the goods are put into the basket, because the customer may want to change his or her mind, and it is undoubtedly the intention of all concerned that this should be possible. The display of goods is therefore an invitation to treat, and not an offer.

With respect to the Court of Appeal, the conclusion that was reached was not necessary to avoid the problem of the customer becoming committed too soon. It would have been quite possible to have said that the display of goods is an offer, but that the customer does not accept that offer until presenting the goods to the cashier. This analysis would, of course, also have meant that the sale took place at the cash desk and that no offence was committed under s 18. Strictly speaking, therefore, the details of the Court of Appeal's analysis in this case as to what constitutes the offer, and what is the acceptance, may be regarded as *obiter*. It has, however, generally been accepted subsequently that the display of goods within a shop is an invitation to treat and not an offer.

2.3.3 Shop window displays

The slightly different issue of the shop-window display was dealt with in *Fisher v Bell* (1961). The defendant displayed in his shop window a 'flick-knife' with the price attached. He was charged with an offence under s 1(1) of the Restriction of Offensive Weapons Act 1959, namely, 'offering for sale' a 'flick-knife'. It was held by the Divisional Court that no offence had been committed, because the display of the knife was an invitation to treat, not an offer.

Lord Parker had no doubt as to the contractual position:

> It is perfectly clear that according to the ordinary law of contract the display of an article with a price on it in a shop-window is merely an invitation to treat. It is in no sense an offer for sale the acceptance of which constitutes a contract.

No authority was cited for this proposition, but the approach is certainly in line with that taken in the *Boots* case. There has never been any challenge to it, and it must be taken to represent the current law on this point. It was followed in *Mella v Monahan* (1961), where a charge of 'offering for sale' obscene articles, contrary to the Obscene Publications Act 1959, failed because the items were simply displayed in a shop window.

These cases lead to the conclusion that, as far the law of contract is concerned, a shopkeeper is not bound by any price that is attached to goods displayed in the shop, or in the window. He or she is entitled to say to the customer seeking to buy the item '... that is a mistake. I am afraid the price is different'. Such action would, however, almost certainly constitute a criminal offence under s 20 of the Consumer Protection Act 1987. This states that:

> ... a person shall be guilty of an offence if, in the course of any business of his, he gives (by any means whatever) to any consumers an indication which is misleading as to the price at which any goods, services, accommodation or facilities are available (whether generally or from particular persons).

An indication is 'misleading' if, *inter alia*, it leads the consumer to think that the price is less than in fact it is (s 21). Thus, if a shop has a window display indicating that certain special packs of goods are on offer at a low price inside, but in fact none of the special packs are available, an offence will almost certainly have been committed. This was the result in *Tesco Supermarkets Ltd v Nattrass* (1971), a case concerning s 11 of the Trade Descriptions Act 1968, which was the predecessor to s 20 of the Consumer Protection Act 1987. Because of this, shopkeepers, and other businesses are unlikely to insist on their strict contractual rights in situations of this kind. The legislative provisions do not, however, affect the right of the shopkeeper to refuse to do business at all with a particular customer. To that extent, the rule that it is the customer who makes the offer, and the shopkeeper who has the choice whether or not to accept it, continues to have practical importance.

2.3.4 Advertisements

Where goods or services are advertised, does this constitute an offer or an invitation to treat? Generally speaking, an advertisement on a hoarding, a newspaper 'display', or a television commercial, will not be regarded as an offer. Thus, in *Harris v Nickerson* (1873), the defendant had advertised that an auction of certain furniture was to take place on a certain day. The plaintiff travelled to the auction only to find that the items in which he was interested had, without notice, been withdrawn. He brought an action for breach of contract to recover his expenses in attending the advertised event. His claim was rejected by the Queen's Bench. The advertisement did not give rise to any contract that all the items mentioned would actually be put up for sale. To hold otherwise would, Blackburn J felt, be 'a startling proposition' and 'excessively inconvenient if carried out'. It would amount to saying that 'anyone who advertises a sale by publishing an advertisement becomes responsible to everybody who attends the sale for his cab hire or travelling expenses'. It follows from this that advertisements should be regarded simply as attempts to make the public aware of what is available. They will in any case generally not be specific enough to amount to an offer. Even where goods are clearly identified, and a price specified, however, there may still not be an offer. A good example of the problem is another criminal law case, *Partridge v Crittenden* (1968).

The defendant put an advertisement in the 'Classified' section of a periodical, advertising bramblefinches for sale at 25s each. He was charged under the Protection of Birds Act 1954 with 'offering for sale' a live wild bird, contrary to s 6(1). It was held that he had committed no offence, because the advert was an invitation to treat and not an offer. The court relied heavily on *Fisher v Bell* (1961), and appeared to feel that this kind of advertisement should be treated in the same way as the display of goods with a price attached. Lord Parker, however, pointed out an additional, and very practical reason for not treating it as an offer. If it was an offer, this would mean that everyone who replied to the advertisement would be accepting it, and would therefore be entitled to a bramblefinch. Assuming that the advertiser did not have an unlimited supply of bramblefinches, this cannot be what he intended. This is an analysis based on 'promisor objectivity' (see 1.3.1 above), looking at what the reasonable advertiser would be taken to have meant by the advert. As a result, the advertisement was properly to be categorised as an invitation to treat.

This does not mean, however, that all newspaper advertisements will be treated as invitations to treat. Provided that the wording is clear, and that there are no problems of limited supply, then there seems no reason why such an advertisement should not be an offer. If, for example, the advertiser in *Partridge v Crittenden* had said, '100 bramblefinches for sale. The first 100 replies enclosing 25s will secure a bird', then in all probability this would be construed as an offer. An advertisement of a similar kind was held to be an offer in the American case of *Lefkowitz v Great Minneapolis Surplus Stores* (1957), where the defendants published an advertisement in a newspaper, stating:

> Saturday 9 am sharp; 3 Brand new fur coats, worth to $100. First come first served, $1 each.

The plaintiff was one of the first three customers, but the firm refused to sell him a coat, because they said the offer was only open to women. The court held that the advertisement constituted an offer, which the plaintiff had accepted, and that he was therefore entitled to the coat.

2.3.5 *Carlill v Carbolic Smoke Ball Co* (1893)

In England, the most famous case of an advertisement constituting an offer is *Carlill v Carbolic Smoke Ball Co* (1893). The manufacturers of a 'smoke ball' published an advertisement at the time of an influenza epidemic, proclaiming the virtues of their smoke ball for curing all kinds of ailments. In addition, they stated that anybody who bought one of their smoke balls, used it as directed, and then caught influenza, would be paid £100. Mrs Carlill, having bought and used a smoke ball, but nevertheless having caught influenza, claimed £100 from the company. The company argued that the advertisement could not be taken to be an offer which could turn into a contract by acceptance. They claimed that it should be regarded as a 'mere puff' which meant nothing in contractual terms. This is certainly true of many advertising slogans (for example, 'Gillette – the Best a Man Can Get', 'The Best Hard Rock Album in the World ... Ever!'). A contractual action based on these would be doomed to failure. In the *Carlill* case, however, there was evidence of serious intent on the part of the defendants. The advertisement had stated that '£1,000 is deposited with the Alliance Bank, showing our sincerity in this matter'. The court took the view that the inclusion of this statement meant that reasonable people would treat the offer to pay £100 as one that was intended seriously, so that it could create a binding obligation in appropriate circumstances, such as those which had arisen. The defendants raised two further objections. First, they argued that the advertisement was widely distributed, and that this was therefore not an offer made to anybody in particular. The court did not regard this as a problem. Offers of reward were generally in the same form, and could be accepted by any person who fulfilled the condition. There was plenty of authority to support this, such as *Williams v Carwardine* (1833) (see 2.8.16 below). Secondly, the defendants said that Mrs Carlill should have given them notice of her acceptance. Again, however, the court, by analogy with the reward cases, held that the form of the advertisement could be taken to have waived the need for notification of acceptance, at least prior to the performance of the condition which entitled the plaintiff to claim. As Lindley LJ put it:

> I ... think that the true view, in a case of this kind, is that the person who makes the offer shows by his language and from the nature of the transaction, that he does not expect and does not require notice of the acceptance apart from notice of the performance.

The Smoke Ball Company cannot have expected that everyone who bought a smoke ball would get in touch with them. It was only those who, having used the ball, contracted influenza, who would do so. This case, therefore, is authority for the propositions that an advertisement can constitute an offer to 'the world', that is, anyone who reads it, and that it may, by the way in which it is stated, waive the need for communication of acceptance prior to a claim under it.

It should be noted that the offer in *Carlill*, in *Lefkowitz*, and the suggested reformulation of the offer in *Partridge v Crittenden* (1968) (see 2.3.4 above), are all offers of a particular kind, known in English law as an offer in a 'unilateral' (as opposed to a 'bilateral') contract. It will be convenient at this point to examine the difference between these two types of contract.

2.4   Unilateral and bilateral contracts

The typical model of the bilateral contract arises where A promises to sell goods to B in return for B promising to pay the purchase price. In this situation, the contract is bilateral, because as soon as these promises have been exchanged there is a contract to which both are bound. In relation to services, the same applies, so that an agreement between A and B that B will dig A's garden for £20 next Tuesday is a bilateral agreement. Suppose, however, that the arrangement is slightly different, and that A says to B 'If you dig my garden next Tuesday, I will pay you £20'. B makes no commitment, but says, 'I am not sure that I shall be able to, but if I do, I shall be happy to take £20'. This arrangement is not bilateral. A has committed himself to pay the £20 in certain circumstances, but B has made no commitment at all. He is totally free to decide whether or not he wants to dig A's garden or not, and if he wakes up on Tuesday morning and decides that he just does not feel like doing so, then there is nothing that A can do about it. If, however, B does decide to go and do the work, that will be regarded as an acceptance of A's offer of £20, and the contract will be formed. Because of its one sided nature, therefore, this type of arrangement is known as a 'unilateral contract'. Another way of describing them is as 'if' contracts, in that it is always possible to formulate the offer as a statement beginning with the word 'if'. 'If you dig my garden, I will pay you £20.' As has been noted above, the arrangements in *Carlill* and *Lefkowitz* were of this type: 'If you use our smoke ball and catch influenza, we will pay you £100'; 'If you are the first person to offer to buy one of these coats, we will sell it to you for $1.'

The distinction between unilateral and bilateral contracts is important in relation to the areas of 'acceptance', and 'consideration', which are discussed further below.

2.5 Tenders

Some confusion may arise as to what constitutes an offer when a person, or more probably, a company, decides to put work out to tender, or seeks offers for certain goods. This means that potential contractors are invited to submit quotations. The invitation may be issued to the world, or to specific parties. Generally speaking, such a request will amount simply to an invitation to treat, and the person making it will be free to accept or reject any of the responses. In *Spencer v Harding* (1870), for example, it was held that the issue of a circular 'offering' stock for sale by tender, was simply a 'proclamation' that the defendants were ready to negotiate for the sale of the goods, and to receive offers for the purchase for them. There was no obligation to sell to the highest bidder, or indeed to any bidder at all. The position will be different if the invitation indicates that the highest bid or, as appropriate, the lowest quotation will definitely be accepted, then it will be regarded as an offer in a unilateral contract. The recipients of the invitation will not be bound to reply, but if they do, the one who submits the lowest quotation will be entitled to insist that the contract is made with them. A similar situation arose in *Blackpool and Fylde Aero Club Ltd v Blackpool Borough Council* (1990). The council had invited tenders for the operation of pleasure flights from an air field. Tenders were to be placed in a designated box by a specified deadline. The plaintiff complied with this requirement, but due to an oversight on the part of the defendant's employees, the plaintiff's tender was not removed from the box until the day after the deadline, and was accordingly marked as having arrived late. It was therefore ignored in the council's deliberations as to who should be awarded the contract. The plaintiff succeeded in an action against the defendant, who appealed. The Court of Appeal noted that, in this type of situation, the invitor of tenders was in a strong position, as he could dictate the terms on which the tenders were to be made, and the basis on which the selection of the successful one, if any, was to be made. There was nothing explicit in this case which indicated that all tenders meeting the deadline would be considered. Nevertheless:

> ... in the context, a reasonable invitee would understand the invitation to be saying, quite clearly, that if he submitted a timely and conforming tender it would be considered, at least if any other such tender were considered.

By applying this test of 'promisee objectivity' to the circumstances, the court concluded that the defendant was in breach of an implicit unilateral contract, under which it promised that if a tender was received by the specified deadline it would be given due consideration. The person inviting tenders must therefore either explicitly state the terms on which responses will be considered, or be bound by the reasonable expectations of those who put in tenders.

2.6 Auctions

The Sale of Goods Act 1979 makes it clear that in relation to a sale of goods by auction the bids constitute offers which are accepted by the fall of the hammer (s 57). The same is also the case in relation to any other type of sale by auction. The normal position will be that the auctioneer will be entitled to reject any of the bids made, and will not be obliged to sell to the highest bidder. If, however, the auction sale is advertised as being 'without reserve', this will be taken as implying an obligation to sell to the highest bidder (*Warlow v Harrison* (1859)). Similarly, in *Harvela Investments v Royal Trust of Canada* (1987), an invitation to two firms to submit sealed bids for a block of shares, together with a commitment to accept the highest offer, was treated as the equivalent of an auction sale. There was an obligation to sell to the highest bidder. This case was complicated, however, by the fact that one of the bids was what was described as a 'referential bid'. That is, it was in the form 'C$2,100,000 or C$101,000 in excess of any other offer'. The House of Lords held that this bid was invalid and that the owner of the shares was obliged to sell to the other party, who had offered C$2,175,000.

2.7 Acceptance

As has been explained above, an offer must be in a form whereby a simple assent to it is sufficient to lead to a contract being formed. It is in many cases, therefore, enough for an acceptance to take the form of the person to whom the offer has been made simply saying 'yes, I agree'. In some situations, however, particularly where there is a course of negotiations between the parties, it may become more difficult to determine precisely the point when the parties have exchanged a matching offer and acceptance. Unless they do match exactly, there can be no contract. An 'offer' and an 'acceptance' must fit together like two pieces of a jigsaw puzzle. If they are not the same, they will not slot together, and the picture will be incomplete. If they do match, however, it is as if they had been previously treated with 'superglue', for once in position it will be very hard, if not impossible to pull them apart.

2.7.1 Distinction from counter-offer

Where parties are in negotiation, the response to an offer may be for the offeree to suggest slightly (or even substantially) different terms. Such a response will not, of course, be an acceptance, since it does not match the offer, but will be a 'counter-offer'. During lengthy negotiations, many such offers and counter-offers may be put on the table. Do they all remain there, available for acceptance at any stage? Or is only the last offer, or counter-offer, the one that can be accepted? This issue was addressed in *Hyde v Wrench* (1840). D offered to sell a farm to P for £1,000. P offered £900, which was rejected. P then purported to accept the offer to sell at £1,000. D refused to go through with the transaction, and P brought an action for specific performance. The court held that a rejection of an offer in effect destroyed it. It could not later be accepted. Moreover, a counter-offer operated in the same way as a rejection. P's counter-offer of £900, therefore, had the effect of rejecting, and destroying, D's original offer to sell at £1,000. P could not accept it. In effect, P's final communication had to be treated, not as an acceptance, but as a further offer to buy at £1,000, which D was free to accept or reject.

The answer to the question posed above, therefore, is that only the last offer submitted survives and is available for acceptance. All earlier offers are destroyed by rejection or counter-offer.

It should be noted, however, that the courts will not necessarily require exact precision, if it is clear that the parties were in agreement. In the unreported case of *Pars Technology Ltd v City Link Transport Holdings Ltd* (1999), the contract was for the settlement of an earlier dispute. The defendant offered by letter of 7 February to pay £13,500 plus a refund of the carriage charges of £7.55 plus VAT. The claimant's letter of 12 February in response stated that the defendant's offer to pay £13,507.55 plus VAT was accepted. The defendant later claimed that this was not a valid acceptance, because it stated that VAT was to be paid on the whole amount, rather than just on the carriage charge. The Court of Appeal agreed with the trial judge that the correspondence as a whole had to be considered, and took the view that the claimant had merely been trying to restate the defendant's offer in a different way. The claimant's letter had clearly stated that the defendant's offer made in the letter of 7 February was being accepted. A contract had therefore been concluded on the terms stated in the defendant's offer letter.

2.7.2 Request for information

In some situations, however, it may be more difficult to determine whether a particular communication is a counter-offer or not. If, for example, a person offers to sell a television to another for £100, the potential buyer may ask whether cash is required, or whether a cheque is acceptable. Such an inquiry is not a counter-offer. It is not suggesting alternative terms for the contract, but attempting to clarify the way in which the contract will be performed, and in particular, whether a specific type of performance will be acceptable. The effect of an inquiry of this type was considered in *Stevenson, Jaques & Co v McLean* (1880). D wrote to P, offering to sell some iron at a particular price, and saying that the offer would be kept open until the following Monday. On the Monday morning, P replied by telegram, saying: 'Please wire whether you would accept 40 for delivery over two months, or if not, longest limit you could give.' D did not reply, but sold the iron elsewhere. In the meantime, P sent a telegram accepting D's offer. P sued for breach of contract. D argued that P's first telegram was a counter-offer, and that therefore the second telegram could not operate as an acceptance of D's offer. The court held that it was necessary to look at both the circumstances in which P's telegram was sent, and the form which it took. As to the first aspect, the market in iron was very uncertain, and it was not unreasonable for P to wish to clarify the position as to delivery. Moreover, as regards the form of the telegram, it did not say 'I offer 40 for delivery over two months', but was put as an inquiry. If it had been in the form of an offer, then *Hyde v Wrench* (1840) would have been applied, but since it was clearly only an inquiry, D's original offer still survived, and P was entitled to accept it.

2.7.3 Battle of the forms

One situation where it may become vital to decide whether a particular communication is a counter-offer or not, is where there is what is frequently referred to as a 'battle of the forms'. This arises where two companies are in negotiation, and as part of their exchanges they send each other standard contract forms. If the two sets of forms are incompatible, as is likely to be the case, what is the result? There are three possibilities:

- the contract is made on the terms of the party whose form was put forward first;

- the contract is made on the terms of the party whose form was put forward last – the 'last shot' approach;

- there is no contract at all, because the parties are not in agreement, and there is no matching offer and acceptance.

Lord Denning has suggested (in *Butler Machine Tool Co Ltd v Ex-Cell-O Corporation (England) Ltd* (1979)) that the first possibility might apply where the second set of terms (supplied by the offeree) is so different that the offeree 'ought not to be allowed to take advantage of the difference unless he draws it specifically to the attention of' the other party. Subject to that, he also suggested, in the same case, that the second possibility would apply where the terms proposed were not objected to by the other party. In fact, however, strict application of the principles outlined above as regards offers, counter-offers, etc suggests that the third of the possibilities is the right answer. There is, however, a reluctance to apply it, because it will often be the case that the parties are willing, or indeed keen, to have a contract, and will often have carried on their business as if such a contract had been validly made. If they are then told by the court that they have no contract at all, it may become very difficult to unscramble their respective rights and liabilities. (This sort of situation may be dealt with by the law of 'quasi-contract' or 'restitution' – for which see Chapter 16 below.)

2.7.4   The traditional view

An example of the way in which the courts have generally tackled the problem is to be found in the case mentioned above, *Butler Machine Tool Co Ltd v Ex-Cell-O Corporation (England) Ltd* (1979). The buyers wished to purchase a machine for their business. On 23 May, the sellers offered to sell them one for £75,535, with delivery in 10 months. The offer incorporated the sellers' standard terms, which were said to prevail over any terms in the buyers' order. It also contained a price variation clause, allowing the sellers to increase the price in certain situations. The buyers responded with an order on 27 May. This order incorporated the buyers' terms, which did not include a price variation clause. It also included a tear-off acknowledgment slip, stating: 'We accept your order on the Terms and Conditions stated therein.' The sellers signed and returned this acknowledgment, together with a covering letter, referring back to their terms as set out in their offer of 23 May. There were no further relevant communications. When the sellers delivered the machine, they tried to enforce the price variation clause, but the buyers insisted that they were only obliged to pay £75,535. The trial judge upheld the sellers' claim, but the Court of Appeal reversed this decision. Lord Denning would have liked to do so on the basis that the overall negotiations between the parties indicated that there was a contract, even if it was not possible to identify a clear, matching, offer and acceptance. He had previously argued for this method of identifying a contract in the Court of Appeal in *Manchester City Council v Gibson* (1979). He recognised, however, that the rejection of such an approach by the House of Lords in *Gibson* precluded his use of it, and so he fell back on the traditional 'offer/counter-offer' analysis. This was the line taken by the other members of the Court of Appeal. On this basis, the court was unanimous in holding that the buyers' terms should prevail. The sellers' original offer of 23 May was met with a counter-offer from the buyers, which, on the basis of *Hyde v Wrench* (1840) destroyed the sellers' original offer. By completing and returning the acknowledgment slip, the sellers were accepting this counter-offer, and their covering letter was thought not to be sufficiently specific so as to revive the detailed terms of the offer of the 23 May. Although the original terms were referred to in that letter, it was, according to Bridge LJ, in language which was 'equivocal and wholly ineffective to override the plain and unequivocal terms of the printed acknowledgement of order'.

The *Butler Machine Tool* case confirmed the courts' adherence to the traditional analysis in terms of looking for what objectively appears to be a matching offer and acceptance. It did little to resolve a true 'battle of the forms' such as might have arisen had there been no acknowledgment slip, but simply an exchange of incompatible terms, followed by the manufacture and delivery of the machinery. In such a situation, a court which followed the traditional line would probably be forced to say that there was no contract. Other possibilities might be to argue that delivery, or taking delivery, of the machinery amounted to *acceptance by conduct*, or that the failure to respond to the last offer sent amounted to *acceptance by silence*. These two concepts are considered below. A further attempt has recently been made by the Court of Appeal, however, to adopt an approach similar to that advocated by Lord Denning, and this needs to be discussed first.

2.7.5   New developments

In *Trentham Ltd v Archital Luxfer* (1993), the plaintiffs (Trentham), were the main contractors on a building contract. They entered into negotiations with the defendants (Archital), for sub-contracts to supply and install doors, windows, etc. The work was done, and paid for, but when the plaintiffs tried to recover a contribution from the defendants towards a penalty which the plaintiffs had had to pay under the main contract, the defendants denied that a binding contract had ever been formed. There had been exchanges of letters, and various telephone conversations, but there was no matching offer and acceptance. In particular, there was a dispute as to whose standard terms should govern the contract. The trial judge held that there was a contract, in that the defendants, in carrying out the work, had accepted Trentham's offer – in other words, acceptance by conduct (as in *Brogden v Metropolitan Rly* (1877), which is discussed further at 2.8.1 below). The defendants appealed. The only full judgment was delivered by Steyn LJ, with whom the other two members of the court agreed. Steyn LJ agreed that there was a contract here. In reaching this conclusion, he started by stating four basic points which he considered relevant to the case:

- The approach to the issue of contract formation is 'objective', and so does not take account of the 'subjective expectations and unexpressed mental reservations of the parties'. In this case, the relevant yardstick was 'the reasonable expectations of sensible businessmen'.

- In the vast majority of cases, the coincidence of offer and acceptance represents the mechanism of contract formation, but 'it is not necessarily so in the case of a contract alleged to have come into existence during and as a result of performance' (for this proposition, he cited *Brogden v Metropolitan Rly* (1877); *New Zealand Shipping Co Ltd v Satterthwaite* (1975); and *Gibson v Manchester City Council* (1979), none of which provides clear authority for it).

- The fact that a contract is executed (that is, performance has taken place, as in this case) rather than executory, is of considerable importance – it will almost certainly preclude, for example, an argument that there was no intention to create legal relations, or that the contract is void for vagueness or uncertainty.

- If a contract only comes into existence during and as a result of performance of the transaction, it will frequently be possible to hold that the contract impliedly and retrospectively covers pre-contractual performance (for this proposition, he cited *Trollope & Colls v Atomic Power Construction Ltd* (1963)).

2.7.6   Application of the new approach

Applying these points to the case before him, Steyn LJ concluded that the judge had sufficient evidence before him to conclude that there was a binding contract. The parties had clearly intended to enter into a legal relationship. The contemporary exchanges, and the carrying out of what was agreed in those exchanges, support the view that there was a course of dealing which on Trentham's side created a right to performance of the work by Archital, and on Archital's side it created a right to be paid on an agreed basis. Thus, although the trial judge had found that there was offer and acceptance, Steyn J was of the view that, in any event:

> ... in this fully executed transaction, a contract came into existence during performance even if it cannot be precisely analysed in terms of offer and acceptance.

Moreover, even if the contract came into existence after part of the work had been carried out and paid for, it impliedly governed pre-contractual performance.

This case is of potentially great significance. The two main points that it raises are, first, the potential retrospective effect of a contract. This is of considerable importance in relation to major contracts, in particular construction contracts, where it is common for at least some work to take place before any formal agreement has been reached. This decision clearly recognises that such work will generally be governed by any later agreement that is entered into. The need to use restitutionary remedies (which are discussed in Chapter 16) will therefore be reduced. The second issue, which is of more importance to the subject matter of this chapter, is the finding that contracts do not necessarily have to be formed by means of a matching offer and acceptance. This unanimous finding by the Court of Appeal is difficult to reconcile, however, with the rejection by the House of Lords in *Gibson* of Lord Denning's similar attempt to weaken the dominance of 'offer and acceptance'. It is true that Steyn LJ emphasises that he is concerned with the particular circumstances of a wholly executed transaction, but nevertheless the case opens the door for broader arguments that the straitjacket of offer and acceptance does not accord with commercial reality, and for that reason should be loosened in appropriate cases. It will be interesting to see whether the House of Lords, when it next has the opportunity to consider the issue, will take any different line from that which it took in *Gibson*.

2.8 Methods of acceptance

We now turn to look in more detail at the issues of acceptance by conduct, or by silence.

2.8.1 Acceptance by conduct

In unilateral contracts, the acceptance will always be by conduct – using the smoke ball, digging the garden, etc – though there are some problems as to just what conduct amounts to acceptance. These will be considered further later (see 2.8.3 below). Can the same apply in bilateral contracts, so that they too can be accepted by conduct? In some everyday situations, this would seem to be the case. In a shop transaction, for example, there may be no exchange of words between the customer and cashier. The customer may simply present the goods selected together with payment, constituting an offer to buy, which will be accepted by the cashier taking the money and, generally, giving a receipt. Can there be acceptance by conduct in more complicated, commercial, transactions? This issue was considered in *Brogden v Metropolitan Railway* (1877). The plaintiffs sent the defendants a draft agreement for the supply of a certain quantity of coal per week from 1 January 1872, at £1 per ton. The defendants completed the draft by adding the name of an arbitrator, signed it, and returned it to the plaintiffs. The plaintiffs' manager simply put the signed agreement into a drawer. Coal was ordered and delivered on the terms specified in the contract for a period of time, until there was a dispute between the parties. The defendants then argued that there was no contract, because the plaintiffs had never accepted their offer, as contained in the signed agreement. The House of Lords confirmed that it was not enough that the plaintiffs should have decided to accept: there had to be some external manifestation of acceptance. In this case, however, that was supplied by the fact that the plaintiffs had placed orders on the basis of the agreement. The defendants should therefore be taken to be bound by its terms.

This decision confirms that a bilateral contract may be accepted by conduct, and there is no need for a verbal or written indication of acceptance. In *Brogden*, the 'external manifestation' of acceptance (that is, the placing of orders) was also a 'communication' to the other party. What is the position if there is conduct which objectively indicates an intention to accept, of which the other party is unaware? It is to that issue that we now turn.

2.8.2   Acceptance by silence

In *Brogden v Metropolitan Railway* (1877), as we have just seen, it was held that you cannot accept a contract simply by deciding that you are going to do so. There must be some external evidence which would lead a reasonable person to believe that your intention was to accept. Does that external evidence have to come to the attention of the third party? Or is it enough that there was agreement, even if one side was in ignorance of it?

In some cases, the issue will be determined by the form of the offer. In unilateral contracts, for example, it has been recognised since *Carlill v Carbolic Smoke Ball Co* (1893) that the offeror may waive the need for communication of acceptance. The court thought that it clearly could not have been intended that everyone who bought a smoke ball in reliance on the company's advertisement should be expected to tell the company of this. It would be perfectly possible, of course, for an offeror to require such notice, but where an offer is made to the world, as in the *Carlill* case, or where a reward is offered for the return of property or the provision of information, the intention to waive such a requirement will easily be found.

2.8.3   Bilateral contracts

In relation to bilateral contracts, the position is different. The leading authority is *Felthouse v Bindley* (1863). An uncle was negotiating to buy a horse from his nephew. The uncle wrote to his nephew offering a particular sum and saying 'If I hear no more about him, I consider the horse mine'. The nephew did not respond, but told an auctioneer to remove this horse from a forthcoming auction. The auctioneer omitted to do so, and the horse was sold to a third party. The uncle sued the auctioneer, and the question arose as to whether the uncle had made a binding contract for the purchase of the horse. It was held that he had not done so, because the nephew had never communicated his intention to accept his uncle's offer. It is true that he had taken an action (removing the horse from the auction) which objectively could be taken to have indicated his intention to accept, but because his uncle knew nothing of this at the time, it was not effective to complete the contract.

This case has long been taken to be authority for the proposition that silence cannot amount to acceptance, at least in bilateral contracts. It is by no means clear that the court intended to go this far. It is uncertain, for example, what the court's attitude would have been had it been the nephew, rather than the uncle, who was trying to enforce the contract. Nevertheless, later courts have taken the principle to be well established. In *The Leonidas D* (1985), for example, Robert Goff J commented:

> We have all been brought up to believe it to be axiomatic that acceptance of an offer cannot be inferred from silence, save in the most exceptional circumstances.

No court has challenged the correctness of the general principle said to be established by *Felthouse v Bindley*, though many commentators have doubted it. In considering the analogous situation of acceptance of a repudiatory breach of contract, the House of Lords (in *Vitol SA v Norelf Ltd* (1996), discussed in more detail at 14.7.1 below) has suggested that silence and inaction can be effective provided that the they can be regarded as 'clear and unequivocal' and the other party has notice. If the same approach can be applied to acceptance of an offer, this will presumably fall within the 'exceptional circumstances' referred to by Robert Goff J. In most cases, however, silence by itself will inevitably be equivocal, in that it will be impossible to tell objectively whether the offeree has decided to accept or reject the offer.

The policy which may be said to lie behind the principle is that one potential contracting party should not be able to impose a contract on another by requiring the other to take some action in order not to be bound. It was felt that someone in the position of the nephew in *Felthouse v Bindley* should not be obliged to tell his uncle if he did not want to accept the offer. He should be entitled to do nothing, and not incur contractual obligations simply by inaction.

2.8.4 Inertia selling

During the 1960s, a related problem arose out of the growing practice of what came to be known as 'inertia selling'. The seller in these transactions would send a person who was thought to be a potential buyer, a copy of a book, for example, with a covering letter stating that, unless the book was returned within a certain time limit, the recipient would be assumed to want to keep it, and would be obliged to pay the purchase price. As we have seen, on the basis of *Felthouse v Bindley* (1863), no binding contract could arise in this way. But, of course, many people were ignorant of their rights under contract law, and were led in this way to pay for items which they did not really want. In order to remedy this, the Unsolicited Goods and Services Act 1971 was passed, which allows the recipient of unsolicited goods, in circumstances such as those outlined above, to treat them as an unconditional gift, with all rights of the sender being extinguished.

2.8.5 Conclusions on 'silence'

The basic rule, therefore, as derived from *Felthouse v Bindley*, and reinforced by the Unsolicited Goods and Services Act 1971, is that acceptance, whether by words or action, must be communicated to the the offeror. It is clear, however, from the decision in *Carlill v Carbolic Smoke Ball Co* (1893), that, in relation to certain types of unilateral contract, the offeror may waive the need for communication of acceptance. What is not clear is whether this can ever be done in a bilateral contract. While it clearly cannot be used as a means of imposing a contract on an unwilling offeree, there is no authority which specifically precludes the possibility of an offeree choosing to enforce a contract against an offeror who has stated that he will presume acceptance from non-communication. To return to *Felthouse v Bindley*, for example, if the horse had not been sold to a third party, would the nephew have been able to hold his uncle to the promise to buy at the price he had specified? There are two arguments which might be raised against allowing this. The first is that it would run contrary to the principle of mutuality that generally underpins the law of contract. If A can sue B, then B ought to be able to sue A. This principle does not apply universally, however. In relation to contracts with minors, for example, there are situations in which the minor is allowed to enforce a contract, even though the adult with whom he has dealt would not be able to do so (see 6.3 below). Moreover, mutuality only operates to a limited extent in unilateral contracts. This objection is not, therefore, conclusive. The second argument against allowing the silent offeree to sue is a practical one. If there is no outward manifestation of acceptance, how does a court (or anyone else) know that it has occurred? In other words, silence fails the test of unequivocality referred to in *Vitol SA v Norelf Ltd* (1996). The rule would have to require some objective evidence that the offeree had decided to accept. What would not be required, however, would be knowledge of this on the part of the offeror. Thus, again using the facts of *Felthouse v Bindley*, the nephew's removal of the horse from the auction could be regarded as an objective indication of his acceptance of his uncle's offer. The fact that the uncle was unaware of this should not preclude the nephew from enforcing the contract, since the uncle had, by the terms of his offer, waived the need for communication of acceptance. In conclusion, however, it must be stressed that, while the above analysis does not directly contradict any existing authority, neither is there any authority which clearly supports it. The issue as to whether an offeror in a bilateral contract can ever be bound if he has waived the need for communication of acceptance remains open.

2.8.6 Acceptance by post

A requirement of communication will not, however, answer all problems. In the modern world communication can take many forms: face to face conversations, telephone, letters, faxes, or e-mail. In some of these, there will be a delay between the sending of an acceptance and its coming to the attention of the offeror. The law of contract has to have rules, therefore, to make clear what is meant by 'communication'. The simplest rule would be to say that no communication is effective until it is received and understood by the person to whom it is addressed. This is in effect the rule that applies to offers, though as we shall see (2.8.16 below) there are some cases which suggest that it may be possible to accept an offer of which you are unaware. These cases are of dubious authority, however, and can only possibly apply in very restricted circumstances. In any case, they simply suggest that in some situations communication of an offer may not be necessary. Where communication of the offer is required, which is the case in virtually all situations, it is safe to say that communication means that the person to whom the offer is addressed is aware of it. Why should the position be any different as regards acceptances?

The problem first arose in relation to the post, where the delay is likely to be longest. Generally speaking, there will be a delay of at least 12 to 18 hours between the sending of an acceptance by post, and its receipt by the addressee. Does the sender of the acceptance have to wait until it is certain that the letter has arrived before being sure that a contract has been made? The issue was considered in *Adams v Lindsell* (1818).

The defendants sent a letter to the plaintiffs offering wool for sale, and asking for a reply 'in course of post'. The letter was misdirected by the defendants, and arrived later than would normally have been the case. The plaintiffs replied at once accepting, but the defendants, having decided that because of the delay the plaintiffs were not going to accept, had already sold the wool elsewhere. The plaintiffs sued for breach of contract. The court decided that to require a posted acceptance to arrive at its destination before it could be effective would be impractical, and inefficient. The acceptor would not be able to take any action on the contract until it had been confirmed that the acceptance had arrived. The court felt that this might result in each side waiting for confirmation of receipt of the last communication *ad infitum*. This would not promote business efficacy. It would be much better if, as soon as the letter was posted, the acceptor could proceed on the basis that a contract had been made, and take action accordingly.

2.8.7 Limitations on the postal rule

The rule that comes from *Adams v Lindsell* (1818) is thus that a posted acceptance is complete on posting. The offeror is therefore bound to a contract without being aware that this has happened. The same rule was applied to telegrams, where a similar, though shorter, delay in communication would occur. Because the rule is a rather unusual one, however, its limitations must be noted. First, it only applies to acceptances, and not to any other type of communication which may pass between potential contracting parties. Offers, counter-offers, revocations of offers, etc must all be properly communicated, even if sent through the post, or by telegram (*Byrne v van Tienhoven* (1880)). Secondly, it only applies where it was reasonable for the acceptance to be sent by post (*Henthorn v Fraser* (1892)). Clearly, where the offer was made by post, then, in the absence of any indication from the offeror to the contrary, it will certainly be reasonable to reply in the same form, and the postal rule will operate. Wherever the parties are communicating over a distance, it is likely to be reasonable to use the post, even if the offer has been made in some other way. As Lord Herschell put it in *Henthorn v Fraser* (1892):

> Where the circumstances are such that it must have been within the contemplation of the parties that, according to the ordinary usages of mankind, the post might be used as a means of communicating the acceptance of an offer, the acceptance is complete as soon as it is posted.

In this case, the fact that the parties were based in towns some distance apart was held to make the use of the post reasonable, despite the fact that the offer had been hand delivered.

The final limitation that must be noted is that the rule can always be displaced by the offeror. The offer itself may expressly, or possibly impliedly, require the acceptance to take a particular form. In *Quenerduaine v Cole* (1883), for example, it was held that an offer that was made by telegram impliedly required an equally speedy reply. A reply by post would not, therefore, take effect on posting. (There seems no reason, however, why it should not take effect on arrival, provided that the offer was still open.) Any implication from the form of the offer should, of course, be looked at alongside the more general rule as to what is reasonable to expect, as set out in *Henthorn v Fraser*. If the offeror wants to be sure that the postal rule will not operate, this should be made explicit in the offer. In *Holwell Securities Ltd v Hughes* (1974), the offer required the acceptance (in fact, the exercise of an option) to be given by 'notice in writing' to the offeror. It was held that this formulation meant that the acceptance would only take effect when actually received by the offeror. The insertion of this phrase is all that is required, therefore, to displace the postal rule. Other language may, of course, be used, provided the intention is clear.

If, however, the postal rule is to operate, the fact that the acceptance is complete on posting has been taken to its logical limit. It does not matter that the letter is delayed in the post, the offeror is still bound. And, in *Household Fire and Carriage Accident Insurance Co v Grant* (1879), it was held that an acceptance that was entirely lost in the post, and never arrived at its destination, was still effective to create a contract.

2.8.8 Acceptance by private courier

The cases that have been discussed in the previous section were all concerned with the service provided by the Post Office. Recently, there has been a growth in the availability of various kinds of private courier service, which might also be used to deliver communications creating a contract. Does the postal rule apply to acceptances sent by such means? There is no authority on this point. There are two possible lines which the law might take. First, it might be argued that the reasons for applying the postal rule in *Adams v Lindsell* (1818) apply equally to communications via a private courier. The acceptor gives the letter to a private courier, and thereby puts the acceptance out of his or her control. It would not be conducive to business efficiency to require the acceptor to wait for notification that the acceptance had been received before being able to take any action on the contract. Provided that it was reasonable for the acceptor to use the courier service, the acceptance should take effect as soon as it is given to the courier.

The second line of argument might resist the notion of extending the postal rule beyond its current application. It might well be said that communications have developed dramatically since 1818, when *Adams v Lindsell* was decided. Nowadays, if an acceptor wants to proceed quickly on the basis of a contract, where the acceptance has been given to a private courier, there is no need to wait a long time to receive confirmation that the acceptance has arrived. A telephone call to the offeror will enable the acceptor to find out very quickly whether this has happened or not. If the need for speed is even greater, then the acceptance could be sent by fax, with a request for confirmation by phone, or return fax, as soon as it has arrived.

It is difficult to predict which line of argument the courts would find more attractive. As will appear from the following section, however, there has been no move by the courts in recent years to extend the postal rule to other media, and this may be an indication of an acceptance that in the modern context the *Adams v Lindsell* approach has much less to recommend it than it did at the time it was decided. While there have been no moves to overrule that decision, or the case law flowing from it, it may be that the tendency will be to limit its scope, and confine it strictly to the area of communications *via* the Post Office, by letter or telegram.

2.8.9 Acceptance by electronic communication

In the modern world, contracts may well be made by much more sophisticated means of communication than the post. Telexes, faxes and e-mail are all widely used, in addition to letters and the telephone, as means of transmitting offers, counter-offers, acceptances and rejections. If one of these methods is used for an acceptance, when and where is it effective?

2.8.10 The *Entores* approach

The starting point for the law in this area is the case of *Entores v Miles Far East Corpn* (1955). This was concerned with communications by telex machine. The primary issue before the court was the question of *where* the acceptance took effect, if it was sent from a telex machine in one country, and received on a telex machine in another country. The answer to this would affect the position as to which country's law governed the contract.

The leading judgment in the Court of Appeal was given by Lord Denning. His approach was to take as his starting point a very simple form of communication over a distance (albeit a rather unlikely one in factual terms), that is, two people making a contract by shouting across a river. In this situation, he argued, there would be no contract unless and until the acceptance was heard by the offeror. If, for example, an aeroplane flew overhead just as the acceptor was shouting his or her agreement, so that the offeror could not hear what was being said, there would be no contract. The acceptor would be expected to repeat the acceptance once the noise from the aeroplane had diminished. Taking this as his starting point, he argued by analogy, that the same approach should apply to all contracts made by means of communication which are instantaneous or virtually instantaneous (as opposed to post or telegram, where there is a delay). On this basis, regarding telex as falling into the 'instantaneous' category, he held that the acceptance by telex took place where it was received, rather than where it was sent.

The same answer must be presumed to apply to all other forms of more sophisticated electronic communication which can be said to be instantaneous in their effect. They will all take effect at the place where they are received.

What is the position if there are problems with the communication? As we have seen, Lord Denning took the view that in instantaneous communications it is generally up to the person sending the communication to ensure that his message gets through. He will in most cases (as with the aeroplane flying overhead) be aware if there is a problem. If, however, the reason for failure to communicate is clearly the responsibility of the recipient, then the position will be different. Thus:

> ... if the listener on the telephone does not catch the words of acceptance, but nevertheless does not trouble to ask for them to be repeated: or the ink on the teleprinter fails at the receiving end, but the clerk does not ask for the message to be repeated: so that the man who sends an acceptance reasonably believes that his message has been received. The offeror in such circumstances is clearly bound, because he will be estopped from saying that he did not receive the message of acceptance.

On the other hand:

> ... if there should be a case where an offeror without any fault on his part does not receive the message of acceptance – yet the sender of it reasonably

concludes that it has got home when it has not – then I think there is no contract.

2.8.11 Time of acceptance

Note, however, that *Entores* was concerned with the *place* of communication, and not the *time* of communication. It provides no direct authority on the issue of the time when a telexed acceptance takes effect. Clearly, the postal rule cannot apply, since that is based on the acceptance taking effect as soon as it is out of the hands of the acceptor, whereas *Entores* requires it to have arrived at the offeror's address. Several other possibilities are possible. It could take effect only when it is actually read by the person to whom it addressed; or when it is read by someone other than the addressee; or when it is received on the addressee's telex machine, although not read by anyone; or when the acceptor would reasonably expect it to have been read.

Two cases subsequent to *Entores* have considered this issue in relation to telexes. In *The Brimnes* (1974), the communication was a not an acceptance, but a notice of the withdrawal of a ship from a charterparty. It was held to be effective when it was 'received' on the charterers' telex machine during office hours, although it was not actually read until the following morning. In *Brinkibon Ltd v Stahag Stahl* (1982), the House of Lords was dealing with a situation virtually identical to that under consideration in *Entores*, and approved the approach taken there. The House refused to indicate whether the same rule should apply in all circumstances, for example, where the message is sent out of office hours, or at night, in the expectation that it will be read at a later time, or where there is some fault with the recipient's machine of which the sender is unaware. As Lord Wilberforce put it:

> No universal rule can cover all such cases: they must be resolved by reference to the intentions of the parties, by sound business practice and in some cases by a judgment where the risks should lie.

This is not particularly helpful but, insofar as any general principle can be read into it, it would seem to be the last of those suggested above, that is that the communication should take effect at the time when the acceptor could reasonably have expected it to be read. In *Mondial Shipping and Chartering BV v Astate Shipping Ltd* (1995), Gatehouse J adopted this approach in relation to a fax giving notice under a contract. The Wilberforce approach suggests that there may be variations according to the type of communication system being used. There does not seem to be any reason for treating faxes differently from telex, but e-mail, sent to an electronic 'post-box' which will only be checked once or twice a day, might well be be said only to be communicated once the expected time for checking has passed. A similar approach might need to be used in relation to messages left on a telephone answering system. That is, the message should only be regarded as communicated once a reasonable time has elapsed to allow it to be heard by the offeror.

If this line is to be taken, it is clearly to the advantage of the acceptor, in that it allows an acceptance to be treated as effective although the offeror may be unaware of it (as is the case under the postal rule). As with *Adams v Lindsell* (1818), the counter-argument to those who say that this gives the acceptor too much of an advantage would be that the courts have always made it clear that the offeror can specify and insist on a particular mode of acceptance. If actual communication is required, this should be spelt out in the offer. If this is not done, the acceptor must be allowed to proceed on the basis that the acceptance will be read at a time which could reasonably be expected in the normal course of events.

2.8.12 Acceptance in internet transactions

It is likely that an increasing amount of business will be conducted over the internet, either by means of e-mail, or, particularly in the case of consumer transactions, via a website. In the latter case, the consumer may be actually receiving a product over the web (for example, downloading a piece of software or a video or music file) or placing an order for goods to be delivered by the post or courier service. How do the principles outlined above apply in these situations?

In relation to e-mail, as has been assumed in the previous discussion, there seems little reason to distinguish between this form of communication and other types of 'instantaneous' communication such as telex or fax. The contract will be formed at the earliest when the acceptance is received by the offeror's e-mail system, and is available to be read. At the latest, it should be regarded as complete once the time has passed at which it would be reasonable to expect the acceptance to have been read. Since most e-mail systems will return an error message to the sender if delivery has not been possible, then there is no real need here for any other procedure for acknowledgment of receipt.

As regards contracting via a website, some of the potential problems were indicated by events in September 1999, when a retailer was found to be indicating on its website that televisions were available for the price of £3 (see (1999) *The Times*, 21 September). This was a mistake: the price should have been £300. But, before it could be rectified, a large number of people had attempted to buy a television at the lower price. The crucial question was whether by responding to the information contained on the website these people were accepting the retailer's offer, or were themselves making an offer to buy at that price. Given that the purchasers would have had to submit credit card details in order to pay for the goods, and the retailer would presumably reserved the right not to accept these as satisfactory, the better view would seem to be that the purchasers are making the offer to buy. The advertisement of the televisions would thus be simply an invitation to treat. The seller would be free to accept or reject the offers from the potential purchasers. The contract would be made where the seller had acknowledged to the purchaser that his offer was accepted, either by means of a direct response on the website, or by a subsequent e-mail.

This area has also been the subject of proposals from the European Commission, which has issued a draft directive dealing with a range of issues on electronic commerce, including the issue of 'time of acceptance'. The first version of the Directive was issued in November 1998 (COM (1998) 586), with a revised version in September 1999 (COM (1999) 427), following consideration by the European Parliament. Both versions are available on the Commission's website, www.europa.eu.int. Article 11 of the latest draft states:

> Member States shall lay down in their legislation that, save where otherwise agreed by professional persons, in cases where a recipient, in accepting a service provider's offer, is required to give his consent through technological means, such as clicking an icon, the contract is concluded when the recipient of the service has received from the service provider, electronically, an acknowledgment of receipt of the recipient's acceptance.
>
> The following principles apply:
>
> (a) acknowledgment of receipt is deemed to be received when the recipient of the service is able to access it;
>
> (b) the service provider is obliged to immediately send the acknowledgment of receipt.

As will be seen, this seems to assume that it is the owner of the website which will be making the offer, and the purchaser who will be accepting it. This is made clear by the notes to the original draft Directive which indicate (at p 26) that it is only attempting to deal with the situation where a concrete offer is made by a service provider: '... the situation in which the service provider only issues an invitation to offer is not covered.' Since, as we have seen, by far the most likely situation under English law is that the service provider will be seen as making an invitation to treat, with the purchaser making the offer, the requirements of the draft directive may well have very little impact. In situations which do involve the possibility of a purchaser making a contract simply by pressing a button on the website, however, the British Government will in due course have to make sure, by legislation if necessary, that a contract is not in fact completed until the directive's requirements for acknowledgment have been met. (The Electronic Communications Act 2000, which deals with electronic signatures and cryptography, does not address this particular issue.)

2.8.13 Acceptance in unilateral contracts

Particular difficulties arise in connection with acceptances in unilateral contracts. We have already seen that one of the characteristics of the unilateral contract is that the acceptance occurs through the performance of an act, rather than the expression of agreement. It has also been noted that in certain cases the offeror in a unilateral contract may be taken to have waived the need for communication of the fact of acceptance, for example, *Carlill v Carbolic Smoke Ball Company* (1893).

A further problem arises as to when acceptance is complete. Is it when the acceptor starts to perform? Or when performance is complete? If I offer a prize of £100 for the first person to walk from the Town Hall in Leicester to Trafalgar Square in London during the month of February, do you accept this offer when you take your first step away from Leicester, or only when you arrive at Trafalgar Square? An acceptor in a unilateral contract is generally regarded as incurring no obligations until the specified act is completed, so that if you decide to give up half way to London, I will have no claim against you for breach of contract. This would suggest that acceptance only occurs with complete performance. There are problems with this, however, in relation to the offeror's power to withdraw the offer. As will be seen below, the offeror is generally free to withdraw an offer at any point before it has been accepted. If, in a unilateral contract, acceptance means complete performance, then this means that the offeror would be able to back out at any point before performance was complete. So, to use the example given above, if you have started out to walk from Leicester to London, and have managed two-thirds of the distance, I would be entitled to come up to you and say: 'I'm sorry, I have changed my mind. My offer of £100 is withdrawn.' You would have no redress, despite the fact that you might be perfectly willing to continue the walk, because we would not at that stage have a contract. The possibility of withdrawal by notice in this type of contract was given judicial recognition in *Great Northern Railway Co v Witham* (1873), but the court did not on the facts need to decide whether, and in what circumstances, it might be allowed.

2.8.14 Prevention of withdrawal by the offeror

This result has been regarded by many as unfair, and there have therefore been attempts to argue that partial performance may in some circumstances amount to a sufficient indication of acceptance so as to prevent withdrawal by the offeror. In *Errington v Errington* (1952), a father had promised to his son and daughter-in-law, that if they paid off the mortgage on a house owned by the father, he would transfer it to them. The young couple started to make the required payments, but made no promise that they would continue. This appeared to be, therefore, a unilateral contract. The father died, and his representatives denied that there was any binding agreement in relation to the house. They argued that his offer could be withdrawn, because there had not been full acceptance. The Court of Appeal refused to allow this conclusion. Lord Denning recognised that this was a unilateral contract, but nevertheless held that the offer could not be withdrawn:

> The father's promise was a unilateral contract – a promise of the house in return for their act of paying the instalments. It could not be revoked by him once the couple entered on performance of the act, but it would cease to bind him if they left it incomplete and unperformed.

The reasons behind this conclusion are not made clear, other than that this was a fair result where the young couple had acted in reliance on the father's promise. This approach has clear links with the idea of estoppel, of which as we shall see (3.8 below) Lord Denning has made inventive use in other areas, but this concept was not raised directly in this case.

The approach taken by Lord Denning in *Errington* received support from the later Court of Appeal decision in *Daulia v Four Millbank Nominees Ltd* (1978). The parties were negotiating over the sale of some properties. The unilateral contract here was that the defendants promised the plaintiffs that if they produced a signed contract plus a banker's draft by 10 am the next morning, the defendants would go ahead with the sale to the plaintiffs. The plaintiffs did what was requested, but the defendants refused to go through with the contract. In the course of his judgment, Goff LJ considered the question of when the offeror in a unilateral contract is entitled to withdraw that offer. He started by confirming that in general the offeror cannot be bound to a unilateral contract until the acceptor has provided full performance of the condition imposed. That general rule is, however, subject to an important qualification, namely:

> ... that there must be an implied obligation on the part of the offeror not to prevent the condition becoming satisfied, which obligation it seems to me must arise as soon as the offeree starts to perform. Until then, the offeror can revoke the whole thing, but once the offeree has embarked on performance it is too late for the offeror to revoke his offer.

Goff LJ provided no authority for this proposition, but it received the support of Buckley LJ. It was not, however, part of the *ratio* of the case, since the court decided against the plaintiffs on other grounds. It seems likely, nevertheless, that the approach taken by Denning and Goff in these two cases would be followed in similar circumstances.

2.8.15 Position in 'reward' contracts

It may be significant, however, that in both *Errington* and *Daulia* the offeror was aware that the other person had embarked upon performance. It is not clear that in a case, such as the offer of a reward or prize, where the offer is made to the world, that precisely the same approach should apply. In the case, for example, of the offer of £100 for the return of a lost dog, it seems right that where a person is seen at the opposite end of the street, bringing the dog home, the offeror should not be able to shout out a withdrawal of the reward. But, suppose the offeror has run into financial problems since offering the reward, and cannot now afford to pay it. Must the offeror remain committed to keeping the offer open as regards anyone who has started looking for the dog, even if the offeror is unaware of this? It would seem more reasonable that the offeror should be allowed, by giving notice in a reasonable manner (perhaps in the same way as which the offer was made), to withdraw the offer. It is an issue on which there is no English authority, so it is not possible to say with any certainty what the approach of the courts would be, but it is submitted that the fairest rule to all parties would be to hold that the *Errington/Daulia* approach should only apply where the offeror is aware that the other person is trying to perform the condition.

2.8.16 Acceptance in ignorance of an offer

It would seem logical that there can be no acceptance of an offer of which the person accepting was ignorant. Some problems have arisen, however, in relation to certain types of unilateral contract. Suppose a reward is offered for the return of a stolen bicycle, belonging to A, and posters are displayed advertising this fact. B, who has not seen any of the posters, finds the bicycle, and recognising it, returns it to A, its rightful owner. Can B claim the reward from A? There is one authority which suggests that he might be able to. That is *Gibbons v Proctor* (1891), where a police officer gave information for which a reward had been offered. At the time that he gave the information, the officer was unaware of the reward, though he had learnt of it by the time the information reached the person who had offered the reward. It was held that the officer was entitled to claim the reward. This decision has not been followed in any later case, however, and must be regarded as being of doubtful authority. The better view seems to be that knowledge is necessary for an effective acceptance. This was accepted as being the case, though without any authority being cited, in the criminal law case of *Taylor v Allon* (1965).

A slightly different issue arises where the person performing the act has previously known of the offer, but is acting from different motives. In the Australian case of *R v Clarke* (1927), it was held that a person who had known of the offer, but was at the time acting purely out of consideration of his own danger, should be treated as acting in ignorance of the offer. On the other hand, in *Williams v Carwardine* (1833), it was held that acting for mixed motives, that is to ease one's conscience, while at the same time having the reward in mind, did not preclude a valid acceptance of the offer.

2.8.17 Cross-offers

The above cases have all been concerned with unilateral contracts. The parallel situation in a bilateral contract is where there are 'cross-offers'. Suppose, for example, that two parties send each other a letter offering respectively to buy and to sell certain goods at a certain price. Suppose, also, that the two offers match precisely. Does this create a contract? If what the courts were concerned with was a 'meeting of the minds', the answer might well be 'yes'. In *Tinn v Hoffman* (1873), however, it was held that such an exchange does not result in a contract. The case is not conclusive on the general issue, because on the facts there were differences between the two offers. It seems likely, however, that given the general enthusiasm of the courts for looking for an 'exchange' of offer and acceptance, rather than simply general agreement, that *Tinn v Hoffman* would be followed, and that cross-offers would not be regarded as forming a contract.

2.9   Acceptance and the termination of an offer

The general rule is that an offer can be revoked at any point before it is accepted (*Payne v Cave* (1789)), though as we have seen that requires some modification in relation to unilateral contracts. In this section the focus will be entirely on bilateral contracts.

The general rule will apply despite the fact that the offeror may have promised to keep the offer open for a specified time (*Routledge v Grant* (1828)). The reason for this is that before there is an acceptance, there is no contract, and if there is no contract, then the offeror cannot be legally bound to a promise. If the offeree has paid for the time allowance in some way (that is, has given consideration for the promise to keep the offer open), as may well be the case with the exercise of an option, then it will be upheld. In the absence of this, however, there can be no complaint if the offer is withdrawn.

2.9.1   Need for communication

Revocation of an offer must be communicated to be effective. This was implicit in the decision in *Byrne v van Tienhoven* (1880) where the withdrawal of an offer, which was sent by telegram, was held not to take effect until it was received. The *Adams v Lindsell* (1818) postal rule does not apply to revocations of offers, but there may still be difficulties as to what exactly amounts to communication, and when a revocation takes effect. The issues are much the same as those dealt with in the section on acceptance by electronic communication (see 2.8.9 above), and are not discussed again here.

It is clear, however, that communication of revocation need not come directly from the offeror. Provided that the offeree is fully aware at the time of a purported acceptance that the offeror has decided not to proceed with the contract, then the offer will be regarded as having been revoked, and no acceptance will be possible. This was the position in *Dickinson v Dodds* (1876), where the plaintiff was told by a third party that the defendant was negotiating with someone else for the sale of properties which he had previously offered to the plaintiff. The defendant had also indicated to the plaintiff that the offer would be kept open for a specified period.

The plaintiff tried to accept the offer within the time limit. The Court of Appeal decided that acceptance was not possible, because the plaintiff knew that the defendant was no longer minded to sell the property to him 'as plainly and clearly as if [the defendant] had told him so in so many words'. The reasoning of at least some of the judges in this case was clearly influenced by the idea of their needing to be a 'meeting of the minds' in order for their to be a contract. Despite the fact that this approach to identifying agreements no longer has any support, *Dickinson v Dodds* is still regarded as good authority for the more general proposition that an offeree cannot accept an offer where he or she has learnt from a reliable source that the offer has been withdrawn, even where that source was acting without the knowledge of the offeror.

2.9.2 Effect of lapse of time

An offer may also become incapable of acceptance because of lapse of time. If the offeror has specified a time within which acceptance must be received, any acceptance received outside that time limit cannot create a contract. At best, it will be a fresh offer, which may be accepted or rejected. If no time is specified, then the offer will remain open for a reasonable time, which will be a matter of fact in each case. In *Ramsgate Victoria Hotel Co v Montefiore* (1866), it was held that a delay of five months meant that an attempt to accept an offer to buy shares was ineffective.

2.10 Retraction of acceptance

As soon as an acceptance takes effect, then a contract is made, and both parties are bound. It would seem, then, that in the normal course of events, retraction, or revocation, of an acceptance will be impossible. This general rule has been modified, however, in relation to certain types of consumer contracts, where it has been deemed desirable that the consumer should have a 'cooling-off' period following the formation of the contract, during which a change of mind is permitted. Examples of this type of provision may be found in s 67 of the Consumer Credit Act 1974, ss 5 and 6 of the Timeshare Act 1992, and the Consumer Protection (Cancellation of Contracts Concluded Away From Business Premises) Regulations 1987. In these cases, a valid contract, in which offer and acceptance have been exchanged, can be set aside purely at the discretion of the consumer contractor. The possibility of withdrawal from a seemingly binding agreement also arises, however, in relation to situations where the law deems acceptance to take effect at a point in time before that at which it actually comes to the attention of the offeror. The most obvious example of this is the *Adams v Lindsell* (1818) postal rule. It may also apply, however, in relation to, for example, acceptances by telex, fax or e-mail, which are received during office hours, but not read until some time later, or messages left on a telephone answering machine. As we have seen, the law as yet provides no clear answer to the question of when acceptance takes effect in such cases, but if it is decided that the relevant time is when the acceptance is received on the offeror's machine, rather than when it is read, there is again a delay between acceptance and actual communication, which may lead to the possibility of a retraction. The rest of this section will discuss the issue in relation to posted acceptances, but the principles should surely apply in the same way to any acceptance where there is a delay between the point in time when the law says that the acceptance takes effect (for example, on posting) and when it is read by the offeror.

2.10.1 Formalist approach

If a 'formalist' approach is taken to this issue (see 1.2.3 above), then the answer must be that no retraction of an acceptance is possible. The general rule of the contract being complete on acceptance should be applied. So, even if the acceptor is able, for example, by telephoning the offeror, to indicate that an acceptance which is in the post is to be ignored, the offeror should be entitled to say 'Too bad! Your acceptance took effect on posting, and we have a contract. If you fail to go through with it, you will be in breach'.

2.10.2 Purposive approach

This is not the only possible approach, however. It might also be argued that the purpose of the postal rule is to provide a benefit to the acceptor. As we have seen, the main reason for the decision in *Adams v Lindsell* (1818) was that such a rule allowed the acceptor to proceed on the basis that a contract had been made, and that this promoted business efficiency. If that is the case, it might be argued that it is a little odd to then apply the rule in a way which is to the acceptor's disadvantage. Moreover, if, as must be the case for there to be any possibility of retraction, we are considering a point in time at which the offeror is as yet unaware of the acceptance, how can there be any harm in allowing the acceptor to withdraw? The offeror cannot in any way have acted on the acceptance, and so can suffer no harm from its retraction. There seems little point in forcing people to go through with a contract, when one party no longer wishes to proceed, and the other party is unaware of the fact that there is a contract at all.

2.10.3 Unfairness to offeror

This argument is said by some to be too favourable to the acceptor. The example is given of an acceptance of an offer to buy shares, or goods which have a greatly fluctuating market price. If retraction of acceptance is allowed, then it is said that this gives the acceptor the best of both worlds. The offer can be accepted by posting a letter, which will bind the offeror. Then, if before the acceptance is read, the market price falls below the contract price, the acceptor can avoid what has now become a bad bargain, by telephoning a withdrawal. This is regarded as unfair. In an argument which is the converse of the one put forward in the last paragraph, it is said that the postal rule exists for the benefit of the acceptor. It is tipping the scales too far in the acceptor's favour, however, to allow the possibility of retraction as well: a possibility which is not available in any other situation.

2.10.4 Guidance from authority

Attempts to argue the case from first principles, then, may lead to different conclusions. Three possibilities have been outlined above, one in favour of allowing retraction, the other two against. This writer's preferred view is the pragmatic one of allowing retraction, but this is by no means widely accepted. Unfortunately, there is little help from case law, either.

The only British case to deal with the issue at all is *Countess of Dunmore v Alexander* (1830). This is a Scottish case, which on one reading appears to support the view that a posted acceptance can be retracted by speedier means. The case is not a strong authority, however, since it is not absolutely clear that the court considered that the communication which was withdrawn was an acceptance, rather than an offer. Two cases from other common law jurisdictions suggest the opposite. In *Wenckheim v Arndt* (1873) (New Zealand) and *A to Z Bazaars (Pty) Ltd v Minister of Agriculture* (1974) (South Africa), it was held that the attempt to withdraw the acceptance was not effective.

An English court faced with this issue would be free to decide it without any clear guidance from authority. The answer that is given will depend on which of the various possibilities outlined above is the more attractive. It is not unlikely that the court's decision in a particular case will be influenced by what the court sees as the best way to achieve justice between the parties, rather than on any preference based on general principle.

2.11   Certainty in offer and acceptance

Even though the parties may have appeared to make an agreement by exchange of a matching offer and acceptance, the courts may refuse to enforce it if there appears to be uncertainty about what has been agreed, or if some important aspect of the agreement is left open to be decided later. In *Scammell v Ouston* (1941), for example, the parties had agreed to the supply of a lorry on 'hire purchase terms'. The House of Lords held that in the absence of any other evidence of the details of the hire purchase agreement (duration, number of instalments, etc) this was too vague to be enforceable, and there was therefore no contract.

This does not necessarily mean that all details of a contract must be finally settled in advance. It is not uncommon, for example, in relation to contracts for the supply of services, for the precise amount to be paid to be left unspecified at the time of the agreement. If a car is left at a garage for repair, it may not be possible to determine at that stage exactly what the repair will cost, because this may depend on what the mechanic finds once work has started. The car owner may well say something along the lines of 'Do the work, but if it looks as though it will cost more than £150, please contact me before going ahead'. It cannot be doubted that there is a contract for repairs up to the value of £150. The court's view of this situation is that there is in effect an agreement that the customer will pay a 'reasonable price', for the work that is done. What is a reasonable price is a question of fact, which can, if necessary, be determined by the courts. This approach now has statutory force by virtue of s 15 of the Supply of Goods and Services Act 1982. The same rule also operates in relation to goods by virtue of s 8(2) of the Sale of Goods Act 1979.

The possibility of the courts giving specific content to an apparently vague phrase can apply in other areas apart from the price to be paid for goods or services. In *Hillas v Arcos* (1932), for example, there was a contract to supply timber 'of fair specification'. It was held that in the context of the agreement, which was between parties who knew each other and the timber trade well, and taking account of the fact that there had been part performance, the phrase 'fair specification' must be capable of being given a meaning. The contract was therefore enforceable.

2.11.1 Meaningless phrases

The decision in *Scammell v Ouston* (1941) (see 2.11 above) might be thought to open the door to an unscrupulous party to include some meaningless phrase in an agreement, which would then allow him to escape from the contract if he wished on the basis of uncertainty. To have such an effect, however, the phrase must relate to some significant aspect of the contract. If it can be deleted and still leave a perfectly workable agreement, then the courts will ignore it. This was the position in *Nicolene v Simmonds* (1953), where the contractual documentation contained the statement 'we are in agreement that the usual conditions of acceptance apply'. Since there were no 'usual conditions', it was held that this was simply a meaningless phrase, which could be ignored. There was nothing left open which needed to be determined.

2.11.2 Incomplete agreements

If an agreement leaves undecided, and undeterminable, some important aspect of the contract, then the courts will not enforce it. This can arise where perfectly clear words are used, about the meaning of which there is no dispute, but which do not settle some significant part of the contractual terms. In *May and Butcher v R* (1934), for example, the agreement provided that the price, and the date of payment, under a contract of sale, was to be 'agreed upon from time to time'. The House of Lords held that there was no contract. The parties had not left the price open – when, as we have seen, a 'reasonable price' would have been payable – they had specifically stated that they would agree in the future. The contract contained an arbitration clause, but the House of Lords considered that this was only meant to be used in the event of disputes, and could not be the means of determining basic obligations. This refusal to give effect to an 'agreement to agree' was followed in *Courtney and Fairbairn Ltd v Tolaini Brothers (Hotels) Ltd* (1975).

This left open the possibility that a 'lock-out' agreement, not to negotiate with any one else, which is sufficiently limited in terms of time, might be enforceable. That this is indeed possible was confirmed by the Court of Appeal in *Pitt v PHH Asset Management Ltd* (1993). The parties were in negotiations over the sale of a property, and the plaintiffs, the prospective purchasers, were concerned that the defendants would accept a higher offer from a third party. An agreement was arrived at under which, in return for the plaintiffs agreeing to exchange contracts within two weeks, the defendants agreed not to consider any further offers within that period. The defendants went back on this agreement, and sold to the third party at a price above that which the plaintiffs had offered. The Court of Appeal held that, in this case, the 'lock-out' agreement was sufficiently specific to be binding, and the plaintiff's action against the defendants for damages for breach of this agreement was therefore successful.

2.11.3 Obligations distinguished from 'machinery'

The contract will not be regarded as incomplete if it provides a machinery for resolving an aspect which has been left uncertain. As we have seen, in relation to the price, the courts will often be prepared to assume that a 'reasonable price' was intended. They will also be prepared to give effect to an agreement where property is to be valued by an independent valuer, or where the price is to be determined by reference to the prevailing market price. In such situations, the contract provides a mechanism by which the uncertainty can be resolved.

In some cases, however, the courts have been prepared to stretch this principle rather further than might have been expected. In *Sudbrook Trading Estate v Eggleton* (1982), the price for exercise of an option to purchase was to be determined by two valuers, one to be nominated by each party. One party refused to appoint a valuer, and claimed that the agreement was therefore void for uncertainty. The House of Lords disagreed. The contract was not uncertain in that it provided a clear machinery by which the price was to be determined. This machinery was not, however, itself an essential term of the contract. It was simply a way of establishing a 'fair' price. If the machinery failed, then the court could substitute its own means of determining what was a fair price. This approach was relied on by the Court of Appeal in *Didymi Corporation v Atlantic Lines and Navigation Co Inc* (1987). The agreement contained a provision under which the hire under a charter of a ship could in some circumstances be increased 'equitably' by an amount 'to be mutually agreed between the parties'. At first sight, this looks like an 'agreement to agree' which would be unenforceable. The court, however, following the lead given by *Sudbrook Trading Estate v Eggleton*, ruled that the reference to 'mutual agreement' was simply part of the 'inessential machinery' by which the hire was to be determined. The agreement was that the hire should be 'equitable', which meant 'fair and reasonable'. There was therefore no reason why the court should not determine this as a question of fact.

An incomplete agreement may nevertheless give rise to some legal obligations between the parties under the doctrine of 'restitution'. This is discussed further in Chapter 16.

OFFER AND ACCEPTANCE

Lack of need for formality

Contracts do not generally need to be in writing, or to use any particular form of words. A verbal offer and acceptance is sufficient.

Exceptions to this exist in relation to contracts concerning land, and consumer credit agreements.

Offer

An offer is an indication by one person that he or she is prepared to contract with one or more others, on certain terms, which are fixed, or capable of being fixed, at the time the offer is made.

Distinction from 'invitation to treat'

An offer can be distinguished from 'invitation to treat': preliminary negotiations, or expressions of interest will be regarded as invitations to treat, rather than offers (*Gibson v Manchester City Council* (1979)).

Displays of goods

Displays of goods in shops, or shop-windows, will generally be regarded as invitations to treat, not offers (*Pharmaceutical Society of Great Britain v Boots* (1953); *Fisher v Bell* (1961)).

Advertisements

Advertisements may be either invitations to treat (*Partridge v Crittenden* (1968)); or offers (*Carlill v Carbolic Smoke Ball Co* (1893); *Lefkowitz v Great Minneapolis Surplus Stores* (1957) (American case)), depending on the precise terms of the advert.

Advertisements which are offers, will normally involve 'unilateral', or 'if' contracts, under which the offeree incurs no obligation prior to performing an act requested by the offeror.

Invitation to tender for work

An invitation to tender for work will normally constitute an invitation to treat, with the responses being offers (*Spencer v Harding* (1870)). There may, however, be a unilateral contract obliging the person inviting the tenders to comply with any procedures set out in the invitation (*Blackpool and Fylde Aero Club Ltd v Blackpool Borough Council* (1990)).

Auctions

Auctions: the bids are offers, which are accepted by the fall of the hammer. An auction advertised as being 'without reserve', however, implies an obligation to sell to the highest bidder (*Warlow v Harrison* (1859)). (Note, also, *Harvela Investments v Royal Trust of Canada* (1987).)

Acceptance

Definition of acceptance: an unconditional assent to an definite offer.

Distinction from counter-offer

Distinction from counter-offer: a response to an offer which introduces new terms or conditions is a 'counter-offer' not an acceptance. A counter-offer prevents later acceptance of the original offer (*Hyde v Wrench* (1840)). A request for information which is not a counter-offer does not have this effect (*Stevenson, Jaques & Co v McLean* (1880)).

Battle of the forms

'Battle of the forms': exchange of incompatible terms between businesses may make it difficult to identify an agreement. Courts have generally used traditional 'offer and acceptance' analysis (*Butler Machine Tool Co Ltd v Ex-Cell-O Corporation* (1979)). Note the more recent broader approach in *Trentham v Archital Luxfer* (1993).

Methods of acceptance

Acceptance may be achieved by various means:

- Acceptance by conduct

  This is possible, as in *Brogden v Metropolitan Rly* (1877), provided the offeror is aware of the acceptance.

- Acceptance by silence

  This is not generally possible (*Felthouse v Bindley* (1863)).

- Acceptance by post

  Acceptance will take effect on posting (*Adams v Lindsell* (1818)) unless:

○ use of the post is unreasonable (*Henthorn v Fraser* (1892)); or

○ the offeror has required actual communication (*Holwell Securities v Hughes* (1974)).

- **Acceptance by private courier**

  There is no authority on this. It is not clear whether the *Adams v Lindsell* rule would apply.

- **Acceptance by electronic communication**

  'Instantaneous' communications, such as telex or e-mail, take effect at the point of receipt (*Entores v Miles Far East Corporation* (1955)). The time at which they take effect is not settled – note *The Brimnes* (1975) and *Brinkibon Ltd v Stahag Stahl* (1983). Advertising goods, etc, on a website probably constitutes an invitation to treat, with the potential purchaser making the offer.

- **Acceptance in unilateral contracts**

  If acceptance equals completion of performance, can the offer be withdrawn before performance is complete (as suggested in *Great Northern Rly v Witham* (1873)). Note *Errington v Errington* (1952) and *Daulia v Four Millbank Nominees* (1978) which suggest that, at least where the offeror is aware of the attempt to perform, withdrawal of the offer will not be allowed.

- **Acceptance in ignorance of the offer**

  The general view (despite *Gibbons v Proctor* (1891)) is that the person accepting must be aware of the offer, though this need not be the sole motive for acting (*Williams v Cawardine* (1833)). *Tinn v Hoffman* (1873) suggests that cross-offers do not make a contract.

- **Acceptance and the termination of an offer**

  The general rule is that an offer can be revoked at any time before acceptance (*Payne v Cave* (1789)), even if there has been a promise to keep it open (*Routledge v Grant* (1828)). Withdrawal of the offer must be communicated (*Byrne v van Tienhoven* (1880)), though this may be done *via* a third party (*Dickinson v Dodds* (1876)). An offer may also lapse after the expiry of a specified, or reasonable, time (*Ramsgate Victoria Hotel v Montefiore* (1866)).

Revocation of acceptance

Revocation of acceptance is not normally possible. The only exception may exist in relation to postal acceptances while they are still in transmission. There is no English authority on this – compare *Dunmore v Alexander* (1830)

(Scottish case, revocation possible), with *Wenckheim v Arndt* (1873) (New Zealand) and *A to Z Bazaars (Pty) Ltd v Minister of Agriculture* (1974) (South Africa) (both of which suggest revocation is not permissible).

Certainty in offer and acceptance

If an agreement is uncertain on some important issue, or leaves it open to be decided, the courts will hold that there is no contract (*Scammell v Ouston* (1941)). This does not prevent contracts to pay a 'reasonable price' for goods or services (s 8(2) of the Sale of Goods Act 1979; s 15 of the Supply of Goods and Services Act 1982).

Meaningless phrases

A meaningless phrase which can be excised without affecting the agreement will not prevent a contract (*Nicolene v Simmonds* (1953)).

Incomplete agreements

An 'agreement to agree' will not be enforced (*Courtney and Fairbairn Ltd v Tolaini Brothers* (1975)), unless the contract itself contains a method for determining the matter left open (*Sudbrook Trading Estate v Eggleton* (1982)).

CHAPTER 3

CONSIDERATION

This chapter is concerned with one of the remaining two elements which the courts look for in deciding whether a binding contract exists. As well as seeking a matching offer and acceptance, they will also look for 'consideration'. In some situations, a clear 'intention to create legal relations' will also need to be identified. This issue is discussed in Chapter 4.

3.1 The nature and role of consideration

The doctrine of consideration is one of the characteristics of English contract law. No matter how much the parties to an agreement may wish it to be legally enforceable, it will not be so unless it contains 'consideration'. What does the word mean in this context? It is important to note that it does not have its ordinary, every day, meaning. It is used in a technical sense. Essentially, it refers to what one party to an agreement is giving, or promising, in exchange for what is being given or promised from the other side. So, for example, in a contract where A is selling B 10 bags of grain for £100, what is the consideration? A is transferring the ownership of the grain to B. In consideration of this, B is paying £100. Or, to look at it the other way round: B is paying A £100. In consideration for this, A is transferring to B the ownership of the grain. From this example it will be seen that there is consideration on both sides of the agreement. It is this mutuality which makes the agreement enforceable. If B simply agreed to pay A £100, or A agreed to give B the grain, there would be no contract. The transaction would be a gift and not legally enforceable.

3.2 Benefit and detriment

It is sometimes said that consideration requires benefit and detriment. The often-quoted, but not particularly helpful, definition of consideration contained in *Currie v Misa* (1875) refers to these elements:

> A valuable consideration, in the sense of the law, may consist either in some, right, interest, profit or benefit accruing to one party or some forbearance, detriment, loss or responsibility, given, suffered or undertaken by the other.

In other words, what is provided by way of consideration should be a benefit to the person receiving it, or a detriment to the person giving it. Sometimes, both are present. For example, in the situation discussed in the previous paragraph, B is suffering a detriment by paying the £100, and A is gaining a benefit. B is gaining a benefit in receiving the grain, A is suffering a detriment by losing it. In many cases, there will thus be both benefit and detriment involved, but it is not necessary that this should be the case. Benefit to one party, or detriment to the other, will be enough. Suppose that A agrees to transfer the grain, if B pays £100 to charity. In this case, B's consideration in paying the £100 is a detriment to B, but not a benefit to A. Nevertheless, B's act is good consideration, and there is a contract. In theory, it is enough that the recipient of the consideration receives a benefit, without the giver suffering a detriment. It is difficult, however, to think of practical examples of a situation of this kind.

3.3   Mutual promises

The discussion so far has been in terms of acts constituting consideration. It is quite clear, however, that a promise to act can in itself be consideration. Lord Dunedin, in *Dunlop Pneumatic Tyre Co Ltd v Selfridge & Co Ltd* (1915), for example, approved the following statement from Pollock, *Principles of Contract*, 7th edn, 1902, Stevens:

> An act or forbearance of the one party, or the promise thereof, is the price for which the promise of the other is bought, and the promise thus given for value is enforceable.

Suppose, then, continuing the example used above, that on Monday, A promises that he will deliver, and transfer the ownership of the grain to B on the following Friday; and B promises, again on Monday, that when it is delivered she will pay £100. There is no doubt that there is a contract as soon as these promises have been exchanged, so that if on Tuesday B decides that she does not want the grain, she will be in breach. But, where is the consideration? On each side, the giving of the promise is the consideration. A's promise to transfer the grain is consideration for B's promise to pay for it, and *vice versa*. The problem is that this does not fit easily with the idea of benefit and detriment. A's promise is only a benefit to B, and a detriment to A, if it is enforceable. But, it will only be enforceable if it is a benefit or a detriment. The argument is circular, and cannot therefore explain why promises are accepted as good consideration. There is no easy answer to this paradox, but the undoubted acceptance by the courts of promises as good consideration casts some doubt on whether benefit and detriment can truly be said to be essential parts of the definition of consideration. It may be that the concept simply requires the performance, or the promise to perform, some action which the other party would like to be done. This approach ignores the actual or potential detriment. Alternatively, if it is thought that the idea of benefit and detriment is too well established to be discarded, the test must surely be restated so that consideration is provided where a person performs an act which will be a detriment to him or a benefit to the other party, or promises to perform such an act. On this analysis, benefit and detriment are not so much essential elements of consideration, as necessary consequences of its performance.

3.4 Consideration need not be 'adequate' but must be 'sufficient'

The view that the element of 'mutuality' is the most important aspect of the doctrine of consideration is perhaps supported by the fact that the courts will not inquire into the 'adequacy' of consideration. By 'adequacy' is meant the question of whether what is provided by way of consideration corresponds in value to what it is being given for. Thus, if I own a car valued at £20,000, and I agree to sell it to you for £1, the courts will treat this a binding contract. Your agreement to pay £1 provides sufficient consideration for my transfer of ownership of the car, even though it is totally 'inadequate' in terms of its relationship to the value of the car. This aspect of consideration was confirmed in *Thomas v Thomas* (1842). The testator, Mr Thomas, before his death, expressed a wish that his wife should have for the rest of her life the house in which they had lived. After his death, his executors made an agreement with Mrs Thomas to this effect, expressed to be 'in consideration of' the testator's wishes. There was also an obligation on Mrs Thomas to pay £1 per year, and to keep the house in repair. It was argued that there was no contract here, because Mrs Thomas had provided no sufficient consideration. The court took the view that the statement that the agreement was 'in consideration' of the testator's wishes, was not using 'consideration' in its technical contractual sense, but expressing the motive for making the agreement. The actual 'consideration' was the payment of £1 and the agreement to keep the house in repair. Either of these was clearly recognised as good consideration, even though the payment of £1 could in no way be regarded as anything approaching a commercial rent for the property.

3.4.1 Economic value

In coming to its conclusion in *Thomas v Thomas*, the court pointed out that consideration must be 'something which is of some value in the eye of the law'. This has generally been interpreted to mean that it must have some economic value. Thus, the moral obligation which the executors might have felt, or been under, to comply with the testator's wishes would not have been sufficient. An example of the application of this principle may perhaps be found in the case of *White v Bluett* (1853). A father promised not to enforce a promissory note (that is, a document acknowledging a debt) against his son, provided that the son stopped complaining about the distribution of his father's property. It was held that this was not an enforceable agreement, because the son had not provided any consideration. As Pollock CB explained:

> The son had no right to complain, for the father might make what distribution of his property he liked; and the son's abstaining from what he had no right to do can be no consideration.

The courts have not been consistent in this approach, however. In the American case of *Hamer v Sidway* (1891), a promise not to drink alcohol, smoke tobacco, or swear, was held to be good consideration, and in *Ward v Byham* (1956) it was suggested that a promise to ensure that a child was happy could be good consideration.

Even in cases which have a more obvious commercial context, the requirement of economic value does not seem to have been applied very strictly. See, for example, *Chappell v Nestlé* (1960). This case arose out of a 'special offer' of a familiar kind, from Nestlés, under which a person who sent in three wrappers from bars of their chocolate could buy a record at a special price. For the purpose of the law of copyright, it was important to decide whether the chocolate wrappers were part of the consideration in the contract to buy the record. The House of Lords decided that they were, despite the fact that it was established that they were thrown away by Nestlés, and were thus of no direct value to them.

The only economic value in the wrappers that it is at all possible to discern is that they represented sales of chocolate bars, which was obviously the point of Nestlés promotion. This is, however, very indirect, particularly as there was no necessity for the person who bought the chocolate to be the same as the person who sent the wrappers in. In contrast to this decision, the House of Lords held in *Lipkin Gorman v Karpnale Ltd* (1992), that gambling chips, given in exchange for money by a gambling club to its customers, did not constitute valuable consideration. This was regarded simply as a mechanism for enabling bets to be made without using cash. Lord Goff, however, took the view that the transaction did involve a unilateral contract under which the club issuing the chips agreed to accept them as bets, or indeed, in payment for other services provided by the club. The conclusion that the chips themselves were not consideration, however, must be regarded as being governed by the situation in which they were provided. There is no doubt that a perfectly valid and binding contract could be made under which plastic tokens are exchanged for money – indeed, the club presumably made such a contract when it bought the chips from the manufacturer or wholesaler. The case does not, therefore, in the end, affect the general approach taken by the courts of refusing to inquire into the value of consideration. An example of the lengths to which the courts will sometimes go to identify consideration is *De La Bere v Pearson* (1908). The plaintiff had written to a newspaper which invited readers to write in for financial advice. Some of the readers' letters, together with the newspaper's financial editor's advice was published. The plaintiff received and followed negligently given advice which caused him loss. Since the tort of negligent misstatement was at the time unrecognised, the plaintiff had to frame his action in contract. But where was the consideration for the defendants' apparently gratuitous advice? The purchase of the newspaper was one possibility, but there was no evidence that this was done in order to receive advice. The only other possibility, which was favoured by the court, was that the plaintiff, by submitting a letter, had provided free copy which could be published. This was thought to be sufficient consideration for the provision of the advice, which it would be implied should be given with due care.

The value of consideration has recently been considered in a different context in *Edmonds v Lawson* (2000). The Court of Appeal was considering whether there was a contract between a pupil barrister and her chambers in relation to pupillage. The problem was to identify what benefit the pupil would supply to her pupilmaster or to chambers during the pupillage. The court noted that the pupil was not obliged to do anything which was not conducive to her own professional development. Moreover, where work of real value was done by the pupil, whether for the pupilmaster or anyone else, there was a professional obligation to remunerate the pupil. This led the court to the conclusion that there was no contract between the pupil and pupilmaster, because of lack of consideration. They came to a different view, however, as to the relationship between the pupil and her chambers. Chambers have an incentive to attract talented pupils who may compete for tenancies (and thus further the development of the chambers). Even if they do not remain at the chambers (for example, if they work in the employed bar or overseas), there may be advantages in the relationships which will have been established. The conclusion was that (*per* Lord Bingham):

> On balance, we take the view that pupils such as the claimant provide consideration for the offer made by chambers ... by agreeing to enter into the close, important and potentially very productive relationship which pupillage involves.

The court was therefore prepared to accept the general benefits to chambers in the operation of a pupillage system as being sufficient to amount to consideration in relation to contracts with individual pupils, without defining with any precision the economic value of such benefits.

As these cases illustrate, the requirement of 'economic value' is not particularly strict. Indeed, in the overall pattern of decisions in this area, it is the case of *White v Bluett* (1853) which looks increasingly out of line.

The issue of the 'sufficiency' of consideration looks to the type, or characteristics, of the thing which has been done or promised, rather than to its value. In addition to the requirement of economic value, which as we have seen is applied flexibly, there are two other issues which must be considered here. The first is the question of so called 'past consideration'. The second is whether the performance of, or promise to perform, an existing duty can ever amount to consideration.

3.5 Past consideration is no consideration

Consideration must be given at the time of the contract or at some point after the contract is made. It is not generally possible to use as consideration some act or forbearance which has taken place prior to the contract. Suppose that I take pity on my poverty-stricken niece, and give her my old car. If the following week she wins £10,000 on the football pools, and says she will now give me £500 out of her winnings as payment for the car, is that promise enforceable? English law says no, because I have provided no consideration for it. My transfer of the car was undertaken and completed without any thought of payment, and before my niece made her promise. This is 'past consideration' and so cannot be used to enforce an agreement. A case which applies this basic principle is *Roscorla v Thomas* (1842). The plaintiff had bought a horse from the defendant. The defendant then promised that the horse was 'sound and free from vice', which turned out to be untrue. The plaintiff was unable to sue on this promise, however, since he had provided no consideration for it. The sale was already complete before the promise was made.

A more recent example of the same approach is *Re McArdle* (1951). William McArdle left a house to his sons and daughter. One of the sons was living in the house, and carried out various improvements to it. He then got each of his siblings to sign a document agreeing to contribute to the costs of the work. The document was worded in a way which read as though work was to be done, and that when it was completed, the other members of the family would make their contribution out of their share of William McArdle's estate. If that had been a true representation of the facts, then, of course, it would have constituted a binding contract. But, as Jenkins LJ pointed out:

> The true position was that, as the work had in fact all been done and nothing remained to be done ... at all, the consideration was a wholly past consideration, and therefore the beneficiaries' agreement for the repayment ... of the £488 out of the estate was *nudum pactum*, a promise with no consideration to support it.

This being so, the agreements to pay were unenforceable.

3.5.1 The exceptions

The doctrine of past consideration is not an absolute one, however. The courts have always recognised certain situations where a promise made subsequent to the performance of an act may nevertheless be enforceable. The rules derived from various cases have now been re-stated as a threefold test by the Privy Council in *Pao On v Lau Yiu Long* (1979). Lord Scarman, delivering the opinion of the Privy Council, recognised that:

... an act done before the giving of a promise to make a payment or to confer some other benefit can sometimes be consideration for the promise.

For the exception to apply, the following must be true:

- The act must have been done at the promisor's request. This derives from the case of *Lampleigh v Braithwait* (1615), where the defendant had asked the plaintiff to seek a pardon for him, in relation to a criminal offence which he had committed. After the plaintiff had made considerable efforts to do this, the defendant promised him £100 for his trouble. It was held that the promise was enforceable.

- The parties must have understood that the act was to be rewarded either by a payment or the conferment of some other benefit. In *Re Casey's Patents* (1892), the plaintiff had managed certain patents on behalf of the defendants. They then promised him a one-third share in consideration of the work which he had done. It was held that the plaintiff must always have assumed that his work was to be paid for in some way. The defendants' promise was simply a crystallisation of this reasonable expectation and was therefore enforceable.

- The payment, or conferment of other benefit, must have been legally enforceable had it been promised in advance. There is little that needs to be said about this. It simply means that the usual requirements for a binding agreement must apply.

The effect of these tests is that consideration will be valid to support a later promise, provided that all along there was an expectation of reward. It is very similar to the situation where goods or services are provided without the exact price being specified. As we have seen, the courts will enforce the payment of a reasonable sum for what has been provided. That is, in effect, also what they are doing in situations falling within the three tests outlined above.

3.6 Performance of existing duties

Can the performance of, or the promise to perform, an act which the promisor is already under a legal obligation to carry out, ever amount to consideration? Three possible types of existing obligation may exist, and they need to be considered separately.

3.6.1 Existing duty imposed by law: public policy

Where the promisee is doing something which is a duty imposed by some public obligation, there is a reluctance to allow this to be used as the basis of a contract. It would clearly be contrary to public policy if, for example, an official with the duty to issue licences to market traders was allowed to make enforceable agreements under which the official received personal payment for issuing such a licence. The possibilities for corruption are obvious. It would be equally unacceptable for the householder whose house is on fire to be bound by a promise of payment in return for putting out the fire made to a member of the fire brigade. The difficulty is in discerning whether the refusal to enforce such a contract is on the basis that it is vitiated as being contrary to public policy (which is discussed further in Chapter 10), or because the consideration which has been provided is not valid. The case law provides no clear answer. The starting point is *Collins v Godefroy* (1831). In this case, a promise had been made to pay a witness, who was under an order to attend the court, six guineas for his trouble. It was held that this promise was unenforceable, because there was no consideration for it. This seems to have been on the basis that the duty to attend was 'a duty imposed by law'.

3.6.2 Existing duty imposed by law: other factors

In cases where the possibilities for extortion are less obvious, there has been a greater willingness to regard performance of an existing non-contractual legal duty as being good consideration, though it must be said that the clearest statements to that effect have come from one judge, that is, Lord Denning. In *Ward v Byham* (1956), the duty was that of a mother to look after her illegitimate child. The father promised to make payments, provided that the child was well looked after, and happy, and was allowed to decide with whom she should live. Only the looking after the child could involve the provision of things of 'economic value' sufficient to amount to consideration. But, the mother was already obliged to do this. Lord Denning had no doubt that this could, nevertheless, be good consideration:

> I have always thought that a promise to perform an existing duty, or the performance of it, should be regarded as good consideration, because it is a benefit to the person to whom it is given.

The other two members of the Court of Appeal were not as explicit as Lord Denning, and seem to have regarded the whole package of what the father asked for as amounting to good consideration. This clearly went beyond the mother's existing obligation, but, as has been pointed out, did not involve anything of economic value. So, on either basis, the decision raises difficulties as regards consideration. Lord Denning returned to the same point in *Williams v Williams* (1957), which concerned a promise by a husband to make regular payments to his wife, who had deserted him, in return for her promise to maintain herself 'out of the said weekly sum or otherwise'. The question arose as to whether this provided any consideration for the husband's promise, since a wife in desertion had no claim on her husband for maintenance, and was in any case bound to support herself. Once again, Lord Denning commented:

... a promise to perform an existing duty is, I think, sufficient consideration to support a promise, so long as there is nothing in the transaction which is contrary to the public interest.

Once again, the other members of the Court of Appeal managed to find in the wife's favour without such an explicit statement. What this quote from Lord Denning makes clear, however, is that he regards the rule against using an existing non-contractual duty as consideration as being based on the requirements of the public interest, which would arise in the examples using government officials of one kind or another. Where this element is not present, however, he is saying that an existing duty of this kind can provide good consideration.

The law on this issue remains uncertain but, in view of subsequent developments in relation to contractual duties, in the case of *Williams v Roffey* (1990) which is discussed below (see 3.6.9), it seems likely that Lord Denning's approach would be followed. In other words, performance of, or the promise to perform, an existing duty imposed by law can be good consideration, provided that there is no conflict with the public interest.

3.6.3 Public duty: exceeding the duty

Whatever the correct answer, it is clear that if what is promised or done goes beyond the existing duty imposed by law, then it can be regarded as good consideration. This applies whatever the nature of the duty, so that even as regards public officials, consideration may be provided by exceeding their statutory or other legal obligations. The point was confirmed in *Glasbrook Bros v Glamorgan CC* (1925). In the course of a strike at a coal mine, the owners of the mine were concerned that certain workers who had the obligation of keeping the mines safe and in good repair should not be prevented from carrying out their duties. They sought the assistance of the police in this. The police suggested the provision of a mobile group, but the owners insisted that the officers should be billeted on the premises. For this, the owners promised to pay. Subsequently, however, they tried to deny any obligation to pay, claiming that the police were doing no more than fulfilling their legal obligation to keep the peace. It was held by the House of Lords that the provision of the force billeted on the premises went beyond what the police were obliged to do. Viscount Cave LC accepted that if the police were simply taking the steps which they considered necessary to keep the peace, etc members of the public, who already pay for these police services through taxation, could not be made to pay again. Nevertheless, if, at the request of a member of the public, the police provided services which went beyond what they (the police) reasonably considered necessary, this could provide good consideration for a promise of payment.

This rule is now generally accepted. In relation to the police the position is now dealt with largely by statute, but the approach taken in *Glasbrook* was confirmed in *Harris v Sheffield Utd FC* (1987), which concerned the provision of policing for football matches. The football club was held liable to pay for the services provided.

3.6.4   Existing contractual duty owed to third party

If a person is already bound to perform a particular act under a contract, can the performance of, or promise to perform, this act amount to good consideration for a contract with someone else? Suppose that A is contractually bound to deliver 5,000 widgets to B by 1 June. B is to use these widgets in producing items which he has contracted to supply to C. C therefore has an interest in A performing the contract for delivery to B on time, and promises A £5,000 if the goods are delivered by 1 June. Can A enforce this payment by C if the goods are delivered to B on the date required? Perhaps somewhat surprisingly, the courts have given a clear positive answer to this question. In other words, they have been quite happy to accept that doing something which forms part, or indeed the whole, of the consideration in one contract can perfectly well also be consideration in another contract. The starting point is the case of *Shadwell v Shadwell* (1860). An uncle promised his nephew, who was about to get married, the sum of £150 a year until the nephew's annual income as a barrister reached 600 guineas. The uncle paid 12 instalments on this basis, but then stopped. The nephew sued the uncle's estate for the outstanding instalments, to which the defence was raised that the nephew had provided no consideration. The nephew put forward his going through with the marriage as consideration. At the time, a promise to marry was as between the parties a legally enforceable contract. Nevertheless, the majority of the court had no doubt that performance of this contract could be used as consideration for the uncle's promise, on the basis that that promise was in effect an inducement to the nephew to go through with the marriage. Erle CJ recognised that there was some delicacy involved in categorising the nephew's marriage to the woman of his choice as a 'detriment' to him, but nevertheless considered that in financial terms it might well be. He put the issue in these terms:

> ... do these facts shew a loss sustained by the plaintiff at his uncle's request? When I answer this in the affirmative, I am aware that a man's marriage with the woman of his choice is in one sense a boon, and in that sense the reverse of a loss: yet, as between the plaintiff and the party promising to supply an income to support the marriage, it may well be also a loss. The plaintiff may have made a most material change in his position, and induced the object of his affection to do the same, and may have incurred pecuniary liabilities resulting in embarrassments which would be in every sense a loss if the income which had been promised should be withheld.

Moreover, a marriage, while primarily affecting the parties to it 'may be an object of interest to a near relative, and in that sense a benefit to him'. Thus, not only was going through with the marriage a 'detriment' to the nephew, it was also a 'benefit' to his uncle. On this basis, there was no doubt that it could constitute good consideration for the promise to pay the annuity.

3.6.5 Duty to third party: commercial application

This decision has been accepted as establishing the general principle that the performance of a contract with a third party can be good consideration. It was subsequently applied in a commercial context in *Scotson v Pegg* (1861), where it was held that a promise to deliver a cargo of coal to the defendant constituted good consideration, even though the plaintiff was already contractually bound to a third party to make such delivery. It was more recently accepted as good law in *The Eurymedon* (1974). Goods were being carried on a ship. The carriers contracted with a firm of stevedores to unload the ship. The consignees of the goods were taken to have promised the stevedores the benefit of an exclusion clause contained in the contract of carriage, if the stevedores unloaded the goods. The House of Lords viewed the stevedores performance of their unloading contract as being good consideration for this promise. As Lord Reid said:

> An agreement to do an act which the promisor is under an existing obligation to a third party to do, may quite well amount to consideration and does so in the present case: the promisee obtains the benefit of a direct obligation which he can enforce.

3.6.6 Performance or promise?

In all three cases so far considered, it has been *performance* of the existing obligation which has constituted the consideration. Can a *promise* to perform an existing obligation also amount to consideration? To take the example used at the start of this section, where A is bound to deliver goods to B on 1 June, and C promises A £5,000 if he does so. We have seen that, if A does deliver by the specified date, he will, on the basis of *Shadwell v Shadwell* (1860) and *Scotson v Pegg* (1861), be able to recover the promised £5,000 from C. What if, however, A also promises to C that he will deliver by 1 June? In other words, the contract, instead of being unilateral ('if you deliver to B by 1 June I will pay you £5,000') becomes bilateral? A promises to deliver; C promises £5,000. Is A's promise to perform in a way to which he is already committed by his contract with B, sufficient consideration for C's promise, so that, if A fails to deliver on time C, as well B, may sue A? The reference by Lord Reid in the quotation given above to '*an agreement* to do an act' would suggest that a promise is sufficient, though the facts of *The Eurymedon* (1974) itself clearly involved a unilateral contract ('if you unload the goods, we promise you the benefit of the exclusion clause'). The issue was, however, addressed more directly by the Privy Council in *Pao On v Lau Yiu Long* (1979), where it was held that such a promise could be good consideration. Citing *The Eurymedon*, Lord Scarman simply stated:

> Their Lordships do not doubt that a promise to perform, or the performance of, a pre-existing contractual obligation to a third party can be valid consideration.

Given the general approach to consideration, under which promises themselves can be good consideration, this decision is entirely consistent. The law on this point is, therefore, straightforward and simple. The fact that what is promised or performed is something which the promisor is already committed to do under a contract with someone else is irrelevant. Provided it has the other characteristics of valid consideration, it will be sufficient to make the new agreement enforceable.

3.6.7   Existing duty to the same promisor

The issue of whether performance of an existing duty owed to the same promisor can be good consideration is the most difficult one in this area. If there is a contract between A and B, and A then promises B additional money for the performance of the same contract, is this promise binding? It would seem that the general answer should be 'no'. It is normally considered that once a contract is made, its terms are fixed. Any variation, to be binding, must be mutual, in the sense of both sides offering something additional. If the promise is simply to carry out exactly the same performance for extra money, it is totally one sided. It would amount to a re-writing of the contract, and so should be unenforceable.

This approach was, until recently, taken to represent English law on this point. The authority was said to be the case of *Stilk v Myrick* (1809). The dispute arose out of a contract between the crew of a ship and its owners. The crew had been employed to sail the ship from London to the Baltic and back. Part way through the voyage some of the crew deserted. The captain promised that if the rest of the crew sailed the ship back without the missing crew, the wages of the deserters would be divided among those who remained. When the ship returned to London, the owners refused to honour this promise. It was held that the sailors could not recover. There was some suggestion that this decision was based on public policy, in that there was a risk in this type of situation of the crew 'blackmailing' the captain into promising extra wages to avoid being stranded. This had been the approach taken in the earlier, similar, case of *Harris v Watson* (1791). In *Stilk v Myrick* (1809), however, Lord Ellenborough seemed to base the decision on the lack of consideration. The remaining crew were only promising to do what they were already obliged to do under their existing contract, and this could not be good consideration. The desertion of part of the crew was just part of the normal hazards of the voyage. Campbell's report records Lord Ellenborough's views in the following way:

> There was no consideration for the ulterior pay promised to the mariners who remained with the ship. Before they sailed from London, they had undertaken to do all that they could under all the emergencies of the voyage. They had sold all their services till the voyage should be completed … the desertion of a part of the crew is to be considered an emergency of the voyage as much as their death; and those who remain are bound by the terms of their original contract to exert themselves to the utmost to bring the ship in safely to her destined port.

It might have been otherwise if they had not contracted for the whole voyage, and had been free to leave at the time of the desertion, or if the captain had 'capriciously' dismissed part of the crew (rather than some sailors having deserted). Such circumstances would fall outside the normal hazards of the voyage. Thus, in either of these cases, the remaining crew might not have been compelled by the original contract to proceed with the voyage, and would therefore have provided good consideration by agreeing to do so. On the facts which had actually occurred, however, they had not provided any consideration for the promise of extra money, and so could not recover it.

3.6.8   Going beyond the existing duty

It is implicit in *Stilk v Myrick* (1809) that if the crew had gone beyond their existing duty, then they would have provided good consideration. In addition to the examples given by Lord Ellenborough, the decision in *Hartley v Ponsonby* (1857) suggests that a certain level of desertion may in fact give rise to a situation falling outside the normal hazards of the voyage. In this case, a ship which had started out with a crew of 36 had, at the time that the relevant promise was made to the plaintiff, only 19 left, of whom only four or five were able seamen. In this situation, it was held that the voyage had become so dangerous that it was unreasonable to require the crew to continue. In effect (though the decision does not use this terminology), the original contract with the plaintiff had been 'frustrated' (see Chapter 13), and therefore a fresh contract on the revised (more favourable) terms could be created. The performance, or promise to perform, actions which are inside an existing duty cannot, however, amount to consideration.

3.6.9   A re-consideration: *Williams v Roffey*

The true basis for the decision in *Stilk v Myrick* (1809) is not without dispute, not least because of the fact that it was reported in rather different ways in the two published reports (see, for example, Luther, 'Campbell, Espinasse and the sailors: text and context in the common law' [1999] Legal Studies 526). Nevertheless, the analysis outlined above (based mainly on Campbell's report) was accepted and applied, almost without question, in many cases (for example, *North Ocean Shipping Co Ltd v Hyundai Construction Co* (1979); *Atlas Express v Kafco* (1989)), until 1990, when a decision of the Court of Appeal cast some doubt on its scope, and continued validity. This was in *Williams v Roffey* (1990) which was concerned with a contract to refurbish a block of flats. The defendants were the main contractors for this work, and had engaged the plaintiffs as subcontractors to carry out carpentry work. The agreed price for this was £20,000. Part way through the contract, the plaintiffs got into financial difficulties, at least in part because the contract price for the carpentry work was too low. The defendants were worried that the plaintiffs would not complete the work on time, or would stop work altogether. There was a penalty clause in the main contract under which the defendants would have been liable in the event of late completion. The defendants therefore promised to pay the plaintiffs a further £10,300, at a rate of £575 for each flat completed. On this basis, the plaintiffs continued to work on the flats, and completed a further eight. Because, at this stage, it seemed that the defendants were going to default on their promise of additional payments, the plaintiffs then ceased work, and subsequently sued for the additional sums in relation to the eight completed flats. The county court judge found for the plaintiffs, and the defendants appealed. The main issue before the Court of Appeal was whether there was any consideration for the promise to make the additional payments.

The defendants argued that since the plaintiffs in completing, or promising to complete, the work on the flats, were only doing something they were already bound to do under the existing contract with the defendants, they provided no new consideration. Glidewell LJ first outlined the benefits (as identified by counsel for the defendants) that accrued to the defendants from the plaintiffs' continuation with the contract. These were:

> ... (i) seeking to ensure that the plaintiff continued work and did not stop in breach of the sub-contract; (ii) avoiding the penalty for delay; and (iii) avoiding the trouble and expense of engaging other people to complete the carpentry work.

In the view of Glidewell LJ and the rest of the Court of Appeal, this was enough to support the defendant's promise to make the additional payments. In reaching this conclusion, all members of the court were at pains to stress that they were not suggesting that the principle in *Stilk v Myrick* was wrong, but that the present case could be distinguished from it.

3.6.10 *Williams v Roffey*: effect on *Stilk v Myrick*

The basis on which the court distinguished *Williams v Roffey* from *Stilk v Myrick* is not wholly clear from the judgments. Similar benefits to those identified could be said to have been present in *Stilk v Myrick* (1809). For example, as a result of his promise, the captain did not have to seek replacement crew, avoided delays, and made sure the existing crew continued to work. The main reason for distinguishing *Stilk v Myrick* seems in fact to have been related to the alternative, public policy, basis for the decision mentioned above. In other words, the court regarded it as significant that there was in *Williams v Roffey* (1990) no question of improper pressure having been put on the defendants. Indeed, it was they who suggested the increased payments.

The result is that the position as regards duties owed to the promisor is closely assimilated to the position in relation to duties owed to third parties. Thus, Glidewell LJ summarised the current state of the law as follows:

> ... (i) if A has entered into a contract with B to do work for, or to supply goods or services to, B in return for payment by B; and (ii) at some stage before A has completely performed his obligations under the contract B has reason to doubt whether A will, or will be able to, complete his side of the bargain; and (iii) B thereupon promises A an additional payment in return for A's promise to perform his contractual obligations on time; and (iv) as a result of giving his promise B obtains in practice a benefit, or obviates a disbenefit; then (vi) the benefit to B is capable of being consideration for B's promise, so that the promise will be legally binding.

Williams v Roffey is clearly very significant as regards defining the limits of valid consideration, and undoubtedly has the effect of widening those limits. Promises to perform existing obligations can now amount to consideration, even between contracting parties. Nevertheless, within these wider limits, consideration must still be found, as Russell LJ makes clear:

> Consideration there must ... be but in my judgment the courts nowadays should be more ready to find its existence so as to reflect the intention of the parties to the contract where the bargaining powers are not unequal and where the finding of consideration reflects the true intention of the parties.

3.6.11 Limitation on *Williams v Roffey*

One limitation on the effect of the decision in *Williams v Roffey* (1990) was made clear by the Court of Appeal in *Re Selectmove* (1995). The case concerned an assertion by a company that it had made a binding contract with the Inland Revenue under which it could, effectively, pay off its tax liabilities by instalments. The Inland Revenue argued that this agreement was not binding on them, because the company provided no consideration for the agreement to accept instalments: it was only promising to do something (paying its debts) which it was already obliged to do. The Court of Appeal, while deciding the case in favour of the Inland Revenue on another point, considered whether *Williams v Roffey* could apply in this situation. The company argued that the arrangement was to the Inland Revenue's 'practical benefit', because it meant that the company could stay in business, and therefore be more likely to meet its debts. The Court of Appeal, however, felt that this would be the case in relation to any agreement to pay by instalments. To treat this as providing consideration would be in direct conflict with the House of Lords' decision in *Foakes v Beer* (1884) (see 3.10 below), which had not even been cited in *Williams v Roffey*. The reversing of that decision was a matter for the House of Lords, or Parliament, and could not be undertaken by the Court of Appeal.

The current position is, therefore, that in relation to a promise to supply goods or services, a renewed promise to perform an existing obligation can be good consideration if the other party will receive a 'practical benefit', but that in relation to debts, a promise to make payment will only be consideration if accompanied by some additional benefit, such as payment early or, perhaps, in a different place.

3.7 Consideration and the variation of contracts

We now turn to consider the way in which the doctrine of consideration affects the freedom of parties to vary the obligations under a contract which they have entered into.

3.7.1 Need for accord and satisfaction

We have already referred to the general principle that for a contract to be altered there must be consideration. To use the language of the courts, 'accord and satisfaction' must be present: 'accord' meaning agreement, and 'satisfaction' essentially consideration. The approach taken in *Stilk v Myrick* (1809), as redefined in *Williams v Roffey* (1990), fits into this general principle. The same approach applies where a contract is brought to an end by mutual agreement. As long as there are outstanding obligations on both sides of the contract, the agreement to terminate will be binding.

3.7.2 The concept of 'waiver'

Over the years, however, this approach, though still applied where appropriate, has often been found in practice too restrictive. Various concepts have been used to allow more flexibility, and to give some force to agreed variations, even where these are not supported by consideration. One such is the concept of 'waiver'. Under this principle, a person who 'waives' (that is, promises not to enforce) certain rights under a contract for a period of time, may be stopped from later insisting on performance in accordance with the letter of the contract. So, in *Hartley v Hymans* (1920), a seller requested to be allowed to make late delivery, and the buyer agreed to this. When the seller delivered, the buyer refused to accept. It was held that the seller was entitled to recover damages, despite the fact that delivery was outside the terms of the contract, and that the buyer's promise to accept late delivery was unsupported by consideration. The buyer had waived the right to insist on delivery at a particular time, and could not go back on that.

Waiver was used by the common law courts, but was taken over by the chancery courts, and is now almost exclusively an equitable concept. It is important to note that waiver may not be permanent in its effect. The person waiving the rights may do so for a fixed period of time, or may be able to revive the original right by giving notice. The latter was the case in *Charles Rickards Ltd v Oppenheim* (1950). The contract here was for the building of a car body to fit a Rolls Royce chassis. The suppliers promised the buyer that they could fulfil the contract in 'six or, at the most, seven months'. The precise specification of the work to be done was agreed on 20 August 1947. The latest time for delivery, according to the suppliers' promise, was therefore 20 March 1948. The suppliers failed to meet this deadline, which was held to be a term of the original contract. The buyer, however, did not sue for breach of contract as soon as the date had passed, but continued to seek delivery. This was regarded as the buyer's having waived the right to delivery at a particular time.

Although there was continued delay, the buyer would not have been able to refuse delivery if the car had been finished in April, May or June 1948. By the end of June, however, the buyer's patience ran out, and on 29 June 1948 he told the suppliers that unless the car was delivered by 25 July 1948 he would not accept it. The car was not in fact finished until 18 October 1948. The suppliers then sued for non-acceptance, on the basis of the buyer's waiver of the original term specifying a date for delivery. The Court of Appeal, however, did not accept that such a waiver was permanent in its effect. As Lord Denning put it:

> It would be most unreasonable if, having been lenient and having waived the initial expressed time, [the buyer] should thereby have prevented himself from ever thereafter insisting on reasonably quick delivery. In my judgment, he was entitled to give a reasonable notice making time of the essence of the matter.

On the facts, the notice of four weeks given on 29 June 1948 was reasonable, and once it had expired, the buyer – having waited many months for his car – was entitled to cancel the contract. A waiver of rights will, therefore, generally be capable of withdrawal on the giving of reasonable notice.

Looked at in this way, the concept of equitable waiver has clear links with the common law concept of estoppel. This is the rule, whereby if A, a party to an action, has made a statement of fact on which the other party, B, has relied, A will not be allowed to deny that the original statement was untrue. This rule only applies to statements of existing fact, however. In *Jorden v Money* (1854), an attempt was made to apply it to a promise not to enforce a debt. Mrs Jorden had made repeated statements that she would not enforce a bond for £1,200 issued by Money, which she held. On the basis of that assurance,

Money married. He then sought a declaration from the courts that the debt had been abandoned. He succeeded at first instance, but the House of Lords took a different view. Lord Cranworth LC, having stated the general principles of the doctrine of estoppel, continued:

> I think that that doctrine does not apply to a case where the representation is not a representation of fact, but a statement of something which the party intends or does not intend to do.

Whereas the former type of statement (representation of fact) may provide the basis of an enforceable estoppel, the latter type (statement as to future intentions) can only become enforceable by being made part of a contract. Mrs Jorden's statements were of the latter type, and therefore, since they had not been made as part of a contract, were not enforceable. This decision established, therefore, that the doctrine of estoppel in the strict sense had no application to promises. Nevertheless, it has become common in recent years, following certain developments which will be looked at in more detail below, to refer to equitable waiver as 'promissory estoppel'.

3.8 The doctrine of promissory estoppel

The modern law on this topic, which gives rise to situations in which a contract can in effect be varied without there being consideration, derives from *Central London Property Trust Ltd v High Trees House Ltd* (1947). The plaintiffs were the owners of a block of flats in London, which they rented to the defendants at a rent of £2,500 pa. Following the outbreak of the Second World War in 1939, the defendants were unable to find sufficient tenants to take the flats, because of the large numbers of people leaving London. As a result the plaintiffs agreed that, in the circumstances, the rent could be reduced by half, to £1,250 pa. This arrangement continued until after the war ended in 1945, and the difficulty in letting the flats ceased. The plaintiffs then sought to return to the original terms of the agreement, and also queried whether they might not be entitled to claim the other half of the rent for the war years, since the promise to accept less was not supported by any consideration. Denning J, as he then was, confirmed that the plaintiffs were entitled to recover the full rent from the end of the war. Their promise to take less had clearly only been intended to last until that point. On the more general issue, however, on which his views were strictly *obiter*, he considered that the plaintiffs would not be able to recover the balance for the war years. The reason for this was that he thought that there was a general equitable principle whereby:

> A promise intended to be binding, intended to be acted upon, and in fact acted on, is binding so far as its terms properly apply.

His main authority for this view was the 'equitable waiver' case of *Hughes v Metropolitan Rly* (1877). The defendant held a lease of certain houses from the plaintiff. The lease contained a covenant of repair within six months of being given notice. The plaintiff gave such notice. The defendant then suggested that a sale might be arranged, and said that they would defer carrying out any repairs until this had been discussed. Some negotiations took place, but they did not result in an agreement for the sale. The plaintiff then served notice to quit, on the basis of the defendant's failure to comply with the original notice to repair. It was held that the plaintiff was not entitled to do this. The effect of the notice had been suspended while the negotiations on the sale were taking place, and time did not start to run again until these had broken down. Lord Cairns stated the general principle in the following famous passage:

> ... it is the first principle on which all Courts of Equity proceed, that if parties who have entered in to definite and distinct terms involving certain legal results – certain penalties or legal forfeiture – afterwards by their own act or with their own consent enter upon a course of negotiation which has the effect of leading one of the parties to suppose that the strict rights arising under the contract will not be enforced, or will be kept in suspense, or held in abeyance, the person who otherwise might have enforced those rights will not be allowed to enforce them where it would be inequitable having regard to the dealings which have thus taken place between the parties.

3.8.1 Implications of *High Trees*

Denning in *High Trees* asserted that this general principle supported his view of the relationship between the parties in the case before him. His own statement of the general principle (see 3.8 above), however, raised considerable controversy. First, taken at face value, it seemed to destroy the doctrine of consideration altogether. Secondly, the application of the 'equitable waiver' approach to the facts of the case, that is, the non-payment of rent, appeared to run counter to the House of Lords' decision in *Foakes v Beer* (1884) which stated that part payment of a debt can never be good satisfaction for the whole. Both of these objections, and their treatment in subsequent case law, must now be considered.

3.9 Promissory estoppel and consideration

The first point to consider is whether the doctrine of promissory estoppel as restated and developed by Lord Denning, does strike at the heart of the doctrine of consideration. The answer to this is that the broad statement of Denning in *High Trees* has been limited by subsequent decisions. There are five suggested limitations, of which four certainly apply: the status of the fifth is less clear.

3.9.1 There must be an existing legal relationship

Promissory estoppel cannot exist in a vacuum. There must be an existing legal relationship between the parties which is being altered by the promissory estoppel. This will generally, though not necessarily, be a contract (*Durham Fancy Goods Ltd v Michael Jackson (Fancy Goods) Ltd* (1968)). As Lord Denning said in *Combe v Combe* (1951), consideration remains 'a cardinal necessity of the formation of a contract, but not of its modification or discharge'.

3.9.2 There must have been (detrimental) reliance

Under the normal rules for the creation of a contract, obligations may arise as soon as promises have been exchanged. There is no need for either side to have relied on the other's promise in order to be able to enforce it. In relation to promissory estoppel, however, the party trying to enforce the promise must have taken some action on it. This simply means doing something as a result of it, for example, paying the lower rent, as in *High Trees*. In some cases, it has been suggested that the promisee must have suffered a detriment from such reliance, but Lord Denning has consistently denied that this is necessary.

In *WJ Alan & Co v El Nasr* (1972), for example, the dispute concerned a letter of credit, which had been opened in sterling rather than in Kenyan shillings, as specified by the contract. The other party had, however, drawn on this credit in relation to various transactions. The judge rejected the argument that this amounted to a binding waiver of the original terms as to currency, because there was no evidence that the party for whose benefit the waiver would operate had acted 'to their detriment'. Lord Denning in the Court of Appeal refused to accept this as a necessary requirement for either waiver or promissory estoppel:

> I know that it has been suggested in some quarters that there must be detriment. But I can find no support for it in the authorities cited by the judge. The nearest approach to it is the statement of Viscount Simonds in the *Tool Metal* case [see 3.9.5 below] that the other must have been led to 'alter his position' ... But that only means that he must have been led to act differently from what he otherwise would have done. And, if you study the cases in which the doctrine has been applied, you will see that all that is required is that the one should have 'acted on the belief induced by the other party'. That is how Lord Cohen put it in the *Tool Metal* case, and is how I would put it myself.

Megaw LJ agreed that there had been a binding waiver, though without dealing with the specific point on 'detriment'. Stephenson LJ left open the question of whether 'any alteration of position' was sufficient, but held that on the facts the party acting on the waiver had suffered a detriment anyway. Despite the fact that there is no absolutely clear authority on the issue, the current general view seems to be that action taken in reliance on the promise is enough, without a specific detriment needing to be shown.

3.9.3 The doctrine can only be used as a 'shield not a sword'

The third limitation derives from *Combe v Combe* (1951). In this case, a husband and wife were getting divorced. Between the *decree nisi* and absolute, the husband agreed to pay his wife £100 per annum net of tax. The husband never paid any money, and after seven years his former wife sued on the basis of his promise. Byrne J held that, while there was no consideration for the husband's promise, the wife could recover on the basis of the *High Trees* decision. The Court of Appeal, including Lord Denning, thought that this was a inappropriate use of the doctrine. It could not form the basis of a cause of action, and would generally only be available as a defence – 'as a shield, not a sword'. As Lord Denning pointed out, it was only in relation to the variation or discharge of contractual obligations that the need for consideration was reduced by the doctrine of promissory estoppel. In relation to the creation of such obligations, consideration remains an essential element.

3.9.4 It must be inequitable for the promisor to go back on the promise

Promissory estoppel is, as we have seen, derived from the concept of equitable waiver. Thus, as an equitable doctrine, its use is in the discretion of the courts, and even if the other elements for the applicability of it exist, it may still not be applied because it would be inequitable in the circumstances to do so. A clear example of the kind of situation where this would apply is the case of *D and C Builders v Rees* (1966). The plaintiff builders had done work for the defendants, and were owed nearly £500. After pressing for payment for some time, the plaintiff agreed to take £300 in satisfaction of the account. Mrs Rees, who knew that the plaintiffs were in financial difficulties, had told them that that was all they were likely to get. Despite their promise to accept the £300 (a promise for which there was no consideration), the builders then sought to recover the balance of the debt. Lord Denning, in the Court of Appeal, held that although there was clearly a promise here of a type which might raise promissory estoppel, the element of intimidation in the defendant's behaviour, knowingly taking advantage of the plaintiffs' circumstances, meant that it was not inequitable to allow the plaintiffs to go back on their promise. (The other members of the Court of Appeal did not think it was even necessary to discuss the doctrine.)

The inequity in *D and C Builders* was fairly obvious. The concept of 'equitability' does not necessarily imply impropriety on the part of the promisee, however. In *The Post Chaser* (1982), the promise was made and withdrawn within a few days. Although the other side had relied on the promise, their position had not in fact been prejudiced by such reliance. It was not, therefore, inequitable to allow the promisor to withdraw the promise.

The question is thus not simply whether the promisee acted in reliance on the promise, but whether there was sufficient reliance to make it inequitable not to enforce the promise. Although Robert Goff J in *The Post Chaser* was clearly supportive of the view noted above (see 3.9.2 above) that such 'reliance' does not require 'detriment', if there has been detriment then inequitability may be much easier to establish. In the absence of detriment, the court will probably look at the effect of allowing withdrawal of the promise. Would this have a significant adverse affect on the promisee, because of the way in which he has organised his affairs in the light of the promise? If not, then withdrawal is unlikely to be regarded as 'inequitable'.

3.9.5 The doctrine is only suspensory in its effect

Does the doctrine have a permanent, or only a suspensory effect? This final limitation on promissory estoppel is the one about which there is most uncertainty. There is no doubt that in some circumstances a promissory estoppel will have a purely suspensory effect. In *Hughes v Metropolitan Rly* (1877), for example, the notice of obligation to repair was simply put in abeyance while the negotiations over a possible sale continued. It is also clear that in relation to some sorts of contract, the effect can be to both extinguish some rights and suspend others. This is what happened in *High Trees* itself. Because the promise was interpreted as having only been intended to be applicable during the war, once that was over, the original terms of the lease automatically revived. Even if the promise is expressed to last indefinitely, however, in some circumstances it may be withdrawn by giving appropriate notice. In *Tool Metal Manufacturing Co v Tungsten Electric Company* (1955), for example, there was a promise to accept a reduced royalty in relation to the operation of some patents. It was held that the promisor could withdraw the promise by giving reasonable notice, from which point the original terms of the agreement would come back into operation. The House of Lords in fact held that the initiation of a previous, unsuccessful, action to escape from the promise constituted notice of withdrawal. It is in relation to this type of continuing contract, therefore, that promissory estoppel operates to both extinguish and suspend contractual rights. The obligations to make the higher payments during the period of the operation in both *High Trees* and the *Tool Metal* case were destroyed. The promisor was unable to recover the additional amounts for that period. The original terms were not in themselves extinguished, however, and could be reinstated for the future.

What is not clear is whether the doctrine of promissory estoppel could be used to extinguish, rather than suspend, an obligation which is not a continuing obligation. If, for example, the issue of inequitability had not arisen in *D and C Builders v Rees* (1966), would promissory estoppel have wiped out, or simply postponed, the payment of the balance? It seems clear that if the doctrine is to have any place at all in relation to this type of obligation, it must have the effect of extinguishing the right altogether. It would make no sense to say that Rees could rely on D and C Builders' promise to remit the balance of the debt, but that at any time the obligation to pay it could be revived by the giving of notice. It should be remembered, however, that it was only Lord Denning who seriously considered applying promissory estoppel in this situation, and that there has been no other reported case in which the doctrine has been applied to this kind of obligation.

The conclusion must be, then, that the precise effect of promissory estoppel, in terms of whether it suspends or extinguishes rights, will depend on the nature of the promise, and the type of contract to which it applies. It is not true to say, however, that promissory estoppel only operates in a suspensory way.

3.10   Promissory estoppel and the part payment of debts

The common law position on the part payment of debts is to be found in *Pinnel's* case (1602), as confirmed by the House of Lords in *Foakes v Beer* (1884). The rule is that part payment of a debt on the date that it is due can never be satisfaction for the full amount owed. The creditor will still be able to recover the balance of the debt, unless the debtor can show that some consideration was supplied in return for the creditor's agreement to take the lesser sum. Thus, if payment is made early, or on the day, but at a different place from that specified in the contract, the debt may be discharged. Equally, if the debtor provides goods, or services, instead of cash, this, if accepted by the creditor, will discharge the debt fully, even if the value of what was supplied is less than the total amount owed: 'the gift of a horse, a hawk, or a robe, in satisfaction is good' (*Pinnel's* case). Thus, the payment of £5 on the due date could never discharge a debt of £100; but if the debtor offered and the creditor accepted a book worth £5 in satisfaction, the creditor could not then claim the balance of £95. The justification for this rather odd rule is that the book must have been regarded by the creditor as more beneficial than money, otherwise it would not have been accepted, and the court will not inquire further into the creditor's motives.

3.10.1   The decision in *Foakes v Beer*

The rule in *Pinnel's* case (1602) was strictly *obiter*, in that the debtor had paid early, and had therefore provided sufficient consideration to discharge the whole debt, but it was confirmed by the House of Lords in *Foakes v Beer* (1884). Dr Foakes owed Mrs Beer a sum of money in relation to a judgment debt. Mrs Beer agreed that Dr Foakes could pay this off in instalments. When he had done so, Mrs Beer sued to recover the interest on the debt, in relation to the delay in the completion of payment resulting from the payment by instalments. The House of Lords held that, even if Mrs Beer had promised to forgo the interest (which was by no means certain), it was an unenforceable promise because Dr Foakes had provided no consideration for it. The Court of Appeal has recently confirmed in two cases that this is still the standard position as regards part payment of debts.

The first is *Re Selectmove* (1995), which is discussed above (see 3.6.11); the second is *Ferguson v Davies* (1997). In this case, the plaintiff started a county court action to recover a debt, originally stated at £486.50 but later increased to £1,745.79. The defendant, as part of his 'defence' in relation to these proceedings sent the plaintiff a cheque for £150, sending letters to the plaintiff and the court indicating that, while he admitted liability to this extent, the cheque was sent in full settlement of his dispute. The plaintiff, having sought advice from the county court, presented the cheque for payment, but continued with his action. The trial judge held that by accepting the £150 the plaintiff had compromised his action by a binding 'accord and satisfaction'. The Court of Appeal disagreed. Henry LJ, with whom Aldous LJ agreed, did so on the basis that there was no consideration here for the plaintiff's alleged agreement to abandon his claim. This was not a situation where a claim for a disputed amount was settled by a compromise involving partial payment by the debtor (a common basis for the settlement of legal actions). On the contrary, the defendant had admitted liability for the £150 sent, and so was giving the plaintiff nothing which could amount to consideration for the plaintiff's alleged agreement to forgo any further claim. By his own admission, he was bound in law to pay the £150, so this payment merely constituted the settlement of an acknowledged debt, and could not serve as consideration for any other promise. The principles of *Foakes v Beer* (1884) and *D and C Builders v Rees* (1966) applied, and the plaintiff was free to pursue his claim for the balance which he alleged was owed to him.

It should perhaps be noted that the other member of the Court of Appeal, Evans LJ, with whom Aldous LJ also agreed, decided the case on the different ground that on the facts there was no true 'accord', in that the defendant's letters could reasonably be interpreted as not being intended to assert that the £150 was sent as full settlement of all claims by the plaintiff. On the consideration issue, Evans LJ specifically indicated that he was expressing no view. Nevertheless, there is no doubt that in the light of these latest Court of Appeal decisions, the principles in *Pinnel's* case and *Foakes v Beer* remain good law in relation to the payment of debts.

What is the effect, if any, of the doctrine of promissory estoppel on these principles? In this context, it is important to note that *Foakes v Beer* was decided in 1884, that is, seven years after *Hughes v Metropolitan Rly*. *Hughes* was not even cited in the later case. Given that several members of the House of Lords in *Foakes v Beer* expressed some unhappiness about the outcome to which they felt that the common law bound them, so that they would gladly have accepted an escape route *via* the equitable doctrine of waiver, if that had been available, it must be assumed that the approach taken in *Hughes* was considered to have no relevance to the situation of part payment of debts. This, then, was a further way in which Lord Denning's decision in *Central London Property Trust Ltd v High Trees House Ltd* (1947) broke new ground. The case was concerned, in effect, with the partial payment of a debt (that is, half the rent for the war years). Nevertheless, Denning felt able to apply to it the *Hughes* principle of 'equitable waiver', and it seems now to be generally accepted that this doctrine, in its new guise of 'promissory estoppel', can mitigate the harshness of the rule in *Foakes v Beer*, in appropriate cases. This is not to say that *Foakes v Beer* would definitely be decided differently if it came before the House of Lords again today. That would depend on what exactly Mrs Beer was found to have promised, and also on whether promissory estoppel can ever be applied to extinguish a 'one-off' debt as opposed to payment obligations under a continuing contract. This issue has been discussed in the previous section, in considering whether promissory estoppel is only suspensory in its effect. It is, however, probably significant that the issue of promissory estoppel was not discussed in either *Re Selectmove* (1995) or *Ferguson v Davies* (1997). This would suggest that the courts remain reluctant to introduce this principle into the area of part payment of simple debts.

3.11 Other types of estoppel

Before leaving this area, we should also note two other types of estoppel which can have an effect on the operation of a contract. First, there is *estoppel by convention*. This arises where the parties to an agreement have acted on the basis that some provision in the contract has a particular meaning. This type of estoppel will operate to prevent one of the parties later trying to argue that the provision means something different. An example of its use is *Amalgamated Investment and Property Co Ltd (AIP) v Texas Commerce International Bank Ltd (TCIB)* (1981). In this case, a contract of guarantee between AIP and TCIB contained a promise by AIP to repay money 'owed to you' (that is, TCIB) by a subsidiary of AIP (ANPP). In fact, ANPP had been lent the money not by TCIB direct, but by a specially created subsidiary of TCIB named 'Portsoken'. When AIP got into financial difficulties, the liquidator sought a declaration that the guarantee was not binding, because there was no money owed to TCIB. It was held, however, that all parties had acted on the basis that the wording of the guarantee referred to the money lent by Portsoken to ANPP and, on that basis, an estoppel by convention operated to prevent AIP arguing for a different meaning.

The second type of estoppel which needs to be noted is *proprietary estoppel*. This operates in relation to rights in land only. It also differs from promissory estoppel (though both are sometimes confusingly referred to as 'equitable estoppel') in that it may be used to found a cause of action. In other words, it can be used as a sword rather than a shield. An example of its use is *Crabb v*

Arun District Council (1975). Mr Crabb owned a plot of land adjacent to a road. He decided to sell one-half of the plot to the Arun District Council (ADC). The ADC built a road along one edge of the piece of land which they had bought. Mr Crabb was allowed access to this road from a particular point on the land which he had retained. Mr Crabb then decided to sell another portion of this land. On the basis of a promise from the council that he would be allowed another access point on to their road, he sold the piece of land containing the first access point. The ADC, despite the fact that they had initially left a gap in their fencing at an appropriate point, then refused to allow the second access. The result was that the piece of land which Mr Crabb had retained was completely blocked in, without any access from either the original road, or the road built by the ADC. Mr Crabb brought an action to compel the ADC to grant him the second access point which had been promised. Although there was no consideration for this promise, Mr Crabb succeeded in his action. The words and actions of the ADC had led Mr Crabb to believe that he would have the second access point, and he had relied on this to his detriment in selling the piece of land containing the first access point. The Court of Appeal therefore allowed him to succeed on the basis of a proprietary estoppel.

3.12 Atiyah's view of consideration

Before we leave the topic of consideration, we should note briefly the views of Professor Atiyah on this issue, as set out, *inter alia*, in 'Consideration: a restatement', reproduced as Chapter 8 of his *Essays on Contract*, 1986, OUP.

Atiyah's view is that 'consideration' originated simply as an indication of the need for a 'reason' for enforcing a promise or obligation, such as the fact that the promisee had given something to the promisor in expectation that the promise would be fulfilled. It became formalised, however, into a rigid set of rules, such as that there must be benefit and detriment; that past consideration is no consideration; that consideration must be of economic value; and that gratuitous promises will not generally be enforced.

In examining how these rules actually operate, however, Atiyah argues that they are not actually followed rigidly by the courts. For example, as regards the need for benefit/detriment, he cites *Chappell v Nestlé* (1960) and *Hamer v Sidway* (1891) (see 3.4.1 above) as indicating that this is not necessary for a contract. Nor is it sufficient, in that contracts in which there is clearly benefit or detriment may still not be enforced, as we shall see in later chapters, because of considerations of illegality, duress, or undue influence. In relation to the need for economic value, *Ward v Byham* (1956) (see 3.4.1 above) may be seen as an exception.

Moreover, the unenforceability of gratuitous promises is not applied where promissory estoppel operates. Atiyah argues that promissory estoppel, as expounded in *High Trees*, was a step in the right direction, following a wrong turning taken as a result of the misinterpretation of *Jorden v Money* (1854) as an authority for the proposition that a statement of intention cannot give rise to an estoppel. That case was actually decided as it was, according to Atiyah, because of the requirements of the Statute of Frauds 1677, which at the time required that a promise given in consideration of marriage (which was the situation in *Jorden v Money*) had to be proved by writing. Because there was no writing, the case could not be pleaded in contract and was therefore pleaded as estoppel, but the court refused to allow this to be used as a means of circumventing the requirements of the Statute of Frauds 1677. *High Trees*, which recognised the enforceability of a statement of intention which had been relied on, should have shown the way forward, but was thrown off course by *Combe v Combe* (1951) (see 3.9.3 above: the 'shield not a sword' case). The real reason for the decision in that case, Atiyah says, was not the fact that the wife was trying to use promissory estoppel as a cause of action, but that justice was not on her side, because she was earning more than her ex-husband. This was a reason (or consideration?) for not enforcing the husband's promise. But, in general, where there has been reasonable reliance on a promise, even if the promisee has not provided what we should recognise as 'consideration' in the technical sense, Atiyah is of the view that the promise should be enforceable. This concept of reliance would, he argues, be a more satisfactory way of determining the existence of contractual obligations, as opposed to the formalistic requirement of consideration, with all its technical limitations.

Atiyah is not trying to substitute his own rigid doctrine of consideration for the current orthodoxy. What he is saying is that we should recognise the original idea of 'consideration' as meaning a reason for enforcing a promise, or acknowledging an obligation. This would be a much more flexible doctrine. The disadvantage, however, is that it would also be rather uncertain and unpredictable, and might depend too much on what the individual judge thinks amounts to a sufficient reason for enforcing a promise on a particular set of facts.

One possible basis on which this might be done is by giving a greater status to the requirement of 'intention to create legal relations'. We shall now return to more orthodox waters, and consider the role which this concept currently plays in determining the existence of contractual obligations.

CONSIDERATION

Consideration may be defined as what one party to an agreement is giving, or promising, in exchange for what is being given or promised from the other side. It provides the mutuality which makes an agreement enforceable.

Consideration involves a detriment to the party providing it, or a benefit to the party receiving it.

Mutual promises are sufficient to constitute consideration.

Consideration need not be 'adequate'. The value of what is provided by way of consideration does not have to match what it being given in exchange (*Thomas v Thomas* (1842)).

Consideration must be 'sufficient'. It must be of economic value (*White v Bluett* (1853)), but this requirement is not applied very strictly (*Chappell v Nestlé* (1960); *De La Bere v Pearson* (1908); *Edmonds v Lawson* (2000)).

Past consideration is no consideration (*Re McArdle* (1951)). But note the exceptions as set out in *Pao On v Lay Yiu Long* (1980), where there is:

- a prior request;

- an expectation of payment;

- the payment would have been legally enforceable if promised in advance.

Performance of existing duties

The performance of existing duties:

- Imposed by law

  This may well not amount to consideration (*Collins v Godefroy* (1831)) unless something additional is provided (*Glasbrook v Glamorgan CC* (1925)). But note Lord Denning's opposing view (for example, *Williams v Williams* (1957)).

- Owed to a third party under another contract

  This will be good consideration (*Shadwell v Shadwell* (1860); *The Eurymedon* (1975); *Pao On v Lau Yiu Long* (1980)).

- Owed to same promisor under a contract

  The position is uncertain. *Stilk v Myrick* (1809) states that this is not good consideration, unless something additional is provided (*Hartley v Ponsonby* (1857)). *Williams v Roffey* (1990) has established a potentially broad exception to this, which does not, however, extend to part payment of debts (*Re Selectmove* (1995)).

Consideration and the variation of contracts

An agreed variation which is supported by consideration will be fully enforceable.

- The concept of waiver

    A party may waive rights under a contract for a fixed period, or until notice is given to terminate the waiver (*Charles Rickards v Oppenheim* (1950)). (This was a common law doctrine, now taken over by equity.) Note the link with estoppel, which operates in a similar way in relation to statements of existing fact only (*Jorden v Money* (1854).)

- The doctrine of 'promissory estoppel'

    Invented by Denning in *Central London Property Trust Ltd v High Trees House Ltd* (1947) (relying on *Hughes v Metropolitan Rly* (1877)) – 'a promise intended to be binding intended to be acted upon, and in fact acted on, is binding in so far as its terms properly apply'.

Promissory estoppel and consideration

Promissory estoppel does not destroy the doctrine of consideration, because:

- it only applies where there is an existing legal relationship (*Durham Fancy Goods Ltd v Michael Jackson (Fancy Goods) Ltd* (1968));

- the promisee must have relied on the promise – though not necessarily to the promisee's detriment (*WJ Alan & Co v El Nasr Export and Import Co* (1972));

- the doctrine can only be used as a shield not a sword (*Combe v Combe* (1951));

- it must be inequitable for the promisor to go back on the promise (*D and C Builders v Rees* (1966); *The Post Chaser* (1982));

- the doctrine is, at least in some circumstances, only suspensory in its effect (*Tool Metal Manufacturing Co v Tungsten Electric Company* (1955)). Note that is not clear to what extent this can or should apply outside the context of 'continuing' contracts (such as leases, or agreements for royalty payments).

Promissory estoppel and the part payment of debts

The doctrine of promissory estoppel and the part payment of debts may be taken to limit the common law rule as laid down in *Pinnel's* case (1602) and *Foakes v Beer* (1884) (that is, that payment of less than is owed on the due date can never satisfy the full debt, though payment early, or at a different place, or with something other than money, may do so).

Other types of estoppel

Note 'estoppel by convention' (*Amalgamated Investment and Property Co Ltd v Texas Commerce International Bank Ltd* (1981)); and, also, 'proprietary estoppel' (*Crabb v Arun District Council* (1975)).

Atiyah's view of consideration

Atiyah argues that 'consideration' originally meant a 'reason for enforcing an agreement'. Problems have arisen from a misunderstanding of the case of *Jorden v Money* (1854), and the development of a rather rigid doctrine of consideration. It would be more satisfactory to return to a concept of 'reasonable reliance' as the basis for enforcing agreements, as opposed to the current very formalistic approach, as exemplified by *Foakes v Beer* (1884).

CHAPTER 4

INTENTION TO CREATE LEGAL RELATIONS

The final element to be considered in deciding whether a binding contract has been made is the parties 'intention to create legal relations'. It is only where the parties themselves have entered into an agreement which they intend to be legally binding that the courts will treat it as a contract. One way of achieving this objective would be through formal requirements. It would be possible to require, for example, that an agreement, to be legally binding, must be in writing, and have within it a clause confirming that it is intended to be legally binding. In one particular situation, relating to the enforceability of collective agreements between trade unions and employers, this is precisely what has been required (see 4.3 below). As has been explained in earlier chapters, however, generally the English law of contract does not require formalities. Verbal agreements are enforceable, and no particular forms of words are required. In many ways, however, the requirements of offer, acceptance and consideration, discussed in Chapters 2 and 3, may be regarded in themselves as indications of an intention to enter into a legally binding contract. If the parties have taken the trouble to specify their obligations in a way which makes them clear and unambiguous (as required by 'offer and acceptance'), and the agreement has the element of mutuality required by the doctrine of consideration, this may reassure a court that legal enforceability was intended. If, for example, a transaction which would otherwise appear as a gift has consideration introduced artificially, this may well be strong evidence of an intention to make a contract. The transfer of the ownership of a valuable painting, worth £50,000, which involves the recipient giving the supplier £1 in exchange would fall into this category. There would be no point in the recipient giving the money, unless the intention is to make the transaction of transfer into a contract, and the parties into 'seller' and 'buyer.' The introduction of consideration is in this case therefore evidence of an intention to create legal relations. Taking this approach to its logical conclusion, Hepple, for example, has argued that there is no need for a separate heading of intention ('Intention to create legal relations' (1970) 29 CLJ 122), and this point will be discussed below (see 4.5 below). The generally accepted view, however, is that although this analysis has some force, there are nevertheless some agreements which may have all the other characteristics of a contract, but which are clearly not meant to be treated as legally binding. If the parties to an apparently binding commercial agreement specifically state that it is not to have legal consequences, surely the courts should pay attention to this? Certain domestic arrangements may also raise difficulties. If, for example, there is an agreement between a man and a woman that he will cook a meal for them both, in return for her providing the wine to go with it, this may involve an offer, acceptance, and consideration, but no one would expect it to be regarded as legally binding. If she failed to turn up, he would not be able to sue for the cost of preparing the meal. Given, however, that no formalities are required, and that offer, acceptance and consideration can be identified, how are those agreements which are intended to be binding to be distinguished from those which are not? The evidence of the parties themselves is likely to be unreliable, so some other means of determining the issue must be found. As stated in *Edmonds v Lawson* (2000):

> Whether the parties intended to enter into legally binding relations is an issue to be determined objectively and not by requiring into their respective states of mind.

In fact, English law operates on the basis of 'presumptions' as to intention, which differ according to whether the agreement is to be regarded as 'domestic' or 'commercial'. These two categories of agreement must therefore be looked at separately.

4.1 Domestic agreements

The leading case in this category is *Balfour v Balfour* (1919). This involved an agreement between husband and wife, resulting from her inability (due to illness), to return with him to his place of work, in Ceylon. He agreed to pay her £30 per month while they were apart. Later the marriage broke up, and the wife sued the husband for his failure to make the promised payments. The Court of Appeal held that her action must fail. Two members of the court centred their decision on the lack of any consideration supplied by the wife. Atkin LJ, however, stressed that even if there were consideration, domestic arrangements of this kind are clearly not intended by the parties to be legally binding. He used the example of the husband who agrees to provide money for his wife in return for her 'maintenance of the household and children'. If this was a contract then each would be able to sue the other for failure to fulfil the promised obligation. As regards this possibility, Lord Atkin commented:

> All I can say is that the small courts of this country would have to be multiplied one hundredfold if these arrangements were held to result in legal obligations. They are not sued upon, not because the parties are reluctant to enforce their legal rights when the agreement is broken, but because the parties, in the inception never intended that they should be sued upon. Agreements such as these are outside the realm of contracts altogether.

The onus was on the wife to establish a contract, and she had failed to do so.

Lord Atkin's judgment is the one which has received most attention in subsequent case law, and has been taken as establishing the position that in relation to domestic agreements there is a presumption that they are not intended to be legally binding.

There are two points to be noted here. First, the notion of the 'domestic' agreement should be taken as relating more to the subject matter than the relationship between the parties. If, for example, a woman agrees to sell her brother her car for £1,500, there seems little reason to deny this agreement the status of a contract. On the other hand, social arrangements between friends who are not related, or household agreements between a couple living together, but not married, should come in to the category of 'domestic', and will therefore be presumed not to be binding. An example of the former situation is *Coward v Motor Insurers' Bureau* (1963) where an agreement between workmates to share the cost of transport to work was held not be legally binding.

Secondly, the rule is simply based on a presumption, and it will be possible for that presumption to be rebutted. In *Merritt v Merritt* (1970), for example, an arrangement between husband and wife similar to that agreed in *Balfour v Balfour*, but here made in the context of the break up of the marriage, was held to be legally binding. Lord Denning distinguished *Balfour v Balfour* in the following terms:

> The parties there [that is, in *Balfour v Balfour*] were living together in amity. In such cases, their domestic arrangements are ordinarily not intended to create legal relations. It is altogether different when the parties are not living in amity but are separated, or about to separate. They then bargain keenly. They do not rely on honourable understandings. They want everything cut and dried. It may safely be presumed that they intend to create legal relations.

The context in which the agreement was made was such therefore that, although it *prima facie* concerned a domestic matter, the support of a wife by her husband, the presumption that it was not intended to be binding was rebutted.

What will be the position in relation to agreements other than between spouses? The same principles apply, as is shown by *Simpkins v Pays* (1955). This involved an agreement which is of relevance to the increasing numbers of people involved in national lottery 'syndicates'. The plaintiff, the defendant, and the defendant's grand-daughter, lived in the same house. They regularly entered a newspaper 'fashion' competition, which required the listing of eight items in order of merit. Each of the three women made a listing, and the three entries were submitted on one form. There was no fixed arrangement as to who paid the entry fee or the postage, but the form was submitted in the defendant's name. When one of the lines won £750, which was paid to the defendant, the plaintiff sued to recover a third share of this. The judge held that there was, on the evidence, an agreement to 'go shares' if one of the lines won, and that this was intended to be legally binding. His reasons for coming to this conclusion are not very clear, but seem to relate to the fact that there was a 'mutuality in the arrangement between the parties'. Having heard the evidence of the parties he felt that their agreement went beyond the 'sort of rough and ready statement' made in family associations which would not be intended to be binding. There was a clear understanding as to what would happen in the event of a win, and this agreement was meant to be enforceable. The fact that all the surrounding circumstances may need to be considered was again stressed by Devlin J in *Parker v Clark* (1960). Here a young couple (the plaintiffs) agreed to live with older relatives (the defendants), and help look after them. In exchange, the plaintiffs were promised that the defendants' house and contents would be left to them. The arrangement did not work out, and the plaintiffs, having moved out, sued for damages. Devlin J noted that:

> ... a proposal between relatives to share a house, and a promise to make a bequest of it, may very well amount to no more than a family arrangement ... which the courts will not enforce.

On the other hand, it was possible for such an arrangement to be legally binding:

> The question must, of course, depend on the intention of the parties, to be inferred from the language they use and from the circumstances in which they use it.

In this case, the fact that the plaintiffs had disposed of their own house in order to move in with the defendants suggested that this was intended to be a binding agreement. The presumption that there is no intention in domestic agreements was again held to be rebutted.

4.2 Commercial agreements

If the agreement is not a 'domestic' one, then it will be regarded as 'commercial'. This will mean that the presumption is that the agreement is intended to be legally binding. It was confirmed in *Edmonds v Lawson* (2000) that this could include an agreement which was primarily educational – as with the agreement between a pupil barrister and her chambers. In *Edwards v Skyways* (1964), Megaw J emphasised that there will be a heavy onus on a party to such an agreement who wishes to argue that the presumption has been rebutted. In that case, the plaintiff was a pilot who had been made redundant. As part of the arrangements for this, he was offered and accepted a payment which was stated to be '*ex gratia*'. The company then found that the terms which had offered would be more expensive for it than it had realised, and denied that there was any legal obligation to make the payment. The judge held that *ex gratia* did not mean 'not legally binding', but simply recognised that prior to the offer being made there had been no obligation to make such a payment. Once it had been made, however, and accepted, as part of the redundancy arrangement, it was capable of being legally binding, and there was no evidence to overturn the presumption that this should be the case.

A similar reluctance to overturn the presumption is shown by the House of Lords' decision in *Esso Petroleum Ltd v Commissioners of Customs and Excise*

(1976). This concerned a 'special offer' of a common type, under which garage owners offered a free 'World Cup Coin' to every purchaser of four gallons of petrol. The coins could be collected to make a set, but had minimal intrinsic value. Promotional advertising will often be considered as a 'mere puff', and not intended to be legally binding. As discussed earlier, in relation to offer and acceptance, however, the case of *Carlill v Carbolic v Carbolic Smoke Ball Co* (1893) (see 2.3.5 above) shows that in appropriate circumstances it can be found to be intended to create a legal relationship, on the basis of a unilateral contract. Similarly, in the *Esso* case, the majority of the House of Lords held that there was a unilateral contract under which the garage proprietor was saying 'If you will buy four gallons of my petrol, I will give you one of these coins'. The minority (Viscount Dilhorne and Lord Russell) felt that there was, however, no intention to create legal relations. As Viscount Dilhorne put it, if this arrangement was held to be a contract:

> ... it would seem to exclude the possibility of any dealer ever making a free gift to any of his customers, however negligible its value, to promote his sales.

Moreover, he did 'not consider that the offer of a gift of a free coin is properly to be regarded as a business matter'. The majority, however, viewed what was being done as clearly a 'commercial' transaction. As Lord Simon commented:

> Esso and the garage proprietors put the material out for their commercial advantage, and designed it to attract the custom of motorists. The whole transaction took place in the setting of business relations ... The coins may have been themselves of little intrinsic value; but all the evidence suggests that Esso contemplated that they would be attractive to motorists and that there would be a large commercial advantage to themselves from the scheme, an advantage in which the garage proprietors would share.

The decision thus emphasises the difficulty faced by a commercial organisation in avoiding legal liabilities in connection with any transaction which it enters into with a view to commercial advantage. The advantage here was indirect (neither Esso nor the garages benefited directly from the exchange of the coins for petrol), but was nevertheless sufficient (that is, in terms of the likely increased sales of petrol which would result) to bring the presumption of an intention to create legal relations into play.

It is possible, however, by using sufficiently explicit wording, to rebut the presumption even in relation to a clearly commercial agreement. *Rose and Frank Co v Crompton Bros* (1925) was concerned with a continuing agency arrangement between two companies. The agreement contained within it an 'Honourable Pledge Clause', which specifically stated that it was not entered into as 'a formal or legal agreement', but was 'only a definite expression and record of the purpose and intention' of the parties. The parties 'honourably pledged' themselves to the agreement in the confidence 'that it will be carried through by each of the ... parties with mutual loyalty and friendly co-operation'. The Court of Appeal held that this should not be regarded as creating a legally binding agreement. To hold otherwise would be to frustrate the clear intentions of the parties:

> I can see no reason why, even in business matters, the parties should not intend to rely on each other's good faith and honour, and to exclude all idea of settling disputes by any outside intervention … If they clearly express such an intention, I can see no reason in public policy why effect should not be given to their intention.

The House of Lords agreed with the Court of Appeal that the overall agency arrangement was not legally binding, and could therefore be terminated without notice. In relation to particular orders placed under the agreement, however, they preferred the dissenting view of Lord Atkin in the Court of Appeal that such orders were enforceable contracts of sale. The 'honour clause' applied only to the general framework agreement, and not to specific orders made under it. Once again, therefore, the presumption of legal enforceability prevails in relation to commercial dealings, and the rejection of this by the parties is interpreted strictly so as to apply only in the limited circumstances to which the rejection most clearly applies.

'Honour clauses' have long been included on football pools' coupons, with the effect that the promoter is under no contractual obligation to pay winnings to a person who has submitted a coupon with a winning line ('the punter') (see, for example, *Jones v Vernons Pools* (1938)). It has now been confirmed by the Court of Appeal that such a clause must be taken to apply also to any agreement between the punter and a collector of coupons who then forwards them to the promoter. In *Halloway v Cuozzo* (1999), the collector had failed to forward the plaintiff's coupon, which contained a winning line. The Court of Appeal held that the collector had no contractual liability towards the punter. Moreover, the lack of intention to create legal relations also prevented the creation of duty of care, so that there was no liability in the tort of negligence either.

Public policy arguments may also influence a decision as to whether there is intention to create legal relations. In *Robinson v HM Customs v Excise* (2000), the claimant was an informer for the Customs and Excise. He tried to bring a contractual claim for the payment of reasonable remuneration and expenses. It was held, however, that there was no intention to create legal relations in respect of the supply of information by the claimant. The payments were discretionary and dependent on results (for example, arrests, seizures of illicit goods) and there were reasons of public policy why the court could not become involved in inquiring into these matters.

4.3   Collective agreements

Some problems of intention to create legal relations have arisen in the area of 'collective agreements'. By this is meant agreements between trade unions and employers, or employers organisations, as to the terms and conditions of work of particular groups of employees. Each employee will have a binding contract of employment with the employer, but some of the terms of this agreement (for example, as to rates of pay) may specifically be stated to be subject to the current collective agreement between employer and trade union. What is the status of the collective agreement itself? It is clearly made in a commercial or business context, and therefore it would seem that there should a presumption of legal enforceability. The issue was considered by the High Court in *Ford Motor Co Ltd v AEF* (1969). Ford were seeking an injunction restraining the trade union from calling strike action by its members. Part of Ford's argument depended on establishing that the collective agreements which it had reached with the AEF were legally binding. In deciding this issue, Geoffrey Lane J took the view that it was necessary to look at the general context in which such agreements were made. An objective view of whether they were intended to be enforceable should take account of not only the wording of the agreements themselves, and their nature, but also 'the climate of opinion voiced and evidence by the extra-judicial authorities' (here, he had in mind the Donovan Report (1968, Cmnd 3623) on industrial relations which had recently been published, and academic writing on the issue). Taking these matters into account:

> Agreements such as these, composed largely of optimistic aspirations, presenting grave practical problems of enforcement and reached against a background of opinion adverse to enforceability, are, in my judgment, not contracts in the legal sense and are not enforceable at law.

To make them legally binding would require 'clear and express provisions' to that effect.

This judgment seems to draw on a much wider range of factors than the other cases in this area in order to determine the issue. It is probably the case, however, that such an approach was a result of the particular sensitive context (that is, industrial relations) rather than being indicative of the way the issue should be dealt with more generally. The *Ford* decision should not, therefore, be regarded as indicating any general departure from the presumption of legal enforceability which attaches to agreements in the commercial area. As far as collective agreements themselves are concerned, the matter is now dealt with by statute. Section 179 of the Trade Union and Labour Relations (Consolidation) Act 1992, provides that collective agreements are 'conclusively presumed not to have been intended by the parties to be' legally enforceable. The only exception is where the agreement is in writing, and expressly stated to be legally enforceable. We thus have here a presumption against legal enforceability which is even stronger than that which operates in relation to domestic agreements. It cannot be rebutted by taking account of verbal statements, or by looking at the context, but only by a clear intention committed to writing. This, therefore, is one of the few occasions in which English law requires formality in the making of an agreement, if it is to be legally enforceable.

4.4   Letters of comfort

Finally, the status of 'letters of comfort' should be noted. Such 'letters' are often used as a means of encouraging a creditor to lend money to a subsidiary, or related, company of the issuer of letter. The effect of a letter of this kind was considered in *Kleinwort Benson v Malaysian Mining Corpn* (1989). The relevant letter had been given by the defendants to the plaintiff bank as part of a loan to a subsidiary of the defendants, MMC Metals Ltd. It stated that 'It is our policy to ensure that the business of MMC Metals Ltd is at all times in the position to meet its liabilities to you'. When the subsidiary went into liquidation, and the bank tried to recover from the defendants, they argued that the letter had never been intended to create a legal relationship. The trial judge disagreed, and held them liable. The Court of Appeal, however, construed the letter as simply stating the defendants' present intentions at the time the letter was issued, and not representing a promise as to future conduct. On that basis, the plaintiff's action failed. But there is nothing in the judgment of the Court of Appeal to suggest that an appropriately worded letter of comfort, stating, perhaps, 'it will at all times be our policy to ensure ...', could not be regarded as intending to create legal relations. Provided that some consideration could be demonstrated as having being given in return, then this would raise the possibility of the promise being enforceable. It might well be argued, however, that this goes against the whole purpose of comfort letters, which are essentially pre-contractual documents, and are given on the basis that there is no contract as yet between the parties. Perhaps this is a situation where the approach taken by *Ford Motor Co Ltd v AEF* (1969) would again be appropriate. In other words, the general context in which the letter is given should be taken into account in deciding whether it was intended to have legal effect: with the answer probably being that it was not intended to do so.

4.5   Is a requirement of intention necessary?

At the beginning of this chapter, reference was made to the argument that the insistence on a requirement of intention in addition to the other elements of validly formed contract (offer, acceptance, consideration) is unnecessary. This view has been taken by, for example, Williston (*Williston on Contracts*, 4th edn, 1990, Lawyers Co-operative Publishing) in the United States, and Hepple in the United Kingdom. (The latter's views are set out in the article 'Intention to create legal relations' (1970) 29 CLJ 122.) He argues that the problems with this area derive largely from a failure to take account of the particular approach to consideration adopted by Lord Atkin in *Balfour v Balfour* (1919). Hepple points out that, in defining consideration in terms of 'mutual promises' or as 'a benefit received by one party or a loss suffered by the other', Lord Atkin failed to add that the benefit or loss, or indeed the mutual promises, 'must be received as the price for the other'. Hepple argues that many domestic agreements may involve mutual promises, 'and yet not be a contract because the promise of the one party is not given as the price for the other'. In other words, the concept of the *bargain* is central to the test of enforceability of contracts under English law and the vital elements in the identification of a bargain are offer, acceptance and consideration. These three elements should be treated *together* as indicating a *bargain*. In other words, an analysis which tries to separate out *agreement* (that is, offer and acceptance) from consideration is missing the point of why the courts started looking for evidence of these three elements in the first place:

> This separation of agreement from consideration ... has resulted in a fundamental point being overlooked. This is that the common law recognised at an early stage that usually parties do not define their intention to enter into legal relations. Consequently, the fact that they have cast their agreement into the form of bargain (offer, acceptance, consideration) provides an extremely practical test of that intention. This test of bargain renders superfluous any *additional* proof of intention.

Accordingly, Hepple regards the courts as falling into error in trying to identify an additional element of intention in cases such as *Ford Motor Co Ltd v AEF* (1969). This only results 'in the use of unnecessary legal fictions'.

The argument may be justified as according with the principle that matters of the intention of the parties must be decided objectively. In other words, can the party who claims that he or she thought that the agreement was intended to be enforceable be said to have acted reasonably in this assumption? The presumption would be that as long as offer, acceptance and consideration were present, and no specific statement had been made about enforceability, then it would be intended to be legally binding. Social and domestic agreements could still be excluded from enforceability either because no reasonable person expects them to be legally binding, and therefore an assumption that they are would be unreasonable, or because what is given in exchange in such agreements is not generally to be regarded as good consideration. In either case, no 'bargain' is created.

This line of argument is in effect introducing a rule of formality into the formation of contracts. The formal requirements become not writing, or signature, but 'offer', 'acceptance' and 'consideration'. The parties who go through the process of making an agreement which contains these elements will, in the absence of specific and explicit evidence to the contrary, be deemed to have made a 'bargain' and therefore a binding agreement. Although this has some attractions, it is submitted that it does not truly represent the English common law approach to contracts. This is based, not only in relation to formation, but in many other areas as well, on the basis that the court is trying to give effect to the intention of the parties. This is the overriding concept, and the evidence which may go towards establishing whether any intention to create a legal relationship existed, and if so, what it was intended to be, is subsidiary. For that reason, the courts legitimately remain concerned to establish the existence or absence of intention, even if other indicators of a binding agreement are present. The existence of the presumption of enforceability in commercial agreements does not contradict such an approach. It simply allows it to operate in a way which is efficient, and does not encourage the parties to an agreement to become involved in unnecessary disputes as to their supposed intentions.

INTENTION TO CREATE LEGAL RELATIONS

Identification of intention

English law does not use formalities as a means of identifying intention to make a legally binding contract, but focuses on offer, acceptance and consideration. If these exist, then the courts will operate on presumptions related to the type of contract concerned – that is, whether it is 'domestic' or 'commercial'.

Domestic agreements

Domestic agreements are identified by their subject matter, rather than the relationship of the parties. Presumed not to be intended to be legally binding (*Balfour v Balfour* (1919)). Presumption can be rebutted, for example, where the agreement is made in connection with the break-up of a marriage (*Merritt v Merritt* (1970)), or one party has undertaken a major commitment indicating an intention to be legally bound (for example, *Parker v Clark* (1960)).

Commercial agreements

Non-domestic agreements will be regarded as 'commercial'. They will be presumed to be legally binding, and this presumption is difficult to rebut (*Edwards v Skyways* (1964)). Even an indirect commercial advantage will be enough to suggest an intention of legal enforceability (*Esso Petroleum Ltd v Commissioners of Customs and Excise* (1976)).

Presumption of enforceability may be overturned by:

- specific provision, such as an 'honour clause' as in *Rose and Frank Co v Crompton Bros* (1925);

- statutory provision – for example, s 179 of the Trade Union and Labour Relations (Consolidation) Act 1992;

- considering all the surrounding circumstances, including the commercial context of the agreement, and the expectations of the parties (*Ford Motor Co Ltd v AEF* (1969)).

Comfort letters

Comfort letters which express a present intention, rather than a promise as to the future, will not be legally binding (*Kleinwort Benson v Malaysian Mining Corpn*

(1989)). It is possible, however, that an appropriately worded comfort letter could be held to be legally binding.

Need for a requirement of intention – Hepple's view

Hepple argues that there is no need for a separate requirement of intention – what is needed is a 'bargain', involving mutuality. This is generally evidenced by offer/acceptance/consideration. Problems have arisen from Lord Atkin's view of consideration in *Balfour v Balfour* (1919), which did not require 'mutuality'. If this element is returned to the analysis of the formation of contracts, the need for a separate requirement of intention disappears.

Hepple's views have not been generally accepted, and arguably give insufficient weight to the identification of the parties' intentions as the primary role of the courts in 'policing' contracts.

CHAPTER 5

PRIVITY

5.1 The doctrine of privity

The doctrine of privity is regarded as one of the fundamental characteristics of the English law of contract, although as will be seen later in this chapter, the courts have recognised a number of exceptions to it and sanctioned a variety of devices for avoiding its effect. In addition, Parliament has recently given parties the opportunity of avoiding a significant part of the doctrine, by virtue of the Contracts (Rights of Third Parties) Act 1999.

The essence of the doctrine of privity is the idea that only those who are parties to a contract can have rights or liabilities under it. It is closely linked to the rule that consideration must move from the promisee, but can be shown to be distinct from it. Suppose, for example, that Aardvark Ltd agrees to buy shares from Bison plc, provided that Cheetah Ltd (which is a subsidiary of Bison) makes a loan to Aardvark. If Cheetah makes the loan, but Aardvark breaks its promise to Bison, who can sue? Not Bison, who has supplied no consideration. But neither can Cheetah, although it has supplied consideration, because it is not a party to the agreement between Aardvark and Bison.

What is the reason for the doctrine? It is clearly justifiable as a general rule that the burden of a contract should not be placed on a third party. It is less clear that the same applies to a benefit. Suppose that Alison promises Bernard that she will pay £100 to Oxfam if Bernard gives up smoking for a year. This is a contract which (subject to the question of intention to create legal relations) is clearly enforceable by Bernard. But, the charity which is to benefit will not at common law be allowed to enforce, because it is not a party to the agreement. Treitel argues that once again, the answer lies with the doctrine of consideration (*Law of Contract*, 10th edn, 1999, Sweet & Maxwell, p 545):

> A system of law which does not give a gratuitous promisee a right to enforce a promise may well be reluctant to give this right to a gratuitous beneficiary who is not even a promisee.

This aspect of the privity doctrine has, however, attracted much criticism, and it is the area in which, following recommendations to this effect from the Law Commission, there has now been legislative intervention. The effect of the Contracts (Rights of Third Parties) Act 1999 is discussed in detail later in this chapter (see 5.4). Since the Act has not replaced the common law, however, we shall start by looking at the development of the common law doctrine.

5.2 Development of the doctrine

There were some decisions dating from the 17th century which allowed a third party beneficiary to enforce a promise, but these pre-dated the strict formulation of the doctrine of consideration. The modern law is generally taken to derive from the case of *Tweddle v Atkinson* (1861). This concerned an agreement reached between the fathers of a couple who were about to get married, under which the father of the bride was to pay £200 and the father of the groom £100, to the bridegroom, William Tweddle, the plaintiff. William sought to enforce his father-in-law's promise, but it was held that he could not. The main justification appears to have been that it was necessary for there to be mutuality of obligations as between those enforcing a contract and having it enforced against them. As Crompton J put it:

> It would be a monstrous proposition to say that a person was a party to the contract for the purpose of suing upon it for his own advantage, and not a party to it for the purpose of being sued.

It is not clear why this proposition should be thought to justify the strong epithet 'monstrous'. There are other situations in the law of contract where there is not mutuality of this kind. In certain situations, unilateral contracts will lack mutuality, as will some contracts made by minors. The better reason for the decision would seem to be that William Tweddle was not the person to whom the promise was made, even though it was intended for his benefit. If he had been, it will be noted that it would have been quite possible for the court to have found that he had provided consideration for the promise. The agreement was clearly made in consideration of William's marriage, and, as we saw in the last chapter, in *Shadwell v Shadwell* (1860), decided just a year before *Tweddle v Atkinson*, going through with a marriage ceremony can be good consideration. This again indicates that the doctrine of privity is properly regarded as separate from, though closely linked to, the doctrine of consideration.

5.2.1 Affirmation by the House of Lords

Tweddle v Atkinson (1861) was a decision of the court of Queen's Bench, but the principle it stated was re-affirmed by the House of Lords in a commercial context in *Dunlop Pneumatic Tyre Co Ltd v Selfridge & Co Ltd* (1915). This concerned an attempt by Dunlop to control the price at which their tyres were sold to the public. They had a contract with Dew & Co, who were wholesalers in motor accessories, that in selling the tyres to retailers they would require the retailer to undertake to observe Dunlop's list price. Selfridge & Co entered into such an agreement with Dew & Co. Dunlop subsequently sought an injunction and damages in relation to alleged breaches of this agreement. The House of Lords held that they could not succeed. The following passage from the speech of Viscount Haldane LC, indicates the approach taken:

My Lords, in the law of England, certain principles are fundamental. One is that only a person who is a party to a contract can sue on it. Our law knows nothing a *jus quaesitum tertio* arising by way of contract. Such a right may be conferred by way of property, as, for example, under a trust, but it cannot be conferred on a stranger to a contract as a right to enforce the contract *in personam*. A second principle is that if a person with whom a contract not under seal has been made is to be able to enforce it consideration must have been given by him to the promisor or to some other person at the promisor's request.

On both grounds, Dunlop were doomed to failure. They were not parties to the agreement between Dew and Selfridge, and moreover, had provided no consideration for Selfridge's promise not to sell below the list price. Note also that, although this was not raised as an issue in the case, Dunlop could not, of course, rely on the terms of their contract with Dew, because Selfridge were not a party to this contract.

The doctrine is not one for which the courts have shown any great affection, but it was again re-affirmed by the House of Lords in 1968 in the case of *Beswick v Beswick*. A nephew had bought his uncle's coal merchant's business, and had promised as part of the deal, to pay his uncle £6.50 a week, and then, when his uncle died, to pay his aunt (if she survived) £5 a week. After his uncle's death, the nephew refused to make the payments to his aunt, and she sued. In the Court of Appeal, Lord Denning tried to open up a broad exception to the doctrine of privity by relying on s 56(1) of the Law of Property Act 1925, which states that:

A person may take an immediate or other interest in land or other property, or the benefit of any condition, right of entry, covenant or agreement over or respecting land or other property, although he may not be named as a party to the conveyance or other instrument.

Lord Denning's view (with which Danckwerts LJ agreed) was that this in effect abolished the doctrine of privity in relation to written contracts, and therefore allowed Mrs Beswick to sue her nephew on the promise made to her husband for her benefit. The House of Lords rejected this argument, deciding that the history and context of s 56 meant that it should be interpreted as not intended to apply to a straightforward contractual situation such as that in *Beswick v Beswick*, although the exact scope of the section remains uncertain (though it received a full consideration in *Amsprop Trading Ltd v Harris Distribution Ltd* (1997)). The case, therefore, fell to be dealt with under common law principles. The House accepted what Lord Reid referred to as the 'commonly held' view that where a contract between A and B contains an obligation to pay money to a third party, X, 'such a contract confers no right on X and X could not sue for the [money]'. In other words, the traditional doctrine of privity applied and Mrs Beswick was therefore prevented from suing in her personal capacity. The House of Lords agreed, however, that as the administratrix of her husband's estate, she could take his place as a party to the contract with the nephew, and thus obtain an order for specific performance of the obligations contained in it. Thus, while affirming the doctrine of privity, the House of Lords found a way to achieve what was clearly a just result.

5.2.2 A special case: multi-party contracts

There is one situation which does not fit neatly within the doctrine of privity, and which should be noted before moving on to consider the more general attempts which have been made to avoid the effects of the doctrine. This is the situation of the 'multi-party' contract.

We normally take as our typical model of a contract a two-party relationship. Nevertheless, there are situations which are clearly governed by contract but which do not fall into this pattern. Where a group of people each contract with one body, for example on joining a sports club, and agree to abide by the body's rules, can one member enforce those rules against another? Or is the only contract between each member and the club itself? The issue was considered in *Clarke v Dunraven* (1897). The case concerned the participants in a race organised by a yacht club. There was a collision during the race, as a result of which the plaintiff's yacht sank. The plaintiff sued the defendant, claiming damages based on provisions in the club rules. The defendant denied that there was any contractual relationship between him and the plaintiff. The House of Lords held that there was. The committee of the club had, in effect, made an offer to prospective entrants to the race to the effect that if they wanted to take part in the race, they would have to abide by the conditions which the committee had laid down. One of the conditions must be deemed to be that (in the words of Lord Esher, in the Court of Appeal):

> ... if you do sail [in a race], you must enter into an obligation with the owners of the yachts who are competing, which they at the same time enter into similarly with you, that if by a breach of any of our rules you do damage or injury to the owner of a competing yacht, you shall be liable to make good the damage you have so done.

There was, in other words, an obligation under a unilateral contract with the club's committee to enter into a contract with every other competitor. Applying this approach, the House of Lords held that there was a contract between all the competitors, which they had each entered into when they entered the race. The plaintiff was therefore entitled to succeed in his action, based on the obligation contained in the regulations governing the race to pay for damage caused by a breach of the rules of racing. Thus, in the example given above, each member of the sports club is in a contractual relationship, based on the rules of the club, with every other member. This analysis avoids any problems of privity, but creates difficulties as regards offer and acceptance. Who exactly is making the offer and acceptance as between the first and last individuals to join? Any attempt to find a way around this, such as making the club the agent for the receipt of both offer and acceptance, is bound to look very artificial.

5.3   Evading the doctrine

The current position as regards the doctrine of privity is that, its status having been confirmed by *Beswick v Beswick* (1968), there has not in recent years been any direct challenge in the courts to either aspect of the doctrine (that is, the conferring of benefits, or the imposition of obligations). There have, however, been various attempts to evade the effects of the doctrine, some of which have been more successful than others. The whole area must now be reconsidered in the light of the Contracts (Rights of Third Parties) Act 1999. This has fundamentally changed the position in relation to the conferring of benefits, but has not altered the common law as regards imposing burdens. The order of treatment will therefore be to look first at the Act; then at the various devices which have been used previously by the courts to confer benefits, and which may still be relevant in situations to which the Act does not apply; and, finally, at the common law rules relating to the imposition of burdens. (Note, also, that some aspects of the law of agency, in particular, the concept of the 'undisclosed principal', can be regarded as exceptions to privity: these are considered further in Chapter 17.)

5.4   The Contracts (Rights of Third Parties) Act 1999

The Act received the Royal Assent on 11 November 1999, and applies to contracts made on or after 11 May 2000. It also applies to contracts made between these two dates if the contract specifically states that the Act is to apply (s 10(2), (3)).

The Act is based on the 1996 Law Commission Report No 242, *Privity of Contract: Contracts for the Benefit of Third Parties* (Cmnd 3329). In one respect, therefore, this may appear as a speedy response to an identified need for law reform. It should not be forgotten, however, that, over 60 years ago, a similar reform was recommended by the Law Revision Committee (Sixth Interim Report, 1937, Cmnd 5449).

5.4.1   The main effect

The simplest reform would have been to say that third parties should be able to sue whenever a contract happens to benefit them. The Law Commission rejected this as being unacceptably wide, and opening the floodgates to litigation. It should only be where the contracting parties *intend* to confer a benefit on the third party that the right of action should arise. Even this would go too far, however. The Law Commission in its Consultation Paper which preceded the Report gave the example of a contract between a building company and a highway authority for the construction of a new road. The road may be intended for the benefit of all road users but it would surely not be acceptable for them all to have a right of action, for example, in the event of delay in completion of the project. The range of potential third party claimants should be narrowed to those on whom the parties to the contract intend to confer an *enforceable legal obligation*.

This objective is put into effect by s 1 of the Act which states:

(1) ... a person who is not a party to a contract (a 'third party') may in his own right enforce a term of the contract if:

(a) the contract expressly provides that he may; or

(b) subject to sub-s (2), the term purports to confer a benefit on him.

(2) Sub-section (1)(b) does not apply if on a proper construction of the contract it appears that the parties did not intend the term to be enforceable by the third party.

Sub-sections (1)(b) and (2) operate to create a rebuttable presumption that if contract appears to confer a benefit on a third party, then such a benefit is intended to be legally enforceable by that third party. A court faced with a promisor who denies that such legal enforceability was intended will have to decide what the 'proper construction' of the contract is. This will presumably mean applying an objective test of what reasonable contracting parties would have thought was meant by the term or terms in question. It also means that care will need to be taken in drafting contracts. If the parties do not want a third party to be able to enforce any benefits under the contract, they will be well advised to say so in specific terms.

The intended third party beneficiary need not be in existence at the time of the contract, but must be expressly identified in the contract by name, or as a member of a class, or as answering a particular description (s 1(3)). Thus, unborn children, future spouses and companies which have not at the time been incorporated all have the potential to benefit. A contract between the partners of the firm, for example, that each of their spouses will in certain circumstances receive benefits from partnership property, will apply both to the spouses of those already married and any future spouses of those who at the time are single.

If the above conditions are satisfied, the third party will be able to enforce the term of the contract (subject to any other relevant terms of the contract – s 1(4)) in exactly the same way as a party to the contract, obtaining damages, injunctions or specific performance in the normal way (s 1(5)). If the term is an exclusion clause, the third party will be able to take advantage of the exclusion or limitation (s 1(6)).

5.4.2 Changing the agreement

An important issue which arises once third party rights are recognised in this way is the extent to which the parties to the contract should be free to change, or even cancel, their agreement. In other words, does the third party have a legal right as soon as the contract is made, or only at some later stage. Normally, of course, the parties to an agreement can change it in any way they wish, provided there is consideration for any such change (see 3.7 above). Clearly, however, the right under s 1 would be of limited effect if the parties could at any time withdraw the promised benefit. At the same time, it would probably be restricting the normal freedom of the parties too greatly to prevent all possibility of such change. The Act deals with this situation by s 2.

The balance of s 2 lies with the freedom of the contracting parties. Section 2(3) provides that they can include a clause in their agreement which removes the need for any consent by the third party to a variation, or which lays down different procedures for consent from those contained in the Act. If no such clause is included, however, the provisions of s 2(1) will operate. This provides that the parties may not rescind or vary the contract so as to extinguish or alter the third party's rights under it if one of three conditions is satisfied. These are that:

- the third party has communicated to the promisor (by words or conduct) his assent to the relevant term (the 'postal rule' (see 2.8.6 above)) does not apply here – s 2(2); or

- the third party has relied on the term and the promisor is aware of this; or

- the third party has relied on the term and the promisor could reasonably be expected to have foreseen that the third party would do so.

Where the situation is that the third party has relied on the promise, that reliance does not have to be detrimental. If, for example, T (the third party) has been promised £1,000 by A under a contract between A and B, the fact that T has, in reliance on that promise, bought goods at a bargain price, or has acquired shares that have subsequently doubled in value, will be enough to prevent A and B cancelling the promise, provided that A knew or could reasonably be expected to have known that T had acted in reliance on the promise.

It is important to remember that these provisions relating to the ability of the parties to change the contract do not set out requirements for the third party right to arise. As soon as a contract is made which satisfies the requirement of s 1 of the Act, the third party acquires legal rights under it, and may enforce the relevant term without having either assented to or relied on the promise. The significance of the provisions in s 2 is simply that, once one of the events specified there has occurred, the promise may not be withdrawn or varied.

5.4.3 Defences

The availability of defences is dealt with by s 3 of the Act. Unless the parties to the contract have agreed otherwise in the contract (s 3(5)), the promisor can raise against the third party any defences (including 'set-offs') that could have been raised against the promisee (that is, the other party to the contract). Thus, if the promisee has induced the contract by misrepresentation (see Chapter 9) or duress (see Chapter 11), the promisor can use that as a defence to the action by the third party. Similarly, if goods are to be supplied by A to B, with B promising to pay the price to be paid to T, B could raise against T the fact that the goods were not of satisfactory quality under the Sale of Goods Act 1979 (see 18.5.3). The main contracting parties may also agree that a set-off arising between them from unrelated dealings may nevertheless be used by the promisor against the third party. The Explanatory Notes to the Act suggest that this could arise where:

> P1 and P2 contract that P1 will pay P3 if P2 transfers his car to P1. P2 owes money under a wholly unrelated contract. P1 and P2 agree to an express term in the contract which provides that P1 can raise against a claim by P3 any matter which would have given P1 a defence or set-off to a claim by P2.

The promisor may also rely on defences, set-offs or counterclaims against the third party which arise from previous dealings between the promisor and third party (s 3(4)). Thus, if T has induced A to contract with B on the basis of a misrepresentation, A can rely use that as a defence to an action by T, whether or not it would have been available against B. Similarly, if A and B contract that A is to pay £1,000 to T, but T already owes A £500, that can be set off by A against any claim by T.

The effect of s 7(2) should also be noted in this context, since it provides additional protection for the promisor. If the third party is taking action for negligent performance of an obligation under the contract, s 2(2) of the Unfair Contract Terms Act 1977 (which restricts the ability of a party to limit liability for loss or damage, other than death or personal injury, caused by the party's negligence – see 8.6), cannot be used to restrict the promisor's ability to rely on an exclusion clause.

Section 3(6) deals with the converse situation to those covered by s 3(2)–(5), that is, where the third party seeks to rely on a term of the contract (the most obvious example being an exclusion clause) in an action brought against him. The sub-section provides that the third party will only be able to enforce the term if he could have done so if he had been a party to the contract.

5.4.4 Protection from double liability

The right of the promisee to enforce the contract is specifically preserved by
s 4. In order that the promisor does not face being liable to both the promisee
and the third party, however, s 5 provides that, where the promisee has
recovered compensation from the promisor in relation to a term falling within
s 1 of the Act, this must be taken into account in any award subsequently
made to the third party. The converse situation is not specifically dealt with,
but it must be presumed that the courts would not allow the promisee to
recover where compensation has already been paid to the third party by the
promisor.

5.4.5 Exceptions

Section 6 excludes certain types of contract from the provisions of the Act.
These include:

- contracts on a bill of exchange, promissory note or other negotiable
  instrument;

- contracts binding on a company and its members under s 14 of the
  Companies Act 1985;

- terms of a contract of employment, as against an employee;

- contracts for the carriage of goods by sea, or, if subject to an international
  transport convention, by road, rail or air.

In relation to carriage contracts, however, the exception does not apply to
reliance by a third party on an exclusion or limitation of liability contained in
such a contract. The 'Himalaya' exclusion clause of the type considered in *The
Eurymedon* (1975) (see 5.9.2) could therefore now apply for the benefit of the
stevedores without the need to rely on agency.

5.4.6 Effect of the Act

The Contracts (Rights of Third Parties) Act 1999 has the potential to lead to
significant changes in the way in which contracts can be enforced by third
parties. For example, if applied to the facts of *Beswick v Beswick* (1968) (above,
5.2.1), the term in the contract between old Mr Beswick and his nephew
purported to confer a benefit on Mrs Beswick (s 1(1)(b)). It is likely that the
court would construe this term as being intended to confer a legally
enforceable benefit on her (s 1(2)). She would therefore be able to sue the
nephew in her personal capacity rather than only in her (fortuitous) capacity
as administratrix of her husband's estate. Similarly, in the commercial context,
in a case like *Woodar v Wimpey* (1980) (see 5.5 below), there was a promise to
pay part of the purchase price of a plot of land to a third party. The contract
specifically identified the third party, and purported to confer a benefit on it.

Again, assuming that the court construed this as being intended to confer a legally enforceable benefit, the third party could sue directly for the breach of the promise to pay. Other possible effects of the Act will be noted in discussing the cases dealt with in the rest of this chapter.

It must be remembered, however, that the main contracting parties are still in control. They can decide that the provisions of the new Act should not apply, and there will be nothing that the third party can do about it. They also have the freedom to change their minds, subject to the provisions restricting variation or cancellation. Where, however, the parties have decided that they wish to confer a benefit on third party, and have put that clearly into their contract, the courts will be able to enforce their wishes directly, rather than having to rely on the range of, at times, rather strained devices which they have been used in the past.

The extent to which these devices can be safely consigned to history is, however, not yet clear. Section 7(1) of the Act specifically states that the Act 'does not affect any right or remedy of a third party that exists or is available apart from this Act'. Moreover, as we have seen, the Act does not apply to all contracts. It is therefore still necessary to consider the ways in which the doctrine of privity has been circumvented prior to May 2000, since some of this law may prove to be of continued relevance.

5.5   Damages on behalf of another

It has been argued in some cases that where a contract is made by one person for the benefit of another, the contracting party should, in the event of breach, be able to recover damages to compensate the potential beneficiary's loss. This was the approach taken by Lord Denning in *Jackson v Horizon Holidays* (1975). Mr Jackson had booked a holiday for himself and his family, which turned out to be a disaster. The hotel for which the booking was made was not completed when the Jacksons arrived, and the alternative offered was of a very poor standard. The facilities did not match what had been promised, and the family found the food distasteful. There was no doubt that the defendants were in breach of contract. The trial judge, however, awarded £1,100 damages, and the defendants appealed against this as being excessive. The Court of Appeal, however, upheld the award, with Lord Denning holding that Mr Jackson was entitled to recover damages on behalf of the rest of his family. In particular, Lord Denning relied on the following quotation from Lush LJ in *Lloyd's v Harper* (1880):

> I consider it to be an established rule of law that where a contract is made with A for the benefit of B, A can sue on the contract for the benefit of B, and recover all that B could have recovered if the contract had been made with B himself.

Lord Denning felt that this indicated that where one person made a contract which was intended to benefit others, such as the father booking a family holiday, a host making a restaurant reservation for dinner, or a vicar arranging a coach trip for the choir, and there was a breach of contract, the father, the host, or the vicar should not only be able to recover lost expenses, but:

> ... he should be able to recover for the discomfort, vexation and upset which the whole party have suffered by reason of the breach of contract, recompensing them accordingly out of what he recovers.

This would have had the potential of opening up a large hole in the doctrine of privity, since all that a third party beneficiary would need to do would be to persuade the contracting party to sue in order to obtain the promised benefit, or appropriate compensation. In *Woodar Investment Development Ltd v Wimpey Construction (UK) Ltd* (1980), the House of Lords rejected the idea that it was possible generally to circumvent the doctrine of privity in this way. The decision in *Jackson* was accepted as being right, either (according to Lord Wilberforce) because it related to a special situation of a kind which perhaps calls for special treatment such as ordering a meal in a restaurant, or hiring a taxi for a group, or, more generally, because, as James LJ had held in the Court of Appeal, Mr Jackson's damages could justifiably be increased to take account of the fact that the discomfort of the rest of the family was part of his loss, in that it contributed to his own bad experience. This did not constitute, however, any significant exception to the doctrine of privity, and the more general basis on which Lord Denning had upheld the award of damages was specifically rejected. Lord Denning was held to have used out of context a quotation from *Lloyd's v Harper* (1880). As Lord Russell pointed out, Lush LJ was clearly concerned with the relationship between principal and agent, and it is to this situation alone that his statement should be taken to refer.

Despite this strong rejection of any general right to claim damages on behalf of a third party, in 1993, the House of Lords seemed to open the door again to claims of this kind. *Linden Gardens Ltd v Lenesta Sludge Disposals Ltd* (1993) concerned a building contract between a property company, P, and a construction company, C, in relation to a development containing shops, offices and flats. Before the building work was complete, P assigned its interests to T. The assignment was made without C's consent, and therefore was not effective to create a contractual relationship between T and C. Defect in the construction work were later discovered. These had taken place after the assignment of the contract. P sued C, but it was argued that P had suffered no loss, because at the time of C's breach of contract, the property had already been assigned to T. The House of Lords, however, drawing on an analogy for the carriage of goods by sea, where a shipper of goods is allowed to sue the shipping contract for the benefit of a third party to whom the goods have been transferred, held that this was a situation where a party to a contract was entitled to recover damages on behalf of another. Here, C knew that P was not going to occupy the premises itself, and therefore could foresee that any breaches would adversely impact on whoever acquired the premises from P.

This exception seems to indicate a retreat from *Woodar v Wimpey*, and has been applied by the Court of Appeal in the subsequent cases of *Darlington BC v Wiltshier Northern Ltd* (1995) and *Alfred McAlpine Construction Ltd v Panatown Ltd* (1998). It would seem unlikely, however, that it will need to be developed further. The availability of the power to confer rights directly on a third party under the Contracts (Rights of Third Parties) Act 1999 means that there is no need to expand the situations where a contracting party can recover damages on behalf of a third party. Indeed, the fact that the parties can now make this provision for third party rights, may well lead the courts to return to a more restrictive line in this area, as suggested by *Woodar v Wimpey*.

5.6 The trust of a promise

The chancery courts developed the concept of the 'trust' to deal with the situation where property was given to one person (the 'trustee') to look after and deal with for the benefit of another (the 'beneficiary'). Whereas the common law regarded the trustee as the legal owner of the property, and therefore as having a free hand to deal with it, in equity, it was held that the trustee had to take account of the claims of the beneficiary, and, moreover, the beneficiary could take action to compel the trustee to act in the beneficiary's interest. This tripartite trust arrangement has obvious possibilities for the development of a way round the doctrine of privity, and this was successfully attempted in *Les Affréteurs Réunis SA v Leopold Walford (London) Ltd* (1919). A contract for the hire of a ship (a 'time charterparty') included a clause promising a commission to the broker (Walford) who had arranged the contract. Walford was not a party to the contract, but was held by the House of Lords to be able to sue to recover the commission, on the basis that the charterers, to whom the promise had been made, were trustees of this promise. The House of Lords was thus ruling that the trust concept could apply to a promise to pay money, as well as to a situation where property was transferred into the hands of the trustee. This opened up a potentially substantial exception to the doctrine of privity. Later case law has, however, made the finding of the existence of a trust subject to some fairly strict requirements which have limited the usefulness of the device. There must have been a definite intention to create a trust and, in looking for this, the court will expect to find a clear intention to benefit the third party, which is intended to be irrevocable.

5.6.1 Intention to create a trust

The intention to create a trust will be easiest to find where the parties actually say that that is what they are doing. The courts are much more reluctant to imply an intention which is not made explicit. Two cases can be contrasted. *Re Flavell* (1883) concerned a partner in a firm of solicitors. When he retired, his partners agreed to pay him an annuity. It was also agreed that, when Flavell died, the annuity would be paid to his personal representatives, to be applied for the benefit of his widow and children. After Flavell's death, his creditors wanted the annuity to be regarded as part of the general assets of the estate, and therefore available to them. The High Court held, and the Court of Appeal confirmed, however, that the words used in setting up the annuity had created a trust in Mrs Flavell's favour. She therefore had a prior claim over the creditors.

Sixty years later, in *Re Schebsman* (1944), a different conclusion was reached. Schebsman was the employee of a company. On his retirement, the company agreed to pay him £5,500 pounds in instalments over six years. If he died within that period, certain sums were to be payable to his widow. Schebsman did die within the six years, shortly after having been declared bankrupt. The trustee in bankruptcy claimed that the payments to Mrs Schebsman were made on the basis of a trust, and therefore should, under the provisions of the relevant bankruptcy legislation, form part of Schebsman's estate, and go to pay off his creditors. The Court of Appeal held that the contract between Schebsman and the company was simply that payments should be made direct to Mrs Schebsman. Mr Schebsman would have had no rights over them. But it was a straightforward contract between Mr Schebsman and the company, not a trust. Mrs Schebsman had no right to enforce this contract, but equally the trustee in bankruptcy had no claim. As the company was willing to pay Mrs Schebsman, effectively she won.

The distinction between *Flavell* and *Schebsman* is clearly a fine one. It may well have been important that in *Flavell* the payment was to be made to the personal representatives, rather than direct to Mrs Flavell. This indicated an arrangement more akin to a trust than a straightforward contract.

5.6.2 Need for a clear intention to benefit the third party rather than the promisee

If the contract is intended to benefit the promisee, then, even if it might incidentally benefit a third party, there will be no trust. Thus, in the Canadian case of *Vandepitte v Preferred Accident Insurance* (1933), a father took a policy of car insurance which was stated to be 'available to any person while legally operating the car'. His daughter drove the car with his permission, and injured the plaintiff. The plaintiff sued the daughter and won. The relevant Canadian legislation provided that this judgment could be enforced against the daughter's insurer. But, the daughter had no insurance contract. The plaintiff argued that the father was the trustee of a promise made by his insurance company for the benefit of his daughter. This argument was rejected by the Privy Council on the basis that the father, in making the contract with the insurers was doing so for his own benefit, not his daughter's. There was no clear intention that she was to benefit, and therefore the trust argument failed.

5.6.3 Intention to benefit must be irrevocable

Whereas the parties to a contract are always free to change it by mutual agreement, a trust, once established, is regarded by the courts as irrevocable because it creates rights for the third party beneficiary which the trustee and the promisor are not entitled to change. This requirement has perhaps been the biggest obstacle to the development of the concept of the 'trust of a promise'. For example, in *Re Sinclair's Life Policy* (1938), a policy of life insurance was taken out for the benefit of the insured's godson. There was a clear intention in this case to benefit the third party. The policy, however, contained a provision enabling the policy to be surrendered for the benefit of the insured. It was not, therefore, irrevocable, and so could not be the subject of a trust.

This was an additional reason for the decision in *Re Schebsman* (1944). The court was not prepared to concede that parties to a contract had given up their right to consensual variation. As Du Parcq LJ put it:

> I have little doubt that in the present case both parties … intended to keep alive their common law right to vary consensually the terms of the obligation undertaken by the company, and if circumstances had changed in the debtor's lifetime injustice might have been done by holding that a trust had been created and that those terms were accordingly unalterable.

An element of discretion as regards who is to benefit will not, however, be fatal to a trust. In *Re Webb* (1941), insurance policies were taken out by a father in favour of his children. The policies allowed him to exercise options which would vary the benefits. This was held not to be fatal to a trust. Similarly, in *Re Flavell* (1883) (see 5.6.1 above), where there was a discretion to pay to the widow or daughters, the trust was upheld. So, the existence of a discretion will only defeat the trust if it enables the benefit to be diverted away from the beneficiaries altogether.

5.6.4 Effects of a trust

If a trust is found to exist, the third party can sue but must join the promisee as a party. The third party is entitled to any money paid or payable under the contract: the promisee has no rights to it, unless the trust fails for some reason.

5.6.5 Conclusion on trust device

The trust of a promise is a true exception to the doctrine of privity. The restrictions outlined above mean, however, that it has limited application. Indeed, it was not even considered in *Beswick v Beswick* (1968). The principle has never been denied, however, and if an appropriate case arose again, no doubt the courts would apply it. On the other hand, the situations where the trust device has been used are ones in which the parties could now generally achieve their objective much more easily by using the provisions of the Contracts (Rights of Third Parties) Act 1999.

5.7   Collateral contracts

A collateral contract generally takes the form of a unilateral contract, under which one party says 'if you enter into contract X, I will promise you Y'. The consideration for the promise, is the entering into contract X. It is quite possible for such an agreement to be made between the two parties to contract X, as in the case of *Esso Petroleum Co v Mardon* (1976), which is discussed below in Chapter 7. In a three-party situation, however, the construction of a collateral contract can be a means of evading the doctrine of privity. In *Shanklin Pier v Detel Products* (1951), the plaintiffs, who were the owners of a pier, were promised by the defendants, who were paint manufacturers, that the defendants' paint, if used to re-paint the pier, would last for seven years. As a result, the plaintiffs instructed the firm of painters who had undertaken the re-painting, to purchase and use the defendants' paint. This they did, but the paint only lasted three months. At first sight, the plaintiffs appeared to have no remedy, since they had provided no consideration for the promise given by the defendants (the paint manufacturers). The only contract which the defendants had made was to sell paint to the painters, and the plaintiffs were not a party to that agreement. It was held, however, that the plaintiffs could recover on the basis of a collateral contract. The consideration for the promise as to the paint's durability was the instruction by the plaintiffs to their painters to purchase the paint from the defendants.

In this case, there was a particular 'main' contract in prospect, that is, the purchase of the paint to re-paint the pier. This will usually be the case, but the device can be used even where there is no such contract specified at the time of the promise. In *Wells (Merstham) Ltd v Buckland Sand and Silica Co Ltd* (1965), the plaintiffs, who were chrysanthemum growers, bought sand produced by the defendants from a third party on the basis of the defendants' assurances as to its iron oxide content. These assurances turned out to be unreliable, and the plaintiffs sued the defendants for the resulting loss on the basis of a collateral contract. The court held that, although at the time the assurance was given there was no specific main contact in contemplation, this did not matter as long as it could be said to be made *animo contrahendi*, that is, with a view to a contract being made shortly. The plaintiffs were entitled to succeed.

The collateral contract device is not, of course, a true exception to the doctrine of privity (in the way that the trust is), because in the end the claimant and defendant are found to be the parties to a contract, albeit a collateral one. The way that it has been used by the courts at times, however, has been clearly as a means of avoiding the doctrine of privity, in that they have not been over-scrupulous in investigating whether the parties themselves thought that they were entering into a contract of the kind alleged, or had any intention of doing so. It may well be that, in the light of the Contracts (Rights of Third Parties) Act 1999, the courts will in future be less willing to find a collateral contract, given that the parties will now usually be able to achieve their objective of benefiting a third party more directly.

5.8 Statutory exceptions

In a number of situations, there has been statutory intervention to mitigate the effects of the doctrine of privity. These are generally connected with insurance, and the need to make sure that the intended beneficiary under an insurance contract is enable to enforce his or her rights. Examples include the Third Parties (Rights against Insurers) Act 1930; s 11 of the Married Women's Property Act 1882; s 148(7) of the Road Traffic Act 1988; and the Carriage of Goods by Sea Act 1992. These statutory exceptions are not affected by the Contracts (Rights of Third Parties) Act 1999.

5.9 Privity and exclusion clauses

One particular situation where the parties to a contract may wish to confer a benefit on a third party is in relation to exclusion clauses. Where some part of the contract is to be performed by employees, or sub-contractors, of one of the parties, that party may wish to extend the benefit of a clause excluding liability to such people. The doctrine of privity stands in the way of this, however. The problem generally arises where some loss or damage has been caused by negligence. If it is the negligence of an employee of a contracting party, then that party may well be protected, as far as breach of contract or vicarious liability in tort is concerned, by an exclusion clause. The employee will not be protected, however, and the injured party may decide to take action directly against him or her in tort, perhaps relying on the fact that the employer may well feel obliged to make good any damages awarded. In *Adler v Dickson* (1955), for example, Mrs Adler was a passenger on a cruise. She was injured when she fell from the ship's gangplank, which had been negligently left insecure. Her contract was with the shipping company, but she sued the master and boatswain personally, alleging negligence. The contract contained a very broadly drawn exemption clause. The Court of Appeal held, however, that this only protected the company, and not its employees, who were not parties to the contract with Mrs Adler. Since in this case the company had made clear that it would reimburse any damages awarded against its employees, the decision had the effect of negating the benefit of the exclusion clause as regards the contracting party as well. On the facts, this was probably justifiable, in that the clause had not purported to protect the employee. If, however, a clause is specifically worded to have this effect, and there is evidence that both parties intended that it should do so, the *Adler v Dickson* approach may have the effect of frustrating their intentions. The courts have therefore sought ways to avoid applying the doctrine of privity in such situations. One possibility, where the plaintiff has specifically promised not to sue the third party, is for the promisee to intervene to seek a stay of the action. This was recognised as a possibility in *Gore v Van der Lann* (1967), where the plaintiff was injured boarding a bus, and sued the bus conductor, rather than the corporation which ran the bus service. On the facts, however, there was no evidence of any contractual obligation on the part of the corporation to re-imburse the conductor, and therefore no grounds for granting a stay of the action. A stay was granted on this basis, however, in *Snelling v Snelling* (1973), though this was not an exemption clause case. The plaintiff, the director of a company, had agreed with his fellow directors that if any of them resigned they would forfeit the balance of a loan which each of them had made to the company. The plaintiff resigned, and sued to recover his loan. The company was not a party to the agreement between the directors, but it was held that they could intervene to stop the plaintiff's action. Ormrod J held that it was a necessary implication of the agreement to forfeit the loan that the plaintiff would not sue the company for its recovery:

> In my judgment, therefore, the second and third defendants have made out an unambiguous case and have shown that the interests of justice required that the plaintiff be not permitted to recover against the defendant company. It follows that this is a proper case in which to grant a stay of all further proceedings in the plaintiff's action against the company.

This principle could therefore be applied in an appropriate case to prevent an action against a third party who was purportedly protected by an exclusion clause, and therefore indirectly to give the third party the benefit of that clause. Its limitation, however, is that is dependent on the existence of a specific promise (express or implied), and also on the willingness of the promisee to intervene on the third party's behalf. Other attempts to avoid the effects of privity in this type of situation have been more broadly based.

5.9.1   Vicarious immunity

In *Elder, Dempster & Co v Paterson, Zochonis & Co* (1924), the House of Lords allowed shipowners to take the benefit of an exclusion clause (which was stated to apply to them), contained in a contract between the charterers of the ship, and the owner of goods being carried on it. The ratio of the decision is not very clear, but one possible basis for it was a principle of 'vicarious immunity', under which those who perform contracts on behalf of a contracting party can take the benefit of exclusion clauses contained in that contract. This analysis, which would constitute a major exception to the doctrine of privity, was, however, subsequently rejected by the House of Lords in *Scruttons Ltd v Midland Silicones Ltd* (1962). The House ruled that the third party stevedores in this case were unable to rely on an exclusion clause contained in a contract of carriage to which they were not parties. It recognised, however, that it might be possible in some situations for a contracting party to be regarded as the agent of someone who was involved in the performance of the contract, for the purpose of bringing them into a contractual nexus with the other party. Lord Reid identified four requirements which would need to be satisfied:

> I can see a possibility of success of the agency argument if [first] the bill of lading makes it clear that the stevedore is intended to be protected by the provisions in it which limit liability; [secondly] the bill of lading makes it clear that the carrier ... is also contracting as agent for the stevedore that these provisions should apply to the stevedore; [thirdly] the carrier has authority from the stevedore to do that, or perhaps later ratification by the stevedore would suffice; and [fourthly] that any difficulties about consideration moving from the stevedore were overcome.

5.9.2 The agency approach

This possibility was developed by the Privy Council in *New Zealand Shipping Company v Satterthwaite & Co (The Eurymedon)* (1975) where Lord Reid's four conditions were found to be fulfilled. The case again concerned the liability of stevedores for the negligent unloading of a cargo. The contract of carriage contained a very detailed exclusion clause, which, among other things, specifically stated that the carrier was to be regarded as acting as agent for any independent contractors carrying out any part of the contract, and that such contractors would have the benefit of the exclusion clause. The majority of the Privy Council found this sufficient to enable them to construct a contract between the owner of the goods and the stevedores. It was in the form of a unilateral contract, under which the owners said 'if you agree to unload these goods, we will give you the benefit of the exclusion clause'. The carriers acted as the stevedores' agents for the receipt of this offer. The consideration provided was the unloading of the goods. The stevedores were of course bound to do this anyway, under their contract with the carriers, but, as discussed in Chapter 3, the performance of an existing contractual duty owed to a third party is perfectly good consideration.

There is no doubt that the contract constructed in *The Eurymedon* was a 'fiction' in the sense that it is highly unlikely that any of the parties intended precisely such an arrangement as the Privy Council found to have existed. On the other hand, the result is clearly commercially convenient, since it is the clear desire and expectation of all concerned in contracts of this kind that third parties who perform part of the contract should be able to take the benefit of any relevant exclusion clause. The decision has not opened a up a major exception to the doctrine of privity: indeed, like the collateral contract device, it is not really an exception at all, since the individual who initially looks like a non-contracting third party, is found to be a party to a contract after all. The approach taken in *The Eurymedon* was applied again by the Privy Council in *The New York*

Star (1981), and must now be regarded as an established principle which can be applied wherever the wording of the clause and the relationships between the various parties make it appropriate.

In *The Mahkutai* (1996), however, the Privy Council, while recognising the general acceptance of *The Eurymedon* principles in relation to exemption clauses and third parties, refused to apply them on the facts. In this case shipowners, who were not party to a contract for the carriage of goods entered into by a charterer of their ship, sought to rely on an exclusive jurisdiction clause contained in the bill of lading. The Privy Council noted, however, that the wording of the relevant clause limited its extension to sub-contractors to the giving of the 'exceptions, limitations, provisions, conditions and liberties'. The Privy Council interpreted this as being limited to terms 'inserted in the bill for the carrier's protection ... It could not therefore extend to a *mutual* agreement, such as an exclusive jurisdiction clause' (emphasis added). In reaching this conclusion, the privy Council also noted the very technical nature of *The Eurymedon* analysis, involving fine points of contract and agency. It considered whether the time might have come to take a further step, and to recognise the situations currently dealt with by this principle as involving 'a fully fledged exception to the doctrine of privity of contract', thus escaping from the technicalities. It concluded, however, that it was not appropriate in the present case to take such a step. Nevertheless, the question has been raised, and there would seem to be a clear invitation to counsel in subsequent cases to try to argue for a general exception to privity, rather than relying on the technical analysis in terms of agency and consideration. The enactment of the Contracts (Rights of Third Parties) Act 1999 makes it much less likely, however, that this invitation will need to be taken up. The benefit of an exclusion clause can now be given to a third party quite straightforwardly, and the further development of the common law if therefore likely to prove unnecessary.

5.9.3   Modification of the duty of care

An alternative way of giving negligent third parties the benefit of an exclusion clause has been recognised in some recent cases. This treats the contract as part of the context in which the negligence occurs, and therefore relevant to defining the defendant's duty of care. In *Southern Water Authority v Carey* (1985), the negligence of subcontractors had caused the loss. The main contract contained an exclusion clause purporting to extend to the subcontractors, and stating that the main contractor contracted on their behalf. The agency argument, based on *The Eurymedon* failed, however, because of the rule of agency that the principal (in this case the subcontractor) for whom an agent acts must be identifiable at the time of the contract. That was not the case here. The judge decided in favour of the subcontractors, on the basis that the existence of the exclusion clause negated any duty of care owed by the subcontractors to the plaintiff. In the absence of a duty of care, the tortious action must fail. The validity of this approach was subsequently confirmed by the Court of Appeal in *Norwich City Council v Harvey* (1989). Once again, the case concerned the negligence of subcontractors, who in this case had set fire to the plaintiffs' premises. The main contract, however, contained a clause placing the burden of insuring against fire on the plaintiff. In this context, the Court of Appeal took the view that the subcontractors were not in breach of any duty of care. As May LJ put it:

> I do not think that the mere fact that there is not strict privity between the employer and the subcontractor should prevent the latter from relying on the clear basis on which all the parties contracted in relation to damage to the employer's building caused by fire, even when due to the negligence of the contractors or subcontractors.

5.10   Restrictive covenants

The exceptions and evasions of the doctrine of privity which we have looked at so far, have all been concerned with the recovery of a benefit by a third party. In this section we are concerned with the possibility of imposing a restriction on a third party's behaviour.

In land transactions, the seller of a piece of land will often wish to restrict the use to which the purchaser can put the land, particularly if the seller is retaining ownership of adjacent land. Of course, as between the original seller and purchaser, this can be achieved by contract. What about someone who buys from the original purchaser, however? Can that person be made subject to the restriction? In *Tulk v Moxhay* (1848), it was held that this could be the case in relation to land, provided that certain conditions were satisfied, in particular, that the original vendor still had an interest to protect (for example, continued ownership of the adjacent land).

5.10.1 Application outside land law

Land law has subsequently developed a complicated set of rules dealing with the enforceability of such 'restrictive covenants'. Outside the land law area, however, the courts have been reluctant to extend this exception to the privity doctrine. In *Taddy v Sterious* (1904), the court refused to apply it to an attempt to restrict the price at which the plaintiff's goods were sold by a third party. The plaintiffs had attached a notice to the packets of tobacco which they manufactured indicating that it was supplied to retailers on condition that it was not sold below the stipulated price. Acceptance of the goods was deemed to be acceptance of these conditions, and where the goods were bought from a wholesaler, the wholesaler was deemed to be the agent of the manufacturer. Despite this elaborate attempt to create an obligation which attached to the goods, in the same way as a covenant may attach to land, it was held that the defendant, who bought the goods from a wholesaler with full knowledge of the conditions, was nevertheless not bound by them. There have, however, been some cases concerned with shipping contracts where an approach analogous to the restrictive covenant has been used to bind a third party. In *De Mattos v Gibson* (1859), for example, the plaintiff had chartered a ship from its owner, C. C had then mortgaged the ship to G, who had notice of the charter. When C ran into financial difficulties, G proposed to sell the ship. The plaintiff successfully obtained an injunction restraining G from acting in a way which was inconsistent with the charter. Knight Bruce LJ said that where a person had acquired property from another with knowledge of a prior binding contract as to the use of the property made with a third party:

> ... the acquirer shall not, to the material damage of the third person, in opposition to the contract and inconsistently with it, use and employ the property in a manner not allowable to the giver or seller.

Moreover, he considered that the rule applied in the same way to both land and personal property. The same line was taken by the Privy Council in *Lord Strathcona SS Co v Dominion Coal Co* (1926). The plaintiffs had chartered a ship which had subsequently been sold. It was held that the new owner, the defendant, could be restrained by injunction from using the ship in a way which would prevent the operation of the charter contract made by the previous owner. It was regarded as significant, however, that the new owner had been aware of the existence of the charter at the time that the ship was bought.

5.10.2 The current position

The further development of this exception to privity was halted by the refusal of Diplock J (as he then was) in *Port Line Ltd v Ben Line Ltd* (1958), to accept the earlier decisions as being correctly based on equitable principles analogous to the law relating to 'restrictive covenants'. He took the view that these cases could be more properly viewed as falling within the area where the law of tort could provide a remedy (see 5.11 below), rather than as examples of a more general exception to the doctrine of privity. This analysis was apparently accepted for the following 20 years, but in 1979 Browne Wilkinson J indicated that there might still be some life in the equitable, restrictive covenant approach outside the area of land law. In *Swiss Bank Corporation v Lloyd's Bank Ltd* (1979), a loan had been made to buy shares. The lender argued that the borrower was contractually bound to repay the loan and interest out of the proceeds of any dealings with the shares. This was said to be a specifically enforceable obligation. The shares were also subject to a charge by Lloyd's Bank (presumably they had been put up as security for a loan). The lender alleged that Lloyd's rights over the shares were subject to the rights of the lender as set out in the original contract of loan. Browne-Wilkinson J held that the obligation to repay the loan out of dealings with the shares was specifically enforceable. This meant that the lender held an equitable interest in the shares, and that Lloyd's rights were subject to this obligation. The Court of Appeal and the House of Lords held that there was no specifically enforceable obligation of the kind alleged, but did not disagree with the judge's analysis of the relationship between the parties if there had been. It seems, therefore, that the equitable approach will still be available in certain appropriate cases. What will be needed is to show that the contract which is alleged to bind the third party has created an equitable interest in property falling within the scope of the contract. The third party will not then be allowed to act in a way which adversely affects this equitable interest. Nevertheless, although this demonstrates the theoretical availability of the 'restrictive covenant' approach in relation to personal property, the tortious action considered in the next section is more likely to work in practice.

5.11 The role of the law of tort

The cases and principles discussed in this section are in many ways the proper concern of the law of tort. But, this is an area (of which there are several) in which the rigid division drawn between tort and contract is unhelpful. The particular tortious action which we need to consider is that of 'wrongful interference with contractual rights'. A person who knowingly, and intentionally, brings about a breach of contract between two others, thereby commits a tort. Moreover, an injunction will generally be obtainable to prevent the interferer acting in this way. To this extent, it can be said that a third party is bound by the provisions of a contract between two other people.

The existence of this tort was recognised and applied in *Lumley v Gye* (1853). Lumley had engaged a singer, Joanna Wagner, to sing at a series of concerts at his theatre. It was a provision of this contract that she should not sing elsewhere. The defendant, who knew of this, persuaded Ms Wagner to sing at his theatre. Lumley first obtained an injunction against Ms Wagner preventing her from breaking her contract in this way. Her response was to leave the jurisdiction, and refuse to sing at either theatre. Lumley then sued Gye, and was awarded damages on the basis of Gye's intentional interference with the contract between Lumley and Wagner. This remedy has also been held to be available where goods are sold subject to a restriction on their disposal. In *BMTA v Salvadori* (1949), the purchaser of a new car agreed not to sell it for a year without first offering it to the plaintiff. The defendant bought the car with knowledge of this restriction, and with the intention of evading its effects, and was again held liable in tort.

As has been noted above, this is an alternative way of analysing the outcome in cases such as *De Mattos v Gibson* (1859) and *Lord Strathcona SS Co v Dominion Coal Co* (1926). It is, however, more limited than the 'restrictive covenant' approach. Such covenants may, in certain circumstances, bind even those who are unaware of them. The tort of interference with contract, on the other hand, requires knowledge on the part of the tortfeasor. It is only where he or she is aware of the other contract, and the fact that rights under it may be affected, that the tortious remedy will be available to restrain, or provide compensation for, the interference.

PRIVITY

The doctrine of privity

The doctrine of privity is regarded as one of the fundamental characteristics of the English law of contract.

- The essence of the doctrine is that only those who are parties to a contract can have rights or liabilities under it.

- The doctrine is linked to, but distinct from, the rule that consideration must move from the promisee.

- Development of the doctrine: *Tweddle v Atkinson* (1861) provides the starting point for the modern law: confirmed by the House of Lords in *Dunlop v Selfridge* (1915) and *Beswick v Beswick* (1968).

- Multi-party contracts: these are a special case (for example, *Clarke v Dunraven* (1897)).

Contracts intended to benefit a third party

The Contracts (Rights of Third Parties) Act 1999 enables parties to give a third party the power to enforce a benefit promised under the contract. The main provisions are:

- the clause must have been intended to confer a legally enforceable benefit;

- the beneficiary must be clearly identified;

- the parties will not be able to change the agreement once the third party has assented to or relied on the promise to confer a benefit;

- the promisor may plead any defences that would have been available against the promisee.

Evading the doctrine: conferring benefits

Various attempts have been made at common law to evade the effects of the doctrine.

- Damages on behalf of another was used in *Jackson v Horizon Holidays* (1975), but was disapproved by the House of Lords in *Woodar Investment Development Ltd v Wimpey* (1980).

- Trust of a promise: a true exception to privity, recognised in *Les Affréteurs Réunis SA v Leopold Walford* (1919), and applied in *Re Flavell* (1883). Strict conditions as regards the intention to create an irrevocable trust (as in, for example, *Re Schebsman* (1944)), which is meant to benefit the third party alone (*Vandepitte v Preferred Accident Insurance* (1933)), have prevented the development of the concept.

- Collateral contracts: the construction of a collateral contract, with consideration in the form of the making of the main contract, may bring parties who would otherwise appear strangers to the contract into such a relationship (*Shanklin Pier v Detel Products* (1951)). This is not a true exception, rather a device used to evade the doctrine by the construction of another contract.

- Statutory exceptions: these mostly concern insurance.

Privity and exclusion clauses

- Sub-contractors and employees included within the scope of exclusion clauses in contracts to which they are not parties will not generally be protected (*Adler v Dickson* (1954)).

- Protection may arise if there is a promise not to sue, and the promisee is willing to intervene (*Snelling v Snelling Ltd* (1973)).

- The doctrine of 'vicarious immunity' (*Elder, Dempster v Paterson Zochonis* (1924)) was rejected by the House of Lords in *Scruttons v Midlands Silicones* (1962).

- Agency, where the promisee is deemed to act as agent for the third party beneficiary, was used by the Privy Council in *The Eurymedon* (1975), and again in *The New York Star* (1981). This involves the construction of a collateral, unilateral contract between promisor and beneficiary.

- In negligence cases, the clause may be taken to have modified or negated the duty of care owed by the third party (*Southern Water Authority v Carey* (1985); *Norwich City Council v Harvey* (1989)).

Evading the doctrine: imposition of burdens

- Restrictive covenants: a means of imposing burdens on third parties, recognised in land law (*Tulk v Moxhay* (1848)). These have been used in some shipping cases (for example, *De Mattos v Gibson* (1859); *Strathcona v Dominion Coal* (1926)), but were rejected in *Port Line v Ben Line* (1958). There has been no recent use, but note *Swiss Bank Corporation v Lloyd's Bank* (1979), which suggests this approach is still possible.

- The role of the law of tort.

  A tort can be committed by intentionally inducing a breach of contract. This was used in *Lumley v Gye* (1853), to restrict the actions of a person who was not party to the contract.

  This provides an alternative explanation of the shipping 'restrictive covenant' cases.

CHAPTER 6

CAPACITY

6.1 Introduction

In order to make a valid, enforceable, contract, both parties must be regarded as having capacity in law to enter into such an agreement. This is not an issue which causes practical problems with any frequency, and the rules are not particularly complicated. Three aspects of this topic are considered in this chapter, namely minors' contracts, mental disability, and intoxication. The problems which can, on occasion, arise concerning the capacity of companies to make particular contracts are not considered here, being regarded as more appropriately the concern of texts on company law.

6.2 Minors' contracts

The basic rule is such that people who have not reached the age of 18 are regarded in English law as 'minors' and as having limited capacity to enter into contracts. The purpose of the rules is largely paternalistic – that is, it is intended to protect minors from the consequences of their own actions. As a result, the law can sometimes appear to operate harshly against those who contract with minors. In particular, the adult party who is unaware that he or she is contracting with a minor, may still find the contract unenforceable. The law starts with a presumption that all minors' contracts are either void or voidable. There are two main exceptions to this, namely contracts for 'necessaries', and 'beneficial contracts of service'. Such contracts may be fully enforceable. In addition, certain contracts which involve a minor obtaining an interest in property which involves continuous or recurring obligations may be voidable. The scope of these various categories will be considered next, before moving on to the consequences of entering into a contract with a minor.

6.2.1 Contracts for necessaries

The first major exception to the rule as to unenforceability relates to contract for 'necessaries'. The reasoning here is that a total rule of unenforceability would act to the minor's disadvantage. If traders knew that any contract with a minor would involve the risk of the minor deciding not to honour it, they would be reluctant to enter into such contracts at all. As a consequence, the minor might have difficulty acquiring the basic requirements of everyday life, such as food or clothing. In reality, of course, the majority of transactions of this type take place on the basis of the simultaneous exchange of goods and payment, where there is little or no risk to the trader. In relation to more complicated transactions, and particularly those which do not involve payment on the spot, the question of whether the contract concerns 'necessaries' will still be important.

6.2.2 The definition of 'necessaries'

The concept of necessaries, which covers both goods and services, was explained in some detail in *Chapple v Cooper* (1844), where it was held that a widow who was a minor was liable in contract for the cost of her husband's funeral. According to Alderson B in this case, 'necessaries' includes not only things which are absolutely necessary for survival, but also all those which are required for a reasonable existence. Food and clothing are obviously covered, but also medical assistance and education. Once the goods or services are of a kind which can be put in the general category of 'necessaries', there is then a further question as to whether they are appropriate to the particular minor. Whether a silk dress can count as a necessary will depend on the minor's normal standard of living. Items of 'mere luxury', however (as opposed to 'luxurious articles of utility'), will not be regarded as necessaries. Nor will articles bought as gifts normally be so regarded (*Ryder v Wombwell* (1868)). The approach of the common law is confirmed as far as goods are concerned by s 3 of the Sale of Goods Act (SGA) 1979 which states:

> ... 'necessaries' means goods suitable to the condition in life of the minor and to his actual requirements at the time of sale and delivery.

As will be noted, this adds to the test stated above the question of whether the minor is already adequately supplied with goods of this kind. The same limitation almost certainly applies to services. Its application in relation to goods is illustrated by *Nash v Inman* (1908). The plaintiff was a tailor, and the defendant an undergraduate at Cambridge University, who had ordered 11 fancy waistcoats. When the plaintiff sued for payment, the defendant pleaded lack of capacity. The plaintiff argued that the waistcoats were in the category of necessaries. There was no doubt that they were among the class of things (that is, clothing) capable of being necessaries. It was up to the plaintiff to prove, however, that the defendant was not already adequately supplied with items of this kind, which he was unable to do. It should be noted that this case made it clear that the trader who is ignorant of the minor's situation will not be protected. The decision is made by looking at matters entirely from the minor's point of view.

6.2.3 Beneficial contracts of service

A person under the age of 18 must have the possibility of being able to earn a living, and so contracts of employment, training, or apprenticeship, will be enforceable. The contract, taken as a whole, must not, however, be oppressive. *De Francesco v Barnum* (1889), for example, concerned a girl of 14 who entered into a contract with the plaintiff as an apprentice dancer. The contract was to last for seven years. During its operation, the girl was forbidden to marry, and could not accept any professional engagements without the plaintiff's consent, but, on the other hand, was not guaranteed work by the plaintiff. The plaintiff could decide to terminate the agreement virtually at his discretion. The Court of Appeal held that the stipulations were of an extraordinary and unusual character, which gave the plaintiff inordinate power without any corresponding obligation. The agreement was, as a whole, not beneficial, and was thus unenforceable.

The inclusion of some disadvantageous terms, however, will not necessarily be fatal. In *Clements v London and NW Rly* (1894), C was employed as a porter. Under his contract he agreed to forgo his rights under the Employers' Liability Act 1880. Instead, he agreed to join an insurance scheme to which the employer contributed. The Court of Appeal held that although the insurance scheme had some disadvantages (for example, lower rates of compensation), it also had wider coverage than the Act in terms of the types of accident included. On balance, the court was not prepared to say that the contract of employment as a whole was disadvantageous.

6.2.4 Other contracts related to work

The rules about beneficial contracts of service extend to contracts related to the way in which the minor earns a living. Thus, in *Doyle v White City Stadium* (1935), a contract between a boxer and the British Boxing Board of Control, under which the boxer received a licence in return for agreeing to abide by the Board's rules, was held to be enforceable, despite the fact that in this particular case the rules operated to the boxer's disadvantage. This decision was relied on in *Chaplin v Leslie Frewin* (1966), where the court upheld a contract relating to the production of the minor's autobiography (he was the son of Charlie Chaplin). The contract enabled the minor to earn money, and to make a start as an author, and for that reason was to be regarded as beneficial.

Trading contracts, on the other hand, will not be enforced. In *Mercantile Union Guarantee v Ball* (1937), the court refused to enforce a hire purchase contract made by a minor who ran a haulage business. The minor businessperson is therefore at a considerable disadvantage, as compared with the minor employee. Once the age of the minor is known to others with whom he or she wishes to trade, it is unlikely that any contracts will be forthcoming. The reason for this is in line with the general paternalistic approach taken in this area, in that it is felt undesirable that the minor should enter into contracts carrying the high financial risks which will often be involved in business agreements. On the other hand, it poses severe restrictions on the teenage entrepreneur who wishes to set up a business producing and dealing in, for example, computer software.

6.2.5 Voidable contracts

Certain contracts are regarded as being valid, unless the minor repudiates them, either during minority, or within a reasonable time of becoming 18. These are, in general, contracts which involve the minor obtaining an interest in property which involves continuous or recurring obligations. So, this rule applies, for example, to contracts involving obligations of shareholding, such as the duty to pay 'calls' (that is, a demand to pay money due in relation to a share price payable by instalments): *Dublin and Wicklow Rly v Black* (1852); partnership agreements: *Goode v Harrison* (1821); marriage settlements: *Edwards v Carter* (1893); and contracts relating to interests in land, such as leases: *Davies v Beynon-Harris* (1931). In relation to the last category, it should be noted that s 1(b) the Law of Property Act 1925, prevents a minor from holding a legal estate in land. The interests concerned will therefore always be equitable.

The repudiation of one of the above contracts during minority is always possible. What constitutes the period after reaching 18 for which this right subsists is not easy to determine. The House of Lords in *Edwards v Carter* (1893) simply felt that repudiation must occur within a 'reasonable' time, and that in the particular case, a period of four years and eight months was too long to be reasonable. It is likely to be regarded as a question of fact in each case as to what is acceptable, and it does not seem possible to lay down any clear rules on this point.

6.3 Effects of entering into a contract with a minor

What are the consequences of entering into a contract with a minor? For example, can property transferred be recovered if the contract is void? And, if the contract is for necessaries, is the minor obliged to pay the full contract price? The answers to these questions will be discussed as they operate in relation to void, voidable, and enforceable contracts.

6.3.1 Void contracts

The first point to note is that, since the passage of the Minors' Contracts Act (MCA) 1987 (repealing s 2 of the Infants Relief Act 1874), it is possible for a void contract to be ratified (expressly or impliedly) on the minor's attaining majority. If this is done, then the contract will take effect as normal, with full enforceability on both sides.

If the contract remains void at the time a dispute arises, the position is more complicated. The Infants Relief Act 1874 declared most such contracts 'absolutely void', but this was an inaccurate representation of reality, and has been repealed by the MCA 1987. The position now is that a contract which has been fully executed will be effective to transfer the ownership of any money or other property which has changed hands under it. A minor who purchases non-necessary goods for cash is not entitled to demand to be allowed to return them. If the minor has performed, it seems that he or she will be able to claim damages (though not specific performance) from the adult party. Money or property transferred will only be recoverable by the minor, however, if there has been a total failure of consideration (*Valentini v Canali* (1889)). If the adult party has performed, in whole or in part, then, if it is services that have been provided, the adult is without a remedy. If property has been transferred, the common law said that it was irrecoverable, but the position has been altered by s 3 of the MCA 1987. This empowers the court, 'if it is just and equitable to do so', to require the minor to transfer to the adult any property transferred, or any property representing it. This is a broad discretion, and the court is given no guidance as to how it should be exercised. But it does provide the opportunity to prevent a minor taking advantage of the situation, and gaining unjust enrichment. Not all such cases are covered, however. As has been noted, the section has no application where it is non-necessary services that have been provided, nor will it provide a remedy where goods, or the proceeds of their sale, have been consumed by the minor.

6.3.2 Voidable contracts

If a minor repudiates a voidable contract, this will not effect obligations which have already fallen due and have been performed. Money or property transferred by the minor will be irrecoverable, unless there has been a total failure of consideration (*Corpe v Overton* (1833)). The position as regards liabilities which have fallen due, but have not been performed at the time of the repudiation is less clear. The point was considered, *obiter,* in *North Western Rail Co v McMichael* (1850). Parke B took the view that a call on shares which had become due was of no effect once repudiation had taken place. In other words, the repudiation was, to that extent, retrospective.

6.3.3 Enforceable contracts

Where a minor has received necessary goods and services, what is the obligation as regards payment? As far as goods are concerned, the position is governed by s 3(2) of the SGA 1979, which states that:

> Where necessaries are sold and delivered to a minor ... he must pay a reasonable price for them.

Two points emerge from this. First, the liability only arises after delivery. The fact that ownership has passed under the SGA 1979 rules for 'passing of property' is irrelevant (see Chapter 18 below). Secondly, the liability is only to pay a reasonable price, which is not necessarily the contract price. This was also the line taken on this issue by Fletcher Moulton LJ in *Nash v Inman* (1908).

It seems, however, that the position may be different as regards necessary services. The relevant authority is *Roberts v Gray* (1913). The defendant was an aspiring billiards player who made a contract to go on a world tour with the plaintiff, who was a leading player. The defendant, however, backed out before the tour began. The Court of Appeal regarded this as a quasi-educational contract, and therefore within the scope of a contract for necessaries. The defendant argued that nevertheless, no damages should be payable, because he had received nothing under the contract. By analogy with contracts for necessary goods, only where services had actually been supplied should a liability to pay for them arise. The Court of Appeal refused to accept this. Hamilton LJ commented:

> I am unable to appreciate why a contract which is in itself binding, because it is a contract for necessaries not qualified by unreasonable terms, can cease to be binding because it is still executory.

Damages were awarded to the extent of the plaintiff's full losses in organising the abortive tour. In effect, then, the minor was made liable on the agreement itself, rather than for what had been received under the agreement. This is also the approach taken to beneficial contracts of service. Thus, it seems to be only in relation to contracts for the supply of necessary goods that there can be no recovery on an executory contract.

6.4   Minors' liability in tort

Although it is perfectly possible for a minor to be liable in tort, there being no age limit in relation to tortious liability, the courts will not allow such an action to be used as a means of indirectly enforcing an otherwise unenforceable contract. The difficulty lies in deciding exactly when that will be the effect of the tortious action.

The first case to consider is *Jennings v Rundall* (1799). The defendant was a minor who had hired a horse for a short journey. In fact it was taken on a long journey, and suffered injury as a result of this overriding. The plaintiff's action in tort failed on the basis that this was in substance an action for breach of contract, which would not have been sustainable because of the defendant's minority.

This must be contrasted with *Burnard v Haggis* (1863). This again concerned the hire of a horse to a minor. The defendant had said that he did not require a horse for jumping, and indeed was specifically told by the owner 'not to jump or lark with it'. The defendant lent the horse to a friend who used it for jumping with the result that the horse fell and was killed. The defendant was held liable in tort to the owner. The distinction between this case and *Jennings v Rundall* appears from the judgment of Willis J, who commented that the act of riding the mare into the place where she was killed was as much a trespass as if:

... without any hiring at all, the defendant had gone into a field and taken the mare out and killed her. It was a bare trespass, not within the object and purpose of the hiring.

Thus, the test is the 'object and purpose' of the contract. Did the tortious act occur as part of the performance of the 'object and purpose'? If so, there will be no liability. So, in *Jennings v Rundall*, the object and purpose was riding the horse on a journey. In *Burnard v Haggis*, however, jumping was outside the object and purpose, and the defendant was therefore liable.

This approach has been confirmed by later cases. Thus, in *Fawcett v Smethurst* (1914), the taking of a hired car on longer journey than indicated at the time of hire was still within the contract's 'object and purpose'. Whereas, in *Ballett v Mingay* (1943), the defendant, who had hired a microphone and amplifier and was found to have lent them to a friend, was held to be altogether outside the scope of the contract, and the defendant was therefore liable in tort.

In so far as there is immunity, it extends not only to torts committed in the course of a contract, but also fraud which induces a contract. Thus, fraudulent misrepresentation of the minor's age will not stop the minor from pleading lack of capacity, and avoiding the contract. Nor will it give the adult party a right to bring an action in tort for deceit. Where property had been transferred as a result of such fraud, equity had developed remedies in certain situations to allow the adult party to recover it (*Stocks v Wilson* (1913)). Although this equitable remedy is still available in theory, the enactment of the more general provision relating to restitution in s 3 of the MCA 1987, means that it is of virtually no practical importance, and so is not discussed further here.

6.5 Mental disability

The law also provides protection for those who make contracts while under some mental disability. There are, of course, degrees of mental disability, unlike the position in relation to minors, where the person is either under 18 or over 18. English contract law recognises three categories. First, there are those whose mental state is such that their affairs are under the control of the court, by virtue of Pt VII of the Mental Health Act 1983. Since the court effectively takes over the individual's power to make contracts, any contracts purported to be made by the individual will be unenforceable against him or her. Secondly, there are those whose mental state is such that, although they are not under the control of the court, they are unable to appreciate the nature of the transaction they are entering into. Contracts made by people in such a condition will be enforceable against them (even if the contract may in some sense be regarded as 'unfair'), unless it is proved that the other party was aware of the incapacity. This was the view taken in *Imperial Loan Co v Stone* (1892), and has more recently been confirmed by the Privy Council in the New Zealand case of *Hart v O'Connor* (1985). The third category consists of those people who are capable of understanding the transaction, but who are, as a result of some mental disability, more susceptible to entering into a disadvantageous contract. Contracts made by such people are binding, unless affected by the rules relating to 'undue influence', which are discussed in Chapter 9 below.

The only exception to the above rules relates to contracts for necessaries. The SGA 1979 applies the same rule as to contracts for necessary goods made by those who 'by reason of mental incapacity ... incompetent to contract' as it does to minors. Thus, the mentally incapacitated individual is liable to pay a reasonable price for goods sold and delivered. It must also be assumed, although there is no recent authority, that rules equivalent to those which apply to minors will operate in relation to necessary services. These rules will apply to people in both of the first two categories listed above.

6.6   Intoxication

Those who as a result of drunkenness, whether voluntary or involuntary, are 'incompetent to contract', are, by virtue of s 3 of the SGA 1979, liable to pay a reasonable price for necessary goods 'sold and delivered'. 'Incompetent to contract' presumably means 'unable to understand the nature of the transaction'. Beyond this, there appears to be little authority on contracts made by those who are intoxicated. It is assumed, however, that similar rules apply as in the case of incapacity through mental disability. This means, amongst other things, that, in contrast to the position in relation to minors, there must be an awareness of the incapacity on the part of the other party before the contract will be unenforceable.

Such cases as there are on this topic, are concerned with intoxication through the consumption of alcohol. There seems no reason why the same rules should not apply to a person who is incapacitated through drug taking.

CAPACITY

Minors' contracts

With regard to minors' contracts:

- The basic rule is that those under the age of 18 have limited capacity to enter into contracts, and it is irrelevant whether the other party is aware of the minor's age. Exceptions exist in relation to necessaries, beneficial contracts of service, and certain voidable contracts.

- Necessaries may be defined as those goods and services which are necessary for a reasonable existence (*Chapple v Cooper* (1844)). They may include 'luxurious items of utility' (for example, food, clothing). They must be appropriate to the particular minor, and to his or her actual requirements (s 3 of the SGA 1979; *Nash v Inman* (1908)).

- Beneficial contracts of service must not be oppressive (*De Francesco v Barnum* (1889)), but the overall effect will be considered, rather than particular terms (*Clements v London and NW Rly* (1894)). Rules extend to contracts related to the way in which the minor earns a living (*Doyle v White City Stadium* (1935)).

- Trading contracts are always unenforceable against the minor.

- Voidable contracts are valid unless repudiated before, or within a reasonable time of, reaching majority (*Edwards v Carter* (1893)). Voidable contracts include 'calls' on shares, partnership agreements and leases.

- Effects of contract with a minor are as follows:

  o void contracts – may be ratified on reaching majority. If not, the adult party cannot enforce against the minor, but may be able to recover property which has been transferred: s 3 of the MCA 1987. The minor will be able to recover property on a total failure of consideration (*Valentini v Canali* (1889)). A contract which has been fully executed will be effective to transfer ownership of property, and will not be rescinded;

  o voidable contracts – repudiation does not effect obligations which have been performed, unless there has been a total failure of consideration from the adult party (*Corpe v Overton* (1893));

  o enforceable contracts – the minor must pay a reasonable price for delivered necessary goods (s 3 of the SGA 1979). May be liable for full compensation in relation to necessary services (*Roberts v Gray* (1913)), and beneficial contracts of service.

- The minor is only liable if tort is outside the 'object and purpose' of the contract (*Burnard v Haggis* (1863)). Immunity extends to fraudulent misrepresentation of age.

Mental disability

Note the different categories of mental disability:

- as regards those whose affairs are controlled by the court under the Mental Health Act 1983, all contracts other than for necessaries, are unenforceable;

- as regards those not under the control of the court, but who are incapable of appreciating the nature of the transaction, they will be liable unless the other party was aware of the disability.

Rules as to necessaries apply here in the same way as to minors (note s 3 of the SGA 1979).

Intoxication

The rules for intoxication *presumably* apply to all types of intoxication whatever the cause.

- The intoxicated party will be liable unless the other party was aware of the intoxication. Intoxication must be such as to render the person unable to understand the transaction.

- Rules as to necessaries apply in the same way as to minors (note s 3 of the SGA 1979).

CHAPTER 7

THE CONTENTS OF THE CONTRACT

7.1 Introduction

This chapter is concerned with the situation where the parties have fulfilled all the requirements for making a valid contract, as described in the previous chapters. It may then become necessary to determine exactly what the obligations are under the contract. Problems may arise in a number of ways. There may, perhaps, have been a lengthy period of pre-contractual negotiation, and it may not be clear which, if any, of the statements which were made at that stage were intended to form part of the contract. The contract may be in writing, and yet one of the parties may allege that it does not truly represent their intentions. Or the contract may be purely verbal, in which case there may be a dispute as to what was said or promised, and by whom. Some of these problems may be resolved by the rules which the courts have developed to enable terms to be implied into a contract. Moreover, in certain situations, terms will be implied by statute, irrespective of the wishes or intentions of the parties.

The order of treatment adopted here is to look first at the question of pre-contractual statements, and the remedies that may be available for them. Secondly, the approach to express terms will be discussed. And finally, the rules relating to the implication of terms, both at common law and by statute, will be considered.

7.2 Distinction between representations and terms

The importance of identifying those pre-contractual statements which do not form part of the contract arises from the question of the remedies that will be available in each case. If a statement amounts to a promise which forms part of a contract, then a person who breaks it will be liable for the full range of contractual remedies discussed in Chapter 15. In particular, the plaintiff will normally be entitled to damages which will compensate for any profits that may have been lost as a result of the broken promise. A statement which is not a term, however, and which turns out to be untrue, or which contains a promise which is broken, may still give rise to a remedy, but on a different, and often more restricted basis. This is discussed in the next section (see 7.3 below) on remedies for pre-contractual statements.

Where there have been statements made prior to a contract, and there is then a dispute as to whether they were intended to form part of the contract or not, how do the courts resolve the issue? The approach is (as in many other areas of contract law) to try to determine the intentions of the parties. Did they intend the statement to be contractually binding? In looking at this, the courts generally adopt an approach based on 'detached objectivity', that is, asking what the reasonable third party would have taken the parties to have intended. The importance apparently attached to the statement by the plaintiff will be very significant in considering this, as in *Bannerman v White* (1861), where a buyer of hops had been assured that sulphur had not been used in their production. He had made it clear that he would not be interested in buying them if it had. When it turned out that sulphur had been used he was entitled to reject them for breach of contract. The undertaking that no sulphur had been used was a 'preliminary stipulation'. If it had not been given then the purchaser would not have bothered to inquire about the price, and would not have continued to negotiate towards a contract. Evidence, such as was given in this case, that the truth of a pre-contractual statement is a pre-condition of any binding agreement being reached, will strongly support the view that it was intended to form part of the contract. In this case, there was, in effect, a guarantee by the seller that sulphur had not been used, breach of which entitled the buyer to reject the goods. It would be possible, of course, to engage in a full scale inquiry in each case as to the evidence of the parties' intentions. In practice, however, the courts have developed three more specific tests which they use as a means of determining this issue. These tend to operate as presumptions of an intention as to whether the statement is part of the contract, which may, of course, be rebutted by other evidence suggesting the contrary intention. The tests focus on: whether the contract was put into written form; whether the plaintiff was relying on the skill and knowledge of the defendant; and the lapse of time between the statement and the contract.

7.2.1 Was the contract put into written form?

As we saw in Chapter 2, there is generally no need for a contract to be put into writing in order for it to be a valid agreement. On the other hand, if the parties have taken the trouble to commit their contract to writing, the courts will be reluctant to find that it does not contain all the terms which were important to either party. Moreover, if a written contract has been signed, the party who has done so may find it virtually impossible to depart from its express provisions (*L'Estrange v Graucob* (1934)). (This case is discussed further in the context of exclusion clauses, in Chapter 8.) This is often referred to as the 'parol evidence rule', by virtue of which the courts will be reluctant to accept oral evidence in order to add to the terms in what appears to be a complete written contract. The rule, and the exceptions to it, are discussed further in the context of the identification of the express terms of a contract, later in this chapter. This was part of the reason for the rejection of an alleged term (relating to the age of a motorcycle), in *Routledge v McKay* (1954). The purchaser of the motor-cycle had prepared a 'written memorandum' at the time of the sale, but this was silent as to the age of the machine. The Court of Appeal was not prepared to say that this definitely precluded any term other than those specified in the memorandum, being part of the contract, but commented that:

> ... as a matter of construction, it would be difficult to say that such an agreement was consistent with a warranty being given at the same time so as to be intended to form part of the bargain then made.

The rule is not an absolute one, however, and if the party can show that the term which was not included was of the utmost importance, then the courts may be prepared to allow it to be added. This is most likely to be the case where the written contract is in a standard form, rather than the result of individual negotiation. An example is *Evans & Son Ltd v Andrea Merzario Ltd* (1976). The plaintiffs had made a contract for the transport of machinery by sea. They had made it clear to the defendants that it was of great importance that the machinery should not be carried on deck. The defendants had given an oral assurance that the plaintiffs' machinery would be carried below deck. The printed standard conditions for the contract, however, allowed for freight to be carried on deck. The plaintiffs' machinery was carried on deck, and was lost overboard. It was held by the Court of Appeal, that in this case the verbal assurance took precedence over the written conditions. The statement that the plaintiffs' goods would be carried below deck was a contractual term, and the plaintiffs were entitled to succeed.

7.2.2 Was the plaintiff relying on the skill and knowledge of the defendant?

If there is an imbalance of skill and knowledge relating to the subject matter of the contract as between the plaintiff and defendant, this will be relevant in deciding whether an oral pre-contractual statement should be treated as a contractual term. The fact that the defendant is in a better position to be able to guarantee the truth of a statement will lend weight to its being regarded as part of the contract. If, on the other hand, it is the plaintiff who is the expert, then the reverse will be true.

Two cases concerning contracts for the sale of cars conveniently illustrate the two sides of this test. The first case to consider (though the later in time) is *Dick Bentley Productions Ltd v Harold Smith (Motors) Ltd* (1965). The plaintiff had bought a car from the defendants, relying on a pre-contractual statement as to its mileage, which later turned out to be untrue. The Court of Appeal held that the test to be applied was that of whether an intelligent bystander would reasonably infer from what was said or done that the statement was intended to be contractual (that is, 'detached objectivity'). Applying this test, the court came to the conclusion that the statement as to the mileage was a term of the contract, on the basis that the defendant was a car dealer who should be taken to have better knowledge of such matters than the plaintiff, who was not involved in the motor trade. In reaching this decision, the court distinguished the earlier case of *Oscar Chess Ltd v Williams* (1957). Here, the defendant was a private individual who had sold a car to a garage. The relevant pre-contractual statement was that the defendant had innocently told the garage that the date of the car was 1948, when in fact it had been first registered in 1939. The garage sued for breach of contract, but the Court of Appeal held that, on the basis of the fact that the plaintiffs here had the greater skill and knowledge of such matters, the statement should not be regarded as a term. The intelligent bystander, looking at all the circumstances, would not say that the seller intended to guarantee the age of the car. The seller was in no position to do so, since all he could rely on were the car's registration documents, and he had no means of determining whether they were accurate. The purchaser, on the other hand, being in the motor trade could, for example, have taken the engine and chassis numbers and checked with the manufacturer.

It should be noted that a case such as *Bentley v Harold Smith*, if the facts recurred, would be more likely nowadays to be dealt with as a negligent misrepresentation under s 2(1) of the Misrepresentation Act (MA) 1967. The remedy in damages for misrepresentations provided by this section was not, of course, available at the time. The MA 1967 is discussed in detail in Chapter 9.

Other cases where the greater skill and knowledge of the defendant has been relevant in giving contractual status to a pre-contractual statement include *Birch v Paramount Estates Ltd* (1956) (developer stating that a house would be as good as the show house), *Schawel v Reade* (1913) (owner selling a horse which he stated was 'perfectly sound'), and *Harling v Eddy* (1951) (owner selling a heifer stating that there was 'nothing wrong' with her).

7.2.3 Was there a significant lapse of time between the statement and the contract?

The courts generally consider that the closer in time that the statement was made to the conclusion of the contract, the more likely it is that it was a matter of importance to the plaintiff, and should therefore be treated as a contractual term. It is certainly true that if there is no significant gap then the statement may well be treated as being intended to be part of the contract, particularly if the agreement is not put into writing. It is by no means clear, however, that the mere existence of a delay should be regarded as in itself reducing the significance of the statement. Such delay may well have been caused by matters irrelevant to the statement, and the plaintiff may have felt that having settled the issue which the statement concerned, there was no need to re-state it at the time of the contract. Nevertheless, whatever the true significance of the delay, it is undoubtedly the case that as far as the courts are concerned it will weaken the plaintiff's case.

An example of the application of this test is the case of *Routledge v McKay* (1954). This concerned the sale of a motorbike. The defendant, who was selling the bike, had told the plaintiff that the date of the bike was 1942. In fact, it dated from 1930. A week elapsed between the defendant's statement, and the making of the contract of sale (which was put into writing). It was held by the Court of Appeal that the defendant's statement was not a term of the contract. The decision may appear a little harsh, but it may be significant that application of both the other tests outlined above would have gone in favour of the defendant. Thus, the written agreement made no mention of the age of the bike, and neither party had any special skill or knowledge. Both were private individuals, and the defendant in making the statement had innocently relied on false information contained in the bike's registration document.

As this last case shows, it must be remembered that none of the tests discussed here is automatically conclusive of the issue. All may need to be considered, and, if they point in different directions, weighed against each other. The ultimate question is whether the statement, viewed objectively, was intended to form part of the contract. All the other tests are simply matters which may provide guidance to the court in determining this issue.

7.3 Remedies for pre-contractual statements

This section is concerned with the situation where the answer to the question raised in the previous section is that the statement is not a term of the contract. What remedies, if any, are available to a person who has made a contract in reliance on such a statement? Although it may be argued that discussion of this issue is out of place in this chapter, since, by definition, such statements are not part of the 'contents of the contract', it is nevertheless helpful to consider them briefly at this stage, in order to fully understand the importance of deciding whether a statement is part of the contract or not. It is only by considering the consequences of that decision, that its significance can be properly appreciated.

There are three possible forms of action which must be considered: the actions for misrepresentation; for breach of a collateral contract; and for the tort of negligent misstatement.

7.3.1 Misrepresentation

The common law and equity recognised two remedies for misrepresentation. Provided that there were no complicating factors, such as the involvement of third party rights, rescission of the contract was the main remedy for all types of misrepresentation. If the misrepresentation was made fraudulently, there was, in addition, the possibility of an action in tort for deceit, which would provide for the recovery of damages (*Derry v Peek* (1889)). Both these remedies are still available in appropriate cases. In addition, however, there is now the possibility of an action for damages for so called 'negligent misrepresentation' under s 2 of the MA 1967.

For any of these remedies to be available, the statement must have been a representation in the strict sense. That is, it must have been a statement of existing fact, not a statement of opinion (*Bisset v Wilkinson* (1927)), nor a statement of law, nor a promise to act in a particular way in the future. Thus, for example, a statement by a seller of a computer system that a 24 hour service facility will be provided is not a 'representation', but a promise. A statement that the system is ideal for a small business may well be a statement of opinion rather than fact (unless it is based on facts which the maker of the statement knows to be untrue: *Smith v Land and House Property Corporation* (1884)). But, a statement that the firm has already sold 1,000 similar systems, or that it has a team of six service engineers, are representations which, if untrue, may give the other party a remedy.

The statement must have induced the contract (*JEB Fasteners v Marks, Bloom & Co* (1983)). This rule, together with other aspects of the law relating to misrepresentations, is discussed in more detail in Chapter 9.

7.3.2 Collateral contract

We have already encountered the concept of the collateral contract, as a means of evading the doctrine of privity, by bringing apparent third parties into a contractual relationship, as in *Shanklin Pier v Detel Products* (1951). As noted there, however, the collateral contract can also be used between parties who themselves subsequently enter into a main contract. The collateral contract will take the form of one party expressly, or impliedly, saying to the other 'if you enter into the main contract, I will promise you X'. It can thus provide a remedy for pre-contractual statements which have not been incorporated into the main contract. It has the advantage over the remedies for misrepresentation in that it is not limited to statements of existing fact. A promise to act in a particular way is clearly covered. Continuing the computer contract example used above, a statement that 'we will answer all service calls within six hours' could not be a misrepresentation, but could found an action for breach of a collateral contract. Statements of fact, or even opinion, may also give rise to a collateral contract, if it can be said that the maker of the statement was guaranteeing its truth.

An example of the use of a collateral contract in a two-party situation is *City of Westminster Properties v Mudd* (1959). A tenant had been in the practice of sleeping in the shop which he rented. When the lease was renewed, the landlord tried to insert a clause stating that the premises should not be used for lodging, dwelling, or sleeping. The tenant objected, but was assured orally that if he signed the lease, he would be allowed to sleep there. In fact, probably due to an oversight, the new clause was omitted, but a provision containing an obligation only to use the premises for the purposes of trade remained. The landlord subsequently tried to rely on this clause to forfeit the lease, claiming that the tenant was in breach of it through sleeping on the premises. It was held that the tenant could rely on a collateral contract, giving him the right to sleep on the premises which, in effect, overrode the clause in the lease itself.

In *Esso v Mardon* (1976), a representative of Esso had given a prospective tenant of a petrol station an estimate of the potential throughput, which was put at 200,000 gallons a year. This failed to take account of the fact that the local planning authority had required the petrol pumps to be sited on a side street, invisible from the main road. The tenant was dubious as to the accuracy of the estimate, but accepted it as being based on Esso's superior knowledge of the petrol-retailing business. He entered into a lease, but the throughput never exceeded 78,000 gallons a year. It was held by the Court of Appeal that the tenant was entitled to recover damages from Esso on the basis of a collateral contract. Although the estimate was an expression of opinion, rather than a statement of fact, or a promise as to the throughput which would be achieved, it contained the implied promise that it was made with reasonable care and skill. As Lord Denning commented:

> They [Esso] knew the facts. They knew the traffic in the town. They knew the throughput of comparable stations. They had much experience and expertise at their disposal. They were in a much better position than Mr Mardon to make a forecast. It seems to me that if such a person makes a forecast – intending that the other should act on it and he does act on it – it can well be interpreted as a warranty that the forecast is sound and reliable in the sense that they made it with reasonable care and skill.

The consideration for the promise that the estimate was made with due care and skill was Mr Mardon's agreement to enter into the lease. A contract collateral to the lease was thus created, and Mr Mardon was entitled to recover damages for Esso's breach of this.

7.3.3 Limitations of the 'collateral contract'

As will be seen from these examples, the collateral contract is a very flexible device. Its disadvantage as compared to the action for misrepresentation is that it will only provide a remedy in damages, and will not allow the plaintiff the possibility of rescinding the main contract. Moreover, the level of damages which can be awarded is more restricted than in the case of actions for deceit, or under s 2(1) of the Misrepresentation Act (MA) 1967.

7.3.4 Negligent misstatement

In 1963, the House of Lords confirmed that the tortious action for negligence could provide a remedy for negligent misstatements which have resulted in purely economic loss (*Hedley Byrne v Heller* (1963)). The development of the law in this area of the past 30 years has been complicated, as the courts have tried to decide exactly when a duty of care as regards such statements can be said to arise. The recent trend, as shown by cases such as *Caparo v Dickman* (1990), has been to limit strictly the number of 'special relationships' which can give rise to such a duty, though this has been softened to some extent by the subsequent decisions in *Henderson v Merrett Syndicates Ltd* (1994) and *White v Jones* (1995). There is little doubt, however, that a duty of this kind may arise between parties who subsequently enter into a contract. The possibility was recognised in *Esso v Mardon* (1976), for example. In practice, however, the existence of the remedies under s 2(1) of the MA 1967 (see 9.3.4 below) means that it is not very likely to be needed in this situation. The action under the MA 1967 has the advantage that the burden of proof as regards negligence is on the defendant (who effectively has to disprove it), and that more extensive damages are available. The only situation where it might be necessary for a party to a contract to look to the common law negligence action is where the statement is not a representation in the strict sense, and it is also impossible to construct a collateral contract. This remedy is discussed further in Chapter 9.

7.3.5 Conclusion on pre-contractual statements

As we have seen, there are a variety of actions which may be available in relation to pre-contractual statements. There is nothing to stop a claimant relying on more than one, as was pointed out by Lord Denning in *Esso v Mardon* (1976). The decision as to which action will be the most appropriate to press, will depend on the type of statement (is it a statement of fact?), and on the remedy which is being sought (is rescission of the contract required, or will damages be adequate?).

7.4 Express terms

In this section, we are concerned with terms that have without doubt been put forward by one or other party as a term of the agreement. There may be disputes, however, as to whether the clause has been incorporated into the contract, as to its proper construction, and as to the consequences of breaking it. In dealing with all these questions, the approach of the courts will again be to try to determine the parties' intention, from an objective viewpoint.

7.4.1 Incorporation

We have already discussed the rules which the courts adopt to decide whether pre-contractual statements should be regarded as having been incorporated into a contract. The situation under consideration here is slightly different, and will generally arise in relation to written contracts in a standard form which have not been signed. One party may object that a particular clause should not be regarded as being included in the contract, because they were unaware of it for some reason, and would have objected to it. The rules that operate in this area have mainly developed in relation to the incorporation of exclusion clauses, and detailed discussion of them will be left until Chapter 8. In appropriate cases, they can apply to other types of clause, however, as is shown by the case of *Interfoto Picture Library v Stiletto Visual Programmes* (1988).

The defendants were an advertising agency. They needed some photographs for a presentation. On 5 March 1984, they contacted the plaintiffs, who ran a library of photographic transparencies, to see if they might have anything suitable. The plaintiffs sent round a packet of 47 transparencies, together with a delivery note. The transparencies were, however, apparently overlooked and not used. They were eventually returned on 2 April, that is, nearly a month after they had been received. The plaintiffs then claimed the sum of £3,783 from the defendants as a 'holding charge' for the transparencies. This was calculated in accordance with the terms laid down in the delivery note, which stated that, in relation to transparencies not returned within 14 days of receipt, a charge of £5 per day plus VAT would be made in respect of each transparency. The issue before the court was thus whether the terms of the delivery note formed part of a contract between the parties; and, if so, whether the plaintiffs could enforce these terms against the defendants. The Court of Appeal held that the clause could not be enforced. They did so by reference to the case law on exclusion clauses and when they are deemed to have been incorporated into a contract. In particular, they relied on *Parker v South Eastern Rly Co* (1877) and *Thornton v Shoe Lane Parking* (1971). *Parker* established the principle that in order to rely on an exclusion clause in an unsigned contract, the defendant had to have taken reasonable steps to bring it to the attention of the plaintiff. *Thornton* added the gloss that the more unusual and onerous the clause, the more that the defendant had to do to draw it to the plaintiff's attention. The court saw no reason why this approach should not apply to the case before them. The clause was particularly, and unusually, onerous in its effect. The plaintiffs had done nothing to draw it to the defendants' attention. It should be regarded as not having been incorporated into the contract.

The approach taken in the *Interfoto* case is an unusual one in relation to a commercial agreement. The use of this aspect of the rule of incorporation has tended to be used mainly as a means of protecting consumers, particularly in relation to exclusion clauses. Where parties are contracting at arms length, in a business context, it would more commonly be the case that the court would expect each party to take care over the obligations to which it was committing itself. If they agree to unfavourable terms then that is their own fault. It is perhaps significant that the *Interfoto* decision has not so far led to other similar reported decisions. An unreported example is to be found in *AEG (UK) Ltd v Logic Resource Ltd* (1995) (which is discussed in detail by Bradgate at (1997) 60

MLR 582), but the majority Court of Appeal decision is strictly *obiter*, since they found that the clause was also unreasonable under the statutory test contained in the Unfair Contract Terms Act 1977 (discussed at 8.8). Indeed, given the statutory control of exclusion and other clauses by this Act and the Unfair Terms in Consumer Contracts Regulations 1999 (also discussed at 8.12), there would seem to be little need to develop further a restrictive rule for incorporation under the common law.

7.4.2   Construction

Even where there is no dispute as to whether a clause is incorporated, the parties may disagree as to what it was intended to mean. It will be necessary to try to construe the clause in order to give effect to it. The courts will adopt the approach of trying to assess objectively what the parties must be taken to have intended. If the contract is in the form of a written document, this will generally be regarded as very strong evidence of the parties' intentions. The parol evidence rule will apply, with the effect that it will not normally be open to one of the parties to argue that some part of the written document should be disregarded, or interpreted in a way which is not consistent with its most obvious meaning. It is thus very important for the parties to make sure that any written document forming part of the contract is clear and explicit as to the obligations which are being imposed on each side. The parol evidence rule is not, however, unchallengeable, and there are certain established exceptions to it.

Exceptions to the parol evidence rule:

*   *Ambiguity*
    Where a word or phrase contained in the written document is ambiguous, then other evidence may be given as to what was actually intended, as in *Robertson v Jackson* (1845).

*   *Written agreement incomplete*
    If either or both of the parties can show that the written agreement was not intended to contain all the terms of the contract then oral, or other extrinsic evidence, may be used to fill it out. In *Allen v Pink* (1838), for example, the written document relating to the sale of a horse was little more than a receipt. It stated the price and the names of the parties, but contained no other terms. In the circumstances, the court was prepared to allow evidence of an oral promise as to the horse's behaviour in harness. This case was fairly clear. It will be more difficult where the written agreement contains some terms. The court will have to consider objectively whether it appears to be complete, or whether it is more likely that the parties intended it to be supplemented by other obligations. The insertion of a clause to the effect that 'this document contains all the terms of the contract' will presumably

make it difficult to rebut the presumption that it is complete, and that any other evidence of additional terms should be excluded.

- *Custom*
Sometimes, a particular word or phrase is used in particular trade, market, or locality, in a way which does not accord with its obvious meaning. In *Smith v Wilson* (1832), evidence was allowed to establish a local custom to the effect that the phrase '1,000 rabbits' meant '1,200 rabbits'. Custom may also be used to fill out an aspect of the contract on which the written document is silent (*Hutton v Warren* (1836)). In this case, a custom as to allowances to be given to an outgoing tenant for seeds and labour used in the last year of the tenancy was held to be incorporated into a lease which contained no such provision. Parke B commented that:

> It has long been settled that, in commercial transactions, extrinsic evidence of custom and usage is admissible to annex incidents to written contracts in matters with respect to which they are silent.

This use of custom overlaps with the use of custom to imply terms, which is discussed further below.

Custom may not be used, however, where it is clearly contradicted by the terms of the contract. Where, for example, a charter provided that the expenses of discharging a cargo should be borne by the charterer, it was not possible to override this by showing a custom that the expenses should be borne by the owner of the ship (*Palgrave, Brown & Son Ltd v SS Turid (Owners)* (1922)).

- *Starting or finishing date*
Extrinsic evidence may be used to establish the date on which a contract is intended to start to operate. In *Pym v Campbell* (1856), evidence was allowed as to an oral provision that the contract should not start to operate prior to the approval of a third party.

- *Other exceptions*
Where it can be argued that a written document was intended simply to record earlier oral agreements, but fails to do so accurately, extrinsic evidence may be allowed to prove this, and thus to 'rectify' the written document. The remedy of 'rectification' is discussed further in Chapter 10. The parol evidence rule may also be circumvented by showing the existence of a collateral contract. An example of this is the decision in *City of Westminster Properties v Mudd* (1959), which has been discussed above (see 7.3.2 above). This is perhaps not a true exception, since it concerns not the interpretation of one contract, but rather a decision as to the priority between two inconsistent contracts. Finally, as we have seen earlier (see 7.1–7.2 above), a pre-contractual statement may become part of the contract, if the courts feel that it related to something of great importance to one or other of the parties. This is perhaps best exemplified by the case of *Evans v*

Andrea Merzario (1976) (see 7.2.1 above) where the statement that the cargo would be carried below deck was held to override the provision in the written contract allowing it to be carried on deck.

Further discussion of the approach to the construction of terms will be found in Chapter 8, since a number of cases deal with this issue in the context of the scope of exclusion clauses.

7.4.3 Conditions, warranties and innominate terms

Not all terms within a contract are of equal importance. In a contract for the provision of a service, for example, terms specifying the dates on which the service is to be provided and the date for payment will be likely to be more important than, for example, a term requiring the supplier of the service to submit an annual account of the work done. The consequence of breach of one of the first two terms is probably going to be more serious than the latter, and may indeed result in the contract as a whole being terminated. The parties may attempt to give effect to such differences in the status of various contractual provisions by the way in which their agreement is drafted in respect of its 'express terms'. There is, in fact, a generally accepted hierarchy of terms, with 'conditions' being more important than 'warranties'. Use of these labels may well indicate an intention by the parties as to the relative status of the terms concerned, though any presumption to this effect may be rebutted by other evidence (*Schuler v Wickman* (1974)) (see 14.4.5 below). As indicated above, the distinction between the status of terms is of most importance when the consequences of a breach are being considered. Breach of 'condition' may well lead to the other party having the right to treat the contract as being at an end as well as suing for damages. Breach of warranty will probably only entitle the other party to claim damages. If no labels are used, and the term is difficult to classify, it may be regarded as an 'innominate' term, in relation to which the consequences of the particular breach which has occurred may determine whether the party not in breach has a right to bring it to an end (*Hong Kong Fir Shipping Co v Kawasaki Kisen Kaisha Ltd* (1962)) (see 14.4.7 below). The context in which the breach occurred will be important, as will its effect on the rest of the contract. The details of the rules which the courts apply in this area are, however, left until Chapter 14, which is concerned specifically with the issues of performance and breach. It is important, however, that the parties should have such issues in mind when drafting their agreement, so that if they wish they can include express terms dealing with the consequences of a breach of any particular obligation. They may also wish to agree in advance the amount of damages which will be recoverable in such circumstances. The principles governing such clauses, known as 'liquidated damages' clauses, are discussed in Chapter 15.

7.5 Implied terms

One or other of the parties to an agreement may wish to claim that although a particular term has not been set out explicitly, either in words or writing, it should nevertheless be implied into the contract. It is also the case that, in some situations, a term will be implied because Parliament has by statute required that all such contracts should contain such a term.

The order of treatment here will be to look first at terms implied by the courts, which can be further divided into terms implied by custom, terms implied in fact, and terms implied by law. Terms implied by statute will then be considered.

7.5.1 Terms implied by the courts

The general approach of the courts is that they are reluctant to imply terms. The parties are generally expected to take the trouble to set out the provisions of their agreement in full. A contract in which certain terms are implicit clearly gives great opportunities for dispute, and the courts have been reluctant to give any encouragement to parties to try to escape from contractual obligations on the basis of some term which was not stated, but which is now alleged to be of great significance. There are certain situations, however, where this reluctance is overcome, and terms are implied. The first of these is where the implication of the term derives from a local or trade custom.

7.5.2 Terms implied by custom

Provided that there is sufficient evidence to establish the custom the courts will be prepared to interpret the contract in the light of it. An early example is *Hutton v Warren* (1836), which has been discussed above, in connection with the parol evidence rule. As will be remembered, a tenant claimed to be entitled, on quitting his tenancy, to an allowance for seed and labour. There was nothing in the lease to this effect, but the court accepted that this was a well established local custom, and implied a term. A different kind of implication was suggested in *British Crane and Hire Corporation Ltd v Ipswich Plant Hire Ltd* (1975). This concerned a contract for the hire of an earth moving machine, together with a driver, and the issue of who was responsible for the cost of pulling it out of marshy land in which it had become stuck. One of the factors which the Court of Appeal regarded as relevant was that there was evidence that it was normal practice in the trade for liability to be placed on the hirer, rather than the owner, in such circumstances. Lord Denning commented:

> The [hirers] themselves knew that firms in the plant hiring trade always imposed conditions in regard to the hiring of plant: and that their conditions were on much the same lines.

This, together with the fact that the hirers had previously contracted with the owners on such terms, led to the implication that liability should rest with the hirer. The issue is thus primarily one of fact. The person wishing to rely on the custom must produce convincing factual evidence of its existence and general acceptance. Assuming that there is sufficient evidence, the courts will imply a term to give it effect.

Such implication will not be possible, however, if the contract contains an express term which is inconsistent with the custom. In that case, the express term will prevail over the custom. In *Les Affréteurs Réunis v Walford* (1919), there was evidence of a custom that a broker's commission was payable only in relation to hire which had been earned under a charter. The contract, however, provided that commission was payable on the signing of the charter. This specific term was held to indicate the parties' intention in relation to this issue. There was therefore no room for a term implied from custom.

7.5.3   Terms implied in fact

The approach here is based on the attempt to determine the true intention of the parties. The courts will imply a term if they consider that it represents the true intention of the parties on a particular issue. In other words, the term is implied not as a matter of law, but on the basis that as a matter of fact, this is what the parties had agreed, though the agreement was implicit rather than explicit. The courts will not easily, however, be convinced that such implication should take place. It is certainly not sufficient that a particular clause would appear to be 'reasonable'. Nor will a term be implied to deal with an eventuality which the parties had not anticipated. If they had not expected a particular circumstance to happen they cannot be said to have intended that a particular term would apply to the situation. This was the view of the Court of Appeal in *Crest Homes (South West) Ltd v Gloucestershire County Council* (1999), where in a construction contract the local planning authority unexpectedly imposed conditions which entailed additional expense and a loss of profit for the builder. The court was not prepared to imply a term that the defendant (which had performed its side of the bargain in accordance with the original contract) should bear any liability for these costs.

7.5.4   The *'Moorcock'* test

The starting point for the law in this area is the case of *The Moorcock* (1889). This concerned a contract which involved the plaintiff's ship mooring at the defendant's wharf in the Thames. The Thames being a tidal river, at low tide the ship, as both parties knew would be the case, settled on the river bed. Unfortunately, the ship was damaged because of a ridge of hard ground beneath the mud of the river bed. There was no express term in the contract as to the suitability of the river bed for mooring a ship there. Nevertheless, it was held by the Court of Appeal that such a term could, and should, be implied. The reason for this was that without such a provision the contract would have effectively been unworkable. It was implicit in the contract for the mooring of the ship, that it would have to rest on the bottom of the river. Both parties must have contracted on the basis that it was safe to do so. On this basis, the court felt that it must have been the parties' intention that the owners of the wharf should warrant that the river bed was suitable for the purpose of the contract. Bowen LJ explained this reasoning as follows:

> Both parties knew that the jetty was let for the purpose of profit, and knew that it could only be used by the ship taking the ground and lying on the ground. They must have known, both of them, that unless the ground was safe the ship would be simply buying an opportunity of danger and buying no convenience at all, and that all consideration would fail unless the ground was safe. In fact, the business of the jetty could not be carried on unless, I do not say the ground was safe, it was supposed to be safe.

Note that the test being applied here is a stringent one. It is not based on the reasonable expectation of the owner of the ship, but rather on what is necessary in order to make the contract work at all. The fact that a contract might work better with a particular term implied would not be sufficient. *The Moorcock* can thus be characterised as having established a test of 'necessity' in relation to the implication of terms.

7.5.5 The 'officious bystander' test

The reason why necessity is a good test for the implication of terms is that it must be regarded as a sure guide as to what the parties intended. If a contract will not work without the inclusion of a particular term, it is a reasonable assumption that the parties intended that term to be included. The courts have been prepared, however, to consider other tests of intention. One of the most commonly used is the test of the 'officious bystander'. This derives from the case of *Shirlaw v Southern Foundries* (1939). MacKinnon LJ suggested that a term may be implied where it is so obvious that it 'goes without saying', so that:

> ... if, while the parties were making their bargain, an officious bystander were to suggest some express provision for it in the agreement, they would testily suppress him with a common 'Oh, of course!'.

The test is again a strict one, in that there will be relatively few provisions of such obviousness that they will satisfy the officious bystander test. Moreover, it is not a particularly easy one to apply, as is perhaps shown by the fact that in *Shirlaw's* case itself there was considerable disagreement between members of the Court of Appeal and House of Lords as to what terms, if any, should be implied into a contract appointing the managing director of a company. Nor is it well suited to complex commercial transactions, in relation to which it may be difficult to formulate an appropriate question for the officious bystander to ask. A final difficulty is that in relation to terms other than those which are 'necessary' in *The Moorcock* sense it may be difficult for a court, after the event to establish what the parties, at the time of the contract, would have agreed. If the matter is before the court, they are by definition in dispute, and identifying an obligation (which will inevitably favour one side of the agreement) to which they would clearly have said 'yes, of course that is included' may be very difficult. Overall, *The Moorcock* test is probably the more satisfactory of the two.

The operation of both *The Moorcock* and the 'officious bystander' tests were considered by Gatehouse J in *Ashmore v Corporation of Lloyd's (No 2)* (1992). The case arose out the problems of Lloyd's 'names' who had made substantial losses out of insurance contracts. The plaintiffs were arguing that Lloyd's had a duty to alert names about matters of which Lloyd's became aware which might seriously affect their interests. One basis for the action was that the duty should be based on an implied term in the names' contracts with Lloyd's. Gatehouse J, however, was unable to find that either of the tests outlined above helped the plaintiffs. Looking first at *The Moorcock* test of business efficacy, many thousands of people had been or were names with Lloyd's under the same contractual arrangements as the plaintiffs. It could not be said that these contracts would not work without the suggested implied term.

As to the officious bystander, Gatehouse J found the suggested question too complicated to be answered by a simple 'yes'. The question was set out in this way by the plaintiff:

> If, at the Rota meeting to admit a new Member, an officious bystander interrupted the proceedings and said, 'You Lloyd's are asking this applicant to engage in a high risk business and, in effect, entrust his entire personal fortune to an underwriting agent approved by you with whom he is not to interfere, and whom you know he relies upon and is by the system you impose forced to rely on: [Question] what if something professionally discreditable is or becomes known to Lloyd's about the underwriting agent which might prejudice the member's underwriting interests, other than matters which in Lloyd's reasonable opinion are not capable of being seriously prejudicial to the member's underwriting interests, would you Lloyd's be obliged to take reasonable steps to alert the applicant, if thought necessary, in confidence, and tell the underwriting agent within a reasonable time thereafter what you have done?' Surely, the answer would be 'of course'.

On the contrary, the response of Lloyd's to such a question, thought Gatehouse J, would have been to refer the question to their lawyers, following which the most likely answer would have been an uncompromising 'no'.

Similarly, in *Wilson v Best Travel Ltd* (1993), the court refused to imply a term into a contract between a tour operator and holidaymaker that a hotel would be reasonably safe. Applying the officious bystander test, the judge did not think the tour operator would have said 'of course' to an inquiry as to whether such a term was included, given that the hotel was not under the operator's control.

These cases illustrate the reluctance of the courts to imply a term, and that the tests to be satisfied are applied quite strictly.

7.5.6 Terms implied by law

The distinction between terms implied in fact, and terms implied by law, was well explained by Lord Denning in *Shell v Lostock Garage* (1977). The case concerned a contract under which a garage owner agreed to buy petrol exclusively from Shell. Subsequently, at a time when there was a petrol 'price war', the garage owner discovered that Shell was supplying other petrol stations in the area at a lower price. This was having a disastrous effect on his business. The garage owner was arguing that a term should be implied to the effect that Shell would not discriminate against him in the terms on which it supplied the petrol. The majority of the Court of Appeal (Bridge LJ dissenting) held that no such term could be implied. In coming to this conclusion, Lord Denning emphasised the difference between terms implied in fact, and by law. As regards the first category, as we have seen, this involves deciding what the parties themselves would have put into the contract had they addressed themselves to the issue. Lord Denning thought that the required term could not be implied on this basis, because it was highly unlikely that Shell would have agreed to the inclusion of such a term if this had been requested by the garage owner. Terms implied by law, however, do not depend on determining the intention of the parties. The court in this case will impose the term on them, whether they would have agreed to it or not. Two conditions need to be satisfied before this can be done, however. First, the contract has to be of a sufficiently common type (for example, seller/buyer, owner/hirer, employer/employee, landlord/tenant) that it is possible to identify the typical obligations of such a contract. Secondly, the matter to which the implied term relates must be one which the parties have not in any way addressed in their contract. There must be a clear gap to be filled. In *Shell v Lostock Garage*, the garage owner failed on the first test. Lord Denning was not prepared to hold that exclusive dealing contracts of this kind were sufficiently common that typical terms could be identified.

7.5.7 *Liverpool City Council v Irwin* (1976)

This type of implication of terms derives from the House of Lords' decision in *Liverpool City Council v Irwin* (1976). The contract in this case was a tenancy agreement in relation to a block of flats. The agreement said nothing about who was to be responsible for the maintenance of the common parts of the block, and in particular the lifts and rubbish chutes. The tenants argued that a term should be implied that the City Council was responsible. It would clearly not have been possible to imply such a term using *The Moorcock*, or the 'officious bystander' tests. It would have been quite possible to have a workable tenancy agreement in which, for example, the responsibility for the common parts was shared among all the tenants of the block. An officious bystander suggesting that a term should be included imposing liability on the landlord alone would have been unlikely to have been considered to be stating the obvious, at least as far as the City Council were concerned. The House of Lords nevertheless decided that it was possible to imply a term to the effect that the landlord should take reasonable steps to keep the common parts in repair. What the House was in effect doing was to say that:

- the agreement was incomplete, in that it was mainly concerned with the tenant's obligations, and contained very little about those of the landlord;

- it was an agreement of a type that was sufficiently common that the court could decide that certain terms would normally be expected to be found in it;

- the term implied was one which the House thought was reasonable in relation to the normal expectations of the obligations as between landlord and tenant.

Despite the fact that Lord Wilberforce insisted on referring the test as one of 'necessity' rather than 'reasonableness', it is clear that in practice it is the latter word which indicates the approach being taken, once the pre-conditions for any implication in law have been met. In other words, if it is established that the agreement is one of 'common occurrence', and that it is 'incomplete', the courts will themselves decide what term should be implied in order to make the contract work 'reasonably' – meaning here 'as would commonly be expected in relation to a contract of this type'.

An example of the term implied by law into an employment contract is to be found in *Malik v BCCI* (1997). The employee had worked for the Bank of Credit and Commerce International which collapsed in 1991, amidst allegations that the bank had operated in a corrupt and dishonest manner. The employee claimed that having worked for BCCI had adversely affected his future employment prospects. On a trial of a preliminary issue as to whether the employee had any cause of action, it was confirmed by the House of Lords that there should be implied into contracts of employment a mutual obligation of 'trust and confidence'. This obligation can be excluded or modified by the parties, but otherwise will operate as a 'default' clause in all contracts of employment. In this case, the implied term had not been amended by the parties, and was held to include the obligation that the employer should not:

> Without reasonable and proper cause, conduct itself in a manner calculated and likely to destroy or seriously damage the relationship of confidence and trust between employer and employee.

Thus, the employee did have the basis for a cause of action against his former employer for the damage caused by the way it was alleged the business had been run.

The possibility of implying a term in law was also raised in *Ashmore v Corporation of Lloyd's (No 2)* (1992), as an alternative to implication in fact. The plaintiff argued that there were many contracts in identical terms between 'names' and Lloyd's, and that therefore this was an appropriate situation in which to use the *Liverpool City Council v Irwin* (1976) approach. Gatehouse J disagreed. What was important was not the number of contracts. Rather, there needed to be a broad category or type of relationship, even though within that type the detailed terms might vary on particular points. The fact that in this case each contract was in identical terms did not create a category, or genus, or contracts, for which typical terms could be found. The plaintiff's attempt to imply a term by this means failed once again.

7.5.8   Terms implied by statute

There are two reasons why it may be appropriate for parliament to enact that certain provisions should be implied into all contracts of a particular type. One relates to efficiency. If it is virtually universal practice for certain terms to be used in particular contractual relationships, there is no need for the parties to state them specifically every time. Rather than having to agree an appropriate wording on each occasion, they can rely on the statutory formulation as representing their obligations. In such a situation, however, there should be the possibility of the parties being able to agree to depart from the statutory wording, if they so wish.

The second reason why terms might need to be implied by statute is for the protection of one of the parties. It may be thought that a particular type of contractual relationship is likely to involve inequality of bargaining power, so that, unless protective provisions are implied, the weaker party may be forced into a very disadvantageous bargain. If this is the reason for the implication, then it may well be that the obligation to include the term should be absolute, without any possibility of its being excluded, or amended, in particular contracts.

Examples of both these bases for implying terms by statute can be found in the history of the implied terms as to quality under the Sale of Goods Acts. The original Sale of Goods Act (SGA) 1893, was intended to represent a codification of current commercial law and practice. Thus, the implied terms as to quality, contained in ss 13–15 were those which merchants of the time would have expected to appear in any contract for the sale of goods. This was an example of the first ground for implying terms, that is, business efficiency. In line with this approach, s 55 of the SGA 1893, allowed the parties to agree to different terms as to quality, or to exclude them altogether, if they so wished. By the time of the enactment of the revised version of the SGA in 1979, however, the atmosphere had changed. The provisions as to quality had come to be regarded as important elements in the law of consumer protection. Their role was therefore at least in part to provide protection for the weaker party in a sale of goods contract. As a result, the Unfair Contract Terms Act (UCTA) 1977 made it impossible in situations where the contract is made between a business and consumer, for the business to exclude the implied terms. Even as between business parties, the exclusion will be subject to a test of 'reasonableness'.

The details of the terms implied by the SGA 1979, and the restrictions on exclusion of them under the UCTA 1977, are discussed in more detail in Chapter 18.

Another example of a term implied on the grounds of protection is to be found in the Equal Pay Act 1970. Section 3 implies into every employment contract an 'equality clause' which has the effect of ensuring that as between men and women employed on 'like work' there is equal treatment in relation to all terms of their contracts.

The implication of terms on this basis runs counter to the normal philosophy of English contract law, which is to make the intentions of the parties paramount. Here the clause is imposed on the parties, whether they like it or not. Even if they expressly agree that it is not to operate, the courts will still give effect to it.

7.6   Statutory controls

As we have seen, the contents of the contract may be subject to statutory control, in that terms may be implied, and exclusion of such terms may be prohibited, by statute (for example, the SGA 1979; UCTA 1977). There is now, however, a broader control of the contents of certain types of consumer contract, which results from the Unfair Terms in Consumer Contracts Regulations 1999. These Regulations prohibit a wider range of contractual clauses than simply the exclusion clauses affected by the UCTA 1977. The Regulations thus represent a further inroad into the traditional common law principle that the intention of the parties is paramount. Since, however, they relate most closely to the type of control contained in the UCTA 1977, and overlap to a considerable extent with that Act, full discussion of these Regulations is left to Chapter 8.

THE CONTENTS OF THE CONTRACT

Distinction between representations and terms

The distinction between representations and terms is important because of remedies. These are more limited as regards representations.

The principal test is the intention of the parties, and the courts will consider:

- the importance of the issue to the parties (*Bannerman v White* (1861));

- whether the contract was put into writing (*Routledge v McKay* (1954); but compare *Evans v Andrea Merzario* (1976));

- relative skill and knowledge of parties (compare *Dick Bentley v Harold Smith* (1965) with *Oscar Chess v Williams* (1957));

- lapse of time between statement and contract (*Routledge v McKay* (1954) – here, one week was too long).

Remedies for pre-contractual statements

The remedies for pre-contractual statements may be based on:

- misrepresentation – this may be innocent, fraudulent (*Derry v Peek* (1889), or negligent (s 2(1) of the MA 1967). Remedies are rescission, and for negligent and fraudulent misrepresentation, damages. To be available, the statement:

  o must be of existing fact; not opinion (*Bisset v Wilkinson* (1927)), nor law;

  o must have induced the contract (*JEB Fasteners v Marks, Bloom & Co* (1983));

- collateral contract – this will cover promises as to future action (*City of Westminster Properties v Mudd* (1959)); guarantees of statements of fact; or warranties that a statement has been made with reasonable care and skill (*Esso v Mardon* (1976));

- negligent misstatement – tortious action developed from *Hedley Byrne v Heller* (1963). It covers a wide range of types of statements, but it may be difficult to establish the existence of a duty of care (*Caparo v Dickman* (1990)).

Express terms

Express terms are identified by:

- incorporation – a clause may be rejected if it is very unusual, and if insufficient notice is given (*Interfoto Picture Library v Stiletto Visual Programmes* (1988)). See, also, the case law on exclusion clauses.

- construction – an objective approach will be taken to interpretation. Only restricted use will be made of parol evidence, for example, to establish a custom (*Smith v Wilson* (1832)), or resolve an ambiguity (*Robertson v Jackson* (1845)). Compare, also, *Evans v Andrea Merzario* (1976).

Implied terms

Terms may be:

- implied by the court:
  - by custom – if custom is established as a question of fact, the court will apply it (*Hutton v Warren* (1836)), unless there is an express term which is inconsistent (*Les Affréteurs Réunis v Walford* (1919));
  - in fact – courts attempt to decide what the parties intended. Courts will use the test of necessity ('does the contract work without the clause?') derived from *The Moorcock* (1889), or the 'officious bystander' test (*Shirlaw v Southern Foundries* (1939)). Neither is easy to satisfy (*Ashmore v Corporation of Lloyd's (No 2)* (1992));
  - by law – this approach derives from *Liverpool City Council v Irwin* (1976). It can be used where the contract is of a 'common type' (for example, sale of goods, employment, landlord/tenant), and there is a clear gap which needs filling (*Shell v Lostock Garage* (1977)). The fact that a lot of contracts have similar provisions does not make them of a 'common type' (*Ashmore v Corporation of Lloyd's (No 2)* (1992));

- implied by statute – they can be used to incorporate terms which are generally accepted, but may be excluded (SGA 1893); or terms which are designed to protect the weaker party (SGA 1979; Equal Pay Act 1970), irrespective of the parties' intentions (see, further, Chapter 18).

CHAPTER 8

EXCLUSION CLAUSES

8.1   Introduction

It will very often be the case that a contract will include a clause exempting or excluding one of the parties from liability in the event of certain types of breach. The exclusion may be total, or may limit the party's liability to a specified sum of money. There is nothing inherently objectionable about a clause of this kind. Provided that it has been included as a result of a clear voluntary agreement between the parties, it may simply indicate their decision as to where certain risks involved in the transaction should fall. If the contract involves the carriage of goods, for example, it may have been agreed that the owner should be responsible for insuring the goods while in transit. In that situation, it may be perfectly reasonable for the carrier to have very restricted liability for damage to the goods while they are being carried. The inclusion of the clause is simply an example of good contractual planning.

Many exclusion clauses, however, are not of this type. They appear in standard form contracts, which the other party has little choice as to whether to accept or not, and may give the party relying on them a very broad exemption from liability, both in tort and contract. (Note that it is quite possible for an exclusion clause in a contract to restrict tortious liabilities, particularly for negligence in the performance of the contract.) When such inequitable clauses began to appear with some frequency in the 19th century, the courts devised ways of limiting their effectiveness. More recently, Parliament has intervened to add a statutory layer of controls on top of the common law rules (that is, the Unfair Contract Terms Act (UCTA) 1977 (see 8.5 below) and the Unfair Terms in Consumer Contracts Regulations (UTCCR) 1999 (see 8.12 below). The common law is still very important, however, not least because its rules apply to *all* contracts, whereas the UCTA 1977 and the UTCCR 1999 only apply in certain situations.

8.2   Common law rules

The approach of the courts to exclusion clauses has not traditionally been to assess them on their merits. In other words, they have not said 'we think this clause is unreasonable in its scope, or unfair in its operation, and therefore we will not give effect to it'. Such an approach would have run too directly counter to the general ideas of 'freedom of contract' which were particularly important to the courts of the 19th century. So, instead, the courts developed and adapted formal rules relating to the determination of the contents of the contract, and the scope of the clauses contained in it. These are issues which we touched on in Chapter 7, but it is in the context of exclusion clauses that they have been most fully developed, and that is why they need to be considered in detail here. The main rules which are used are those of 'incorporation' and 'construction', though we will also need to note the so called 'doctrine of fundamental breach'.

8.3   Incorporation

A clause cannot be effective to exclude liability if it is not part of the contract. The ways in which the courts determine the contents of a contract have been considered in the previous chapter. The rules discussed there, including the parol evidence rule and its exceptions, are also relevant to the decision as to whether an exclusion clause is part of the contract. It will almost always be the case that an exclusion clause will be in writing – though there is no principle which prevents a party stating an exclusion orally, as with any other contractual term. The first question will be, therefore, whether that written term can be regarded as part of the contract. The courts have generally been concerned to limit the effect of exclusion clauses (particularly as regards consumers), and they have, therefore, in this context applied fairly strict rules as to the incorporation of terms. The rules are based on the general principle that a party must have had reasonable notice of the exclusion clause at the time of the contract in order for it to be effective. If, however, the contract containing the clause has been signed by the plaintiff, there will be little that the courts can do. In *L'Estrange v Graucob* (1934), for example, the clause was in small print, and very difficult to read, but because the contract had been signed, the clause was held to have been incorporated. Scrutton LJ made it clear that in such cases questions of 'notice' were irrelevant:

> In cases in which the contract is contained in a railway ticket or other unsigned document, it is necessary to prove that an alleged party was aware, or ought to have been aware, of its terms and conditions. These cases have no application when the document has been signed. When a document containing contractual terms is signed, then, in the absence of fraud, or, I will add, misrepresentation, the party signing it is bound, and it is wholly immaterial whether he has read the document or not ...

Where, on the other hand, the contract has not been signed, the court will be concerned with such matters as the time at which the clause was put forward, the steps which were taken to draw attention to it, the nature of the clause, and the type of document in which it was contained. These matters will now be considered in turn.

8.3.1   Relevance of time

If a contract containing the clause has not been signed, then the *time* at which it is put forward will be important. If it is not put forward until after the contract has been made then it clearly cannot be incorporated. All the main terms of the contract must be settled at the time of acceptance. This is, in effect, the same rule as was applied in *Roscorla v Thomas* (1842) (see 3.5 above), preventing a promise made after the agreement from being enforced, because no fresh consideration was given for it. In the same way, the promise by one party to give the other the benefit of an exclusion clause will be unenforceable if made after the formation of the contract. Thus, in *Olley v Marlborough Court Hotel* (1949), the plaintiff made the contract for the use of a hotel room at the reception desk. A clause purporting to exclude liability for lost luggage was displayed in the room itself. It was held that this came too late to be incorporated into the contract. The position might have been different if the plaintiff had been a regular user of the hotel, and therefore as a result of a long and consistent 'course of dealing' could be said to have had prior notice of the clause (*Hardwick Game Farm v Suffolk Agricultural, etc, Association* (1969)). The defendant would be entitled to assume that the plaintiff has previously read the clause even if this was not in fact the case.

In the *Hardwick Game Farm* case, the contract was between buyers and sellers of animal feed. They had regularly contracted with each other on three or four occasions each month over a period of three years. On each occasion, a 'sold note' had been issued by the seller, which put responsibility for latent defects in the feed on the buyer. The buyer tried to argue that it did not know of this clause in the sold note. However, the House of Lords held that it was bound. A reasonable seller would assume that the buyer, having received more than 100 of these notes containing the clause, and having raised no objection to it, was agreeing to contract on the basis that it was part of the contract. Regularity is important, however, and the *Hardwick Game Farm* case was distinguished in *Hollier v Rambler Motors* (1972) where there had only been three or four contracts over a period of five years. It was held that an exclusion clause contained in an invoice given to the plaintiff after the conclusion of an oral contract for car repairs was not incorporated into the contract. Inconsistency of procedure may also prevent incorporation. In *McCutcheon v MacBrayne* (1964), the plaintiff's agent had regularly shipped goods on the defendant's ship. On some occasions, he was required to sign a 'risk note' containing an exclusion clause, on other occasions the contract was purely oral. The agent arranged for the carriage of the plaintiff's car which was lost as a result of the negligent navigation of the ship. No risk note had been signed, and the House of Lords refused to accept that the exclusion clause could be incorporated from the agent's previous dealings. There was no consistent course of conduct sufficient to allow such an argument to succeed.

8.3.2 Requirement of 'reasonable notice'

More commonly, the clause will be presented as part of a set of standard terms, which the other party will be given or referred to at the time of making the contract. In that situation, the test is whether 'reasonable notice' of the clause has been given (*Parker v South Eastern Rly* (1877)). In this case, the clause was contained on a cloakroom ticket, given in exchange for the deposit of a bag. The front of the ticket, which contained a number and date, also said 'See back'. On the other side of the ticket were various clauses, including one excluding liability for goods exceeding the value of £10. The plaintiff's bag, worth £24.50, had been lost. The jury had found that the plaintiff had not read the ticket, nor was he under any obligation to do so. On that basis, the judge had directed that judgment should be given for the plaintiff. The Court of Appeal, however, ordered a new trial, on the basis that the proper test was whether the defendants had given reasonable notice of the conditions contained on the ticket.

The standard to be applied is what is reasonable as regards the ordinary adult individual, capable of reading English. Thus, in *Thompson v London, Midland and Scottish Rly* (1930), the fact that the plaintiff was illiterate did not help her. The position might be different, however, if the defendant had actual knowledge of the plaintiff's inability to read the terms and conditions. In such a case, the giving of reasonable notice might require rather more of the party wishing to rely on the clause. In *Thompson's* case, the Court of Appeal in addition held that stating on a ticket 'Issued subject to the conditions and regulations in the company's time-tables and notices' was sufficient to draw the other party's attention to the existence of the terms, and thereby to incorporate them into the contract. The contractual document itself, therefore, does not need to set out the exclusion clause, if it gives reasonable notice of the clause's existence, and indicates where it can be read. What is reasonable will, of course, depend on all the circumstances. In *Thompson*, for example, the court placed some stress on the fact that the ticket was for a specially advertised excursion, at a particularly low price, and not for a regular service. There is some suggestion in the judgments, though the point is not made very clearly, that a different standard of notice might be required in relation to full priced regular services. The point seems to be that special conditions, including the possibility of limited liability, were reasonably to be expected in relation to a cheap excursion, whereas there would not be the same level of expectation in relation to regular services.

8.3.3 Incorporation and unusual exclusions

The *Thompson* decision is clearly helpful to the defendant. More recently, the courts have adopted an approach which requires an assessment of the nature of the clause alongside the amount of notice given. Thus, the more unusual or more onerous the exclusion clause, the greater the notice that will be expected to be given. In *Spurling v Bradshaw* (1956), for example, Lord Denning commented that:

> Some exclusion clauses I have seen would need to be printed in red ink on the face of the document with a red hand pointing to it before the notice could be held to be sufficient.

In *Thornton v Shoe Lane Parking Ltd* (1971), this approach was applied, so that a clause displayed on a notice inside a car park, containing extensive exclusions, was held not to be incorporated into a contract which was made by the purchase of a ticket from a machine. The Court of Appeal did not decide definitively the point at which the contract was made, but it was probably when the customer accepted the car park owner's offer by driving up to the barrier, thus causing the machine to issue a ticket. If that was the case, then any conditions, or reference to conditions contained on the ticket came too late – the contract was already made. It was not feasible, as would be possible if dealing with a human 'ticket issuer', for the recipient to inquire further about the conditions, or to reject the ticket. Even if the ticket could be a valid means of giving notice, however, or if the customer could be required as being put on inquiry by a notice at the entrance stating 'All cars parked at owner's risk', there was an issue about the degree of notice required. The exclusion clause in this case was very widely drawn, and purported to cover negligently caused personal injuries (which the plaintiff had in fact suffered). As a result the court felt that the defendant needed to take more specific action to bring it to the attention of customers. In the view of Megaw LJ:

> ... before it can be said that a condition of that sort, restrictive of statutory rights [that is, under the Occupiers' Liability Act 1957], has been fairly excluded there must be some clear indication which would lead an ordinary sensible person to realise, at or before the time of making the contract, that a term of that sort, relating to personal injury, was sought to be included.

In cases such as this, therefore, the nature and scope of the attempted exclusion becomes a relevant factor in relation to incorporation. The issue is not solely procedural, but is affected by the substance of the clause. We have seen that the same approach may be used in relation to other types of clause. Thus, in Chapter 7 (see 7.4.1 above), it was noted that the same rule operated in *Interfoto Picture Library v Stiletto Visual Programmes* (1989) to prevent the incorporation of a clause which was not an exclusion clause, but which was nevertheless exceptional, and unusually onerous. It has been argued that these cases (together with the unreported Court of Appeal decision in *AEG (UK) Ltd v Logic Resource Ltd* (1995)) have, in effect, created a common law test of the 'reasonableness' of exclusion clauses (see Bradgate, 'Unreasonable standard terms' (1997) 60 MLR 582). These cases should, however, be regarded as exceptional. The need for such a common law test is also unclear (as Bradgate recognises) given the statutory tests contained in the Unfair Contract Terms Act 1977, and the Unfair Terms in Consumer Contracts Regulations 1999 (both of which are discussed below, at 8.8 and 8.12). In *AEG's* case, for example, the Court of Appeal also held the clause to be unreasonable under the 1977 Act.

8.3.4 Need for a 'contractual' document

In order to be effectively incorporated, the exclusion clause must generally be contained, or referred to, in something which can be regarded as a contractual document. This is an aspect of the rule that reasonable notice must be given. Notice is unlikely to be regarded as reasonable if the clause appears in something which would not be expected to contain contractual terms. Thus, in *Chapelton v Barry UDC* (1940), the plaintiff wished to hire a deck chair. He took a chair from a pile near a notice indicating the price and duration of hire, and requesting hirers to obtain a ticket from the attendant. The plaintiff did so, but when he used the chair it collapsed, causing him injury. It was accepted that the collapse of the chair was due to the negligence of the defendant (Barry UDC), but the council argued that it was protected by a statement on the ticket that: 'The council will not be liable for any accident or damage arising from hire of chair.' It was held by the Court of Appeal, however, that the ticket was a mere receipt. It was not a document on which the customer would expect to find contractual terms, and the exclusion clause printed on it was therefore not incorporated. The purpose of the ticket was simply to provide evidence for the hirer that he had discharged his obligation to pay for the chair. It was, the court felt, distinguishable from, for example, a railway ticket 'which contains upon it the terms upon which a railway company agrees to carry the passenger'. The test of which category the document should fall into will, presumably, depend on what information, terms, etc, the court thinks that a reasonable person would expect to find on it. In fact, in this case, the ticket was in any case provided too late, as it was held that the contract was formed when the deck chair was first taken for use, whereas the ticket was not handed over until after this had been done.

8.4 Construction

Once it has been decided that a clause has been incorporated into the contract, the next issue is whether it covers the breach that has occurred. In other words, the wording of the clause must be examined to see if it is apt to apply to the situation which has arisen. This is the called the rule of 'construction', but might equally well be called the rule of 'interpretation'. The clause is being 'constructed' or 'interpreted' to determine its scope.

8.4.1 *Contra proferentem* rule

The rules of construction, like the rules for incorporation, are of general application, and can be used in relation to all clauses within a contract, not just exclusion clauses. It is in relation to exclusion of liability, however, that most of the case law has arisen. In this context the courts have traditionally taken a strict approach. The rule of construction has been used as a means of limiting the effect of exclusion clauses, and a person wishing to avoid liability has been required to be very precise in the use of language to achieve that aim. One aspect of this is the *contra proferentem* rule, whereby an exclusion clause is interpreted against the person putting it forward. Thus, in *Andrews v Singer* (1934), a clause excluding liability in relation to *implied* terms was ruled ineffective to exclude liability for breach of an *express* term. Similarly, in *Wallis, Son and Wells v Pratt* (1911), it was held that a clause stating that the suppliers of goods gave no 'warranty' in relation to them did not protect them from being liable for a breach of 'condition' (for the distinction between warranties and conditions, see 7.4.3 above). Moreover, if there is ambiguity in the language used, this will be construed in the plaintiff's favour. Thus, it has been held that a reference in an insurance contract to excess 'loads' did not apply where a car was carrying more passengers than the number which it was constructed to carry (*Houghton v Trafalgar Insurance* (1954)). Particular difficulty can arise where the defendant seeks to exclude liability for negligence in the performance of a contract. In *Hollier v Rambler Motors* (1972), the plaintiff's car was at the defendant's premises when it was damaged by fire, caused by the defendant's negligence. There was a clause in the contract which stated 'the company is not responsible for damage caused by fire to customers' cars on the premises'. In the Court of Appeal, the view was taken that customers would assume that this clause related to fires which arose without negligence on the part of the defendant (though as a matter of law there would in fact be no liability in such a case). If the defendant wanted to exclude liability for negligence, then this should have been done explicitly. This is possible by using a general phrase, such as 'no liability for any damage, *howsoever caused*' (*Joseph Travers & Sons Ltd v Cooper* (1915)).

Note, however, that the position is different if the only basis of liability which the plaintiff would think existed is negligence liability (*Alderslade v Hendon Laundry* (1945)). In this case, the plaintiff had not received certain handkerchiefs which he had left with the defendant laundry. A clause in the contract stated that: 'The maximum amount allowed for lost or damaged articles is 20 times the charge made for laundering.' Lord Greene MR took the view that as regards loss (as opposed to damage), the laundry could not be regarded as undertaking a strict obligation, but only to take reasonable care of items (that is, not to be negligent). On that basis, the clause was apt to cover negligence liability. Salmon LJ in *Hollier v Rambler Motors*, however, in discussing this case, took the view that it was the perception of the customer that was important:

> I think that the ordinary sensible housewife, or indeed anyone else who sends washing to the laundry, who saw that clause must have appreciated that almost always goods are lost or damaged because of the laundry's negligence, and, therefore, this clause could apply only to limit the liability of the laundry, when they were in fault or negligent.

This must be regarded as having modified the approach taken by the Court of Appeal in *Alderslade* itself. The position thus now seems to be that where the reasonable plaintiff would read a clause as covering negligence the courts will be prepared to allow exclusion without any specific reference to negligence, or the use of a general phrase clearly including negligence (*Rutter v Palmer* (1922)). In the end, it is a matter of attempting to assess the intentions and reasonable expectations of the parties.

8.4.2 Relaxation of the rule

The position as regards exclusion of liability for negligence was significantly affected by the UCTA 1977. More generally, the existence of stricter statutory controls over exclusion clauses has encouraged the courts to take the line that there is no need for the rule of construction to be used in an artificial way to limit their scope. The consumer and the standard form contract are dealt with by the UCTA 1977 (and now also by the UTCCR 1999 (see 8.12 below)). Businesses negotiating at arms length should be expected to look after themselves. If they enter into contracts containing exclusion clauses, they must be presumed to know what they are doing. Thus, on three occasions since the passage of the UCTA 1977, the House of Lords has criticised an approach to the interpretation of exclusion clauses in commercial contracts, which involves straining their plain meaning in order to limit their effect. Thus, in *Photo Production v Securicor* (1980), Lord Wilberforce commented that in the light of parliamentary intervention to protect consumers (by means of the UCTA 1977 (see 8.5.4 below)):

> ... in commercial matters generally, when the parties are not of unequal bargaining power, and when risks are normally borne by insurance, not only is the case for judicial intervention undemonstrated, but there is everything to be said, and this seems to have been Parliament's intention, for leaving the parties free to apportion the risks as they think fit and for respecting their decisions.

Lord Diplock, agreeing with Lord Wilberforce, commented that:

> In commercial contracts negotiated between businessmen capable of looking after their own interests and of deciding how risks inherent in the performance of various kinds of contract can be most economically borne (generally by insurance), it is, in my view, wrong to place a strained construction on words in an exclusion clause which are clear and fairly susceptible of one meaning only ...

Similarly, in *Ailsa Craig Fishing Co v Malvern Fishing Co* (1983), Lord Wilberforce again expressed the view (particularly in relation to clauses limiting liability, rather than excluding it altogether) that:

> ... one must not strive to create ambiguities by strained construction, as I think the appellants have striven to do. The relevant words must be given, if possible, their natural, plain meaning.

Lord Fraser agreed that limitation clauses need not:

> ... be judged by the specially exacting standards which are applied to exclusion and indemnity clauses ... It is enough ... that the clause must be clear and unambiguous.

Finally, in *Mitchell (George) v Finney Lock Seeds* (1983), Lord Bridge re-affirmed the need for straightforward interpretation:

> The relevant condition, read as a whole, unambiguously limits the appellants' liability to replacement of the seeds or refund of the price. It is only possible to read an ambiguity into it by the process of strained construction which was deprecated by Lord Diplock in the *Photo Production* case ... and by Lord Wilberforce in the *Ailsa Craig* case.

8.4.3   Fundamental breach

At one time, the view was taken by some courts, and in particular the Court of Appeal, that some breaches of contract are so serious that no exclusion clause can cover them. This was expressed in the so called doctrine of fundamental breach. This doctrine found its origins in shipping law, where there is strong authority that if a ship 'deviates' from its agreed route, there can be no exclusion of liability in relation to events which occur after the deviation (for example, *Joseph Thorley Ltd v Orchis SS Co Ltd* (1907)). Applied more generally to the law of contract, it took two forms. One was that there are certain terms within the contract which are so fundamental that there cannot be exclusion for breach of them. Such would be the situation where the contract stipulated for the supply of peas, and beans were provided instead (*Chanter v Hopkins* (1838)). The supplier in such a case has departed so far from the basic contractual obligation that some courts felt that it could not be justifiable to allow him to exclude liability. To do so would appear to make a mockery of the whole idea of a contractual obligation. If, for example, a person who has contracted to sell potatoes supplies the same weight of coal, it surely ought not to be permissible to allow reliance on a broadly written exclusion clause which states 'the supplier may substitute any other goods for those specified in the contract'. The rules of incorporation and construction do not have any necessary effect on such a clause. The answer appeared to be to treat the promise to supply potatoes as a 'fundamental term'. Any breach of this term would provide a remedy to the other party irrespective of an exclusion clause. Stated in this form the doctrine had close links with the 'deviation' principle in shipping law, which similarly is concerned with the breach of a specific obligation regarded as being central to the contract. The second form of the doctrine of fundamental breach was different in that it looked not at the particular term which had been broken, but at the overall effects of the breach which had occurred. If the breach was so serious that it could be said to have destroyed the whole contract, then again, exclusion of liability should not be possible. Two cases illustrate these two aspects of the doctrine (*Karsales v Wallis* (1956) and *Harbutt's Plasticine v Wayne Tank and Pump Co Ltd* (1970)). In *Karsales v Wallis,* the contract was for the supply of a Buick car, which the plaintiff had inspected, and found to be in good condition. When delivered (late at night), however, it had to be towed, because it was incapable of self-propulsion. Amongst other things, the cylinder head had been removed, the valves had been burnt out, and two of the pistons had been broken. The defendant purported to rely on a clause of the agreement which stated:

> No condition or warranty that the vehicle is roadworthy, or as to its age, condition or fitness for purpose is given by the owner or implied herein.

The county judge held for the defendant, but the Court of Appeal reversed this. The majority of the court (Lord Denning reached the same conclusion, but on slightly different grounds) held that what had been delivered was not, in effect, a 'car'. The defendant's 'performance' was totally different from that which had been contemplated by the contract (that is, the supply of a motor vehicle in working order). There was, therefore, a breach of a fundamental term of the agreement, and the exclusion clause had no application.

In *Harbutt's Plasticine*, the contract involved the supply of pipework in the plaintiff's factory. The type of piping used was unsuitable, and resulted in a fire which destroyed the whole of the plaintiff's factory. The obligation to supply piping that was fit for its purpose could clearly have been broken in various ways, not all of which would have led to serious damage to the plaintiff's premises. In this case, however, the consequences of the defendant's failure to meet its obligation in this respect were so serious that the Court of Appeal regarded it as a 'fundamental breach' of the contract, precluding any reliance on an exclusion clause.

These two Court of Appeal decisions illustrate that a 'fundamental breach' could occur either through the breach of a particularly important term, or through a breach which had the consequences of destroying the whole basis of the contract.

In arriving at its decision in *Harbutt's Plasticine*, however, the Court of Appeal had to deal with the views expressed by the House of Lords in *Suisse Atlantique Société d'Armemente SA v NV Rotterdamsche Kolen Centrale* (1967). The case concerned a charter which included provisions whereby if there were delays the charterers' liability was limited to paying $1,000 per day 'demurrage'. The owners attempted to argue that the charterer's breach was so serious that the demurrage clause should not apply, and that they should be able to recover their full losses. The House of Lords rejected this, and in so doing expressed strong disapproval of the argument that there was a substantive rule of law which meant that certain types of breach automatically prevented reliance on an exclusion clause. As Viscount Dilhorne commented:

In my view, it is not right to say that the law prohibits and nullifies a clause exempting or limiting liability for a fundamental breach or breach of a fundamental term. Such a rule of law would involve a restriction on freedom of contract and in the older cases I can find no trace of it.

As this quotation illustrates, the House was of the opinion that the parties should generally be allowed to determine their obligations, and the effect of exclusion clauses in their contract. If there was a breach which appeared fundamental, then it was a question of trying to determine the parties' intentions as to whether such a breach was intended to be covered by any exclusion clause. Of course, as Lord Wilberforce noted, 'the courts are entitled to insist, as they do, that the more radical the breach the clearer must be the language if it is to be covered', but the question is one of the proper construction of the clause, and not a rule of law.

In *Harbutt's Plasticine,* the Court of Appeal attempted to distinguish *Suisse Atlantique* on the basis that in that case the parties had continued with the charter even after the alleged fundamental breach. The Court of Appeal therefore argued that the principles outlined by the House of Lords in *Suisse Atlantique* should only apply where there was an affirmation of the contract by the parties following the breach, and not where the breach itself brought the contract to an end. In the latter type of situation, there should be no possibility of reliance on an exclusion clause. The difficulty with this argument was that it is a well established principle in contract law (discussed further in Chapter 14), that a breach never in itself brings a contract to an end. The party not in breach always has the option (if the breach is a serious one) of either accepting the breach and terminating the contract, or affirming the contract and suing for damages. Suppose, for example, there is a contract for the sale of components which are to be supplied with certain fixing holes drilled in them. If, when delivered, the fixing holes are not there, this will amount to a breach of 'condition' (by virtue of s 13 of the Sale of Goods Act 1979 (see 18.5 below)). The buyer will have the right to accept the breach, reject the goods, and sue for damages. Alternatively, however, the buyer may affirm the contract, accept the goods, and simply sue for the cost of having the holes drilled, and any other consequential losses. The Court of Appeal in *Harbutt's* took the view that this did not apply to certain fundamental breaches of contract, which themselves brought the contract to an end, without the need for acceptance by the party not in breach. This view, was, however, firmly rejected by the House of Lords in *Photo Production Ltd v Securicor Transport Ltd* (1980), which overruled *Harbutt's Plasticine,* and finally disposed of the argument that certain types of fundamental breach could never be covered by an exclusion clause.

The facts of the *Photo Production* case were that the plaintiffs owned a factory, and engaged the defendants to provide security services, including a night patrol. Unfortunately, one of the guards employed by the defendants to carry out these duties, started a fire on premises which got out of control, and destroyed the entire factory. Thus, rather than protecting the plaintiffs' property, as they had been contracted to do, the defendants could be said to have achieved the exact opposite. The contract, however, contained a very broadly worded exclusion clause, which, on its face, seemed to cover even the very serious breach of the agreement which had occurred. The Court of Appeal took the view that this could not protect the defendants. There had been a fundamental breach, and the exclusion clause was ineffective. The House of Lords, however, took this opportunity to state its position with no possible ambiguity. It ruled that there was no rule of law that a fundamental breach of contract prevented an exclusion clause from being effective. The so called doctrine of fundamental breach was in fact no more than an aspect of the doctrine of construction. Of course, it was the case that the more serious the breach of contract, the clearer the words would need to be which would exclude liability for it. But, if two businesses had negotiated an agreement containing a clause which on its plain wording covered such a breach, there was no reason why the courts should not give effect to it. In the present case, the House, while noting the breadth of the exclusion clause, also noted that the plaintiffs were paying a very low rate for the defendants' services. It was therefore not unreasonable that the defendants should have a low level of liability. The *ratio* of the case was not, however, that the clause was reasonable in all the circumstances, but that on its true construction it covered the breach.

8.4.4   The current position

The demise of the doctrine of fundamental breach as a rule of law (and there has been no attempt to revive it since the *Photo Production* decision) has to some extent simplified the law in this area. It may be still be difficult to decide in particular cases, however, what to do where a breach effectively negates the whole purpose of the contract. It is a matter of looking at the precise wording of the exclusion clause, and trying to determine the intentions of the parties in relation to it. The likelihood of exclusion being effective will decrease with the seriousness of the breach, but it is now always a question of balance, rather than the application of a firm rule.

Where the contract involves a consumer, this process is generally rendered unnecessary because of the statutory provisions contained in the UCTA 1977 and the UTCCR 1999, to which we now turn.

8.5   Unfair Contract Terms Act 1977

The UCTA 1977 has had a very significant effect on the law relating to exclusion clauses. Where it applies, it has to a large extent replaced the common law rules. Although strictly speaking the rules of incorporation and construction are logically prior to any consideration of the statutory provisions, so that if a clause is not incorporated or does not cover the breach it can have no effect at all, and the UCTA 1977 is irrelevant, the Act will in practice often be looked at first. It must be remembered, however, that the UCTA 1977 does not apply to all contracts. The first point for discussion here is therefore the precise scope of the Act.

8.5.1 Scope of the UCTA 1977

There are certain contracts, listed in Sched 1, which are not within the scope of ss 2–4 (which are the main protective provisions) at all. These include:

- contracts of insurance;

- contracts concerning the creation or transfer of interests in land: this includes continuing covenants under a lease – *Electricity Supply Nominees v IAF Group* (1993);

- contracts concerning the creation or transfer of intellectual property rights (copyright, patent, etc);

- contracts relating to the formation, dissolution, or constitution of a company, partnership, or unincorporated association;

- contracts relating to the creation or transfer of securities.

The UCTA 1977 also has only limited application in relation to various types of shipping contract, including carriage of goods by sea. In relation to contracts of employment, s 2(1) and (2) (which deal with exclusion of liability for negligence) do not apply other than in favour of an employee. It was confirmed in *Brigden v American Express* (2000) that an employee can potentially use the Act against terms put forward by an employer (though on the facts the claim failed).

It is always advisable to check the provisions of Sched 1 in relation to contracts falling into the above categories.

8.5.2 'Business' liability

The next limitation on the scope of the UCTA 1977 which must be noted appears in s 1(3). This states that ss 2–7 apply only to:

> ... business liability, that is, liability for breach of obligations or duties arising (a) from things done or to be done in the course of a business ...; or (b) from the occupation of premises used for the business purposes of the occupier.

In general, therefore, the non-business contractor is free to include exclusion clauses, without their being controlled by the UCTA 1977 (though the scope of s 6, which deals with sale of goods contracts, is wider – see Chapter 18 below). In many situations, the test of whether obligations arise in the course of a 'business' will not give rise to problems, but it is perhaps unfortunate that the Act does not contain a comprehensive definition of what is meant by 'business'.

8.5.3 Meaning of business

Section 14 states that '"business" includes a profession and the activities of any government department or local or public authority'. This leaves open the position of organisations such as charities, or universities, which may engage in business activities, but might not be thought to be contracting 'in the course of a business'. The protective policy of the UCTA 1977 would suggest that such situations ought to be covered. The phrase 'in the course of a business' has, however, been interpreted fairly restrictively in relation to its use in another context within the Act. Section 12 uses it as part of the definition of whether a person 'deals as a consumer' for the purposes of buying goods, which is an important consideration in relation to the application of s 6. In *R and B Customs Brokers v UDT* (1988), the plaintiff was a private company involved in the export business. A car was bought by the company for the personal and business use of the directors. It was held by the Court of Appeal that it was not bought 'in the course of a business', because the plaintiff's business was not that of buying and selling cars. If this approach is taken in relation to s 1(3), it would mean, for example, that a university which provides car parking facilities on its site in return for payment, or a charity which makes money by organising a 'car boot' sale, and selling 'pitches', would not be covered by the UCTA 1977. It is difficult to see, however, why the other contracting party should be any less protected in such a situation than if dealing with a commercial organisation, which might well be in no better position to meet financial liabilities, or to ensure against them, than the university or charity.

Some doubt about the correctness of the decision in *R and B Customs Brokers* was expressed by the Court of Appeal in *Stevenson v Rogers* (1999) (discussed further at 18.5.3) in considering whether a sale was 'in the course of business' for the purposes of s 14 of the Sale of Goods Act 1979. It was suggested there that the earlier decision should be confined to its particular facts, that is, the interpretation of s 12 of the UCTA, and not necessarily applied elsewhere. The court therefore refused to apply the same approach in interpreting the Sale of Goods Act 1979. It would be difficult (though not impossible), however, to argue that within one statute the same phrase has been used with different meanings. It remains the case, therefore, that pending a decision to the contrary by the House of Lords, the interpretation of 'in the course of a business' where that phrase is used in UCTA should follow the approach taken in *R and B Customs Brokers*.

8.5.4 Disclaimers

The final issue in relation to the scope of the UCTA 1977 concerns the type of clauses which are covered. In drawing up a contract, it is possible to attempt to avoid liabilities in a number of ways. The most obvious is by an exclusion clause which states that in the event of a breach there will be no liability, or that it will be limited to a particular sum. It is also possible, however, to attempt to achieve the same objective by clauses which define the obligations arising under the contract restrictively ('disclaimers'), or make the enforcement of a liability subject to restrictive conditions (for example, 'all claims must be made within 48 hours of the conclusion of the contract'). Section 13 makes it clear that all clauses of this kind which have the effect of excluding or restricting liability are caught by the Act's provisions. It states:

(1) To the extent that this Part of the Act prevents the exclusion or restriction of any liability, it also prevents:

(a) making the liability or its enforcement subject to restrictive or onerous conditions;

(b) excluding or restricting any right or remedy in respect of the liability, or subjecting a person to any prejudice in consequence of his pursuing any such right or remedy;

(c) excluding or restricting rules of evidence and procedure;

and (to that extent) ss 2 and 5–7 also prevent excluding or restricting liability by reference to terms and notices which exclude or restrict the relevant obligation or duty.

(2) But an agreement in writing to submit present or future differences to arbitration is not to be treated under this Part of this Act as excluding or restricting any liability.

In *Smith v Bush* (1989), the House of Lords confirmed that s 13 extends s 2 of the UCTA 1977 to a clause which is in the form of a disclaimer, which in this case was given by a surveyor providing a valuation of a property to the plaintiff, *via* a building society. The valuation was stated to be given without any acceptance of responsibility as to its accuracy. This was held to be an 'exclusion clause' within the scope of the UCTA 1977, and to fall foul of its requirement of 'reasonableness' (see 8.8 below). Similarly, in *Stewart Gill v Horatio Myer & Co Ltd* (1992), the Court of Appeal held that a clause restricting a right of set-off or counterclaim could be regarded as an exclusion clause, and therefore within the scope of the UCTA 1977.

8.6 Exclusion of negligence under the UCTA 1977

Section 2 of the UCTA 1977 is concerned with clauses which attempt to exclude business liability for 'negligence', which is defined for the purposes of the Act in s 1(1) to cover the breach:

(a) of any obligation, arising from the express or implied terms of a contract, to take reasonable care or exercise reasonable skill in the performance of the contract;

(b) of any common law duty to take reasonable care or exercise reasonable skill (but not any stricter duty);

(c)   of the common duty of care imposed by the Occupiers' Liability Act 1958.

Thus, it applies to negligent performance of a contract (sub-s (a)), the tort of negligence independent of any contract (sub-s (b)), and the statutory duty of care imposed on occupiers towards lawful visitors (sub-s (c)).

Section 2 states:

(1) A person cannot by reference to any contract term or to a notice given to persons generally or to particular persons exclude or restrict his liability for death or personal injury resulting from negligence.

(2) In the case of other loss or damage, a person cannot so exclude or restrict his liability for negligence except in so far as the term or notice satisfies the requirement of reasonableness.

(3) Where a contract term or notice purports to exclude or restrict liability for negligence a person's agreement to or awareness of it is not of itself to be taken as indicating his voluntary acceptance of such a risk.

The level of control imposed by s 2 thus depends on the consequences of the negligence. To the extent that the exclusion clause attempts to limit liability for death or personal injury resulting from negligence it will be totally ineffective (s 2(1)). As regards any other types of loss or damage, the clause will be effective to the extent that the clause satisfies the 'requirement of reasonableness' set out in s 2(2) of the UCTA 1977. (This is discussed further, at 8.8 below.) It is not clear what the approach of the courts will be towards a clause which attempts to exclude or limit liability for all loss or damage (including death or personal injury) resulting from negligence by the use of a general phrase such as 'no liability for any loss, injury or damage, howsoever caused'. Clearly, the clause will not be effective in relation to death or personal injuries resulting from negligence. However, this does not mean that the clause is totally without effect. The Act does not invalidate a clause altogether simply because it attempts to exclude liability for personal injuries. It may be arguable, however, that in relation to other losses the breadth of the clause makes it unreasonable. The answer to this will depend on the precise interpretation of the requirement of reasonableness, and we will return to this issue in the context of that discussion.

8.7   Standard terms and consumer contracts

Whereas s 2 is only concerned with the exclusion of negligence liability, s 3 covers all types of liability arising under a contract, including strict liability, but is limited in the types of contract which it effects. It states:

(1) This section applies as between contracting parties where one of them deals as a consumer, or on the other's written standard terms of business.

(2) As against that party, the other cannot by reference to any contract term:

(a) when himself in breach of contract, exclude or restrict any liability of his in respect of the breach; or

(b) claim to be entitled:

    (i) to render a contractual performance substantially different from that which was reasonably expected of him; or

    (ii) in respect of the whole or any part of his contractual obligation, to render no performance at all,

except in so far as (in all of the cases mentioned above in this sub-section) the contract term satisfies the requirement of reasonableness.

The section is thus directed at situations where there is inequality of bargaining power, and the plaintiff may have effectively been forced to accept a wide ranging exclusion clause, which may appear to operate unfairly. The section operates in relation to two types of contract. First, it covers contracts where the plaintiff 'deals as a consumer'. The definition of 'dealing as a consumer' is to be found in s 12. A party 'deals as a consumer' if:

(a) he neither makes the contract in the course of a business nor holds himself out as doing so; and

(b) the other party does make the contract in the course of a business.

8.7.1 Meaning of 'in the course of a business'

The scope of the phrase 'in the course of a business' as defined in *R and B Customs Brokers v UDT* (1988) has been discussed (see 8.5.3 above). As we have seen, it means that it is not simply the private individual who can claim to deal 'as a consumer'. Businesses will apparently be able to do so in relation to contracts which do not form a regular part of their business. Despite the doubts as to whether this was what Parliament intended, and the refusal of the Court of Appeal to follow this interpretation in relation to the same phrase where used in the Sale of Goods Act 1979 (in *Stevenson v Rogers* (1999), see 18.5.3), the *R and B Brokers* approach remains the governing authority in relation to the UCTA.

A person claiming to deal as a consumer does not have to prove this: the burden of proof is on the party claiming that a person is *not* dealing as a consumer (s 12(3)).

8.7.2 Standard terms of business

The second type of contract which is covered by s 3 is one which is made on the basis of the defendant's 'written standard terms of business'. This phrase is not further defined, but it is to be assumed that the individual negotiation of some of the terms of the agreement will not prevent them from being 'standard'. The exclusion clause itself will, however, presumably have to be part of the standard package. It is important to remember that this provision is not concerned directly with inequalities in bargaining power. It is likely in practice (because of the way in which the requirement of reasonableness operates) to benefit the weaker party more frequently, but there is no reason in theory why it should not be relied on by a large corporation which happens to have made a contract on the basis of a much smaller and less powerful business's standard terms. It is also important to note that this category is unlikely to be needed to be used by the private individual, despite the fact that many contracts between individuals and businesses are made on the business's standard terms. The reason for this is, of course, that the private individual will contract 'as consumer', and will therefore be within the other category covered by s 3.

8.7.3   Effect of s 3

The effect of s 3 is that, in relation to any contract within its scope, any attempt to exclude or restrict liability by the non-consumer, or the party putting forward the standard terms, will be subject to the requirement of reasonableness (s 3(2)(a)). Moreover, s 3(2)(b) goes on to make it clear that this extends also to any contractual term by virtue of which such a party claims to be entitled:

(i)   to render a contractual performance substantially different from that which was reasonably to be expected of him; or

(ii)   in respect of the whole or any part of his contractual obligation, to render no performance at all ...

The point of the provisions in s 3(2)(b) is similar to that of s 13. It is trying to anticipate attempts to exclude liability indirectly by the use of clauses which define a party's obligations very restrictively. It would apply, for example, to a clause such as that used in *Karsales v Wallis* (1956) (see 8.4.3 above) purporting to allow the supplier of a 'car' to deliver something which was incapable of self-propulsion (though such a clause would probably also fall foul of the special provisions relating to sale of goods contracts), or to a clause allowing a party who had agreed to provide a cleaning service each month to miss several months in a row without penalty. Such clauses are permissible, but only to the extent which they satisfy the requirement of reasonableness. This enables a court to distinguish clauses which are genuine and legitimate attempts to set out the parties' contractual obligations, from those which are being used to escape any substantial liability at all. The test of legitimacy, as indicated by s 3(2)(b)(i) above, is likely to be the reasonable expectations of the other party.

The overall effect of s 3 is that, because the vast majority of exclusion clauses will be in either a consumer contract, or one which is on standard terms, there will be very few situations in which an exclusion clause is not at least subject to the requirement of reasonableness. It gives the Appeal Courts the opportunity to indicate the acceptable limits of exclusion of liability, though as will be seen (see 8.8 below), it is not one which they have shown any great willingness to take.

8.8 The requirement of reasonableness

The test to be applied to determine whether a clause meets the requirement of reasonableness is set out in s 11 of the UCTA 1977. The central element of the test is stated in s 11(1) as being whether the clause was:

> ... a fair and reasonable one to be included having regard to the circumstances which were, or ought reasonably to have been, known to or in the contemplation of the parties when the contract was made.

This very general test imposes no very significant restrictions on the exercise of a court's discretion in relation to a clause, and therefore makes things difficult for the parties in terms of contractual planning. It will be very difficult to predict whether a particular clause is likely to fall foul of this test. A few guidelines to its operation can be found, however, both within the UCTA 1977 itself and from case law.

8.8.1 Interpretation of reasonableness

Starting with the wording of s 11, it is clear that the point at which the clause should be assessed is when the contract was created, and that the test is directed at the clause itself, not at any particular application of it. It is submitted that *obiter* statements to the contrary by the Court of Appeal in *Overseas Medical Supplies Ltd v Orient Transport Services Ltd* (1999) (see 8.8.5 below) should be regarded with caution, as running against the clear wording of s 11. Thus, the issue should be whether the clause is one which at the time the parties made the contract could be regarded as fair and reasonable. Subsequent events should not be relevant in deciding this issue. In particular, the actual breach which has occurred and for which the clause is claimed to provide exclusion or limitation of liability, should not, in theory, be considered. The strict reading of the section makes it clear that it is quite possible for a court to feel that it would be reasonable for the defendant to have excluded liability for the particular breach which has occurred, but that the clause is too widely worded to be reasonable, and should therefore fail. This is in line with a policy which aims to discourage the use of unnecessarily wide clauses, rather than simply trying to provide a just solution to individual disputes. The Court of Appeal in *Stewart Gill v Horatio Myer & Co Ltd* (1992) confirmed that it is the reasonableness of a clause as a whole, rather than the part of it which is being relied on in the particular case, that must be considered.

Where the clause is one which attempts to limit liability to a specific sum of money, rather than excluding it altogether, s 11(4) directs the court to take into account, in assessing the reasonableness of the clause:

(a)   the resources which [the defendant] could expect to be available to him for the purpose of meeting the liability should it arise; and

(b)   how far it was open to him to cover himself by insurance.

This recognises that it may be quite reasonable for a contracting party who is impecunious, or is engaging in a particularly risky activity, to put a financial ceiling on liability.

Finally, s 11(5) states that:

> It is for those claiming that a contract term or notice satisfies the requirement of reasonableness to show that it does.

This makes it clear that the burden of proof as regarding reasonableness lies on the party seeking to rely on the clause.

8.8.2   Guidelines in Sched 2

The only other part of the UCTA 1977 which provides guidance on the operation of the reasonableness test is Sched 2. The role of the Schedule is indicated by s 11(2):

> In determining for the purposes of s 6 or 7 above whether a contract term satisfies the requirement of reasonableness, regard shall be had in particular to the matters specified in Sched 2 to this Act; but this subsection does not prevent the court or arbitrator from holding, in accordance with any rule of law, that a term which purports to exclude or restrict any relevant liability is not a term of the contract.

Strictly speaking, therefore, the 'guidelines' which it contains are only to be used in relation to exclusion clauses which attempt to limit liability for breach of the statutorily implied terms under sale of goods and hire purchase contracts. In practice, however, the considerations set out are likely to be regarded as relevant whenever reasonableness is in issue (see, for example, *Overseas Medical Supplies Ltd v Orient Transport Services Ltd* (1999); see 8.8.5 below). There are five factors listed, covering the following areas:

* The relative strength of the bargaining position of the parties – in particular, did the plaintiff have any option about contracting with the defendant, or were there other means by which the plaintiff's requirements could have been met?

* Whether the plaintiff received an inducement (for example, a discount) to agree to the term; could the same contract have been made with other persons without the exclusion clause?

* Whether the plaintiff knew or ought reasonably to have known of the existence and extent of the term. (Note that there is a clear overlap here with the common law requirement of incorporation.)

- Whether at the time of contract it was reasonable to expect that compliance would be practicable with any condition which, if not complied with, leads to the exclusion or restriction of liability.

- Whether goods were manufactured, processed or adapted to the special order of the customer. (Note that this consideration is specifically linked to contracts for the supply of goods: put into general terms it would require the court to consider whether the contract was specially negotiated to meet the plaintiff's requirements.)

The weight to be given to any of these considerations is left entirely to the discretion of the court. Moreover, since they are only 'guidelines' there is no obligation to look at them at all. It is unlikely, for example, that the Court of Appeal would overturn a judge's decision on the reasonableness issue simply because one of the above guidelines had not been considered, even in relation to a contract for the supply of goods. The list is not exhaustive, and other matters may be taken into consideration, if the court feels that this is appropriate.

8.8.3   Judicial approach to 'reasonableness' – pre-UCTA 1977

As far as the case law on 'reasonableness' is concerned, there are two House of Lords' decisions which are worth noting, one applying a test of reasonableness which pre-dated the UCTA 1977, the other dealing with the UCTA 1977 itself.

The first case is *George Mitchell v Finney Lock Seeds* (1983). This concerned a contract for the sale of cabbage seed which turned out not to match its description, with the result that the entire crop failed, and the purchaser suffered a loss of £63,000. The contract contained an exclusion clause, limiting the liability of the seller to the price of the seed, which was under £200. The clause was subject to the test of reasonableness (now superseded by the UCTA 1977) contained in s 55(4) of the Sale of Goods Act 1979 (as set out in Sched 1), which required the court to decide whether it was fair and reasonable to allow reliance on the clause. The trial judge and the Court of Appeal held that the clause did not on its true construction cover the breach. The House of Lords differed on the construction issue, holding that the wording was apt to cover the breach, and so had to go on to consider the question of reasonableness. The House emphasised that it was best on this issue, wherever possible, for the appeal courts to accept the judgment of the trial judge, who had the benefit of hearing all the witnesses. (This point was also made in the later case of *Phillips v Hyland* (1987).) Since that was not possible here, however, the House went on to determine the 'reasonableness' issue itself. It approached it as an exercise in 'balancing' various factors against each other. On the one hand, the clause was a common one in the trade, and had never been objected to by the National Union of Farmers. Moreover, the magnitude of the damage in proportion to the price of the goods sold also weighed in the defendants' favour. Lord Bridge, however, found three matters to put into the other side of the balance. First, the fact that the wrong seed was supplied was due to negligence (albeit of the defendants' sister company, rather than the defendants themselves). Secondly, the trial judge had found that the defendants would have been able to take out insurance against crop failure, without needing to increase the price of the seeds significantly. Thirdly, and in Lord Bridge's view most importantly, there was evidence from a number of witnesses (including the chairman of the defendants) that it was general practice in the trade *not* to rely on this clause in cases like the one which the House was considering, but to negotiate more substantial compensation. As Lord Bridge put it:

> This evidence indicates a clear recognition by seedsmen in general, and the [defendants] in particular, that reliance on the limitation of liability imposed by the relevant condition would not be fair and reasonable.

This indicates that where the courts are dealing with a common type of contract within a particular area of business activity, the practices of the trade or business are likely to be of considerable relevance. In addition, the fact that *all* the circumstances must be considered, and that the appeal courts' are reluctant to interfere with decisions of the trial judge, means that it is not necessarily the case that because a particular exclusion clause has been found unreasonable in one situation, that it will be precluded from use in others. This element of uncertainty will pull in two directions. It will make those who wish to include exclusion clauses cautious, and may encourage them to word clauses narrowly and precisely. On the other hand, the plaintiff who wishes to challenge a clause may well be deterred by the fact that the outcome of such a challenge will be very unpredictable.

8.8.4 The UCTA 1977 in the House of Lords

The second House of Lords' case which has discussed the concept of 'reasonableness' is *Smith v Bush* (1989). The case concerned a 'disclaimer' of liability for negligence put forward by a surveyor carrying out a valuation of a property for a building society, which was relied on by the purchaser of the property. Having decided that this disclaimer did constitute an exclusion clause, by virtue of s 13 of the UCTA 1977 (see 8.5.4 above), the House then had to consider whether it satisfied the requirement of reasonableness. The factors which were considered relevant to this issue were set out most clearly in the speech of Lord Griffiths. He thought that there were four matters which should *always* be considered in deciding this issue. They were:

- Were the parties of equal bargaining power? (This also appears in the guidelines in Sched 2 to the UCTA 1977.)

- In the case of advice, would it have been reasonably practicable to obtain the advice from an alternative source taking into account considerations of costs and time? In this case, although the purchaser could have obtained another survey, it was relevant that the house was 'at the bottom end of the market', which made it less reasonable to expect the purchaser to pay for a second opinion.

- How difficult is the task being undertaken for which liability is being excluded? The more difficult or dangerous the undertaking, the more reasonable it is to exclude liability.

- What are the practical consequences of the decision on reasonableness? For example, if the risk is one against which a defendant could quite easily have insured, but which will have very serious effects on a plaintiff who is required to bear the loss, this will suggest that exclusion is unreasonable. It might be otherwise if a finding of liability would 'open the floodgates' to claims.

With these considerations in mind, and in addition, the fact that this was an individual private house purchase, not a deal in relation to commercial property, the House decided that the disclaimer of liability did not meet the requirement of reasonableness.

8.8.5   'Reasonableness' in the Court of Appeal

Several Court of Appeal decisions have involved a consideration of the test of reasonableness. Two of these, *Phillips Products v Hyland* (1987) and *Thompson v Lohan (Plant Hire)* (1987), involved differing interpretations of the same clause, but did not add significantly to the guidelines on how the test should be applied as indicated by the *George Mitchell v Finney Lock Seeds* (1983) and *Smith v Bush* decisions.

In *Phillips Products v Hyland*, however, Slade LJ noted, and followed, the injunction from Lord Bridge in *George Mitchell* that Appeal Courts should be very reluctant to interfere with the trial judge on this issue. Lord Bridge, having pointed out that the test of reasonableness involves a balancing of considerations, commented that:

> There will sometimes be room for a legitimate difference of judicial opinion as to what the answer should be, where it will be impossible to say that one view is demonstrably wrong, and the other demonstrably right. It must follow, in my view, that, when asked to review such a decision on appeal, the appellate court should treat the original decision with the utmost respect and refrain from interference with it unless satisfied that it proceeded on some erroneous principle or was plainly and obviously wrong.

With this in mind, Slade LJ concentrated his consideration of the first instance judgment on the issue of whether the judge had directed himself to the correct issues. Given that he appeared to have done so, and that his conclusion was not 'plainly or obviously wrong', the court did not feel it appropriate to interfere. It also followed from this approach, however, that:

... our conclusion on the particular facts of this case should not be treated as a binding precedent in other cases where similar clauses fall to be considered but the evidence of the surrounding circumstances may be very different.

Two more recent Court of Appeal decisions have, however, given some further guidance as to factors which are relevant in applying the test. In *Schenkers Ltd v Overland Shoes Ltd* (1998), the clause was contained in the standard trading conditions of the British International Freight Association (BIFA). The Court of Appeal felt that it was relevant, particularly where the parties were of equal bargaining power, that the clause was one which was in common use and well known in the trade. It could therefore be taken to reflect a general view as to what was reasonable in the trade concerned. Although in *George Mitchell v Finney Lock* it had been found that there was an expectation in the trade that an exclusion clause which was in common use would not in practice be relied on, that had not been shown to be the case here. Although there was 'no ready or frequent resort to the clause', there was no evidence of a recognition in the trade that the clause was unreasonable.

The second case is *Overseas Medical Supplies Ltd v Orient Transport Services Ltd* (1999), which was also concerned with a clause (though a different one) contained in BIFA's standard trading conditions. The trial judge in this case held that the clause was unreasonable, and this was upheld by the Court of Appeal. In coming to that conclusion, Potter LJ outlined various factors which are relevant to the decision on reasonableness:

(1) the way in which the relevant conditions came into being (for example, are they part of the standard conditions used in a particular trade);

(2) the guidelines in Sched 2 to UCTA (even where the contract is not concerned with sale of goods, and is not a consumer transaction);

(3) in relation to equality of bargaining position, the question of whether the customer was obliged to use the services of the supplier and how far it would have been practical or convenient to go elsewhere;

(4) the clause must be viewed as a whole, rather than taking any particular part of it in isolation. It must also be viewed 'against a breach of contract which is the subject matter of the present case' [but see the comment on this below];

(5) the reality of the consent of the customer to the supplier's clause;

(6) in cases of limitation, the size of the limit in comparison with other limits in widely used standard terms;

(7) the availability of insurance (though this is by no means a decisive factor);

(8) the presence of a term allowing for an option to contract without the limitation clause but with an increase in price.

All of these factors are sensible ones for the court to consider. In relation to the second sentence of (4) above, however, which derives from *AEG Ltd v Logic Resource Ltd* (1995), it seems to be incompatible with the wording of s 11 of the UCTA which, as we have seen (8.8.1 above), states that the test is whether the clause was a reasonable one to *include in the contract* having regard to the parties state of knowledge *at that time*. The nature of the breach which has actually occurred ought therefore not to be relevant to the assessment of the reasonableness of the clause. The statement to the contrary by Potter LJ is clearly *obiter*, and it is submitted that it should not be relied upon pending further clarification by the appellate courts.

In both *Schenkers Ltd v Overland Shoes Ltd* and *Overseas Medical Supplies Ltd v Orient Transport Services Ltd*, the Court of Appeal again emphasised that the appeal courts should be reluctant to interfere with a decision on this issue by the trial judge, and in both cases upheld the first instance decision. Appealing decisions on 'reasonableness' may well turn out to be a fruitless exercise.

8.9   Indemnities

Section 4 deals with 'indemnities'. It states:

(1) A person dealing as a consumer cannot by reference to any contract term be made to indemnify another person (whether a party to the contract or not) in respect of liability that may be incurred by the other for negligence or breach of contract, except in so far as the contract term satisfies the requirement of reasonableness.

(2) This section applies whether the liability in question:

(a) is directly that of the person to be indemnified or is incurred by him vicariously;

(b) is to the person dealing as consumer or to someone else.

The section is designed to deal with attempts to impose liability on a person dealing as a consumer by way of an obligation to indemnify another for liability for negligence or breach of contract. This can only be done in so far as the clause satisfies the requirement of reasonableness.

This might be attempted where, for example, a consumer sues in tort an individual employee who has acted negligently in the course of employment. The employee may well be entitled to be indemnified by his or her employer, and the employer may in return have provided for an indemnity in the contract with the consumer. By virtue of s 4, this will only be enforceable if it satisfies the requirement of reasonableness.

8.10 Guarantees of consumer goods

Section 5 is concerned with guarantees given by the manufacturers of consumer goods. It states:

> (1) In the case of goods of a type ordinarily supplied for private use or consumption, where loss or damage:
>
> (a) arises from the goods proving defective while in consumer use; and
>
> (b) results from the negligence of a person concerned in the manufacture or distribution of the goods,
>
> liability for the loss or damage cannot be excluded or restricted by reference to any contract term or notice contained in or operating by reference to a guarantee of the goods.
>
> (2) For these purposes:
>
> (a) goods are to be regarded as 'in consumer use' when a person is using them, or has them in his possession for use, otherwise than exclusively for the purposes of a business; and
>
> (b) anything in writing is a guarantee if it contains or purports to contain some promise or assurance (however worded or presented) that defects will be made good by complete or partial replacement, or by repair, monetary compensation or otherwise.
>
> (3) This section does not apply as between the parties to a contract under or in pursuance of which possession or ownership of the goods passed.

The type of situation to which this section is directed is where a 'guarantee' provided by the manufacturer of goods, for example, tries to limit a consumer's rights, by giving, for example, a right to replacement, but denying any other liability. Where the goods have proved defective while 'in consumer use' (that is, other than exclusively for the purposes of a business (s 5(2)(a)), and this results from the negligence of the defendant, then the limitation of liability will be ineffective (s 5(1)).

Note that this section does not apply to guarantees given by a seller, or hirer, of goods (s 5(3)). The effect of such provisions in these contracts is covered by ss 6 and 7 of the UCTA 1977, which are discussed below.

8.11 Other cases – sale, hire purchase, misrepresentation

There are special provisions under the Act in relation to contracts for the supply of goods (ss 6 and 7) and liability for misrepresentations (s 8). These are dealt with in the chapters concerned with these topics (that is, 18 and 9 respectively).

8.12 Unfair Terms in Consumer Contracts Regulations 1999

From 1 July 1995, certain contracts have been subject to Regulations deriving from the European directive on unfair terms in consumer contracts (Directive 93/13/EC). The first set of Regulations were issued in 1994, but a revised set replaced these in 1999. The current Regulations are the Unfair Terms in Consumer Contracts Regulations (UTCCR) 1999 (SI 1999/2083).

8.12.1 Application of the Regulations

The application of the Regulations is in some respects narrower than the UCTA 1977, but in other respects broader. It is narrower in that they apply only to contracts between a seller or supplier of goods or services and a 'consumer'. A consumer is defined in the regulations as being 'a natural person ... acting for purposes which are outside his trade, business or profession' (reg 3(1)). As we have seen, most of the provisions of the UCTA 1977 apply to contracts between businesses, even though they may do so in a different way to consumer contracts. Moreover, the case of *R and B Customs Brokers v UDT* (1988) shows that, in some circumstances, a 'business' can be treated as a consumer. The UTCCR 1999, however, do not apply to contracts between businesses, and only natural persons can be consumers under them.

The UTCCR 1999 are broader than the UCTA 1977 in that they potentially apply to all types of contract term, not just exclusion clauses. They do not, however, apply to any clause which is 'individually negotiated' (reg 5(1)). The purpose of the UTCCR 1999 is to regulate standard form consumer contracts.

Apart from these general provisions as to the application of the Regulations, reg 4 also excludes from their scope terms which are included in a contract to comply with or reflect any UK statutory or regulatory provisions, or the provisions of any international conventions to which the Member States of the European Community, or the Community itself, are party.

8.12.2 Terms attacked

Regulation 8(1) provides that any 'unfair term' in a consumer contract 'shall not be binding on the consumer'. The test of 'unfairness' is contained in reg 5(1), and covers:

> ... any term which contrary to the requirement of good faith ... causes a significant imbalance in the parties' rights and obligations under the contract to the detriment of the consumer.

This definition, with its reference to 'good faith' reveals the European origins of the Regulations. English consumer law has no general concept of 'good faith', and so it is unpredictable how the courts might treat this definition. It is to be expected that they will concentrate on the questions of 'imbalance' and 'detriment' which are more familiar. The 1994 Regulations contained a Schedule setting out some factors which the court should have regard to in assessing the issue of good faith. These were:

(a)   the strength of the bargaining position of the parties;

(b)   whether the consumer had an inducement to agree to the term;

(c)   whether the goods or services were sold or supplied to the special order of the consumer; and

(d)   the extent to which the seller or supplier has dealt fairly and equitably with the consumer.

This list has not been reproduced in the 1999 Regulations. It is hard to believe, however, that the factors listed will not in practice be among those that a court will consider in assessing 'good faith'. In the first reported case on the Regulations (*Director General of Fair Trading v First National Bank plc* (2000), dealing with the 1994 Regulations), the Court of Appeal expressed its approach to the good faith issue as follows (drawing on statements in *Anson's Law of Contract*):

> ... the good faith element seeks to promote fair and open dealing, and to prevent unfair surprise and the absence of real choice. A term to which the consumer's attention is not specifically drawn but which may operate in a way which the consumer might reasonably not expect may offend the requirement of good faith. Terms must be reasonably transparent and should not operate to defeat the reasonable expectations of the consumer. The consumer in choosing to whether to enter into a contract should be put in a position where he can make an informed choice.

This puts the emphasis on openness and information. Anything which suggests that a clause has been concealed from the consumer, or not drawn to his attention when its results may be unexpected, will encourage the court towards a finding of lack of good faith. In the case before it, the Court of Appeal was considering a term in a loan agreement issued by a bank. This provided that if the consumer defaulted on an instalment the full amount of the loan became payable. This is not unusual, but the term to which exception was taken, and about which the Director General received complaints, was to the effect that interest on the outstanding debt would remain payable even after a judgment of the court. Thus, a court might order the consumer to pay off the debt by specified instalments, but the effect of the contract was that interest would continue to accrue at the contractual rate while the instalments were being paid. This would not normally happen with a court order. The Court of Appeal therefore concluded that the term created 'unfair surprise' and did not meet the requirement of 'good faith'.

The 1999 Regulations contain another type of guidance for the courts, which was also in the 1994 Regulations. This is contained in Sched 2 to the 1999

Regulations and consists of an 'indicative and illustrative' list of terms which may be regarded as unfair. The inclusion of a term on the list does not necessarily mean that *any* clause of that type will be unfair: it will depend on the context in which it is put forward. Nor, on the other hand, is the list exhaustive. A clause of a type which does not appear in it may nevertheless be found to be unfair. The list contained in the Schedule is lengthy, and there is not space to reproduce it in full here. It contains some provisions which are familiar from the controls imposed by the UCTA 1977, such as clauses restricting liability for death or personal injury, or allowing the seller or supplier to provide inadequate performance, or a different product or service to that contracted for. Others reflect the common law rules relating to exclusion clauses, such as the restriction on clauses with which the consumer had no real opportunity of becoming acquainted before the contract. In general, the list is concerned with clauses which allow the seller or supplier to impose on the consumer, for example, by allowing the seller or supplier to cancel the contract without notice, or giving the seller or supplier exclusive rights of interpretation, or requiring the consumer to pay disproportionately high compensation for a breach.

The assessment of whether a clause is unfair must take account of the nature of the goods or services supplied, and all the surrounding circumstances (reg 6(1)).

The UTCCR 1999 do not, however, apply to simple bad bargains. Clauses which define the main subject matter of the contract, or concern the adequacy of the price or remuneration for goods or services supplied, will not be assessed, provided they meet the criterion of intelligibility (see 8.12.3 below) (reg 6(2)). The consumer who has agreed to pay over the odds for goods or services will not be helped by these regulations. This limitation only applies to terms which fall within the strict wording of reg 6(2). It does not apply to terms which are simply part of the 'core terms' of an agreement: *Director General of Fair Trading v First National Bank plc* (2000).

8.12.3 The requirement of 'plain, intelligible language'

Regulation 7 requires that the seller or supplier should ensure that the terms of the contract are expressed in 'plain, intelligible language': if there is doubt about the meaning of a term, the interpretation most favourable to the consumer will prevail. The latter part of this regulation simply gives statutory effect to the common law *contra proferentem* rule (see 8.4.1 above). The requirement to use plain, intelligible language goes further, however, and clearly strikes against the use of complex, though unambiguous, legal jargon. There is no apparent sanction for a failure to meet this standard, however. It does not of itself render the term unfair, though presumably it could be a factor in such an assessment. The weight that is given to it will have to await the view of the courts.

8.12.4 General supervision

The Director General of Fair Trading is given a general supervisory role under reg 10. This includes the power to receive complaints, and to seek injunctions restraining the use of unfair terms (reg 12). The 1999 Regulations also contain a new power (in reg 13) to require traders to produce copies of their standard contracts in order to facilitate the consideration of a complaint, or to monitor compliance with any undertaking or court order relating to the continuing use of an unfair term. These supervision and enforcement powers may also be exercised, subject to supervision by the Director General, by the 'qualifying bodies' listed in Sched 1 to the Regulations. These include various statutory regulators (that is, data protection, gas, electricity, water, telecommunications), local authority trading standards departments and the Consumers Association. The Director also has a power (though not a duty) to disseminate information and advice about the operation of the Regulations.

The first reported case under the Regulations, *Director General of Fair Trading v First National Bank plc* (2000), noted above, involved an application for an injunction, following complaints by consumers, and a consequent exchange of correspondence between the Director General and the bank.

EXCLUSION CLAUSES

Common law rules

The common law developed formal rules to protect the 'weaker party' from exclusion clauses.

- Incorporation

  If the contract is not signed (*L'Estrange v Graucob* (1934)), reasonable notice must be given, at or before the time of contract (*Olley v Marlborough Court Hotel* (1949); *Parker v South Eastern Rly* (1877)).

  The degree of notice required will vary according to the scope of the clause (*Spurling v Bradshaw* (1956); *Thornton v Shoe Lane Parking* (1971); *Interfoto Picture Library v Stiletto Visual Programmes* (1989)). The clause must be contained in a 'contractual' document (*Chapelton v Barry UDC* (1940)).

- Construction

  Clauses will be construed *contra proferentem* (*Andrews v Singer* (1934)). Negligence liability may need to be specifically excluded (*Hollier v Rambler Motors* (1972)), unless it is the only type of liability possible (*Alderslade v Hendon Laundry* (1945)). The UCTA 1977 has led to some relaxation in the rule of construction.

- Fundamental breach

  This was rejected as a rule of law by the House of Lords in *Photo Production v Securicor* (1980). It now exists simply as an aspect of the rule of construction.

Unfair Contract Terms Act 1977

The UCTA 1977 has in practice replaced the common law in many areas, though it does not apply to all contracts.

- Scope of the UCTA 1977

  Some types of contract (for example, concerning land) are altogether outside its scope (Sched 1). In other cases, it generally only applies to 'business liability' (s 1(3)). This concept has been narrowly defined in *R and B Customs Brokers v UDT* (1988).

  Disclaimers, and other attempts to avoid liability by narrowing obligations, are to be treated as exclusion clauses (s 13, and *Smith v Bush* (1989)).

- Negligence liability

  This is dealt with by s 2. There can be no exclusion in relation to liability for death or personal injury (s 2(1)). Other losses caused by negligence can be excluded, if the clause is 'reasonable' under s 11.

- Standard term and consumer contracts

  These are dealt with by s 3. All attempts to exclude or restrict liability, or to re-define obligations so as to avoid liability, will be subject to the requirement of reasonableness in s 11.

The requirement of reasonableness

The clause must be a 'fair and reasonable one to be included' in the contract, at the time it was made. The burden of proof is on the defendant (s 11(5)).

The clause must be assessed as a whole (*Stewart Gill v Horatio Myer & Co* (1992)).

If it restricts liability to a specific sum the defendant's resources, and the availability of insurance, must be considered (s 11(4)). Note, also, the guidelines under Sched 2 which cover such things as the relative bargaining strength of the parties, and the plaintiff's knowledge of the term.

- Reasonableness in the courts

  In *Smith v Bush* (1989), the House of Lords set out some guidelines as to what should be considered, which included bargaining strength, availability to the plaintiff of alternatives, the difficulty of the task, and the availability of insurance.

The relevant factors have been summarised by the Court of Appeal in *Overseas Medical Supplies Ltd v Orient Transport Services Ltd* (1999).

Other clauses within the UCTA 1977

Note that the UCTA 1977 also contains provisions dealing with indemnities (s 4), guarantees of consumer goods (s 5), contracts for the sale or hire purchase of goods (ss 6 and 7), and liability for misrepresentations (s 8).

Unfair Terms in Consumer Contracts Regulations 1999

The UTCCR 1999 place controls over unfair standard terms in consumer contracts. They apply alongside the UCTA 1977 and the common law, but are not limited to exclusion clauses. The test of unfairness is based on good faith, and the balance between the parties. Certain clauses are listed in Sched 2 as potentially unfair. Note, also, the requirement of intelligibility, the supervisory role of the

Director General of Fair Trading and the first case under the Regulations: *Director General of Fair Trading v First National Bank* (2000).

CHAPTER 9

MISREPRESENTATION

9.1 Introduction

A party to a contract which has been validly formed, and in which all the terms are clearly agreed, may nevertheless decide that it has turned out not to be quite what was anticipated when it was made. This may be the result of a misrepresentation by the other party, or of a mistake made by either or both parties. In such a situation, the party may wish to escape from the agreement altogether, or to seek compensation of some kind. This chapter discusses the situations where English law allows this to occur, on the basis of the rules relating to 'misrepresentation'. Chapter 10 deals with 'mistake'.

9.2 Misrepresentation

The basic requirements that are necessary in order for there to be a remedy for a pre-contractual misrepresentation are as follows. The statement must have been made by one of the contracting parties to the other; it must be a statement of fact, not opinion or law; and the statement must have induced the other party to enter into the contract.

9.2.1 Statement by one party to the other

If a person has entered into a contract on the basis of a misrepresentation by a third party, this will have no effect on the contract, or on the person's legal relationship with the other contracting party. A person who buys shares in a company on the basis of a third party's statement that it has just made a substantial profit, cannot undo the share agreement if the statement turns out to be untrue. This general principle has been affected, at least in certain circumstances, however, by the House of Lords' decision in *Barclays Bank v O'Brien* (1993). In this case, a husband made a misrepresentation to his wife as to the extent to which the matrimonial home was being used as security for his business debts. On the basis of this misrepresentation, the wife entered into a contract of guarantee with the bank, using the house as security. The House of Lords held that because the bank should have been aware of the risk of misrepresentation by the husband, but had taken no steps to encourage the wife to take independent legal advice, it could not enforce the contract of guarantee against her. In effect, therefore, a misrepresentation made by a person who was not the other contracting party was being used to rescind the contract. This decision, and subsequent case law is discussed in detail in Chapter 11. There is no reason to expect it to result in a broad exception to the general principle stated above. It does open the door, however, to similar arguments in other circumstances where a party may reasonably expect a third party to make misrepresentations. This is discussed in Chapter 11 (see 11.9.3–11.9.10 below).

9.2.2 Statement of existing fact

The statement must be one of fact, not opinion or law. This has already been discussed in Chapter 7 (see 7.3.1 above). Thus, in *Bisset v Wilkinson* (1927), a farmer told the prospective purchaser of his land that it would support 2,000 sheep. It was held by the Privy Council that this was not a misrepresentation, even though it turned out to be inaccurate. The farmer had not at any point carried on sheep-farming on the land, and the purchaser was aware of this. In the circumstances, therefore, the farmer's view on the matter was no more than an expression of opinion, and not a statement of fact. But, the opinion must not be contradicted by known facts. The statement in *Smith v Land and House Property Corpn* (1884) that a tenant was 'most desirable', while on its face an opinion, was treated as a misrepresentation because the maker of the statement knew that the tenant had in fact been in arrears with his rent for some time. One further point should be noted here. A statement of an intention to act in a particular way in the future may be interpreted as a statement of fact, if it is clear that the person making the statement did not, at that time, have any intention of so acting. In *Edgington v Fitzmaurice* (1885), a company prospectus, designed to attract subscribers, contained false statements about the uses to which the money raised would be put. It was held this statement of intention could be treated as a representation as to the directors' state of mind at the time that the prospectus was issued, and could thus be treated as a statement of fact. As Bowen LJ put it:

> ... the state of a man's mind is as much a fact as the state of his digestion. It is true that it is very difficult to prove what the state of a man's mind at a particular time is, but if it can be ascertained it is as much a fact as anything else. A misrepresentation as to the state of a man's mind is, therefore, a misstatement of fact.

A similar lack of belief in the truth of what is being said may also turn a statement of opinion or, presumably of law, into a misrepresentation. It is a false statement of the person's current state of mind.

A misrepresentation can be made by actions as well as words. This is illustrated by the recent case of *Spice Girls Ltd ('SGL') v Aprilia World Service BV ('AWS')* (2000). SGL, the company formed to promote the pop group, the 'Spice Girls', was in the process of making a contract for the promotion of AWS's scooters. Shortly before the contract was signed, the members of the group all took part in the filming of a commercial for AWS. At that time, they knew that one member of the group intended to leave, as she did shortly after the contract had been signed. The group's participation in the filming was held to amount to a representation that SGL did not know and had no reasonable ground to believe that any of the existing members had at that time a declared intention to leave. This was untrue, and therefore the participation in the filming amounted to a misrepresentation by conduct.

9.2.3 Misrepresentation by silence

In general, there is no misrepresentation by silence. Even where one party is aware that the other is contracting on the basis of a misunderstanding of some fact relating to the contract, there will generally be no liability. There are, however, some exceptions to this. First, the maker of the statement must not give only half the story on some aspect of the facts. Thus, in *Dimmock v Hallett* (1866), the statement that flats were fully let, when in fact the tenants had given notice to quit, was capable of being a misrepresentation. Secondly, if a true statement is made, but then circumstances change, making it false, a failure to disclose this will be treated as a misrepresentation. In *With v O'Flanagan* (1936), for example, a statement was made by the vendor of a medical practice that its income was £2,000 per annum. This was true at the time, but as a result of the vendor's illness the practice declined considerably over the next few months, so that by the time it was actually sold its value had reduced significantly. It was held by the Court of Appeal that the failure to notify the purchaser of the fact that the earlier statement was no longer true amounted to a misrepresentation. Thirdly, certain contracts, such as those for insurance, are treated as being 'of the utmost good faith' (*uberrimae fidei*), and as requiring the contracting party to disclose all relevant facts. In an insurance contract, for example, there is an obligation to disclose material facts, even if the other party has not asked about them. Thus, in *Lambert v Co-Operative Insurance Society* (1975), a woman who was renewing the insurance on her jewellery should have disclosed that her husband had recently been convicted of conspiracy to steal. The fact that she had not mentioned that when some of her jewellery was subsequently stolen meant that the insurance company was entitled not to compensate her under the policy. The obligation most frequently operates to the disadvantage of the insured person, but that it can also apply to the insurer was confirmed by the House of Lords in *Banque Financière v Westgate Insurance* (1990), which concerned the failure by the insurer to disclose wrongdoing by its agent. A similar obligation applies to contracts establishing family settlements. Thus, in *Gordon v Gordon* (1816), a settlement was made on the presumption that an elder son was born outside marriage, and was therefore illegitimate. In fact, the younger son knew that his parents had been through a secret marriage ceremony prior to the birth of his elder brother. The fact that he had concealed this knowledge, which was clearly material, meant that the settlement had to be set aside. Finally, there are come contracts which involve a fiduciary relationship, and this may entail a duty to disclose. In this category are to be found contracts between agent and principal, solicitor and client, and a company and its promoters. Other similar relationships which have a fiduciary character will be treated in the same way, and the list is not closed.

9.2.4 Misrepresentation must induce the contract

It is not enough to give rise to a remedy for misrepresentation, for A to point to some false statement of fact made by B prior to a contract which they have made. It must also be shown that that statement formed some part of the reason why A entered into the agreement. In *JEB Fasteners Ltd v Bloom* (1983), for example, which was concerned with this issue of reliance in the context of an action for negligent misstatement at common law, it was established that the plaintiffs took over a business having seen inaccurate accounts prepared by the defendants. Their reason for taking over the business, however, was shown to have been the wish to secure the services of two directors. The accounts had not induced their action in taking over the business.

On the other hand, it is not necessary for the misrepresentation to be the *sole* reason why the contract was entered into. In *Edgington v Fitzmaurice* (1885), the plaintiff was influenced not only by the prospectus, but also by his own mistaken belief that he would have a charge on the assets of the company. His action based on misrepresentation was nevertheless successful. Provided the misstatement was 'actively present to his mind when he decided to advance the money', then it was material. The test is, according to Bowen LJ:

> ... what was the state of the plaintiff's mind, and if his mind was disturbed by the misstatement of the defendants, and such disturbance was in part the cause of what he did, the mere fact of his also making a mistake himself could make no difference.

Nor does it matter that the party deceived has spurned a chance to discover the truth. In *Redgrave v Hurd* (1881), false statements were made by the plaintiff about the income of his practice as a solicitor, on the strength of which the defendant had entered into a contract to buy the plaintiff's house and practice. He had been given the chance to examine documents which would have revealed the true position, but had declined to do so. This did not prevent his claim based on misrepresentation.

Related to this is the question of whether the reliance on the statement has to be 'reasonable'. This issue was considered in *Museprime Properties Ltd v Adhill Properties Ltd* (1990). Property owned by the defendant was sold by auction to the plaintiffs. There was an inaccurate statement in the auction particulars, which was re-affirmed by the auctioneer, to the effect that rent reviews of three leases to which the properties were subject had not been finalised. The plaintiffs sought to rescind the contract for misrepresentation. *Inter alia*, the defendants argued that the misrepresentation was not material because no reasonable bidder would have allowed it to influence his bid. Scott J held, approving a passage to this effect in Goff and Jones, *The Law of Restitution* (1993, 4th edn, Sweet & Maxwell, p 168), that the materiality of the representation was not to be determined by whether a reasonable person would have been induced to contract. As long as the plaintiff was *in fact* induced, as was the case here, that was enough to entitle him to rescission. The reasonableness or otherwise of his behaviour was relevant only to the burden of proof: the less reasonable the inducement, the more difficult it would be for the plaintiff to convince the court that he had been affected by the misrepresentation.

It is difficult to be sure how far this principle can be taken. Suppose, for example, I am selling my car and, prior to the contract, I tell the prospective purchaser that the car is amphibious and will go across water. Can the purchaser later claim against me because this ridiculous statement turns out to be untrue, as he has discovered now that the car is at the bottom of the river? Clearly, there may be difficulties of proving that there was reliance in fact, as noted above, but assuming that it is established that the statement was believed by the purchaser (for example, by the fact that he tried to drive across a river), the *Museprime* approach would give a remedy in misrepresentation. Would the courts go this far? Or would some degree of reasonable reliance be introduced, where, for example, no reasonable person would ever have believed the statement to be true?

9.3   Remedies for misrepresentation

The remedies for misrepresentation depend to some extent on the state of mind of the person making the false statement. If the statement is fraudulent, the remedies may be more extensive than if it is made negligently or innocently. There are remedies available under common law and equity and also under the Misrepresentation Act (MA) 1967.

9.3.1   Rescission

The principal remedy under English law for a misrepresentation was for a long time the equitable remedy of rescission. This allows the parties to be restored to their original position. Thus, if the contract is one for the sale of goods, both the goods, and the price paid for them, must be returned. It is still available in relation to all types of misrepresentation. Prior to the MA 1967, there could be no rescission for misrepresentation where either the false statement had become part of the contract, or where the contract had been performed. This was changed by s 1 of the MA 1967, which states:

> Where a person has entered into a contract after a misrepresentation has been made to him, and:
>
> (a) the misrepresentation has become a term of the contract; or
>
> (b) the contract has been performed;

or both, then, if otherwise he would be entitled to rescind the contract without alleging fraud, he shall be so entitled, subject to the provisions of this Act, notwithstanding the matter mentioned in paras (a) and (b) of this section.

Because the remedy is equitable, however, certain bars operate in relation to it. The remedy will be lost in the following situations:

- Affirmation of the contract by the other party – that is, the party, having knowledge of the other side's misrepresentation nevertheless continues with the contract

In *Long v Lloyd* (1958), for example, a representation was made as to the fuel consumption of a lorry by the seller (the defendant). After buying the lorry, the plaintiff discovered that this statement was untrue, and that the lorry had various other defects. The defendant offered to contribute towards the cost of repairs. The plaintiff accepted this offer, and later sent the lorry on a long journey during which it broke down. He then tried to rescind the contract for misrepresentation. It was held that he had affirmed the contract with full knowledge of the false statement, and had therefore lost the right to rescind.

- Lapse of time

In *Leaf v International Galleries* (1950), the purchaser of a picture stated to be by John Constable discovered, on trying to sell it some five years later, that this statement was false. His attempt to rescind for misrepresentation failed because of the lapse of time. This case was fairly clear. In other situations, it will be a matter for the court to consider in all the circumstances whether the lapse of time is sufficient to preclude rescission. It may be significant that in *Leaf v International Galleries* Lord Denning drew an analogy with the rules relating to the acceptance of goods under the Sale of Goods Act 1893. These are discussed in detail in Chapter 18. It will be seen there that the case law suggests that a fairly short time from contract, measured in days or weeks rather than years, will be sufficient to amount to 'acceptance' (and thereby prevent rejection for breach of contract). It is likely that a similar approach will be taken to assessing the time at which the loss of the right to rescind for misrepresentation will occur.

- Restitution impossible

As, for example, where goods have been destroyed, consumed, or irretrievably mixed with others. Thus, in *Clarke v Dickson* (1858), the purchaser of shares in a company was unable to rescind the contract because he had:

> ... changed the nature of the article: the shares he received were shares in a company on the cost-book principle; the plaintiff offers to restore them after he has converted them into shares in a joint stock corporation.

Moreover, the company was at the time in the course of being wound up, so there was no chance of a profit being made from them. A simple decline in value will not, however, be sufficient to bar rescission (*Armstrong v Jackson* (1917)). (Cf *Cheese v Thomas* (1993) discussed in Chapter 11.)

• If rescission would affect the rights of third parties. This is a major limitation where goods obtained on the basis of a (probably fraudulent) misrepresentation have been sold on to an innocent third party. The courts will not, in such a situation, require the third party to disgorge the goods. This has caused particular problems for plaintiffs where there has been a misrepresentation as to the identity of a purchaser, which is relevant to credit-worthiness. As a result, attempts have been made (generally unsuccessfully) to argue that such contracts are void for mistake. See, for example, *Phillips v Brooks* (1919), discussed in Chapter 10 (see 10.5.3 below).

9.3.2 Damages at common law

At common law, damages are only available in relation to fraudulent misrepresentations, under the tort of deceit. The leading case is *Derry v Peek* (1889). A prospectus for a tram company indicated that it had the right to use steam power. In fact, the Board of Trade refused permission, and the company failed. The plaintiff had bought shares in reliance on the statement in the prospectus, and sought damages for the tort of deceit. The House of Lords held that in order for an action for deceit it was necessary to show fraud. This meant that, in the words of Lord Herschell, that a false representation must be proved to have been made:

> (1) knowingly; or (2) without belief in its truth; or (3) recklessly, careless whether it be true or false.

On the facts, the defendants were not liable, because they honestly believed the truth of their statement in the prospectus. The requirements for deceit remain, however, as set out in this case. As can be seen, mere negligence is not enough – knowledge of the falsity, or a reckless disregard for the truth is needed. Once deceit is established, damages will be assessed according to the tortious measure, which aims to put the parties in the position they would have been in had the tort not occurred, that is, in this context, if the false statement had not been made. (A contractual measure would aim to put them in the position they would have been in had the statement been true – see Chapter 15.) The damages may be more extensive than is usually the case in tort, however, since in *Doyle v Olby (Ironmongers) Ltd* (1969) it was held that the defendant will be liable for all losses which can be shown to be the consequences of the false statement, without being limited by the normal rules of 'remoteness' (for which, see Chapter 15). The effect of this rule was demonstrated in the recent House of Lords' decision in *Smith and New Court Securities Ltd v Scrimgeour Vickers (Asset Management) Ltd* (1996). The case concerned the sale of a parcel of shares in F Ltd owned by the defendants. They offered them to the plaintiffs, but fraudulently claimed that other bids had been received. This fraudulent misrepresentation led the plaintiffs to increase their offer from 78p per share, to 82.25p per share. This offer was accepted, and the parcel of over 28 million shares was sold to the plaintiffs for just over £23 million. It then transpired that F Ltd had been the victim of another unrelated fraud, and its share price plummeted. The plaintiffs resold the shares, suffering a loss of over £11 million. The plaintiffs claimed this in damages from the defendants; the defendants claimed that they should be limited to the difference between the price they would have been prepared to pay without the misrepresentation (78p per share) and the contract price (82.25p per share). The defendants succeeded in the Court of Appeal, but the House of Lords held that the application of *Doyle v Olby* entitled the plaintiffs to recover their full losses. The plaintiffs would not have made the contract but for the misrepresentation (the offer of 78p would not at the time have been acceptable to the defendants), and they were, therefore, as a result of the misrepresentation 'locked into the property'. Their full consequential losses were therefore recoverable. Moreover, in *East v Maurer* (1991), it was held that the attempt to put the plaintiff into the position he would have been in had the misrepresentation not been made, may allow the recovery of certain types of lost profit. The false statement here related to a hairdressing business which the plaintiff bought. The defendant had stated that he had no intention of opening another hairdressing shop in the area. This was untrue, and when he did open such a shop, the plaintiff's sued for damages resulting from their loss of business. If the statement had been true, the plaintiff would have been likely to have made substantial profits from the business which they had bought. Such profits would only, however, be recoverable in an action for breach of contract, where 'expectation interests' are compensated (see Chapter 15). On the other hand, if the statement had not been made, the plaintiff would probably have bought a different business, and would have made some (though not as extensive) profits from that. The court felt that these hypothetical profits should be recoverable. The action for fraudulent misrepresentation may thus come very close to providing the same level of damages as are available for breach of contract.

It should be noted here that in certain situations damages for the tort of negligence may be recoverable in relation to misstatements. The law governing this area derives from the House of Lords' decision in *Hedley Byrne v Heller* (1964). In this case, the plaintiffs had asked their bank to give an opinion on the financial standing of another firm. The bank gave a positive report, and the plaintiffs entered into contracts with the firm. Shortly afterwards the firm went into liquidation, owing substantial sums to the plaintiffs. They sued the bank, alleging that the statements as to the financial status of the firm had been made negligently. On the facts, the House of Lords held that the bank was protected by a 'without responsibility' disclaimer which it had attached to its advice. It held, however, that in the absence of this the bank would have been liable. This established the possibility, therefore, of taking action in the tort of negligence in relation to statements made without proper care, which result in loss. For this to be available, however, a 'duty of care' must be shown to exist between the maker of the statement and the person who has acted on it. Much of the extensive subsequent case law on this area has been concerned with the question of when such a duty will arise, which it has been suggested depends on there being a 'special relationship' between the parties. At times, however, it seemed that all that was needed was that the maker of the statement could reasonably foresee that the person to whom the statement was made would rely on it, and would suffer loss if it turned out to be untrue. The House of Lords' decision in *Caparo v Dickman* (1990) severely restricted the circumstances in which such a duty will be found to exist, though this has been softened to some extent by the subsequent decisions in *Henderson v Merrett Syndicates Ltd* (1994) and *White v Jones* (1995). The current position seems to be that, in addition to the reasonable foreseeability of reliance and harm, there must be sufficient 'proximity' between the parties, and that it must be just and reasonable for the duty to be imposed. The issue of proximity is the most difficult, but will normally be satisfied where the statement is made in a context where the parties are anticipating that a contract will be made between them. It was held by the Court of Appeal in *Esso v Mardon* (1976) that a common law duty of care could arise in such a situation, and this has been confirmed in the more recent cases of *Gran Gelato v Richcliff* (1992), and *Henderson v Merrett Syndicates* (1994). The need for the *Hedley Byrne* action for contracting parties was reduced by the enactment of the MA 1967 (see 9.3.4–9.3.6 below), which for the first time introduced a remedy in damages for non-fraudulent misrepresentations. Nevertheless, there are still situations where it may be useful to plead common law negligence alongside, or as an alternative to liability under the Act. One advantage of the *Hedley Byrne* action, for example, is that it applies to *all* types of statement, not just statements of fact.

A negligently expressed opinion may therefore give rise to the possibility of action in tort, where an action in contract would not be available (because the statement is not one of fact), unless the plaintiff proved that the opinion was not genuinely held, or that the expresser of the opinion was aware of facts which rendered it untenable. In general, however, an action under s 2 of the MA 1967, will be the preferred choice for the plaintiff because it offers, as will be seen below, advantages in terms of the burden of proof, and the extent of damages which are recoverable.

9.3.3 Indemnity at common law

As has been indicated above, the primary remedy for misrepresentation at common law was rescission. There was also, however, in certain circumstances a right to claim an indemnity for expenses incurred, in addition to rescission. As is shown by *Whittington v Seale-Hayne* (1900), however, such expenses must have been directly related to the obligations of the contract. The case concerned the lease of premises for poultry breeding which the landlord had stated were in good sanitary condition. The lease included a covenant under which the tenant was obliged to effect certain repairs (in line with local authority requirements). In fact, the premises were not sanitary, and the plaintiffs decided to rescind for misrepresentation. They also claimed, in addition to a refund of the rent, compensation in relation to rates paid, repairs carried out, loss of stock, medical and removal expenses. It was held that they could only recover the cost of the rates, and of repairs carried out under the covenant. These were obligations which arose directly from the contract, and were recoverable on an 'indemnity' basis. The other items came into the category of a claim for damages, and so were not recoverable. The test is whether the expenses or losses were *necessarily* incurred as a result of entering into the contract. Thus, the claim for an indemnity is very limited in scope.

The availability of an action for damages under the MA 1967 means that the only situation nowadays when the plaintiff might wish to consider claiming for an indemnity is where the contract is being rescinded for a totally innocent, non-negligent, misrepresentation.

9.3.4 Damages under s 2(1) of the Misrepresentation Act 1967

The MA 1967 introduced a statutory remedy in damages (whether or not rescission is also granted) for what is commonly referred to as 'negligent misrepresentation'. In fact, s 2(1) does not use this phrase, but makes the remedy available where the person making the misrepresentation would have been liable to damages if it had been made fraudulently:

> (1) Where a person has entered into a contract after misrepresentation has been made to him by another party thereto and as a result thereof he has suffered loss, then, if the person making the misrepresentation would be liable to damages in respect thereof had the misrepresentation been made fraudulently, that person shall be so liable notwithstanding that the misrepresentation was not made fraudulently, unless he proves that he had reasonable grounds to believe and did believe up to the time the contract was made that the facts represented were true.

The test of what is a misrepresentation will be as set out above. As will be noted from the final part of the section, this action is advantageous to the plaintiff in that, once it is established that a false statement was made, the burden of proof shifts to the defendant to establish that there were reasonable grounds for believing it to be true. Moreover, the courts seem to be prepared to be fairly strict as to what will be regarded as reasonable grounds. In *Howard Marine Dredging v Ogden* (1978), the Court of Appeal held that an incorrect statement as to the weight of a vessel gave rise to an entitlement to damages under s 2(1) because, even though the incorrect figure appeared in a usually authoritative publication (*Lloyd's Register*), the defendant had previously seen the correct figure in the shipping documents.

9.3.5 Measure of damages under s 2(1)

One difficulty which has arisen with s 2(1) is the measure of damages – should it be contractual or tortious? In *Watts v Spence* (1976), there was some suggestion that it should be contractual. The Court of Appeal, however, in *Sharneyford v Edge* (1987), ruled that it should be tortious. The issue was considered further in *Royscot Trust Ltd v Rogerson* (1991). A car dealer misrepresented to the plaintiff finance company the amount of a deposit paid by a customer in connection with a hire purchase agreement. The finance company would not have been prepared to lend as much as it did had it known of the true value of the deposit. The finance company suffered a loss when the customer defaulted on his payments, after having sold the car to an innocent third party (who obtained good title under the Hire Purchase Act 1964). In an action by the plaintiff against the dealer for non-fraudulent misrepresentation, the only dispute was as to the amount of damages payable. The measure used by the judge at first instance was supported by neither party in the appeal, so that the Court of Appeal effectively had to decide the matter *de novo*. It confirmed that in an action for misrepresentation under s 2(1) of the MA 1967, the correct measure of damages is tortious rather than contractual. Moreover, since the wording of s 2(1) makes liability conditional on the situation where 'the person making the misrepresentation would be liable to damages in respect thereof had the misrepresentation been made fraudulently', damages should be assessed in the same way as for fraudulent misrepresentation. This meant that the defendant was liable for *all losses* flowing from the defendant's misrepresentation (as is the case with the tort of deceit: *Doyle v Olby* (1969) (see 9.3.2 above)), and not simply for those losses which were reasonably foreseeable. Although the wording of the section itself gives rise to the so called 'fiction of fraud' alluded to above, the weight of academic opinion, as evidenced by all the leading contract textbooks, has been in favour of applying the negligence remoteness rules, because to apply the deceit rule would operate too harshly in a situation where the defendant has been negligent rather than deliberately fraudulent. The Court of Appeal, in this case, however, was not prepared to be swayed by these arguments of policy. They found that s 2(1) aligned liability under it with liability for fraud. The wording of the section was clear and the court saw no reason to depart from its literal meaning. This approach appeared to be treated with some scepticism by the House of Lords in *Smith New Court Securities Ltd v Scrimgeour Vickers (Asset Management) Ltd* (1996), but the issue was not directly before them, and so no final view was expressed. For the moment, at any rate, the 'fiction of fraud' analysis remains good law. This presumably also means that, assuming the decision in *East v Maurer* (1991) (see 9.3.2 above) is followed, that certain types of lost profits may be recoverable. The damages under s 2(1) may therefore be almost as extensive as for breach of contract, particularly since they are not restricted by any rule of remoteness (see 15.4.1 below). One effect of this may be to lead the courts to be more reluctant to find that there has been a misrepresentation – as in *Avon Insurance plc v Swire Fraser Ltd* (2000).

9.3.6   Damages under s 2(2) of the Misrepresentation Act 1967

Section 2(2) of the MA 1967 allows a court to award damages *in lieu* of rescission, whether or not they are also awarded under s 2(1). This power is to be exercised if the court is:

> ... of opinion that it would be equitable to do so, having regard to the nature of the misrepresentation and the loss that would be caused by it if the contract were upheld, as well as to the loss that rescission would cause to the other party.

Since the power is stated to be *in lieu* of rescission it has been presumed that it will be lost if the right to rescind has been lost, for example, by lapse of time, or the intervention of third party rights (see 9.3.1 above). This was not accepted in *Thomas Witter Ltd v TBP Industries* (1996) where it was suggested that the power to award damages was not dependent on the continued availability of the right to rescind. As regards the *measure* of damages under s 2(2), there is no binding authority, but some guidance has been provided by *obiter* statements in *William Sindall plc v Cambridgeshire County Council* (1994). Hoffman and Evans LJJ agreed that the measure must be different from that applying under s 2(1). This must be so, given that s 2(3) recognises the possibility (or even likelihood) that damages under s 2(2) will be less than under s 2(1). Where, as in this case, the contract concerned the sale of property, the measure should simply be an amount that would compensate the plaintiff for the loss he had suffered on account of the property not being that which it was represented to be. As Evans LJ put it, it should be 'the difference in value between what the plaintiff was misled into believing he was acquiring, and the value of what he in fact received'. The assessment should be made at the time of the contract, and subsequent losses caused by a fall in market value should not be taken into account. There is no suggestion in these statements that any account should be taken of consequential losses, and this is surely right. To compensate for these would go beyond replacing the value of the right to rescind, and is surely better left to be dealt with under s 2(1).

9.4   Exclusion of liability for misrepresentation

Section 3 of the MA 1967, as amended by s 8 of the Unfair Contract Terms Act (UCTA) 1977, restricts the possibility of exclusion of liability for misrepresentation. It states:

If a contract contains a term which would exclude or restrict:

(a) any liability to which a party to a contract may be subject by reason of any misrepresentation made by him before the contract was made; or

(b) any remedy available to another party to the contract by reason of such misrepresentation,

that term shall be of no effect except in so far as it satisfies the requirement of reasonableness as stated in s 11(1) of the Unfair Contract Terms Act 1977; and it is for those claiming that the term satisfies that requirement to show that it does.

Thus, as regards any contract term which attempts to restrict either liability for misrepresentation, or any remedy available in relation to it, this will only be effective if it satisfies the requirement reasonableness under s 11 of the UCTA 1977 (see Chapter 8). This requirement will also apply to clauses which purport to make it a term of the contract that it is not entered into 'in reliance wholly or in part on any statement or representation (written or oral) mader by' the other party – see *Inntrepreneur Estates (CEC) Ltd v Worth* (1996) (in which a clause in those terms was held in all the circumstances to be unreasonable).

MISREPRESENTATION

For a misrepresentation to give rise to a remedy, it must:

- be a statement by one contracting party to another;

- be a statement of existing fact, not opinion or law. But, a false statement of intention is a statement of fact (*Edgington v Fitzmaurice* (1885));

- induce the contract (*JEB Fasteners Ltd v Bloom* (1983)). It need not be the *only* reason for contracting (*Edgington v Fitzmaurice* (1885)), and the reliance need not be 'reasonable' (*Museprime Properties Ltd v Adhill* (1990)).

Remedies for misrepresentation

Remedies depend on the state of mind of the misrepresentor. A range of remedies exist at common law, in equity, and under the MA 1967.

- Rescission

  This is the principal remedy. It requires the parties to be restored to their original positions. The remedy is equitable, and will be lost by:

  o affirmation (*Long v Lloyd* (1958));

  o lapse of time (*Leaf v International Galleries* (1950));

  o impossibility of restitution – for example, where goods have been destroyed;

  o involvement of third party rights.

- Damages at common law

  These are only available in relation to fraudulent misrepresentations (that is, made with knowledge or recklessness as regards the falsehood). They will cover all consequential losses (*Doyle v Olby (Ironmongers) Ltd* (1969)), including certain types of lost profit (*East v Maurer* (1991)).

- Damages under s 2(1) of the MA 1967

  These are available as regards 'negligent' misrepresentations (that is, the misrepresentor had no reasonable grounds for believing the statement to be true). The measure of damages is the same as for fraudulent misrepresentation (*Royscot Trust Ltd v Rogerson* (1991)).

- Damages under s 2(2) of the MA 1967

  These are available at the court's discretion *in lieu* of rescission. The measure should be based on the difference in value between what the plaintiff actually received under the contract, and what he thought he was receiving on the basis of the misrepresentation (*William Sindall plc v Cambridgeshire CC* (1994)).

- Exclusion of liability for misrepresentation

  By virtue of s 3 of the MA 1967, this is only permissible where the exclusion clause satisfies the requirement of reasonableness under s 11 of the UCTA 1977.

CHAPTER 10

MISTAKE

10.1 Introduction

This chapter is concerned with the situations where a contract may be prevented from coming into existence, or brought to an end as a result of a mistake by either or both of the parties. The rules impose fairly heavy burdens on those arguing that a mistake has been made. This is not surprising. It would not be satisfactory if a party to a contract could simply, by saying 'I'm sorry, I made a mistake', unstitch a complex agreement without any thought for the consequences for the other party, or any third parties who might be involved. To allow this to be done would be to strike at the whole purpose of the law of contract, which has as one of its main functions the provision of a structure within which people can organise their commercial relationships with a high degree of certainty. On the other hand, a fundamental principle of the English law of contract is that, as far as possible, the courts should give effect to the intentions of the parties. If either, or both, of the parties has genuinely made a mistake as to the nature of their contract, to enforce it may run counter to their intentions. The courts do, therefore, recognise the possibility of mistakes affecting, or even destroying, contractual obligations which would otherwise arise. The power to intervene in this way is, however, used with considerable circumspection.

This general reluctance to allow mistakes to affect a contract does not, of course, prevent the parties themselves agreeing that a mistake will allow the party who has made the mistake to rescind the contract. This most frequently occurs in relation to consumer contracts made with large chain stores. These organisations often feel able (presumably because of their volume of business, and their strength of position in the market) to allow customers who have simply changed their minds to exchange or return goods even though they are in no way defective. It was also noted in Chapter 2 that there are some statutory provisions which allow consumers a short period in which to change their minds about particular sorts of contracts, particularly those involving long term credit arrangements (see, for example, s 67 of the Consumer Credit Act 1974, ss 5 and 6 of the Timeshare Act 1992, and the Consumer Protection (Cancellation of Contracts Concluded Away From Business Premises) Regulations 1987). In such a situation, the consumer who realises that he has made a mistake of some kind in relation to the contract will be able to escape from it, provided that he acts within the specified time limits. These arrangements are, however, exceptions to the general position under the common law, which will only allow a party to undo the agreement in a limited range of circumstances.

10.2 Categories of mistake

There are various ways in which a party may make a mistake in relation to the contract. It may, for example, relate to the subject matter, the identity of the other contracting party, or the specific terms of the contract. The only mistakes which are relevant as far as the law is concerned, however, are those which strike at the agreement between the parties.

As pointed out by Lord Atkin in *Bell v Lever Bros* (1932), there are two types of mistake which may affect a contract, those which 'nullify consent' and those which 'negative consent' ('consent' meaning here 'agreement'). A mistake which has the effect of nullifying consent means that although the parties were in agreement, they were both labouring under the same misapprehension relating to an important element of the contract (for example, the existence of the subject matter) which means that the agreement should be set aside. This type of mistake is often referred to as a 'common' mistake. A mistake 'negativing' agreement occurs where the mistake has the effect of preventing the parties ever reaching an agreement. It may take two forms. First, the parties may simply be at cross-purposes, as where they have each assumed that they were contracting about a different item. This may be labelled as a 'mutual mistake'. Secondly, one of the parties may be aware of the other's mistake, but nevertheless keep quiet (as, for example, where the innocent party is mistaken as to the identity of the other party). This may be described as a 'unilateral mistake'. It is in relation to this type of mistake that there is most likely to be an overlap with misrepresentation.

In what follows, the division into common, mutual, and unilateral mistakes will be adopted.

10.3 Common mistake

The clearest type of common mistake which will be regarded as rendering the contract void for mistake is where the parties have made a contract about something which has ceased to exist at the time the contract is made. (Where the subject matter ceases to exist *after* the contract is made the doctrine of 'frustration', which is dealt with in Chapter 13, applies, rather than mistake.) If, for example, the contract concerns the hire of a boat which, unknown to either party, has been destroyed by fire the day before the contract was made, the agreement will undoubtedly be void for common mistake. The parties have reached agreement, but that agreement is nullified by the destruction of the subject matter. This type of common mistake is sometimes referred to by the Latin tag of *res extincta*. An example from the cases is *Galloway v Galloway* (1914). The parties, who thought they had been married to each other, made a separation agreement. It was then discovered that their supposed marriage was invalid, because the husband's previous wife was still alive. As a result, the separation agreement was void, and the 'husband' had no liability under it.

As regards contracts for the sale of goods, the common law rule is given statutory effect by s 6 of the Sale of Goods Act (SGA) 1979. This states that:

> Where there is a contract for the sale of specific goods, and the goods without the knowledge of the seller have perished at the time when the contract is made, the contract is void.

The word 'perished' almost certainly encompasses more than simply physical destruction, as is shown by the pre-SGA 1893 case of *Couturier v Hastie* (1856). The contract concerned a contract for the purchase of a cargo of corn. At the time of the contract, the cargo had, because it was starting to deteriorate, been unloaded and sold to someone else. The purchaser was held to have no liability to pay the price. There are some doubts, however, as to the true basis for the decision in this case, which are referred to in the next paragraph.

10.3.1 Subject matter which never existed

The cases we have been considering deal with the situation where the subject matter *did* exist at one point, but has ceased to do so by the time of the contract. The position is more difficult where the subject matter has *never* existed. There seems no logical reason why the contract should not equally be void for mistake in such a case, but this was not the view of the High Court of Australia in *McRae v Commonwealth Disposals Commission* (1951). The Commission had invited tenders for a salvage operation in relation to an oil tanker, said to be 'lying on the Jourmand Reef'. The plaintiffs were awarded the contract, but on arrival found that neither the tanker nor the reef existed. The Commission claimed that the contract was void for mistake, and that they therefore had no liability. The court held, however, that there was a contract, in that the Commission had to be taken to have warranted the existence of the tanker. The plaintiffs were entitled to damages to compensate for their costs in putting together the abortive enterprise. In reaching this conclusion, the court did not accept that the decision in *Couturier v Hastie* (1856) was truly based on 'mistake'. It was simply that the plaintiff's claim in that case that the price was payable on production of the shipping documents could not be upheld as being part of the contract. It is certainly true that the House of Lords in *Couturier v Hastie* never mentioned mistake as the basis for their decision. The case is perhaps in the end best regarded as an example of the kind of situation in which an operative mistake could occur, and which would now fall within s 6 of the SGA 1979, rather than as a direct authority on the issue.

10.3.2 Impossibility of performance

An operative common mistake may also arise where, although the subject matter of the contract has not been destroyed, performance is, and always was, impossible. This may result from a physical impossibility (as in *Sheikh Bros v Ochsner* (1957): land not capable of growing the quantity of crop contracted for), or legal impossibility (as where the contract is to buy property which the purchaser already owns: *Cooper v Phibbs* (1867)). There is also one case, *Griffith v Brymer* (1903), where a contract was found void for what Treitel (*Law of Contract*, 10th edn, 1999, Sweet & Maxwell, p 264) refers to as 'commercial impossibility'. The contract was to hire a room to view an event which, at the time of the contract, had already been cancelled. Performance of the contract was physically and legally possible, but would have had no point. (Compare the frustration cases on similar situations in Chapter 13.)

10.3.3 Mistake as to quality

Can there be an operative common mistake where the parties are mistaken as to the quality of what they have contracted about? Suppose A sells B a table, both parties being under the impression that they are dealing with a valuable antique, whereas it subsequently turns out to be a fake? Can B avoid the contract on the basis of mistake? (Often, this type of situation will in practice be dealt with by the provisions of the SGA 1979 – see Chapter 18 – but that does not prevent us using the example as a means of exploring the principles of mistake.) The leading House of Lords' authority is *Bell v Lever Brothers* (1931). The plaintiffs (Lever Brothers) had reached an agreement for compensation with the defendant over the early termination of contract of employment. This termination agreement was itself a contract, providing for the payment of £50,000. The plaintiffs then discovered that the defendant had previously behaved in a way which would have justified termination without compensation. They therefore argued that the compensation contract should be regarded as being void for mistake. The House was reluctant to allow a mistake as to the quality, or value, of what had been contracted for to be regarded as an operative mistake. As Lord Atkin put it:

> In such a case, a mistake will not affect assent unless it is the mistake of both parties and is as to the existence of some quality which makes the thing without the quality essentially different from the thing as it was believed to be.

This would not be the case in an example such as that of the antique which turns out to be a fake. Lord Atkin again comments:

> A buys a picture from B: both A and B believe it to be the work of an old master, and high price is paid. It turns out to be a modern copy. A has no remedy in the absence of representation or warranty.

Applying this approach to the case before the House, the conclusion was that there was no operative mistake. The plaintiffs had obtained exactly what they had bargained for, that is, the release of the contract with the defendant. The fact that the plaintiffs could have achieved the same result without paying compensation by relying on the defendant's earlier conduct was immaterial.

10.3.4 Effect of *Bell v Lever Brothers*

This conclusion has sometimes been regarded as indicating that there can never be an operative mistake as to quality. But the decision does not go quite that far, as the first quotation from Lord Atkin, above, shows. He specifically recognises the possibility that a mistake as to whether the subject matter of the contract has a particular quality may nullify consent provided it is a quality, the absence of which makes the subject matter 'essentially different'. The difficulty is that if, as was held in *Bell v Lever Brothers* (1931), a mistake worth £50,000 does not make a contract essentially different, then what kind of mistake will do so? The fact that *Bell* did not shut the door on operative mistakes as to quality was, however, noted by Steyn J in *Associated Japanese Bank Ltd v Credit du Nord SA* (1988). He held that a contract of guarantee which was given on the basis of the existence of certain packaging machines, was void at common law when it turned out the machines did not exist at all. B, as a means of raising capital, had entered into an arrangement with the plaintiff bank, under which the bank bought the four machines from B for £1,021,000. The bank then immediately leased the machines back to B. B, of course, had obligations to make payments under this lease to the plaintiff. These obligations were guaranteed by the defendant bank. B was unable to keep up the payments, and the plaintiff sought to enforce the guarantee against the defendant, by which time it had been discovered that the machines had never existed. This mistake, which had been made by both plaintiff and defendant, of course, had great significance for the guarantee. There is no doubt that the defendant would not have given the guarantee if it had known the truth. But, was the guarantee rendered void by this mistake? Steyn J refused to accept that *Bell* precluded an argument based on common mistake as to quality. His view was that, on the facts, such a mistake was not operative in *Bell*, not least because it was by no means clear that Lever Brothers would have acted any differently even if they had known the truth. It was open, therefore, to consider whether the mistake was operative in the case before him. It should be noted that this was not a case of *res extincta*, though it comes close. The machines were not the subject matter of the contract under consideration. The subject matter was in fact a contract in relation to the machines the performance of which had been supported by a guarantee given by the defendant. Steyn J concluded:

> For both parties, the guarantee of obligations under a lease with non-existent machines was essentially different from a guarantee of a lease with four machines which both parties at the time of the contract believed to exist.

The contract of guarantee was therefore void for common mistake at common law. The position would therefore seem to be that some mistakes as to the quality, or value, of the subject matter of the contract can give rise to an operative mistake provided that the mistake has a sufficiently serious effect in relation to matters which are fundamental to the contract. There are *obiter* statements in *Nicholson and Venn v Smith-Marriott* (1947) (mistake as to the provenance of antique table linen) which would also support such a view, though equally, in *Leaf v International Galleries* (1950) (mistake as to whether a picture was painted by Constable), there are *obiter* statements which envisage a very limited role for this type of mistake.

10.3.5 Effect of an operative common mistake

The effect of an operative common mistake at common law is to render the contract void *ab initio*. It is as if the contract had never existed, and therefore, as far as is possible, all concerned must be returned to the position they were in before the contract was made. This applies equally to third parties, so that the innocent purchaser of goods which have been 'sold' under a void contract will be required to disgorge them, and hand them back to the original owner. These powerful and far reaching consequences perhaps explain why the courts have shown a reluctance to extend the scope of common mistake too far, preferring to allow the flexible application of equitable remedies to pick up the pieces in the majority of cases (see 10.6 below).

10.4 Mutual mistake

'Mutual mistake' refers to the situation where the parties are at cross-purposes. This may relate to the subject matter of the contract, or the identity of the other contracting party. If the mistake is sufficiently fundamental that it means in effect that there was no agreement between the parties (that is, a mistake 'negativing' agreement), then there can be no contract, and any actions taken on the basis that there was a contract will have to be undone.

A classic example of a situation which can give rise to this kind of mistake is to be found in *Raffles v Wichelhaus* (1864). The alleged contract was for the purchase of a cargo of cotton due to arrive in England on the ship *Peerless*, from Bombay. There were two ships of this name carrying cotton from Bombay, one which left in October, the other in December. The plaintiff offered the December cargo for delivery, but the defendants refused to accept this, claiming that they intended to buy the October cargo. The plaintiff tried to argue that the contract was simply for a certain quantity of cotton, and that the ship from which it was to be supplied was immaterial. The defendants, however, put their case in these terms:

> There is nothing on the face of the contract to shew that any particular ship called the *Peerless* was meant; but the moment it appears that two ships called the *Peerless* were about to sail from Bombay there is a latent ambiguity, and parol evidence may be given for the purpose of shewing that the defendant meant one *Peerless*, and the plaintiff another. That being so, there was no *consensus ad idem*, and therefore no binding contract.

The court stopped argument at this point, and held for the defendant. There is, however, no report of any judgment, so it is impossible to be certain of the exact basis of the decision. It is perhaps significant, however, that a few years later the case was cited by Hannen J in *Smith v Hughes* (1871) as authority for the proposition that:

> ... if two persons enter into an apparent contract concerning a particular person or ship, and it turns out that each of them, misled by a similarity of name, had a different ship or person in his mind, no contract would exist between them.

Whatever the precise basis for the decision in *Raffles v Wichelhaus* itself, therefore, there seems no doubt that if the parties are at cross-purposes the contract will be void for mutual mistake. This will, of course, only apply where there is a fundamental ambiguity in the contract, and no objective means of resolving it.

10.4.1 Subjective or objective approach?

Raffles v Wichelhaus (1864) shows the court using a combination of a subjective and objective approaches to the agreement. No doubt, if the parties had in fact been in agreement about which ship was meant, then the contract would have been upheld. In the absence of such agreement, the question to be asked is what would a reasonable third party, looking at what was said and done, think that they had intended, or what would a reasonable offeror have thought was being offered. In *Raffles,* the confusion was such that it was not possible to give a definite answer to such questions. A similar result occurred in *Scriven Bros v Hindley* (1913), where there was confusion as to the nature of two lots in an auction, one being 'hemp', the other being much less valuable 'tow'. The defendant who had bid an unusually high price for the tow, in the mistaken belief that it was hemp, was allowed to avoid the contract. In *Smith v Hughes* (1871), however, which again concerned an alleged mutual mistake in relation to the subject matter of the contract, a different view was taken. The plaintiff had offered to sell oats to the defendant. The defendant thought that he was buying 'old' oats. When delivered, they turned out to be 'new', and of no use to the defendant. The trial judge directed the jury that if they thought that the defendant believed that he was contracting for old oats, they should give a verdict for the defendant, which they did. On appeal, however, the Queen's Bench held that it was not enough that the defendant had made a mistake. To allow him to escape from the contract, it would be necessary to show that the defendant thought that it was a *term of the contract* that the oats were 'old', *and that the plaintiff was aware that the defendant thought this* (that is, a 'unilateral', rather than 'mutual', mistake). Looked at objectively, it appeared to be simply a contract for the sale of a specific parcel of oats, about which there was no ambiguity.

The approach here, therefore, as in general with issues as to the creation of an agreement, is to concentrate on what can be deduced objectively from what the parties have said or done, rather than to try to determine their precise state of mind at the time of the alleged agreement.

10.5 Unilateral mistake

As we have seen, the court in *Smith v Hughes* (1871) thought that the result would have been different if the plaintiff had been aware that the defendant was acting on the basis of a mistake as to a term of the contract. In such a situation there will often have been a misrepresentation which will provide the other party with a remedy. If there was no such misrepresentation, however, or the remedies available for misrepresentation are inadequate, there may be a remedy on the basis of a 'unilateral mistake'. Where one party knowingly takes advantage of the other's mistake, this will lead to the contract being held either void at common law, if it is a mistake such as would be regarded as an operative common mistake, or non-existent if it is of a kind which would prevent an agreement arising on the basis of mutual mistake.

10.5.1 Mistaken identity

Unilateral mistake may arise in relation to any aspect of the contract. The majority of reported cases, however, concern mistakes as to the identity of the other contracting party. The general rule is that the mistake to be operative must relate to the *identity* of the person with whom you are contracting, not his or her *attributes*. This is a distinction which may be easier to state than to apply. Indeed, Lord Denning suggested in *Lewis v Averay* (1972) that it was a 'distinction without a difference':

> A man's name is one of his attributes. It is also a key to his identity. If, then, he gives a false name, is it a mistake as to his identity? or a mistake as to his attributes? These fine distinctions do no good to the law.

Nevertheless, it is submitted that the distinction does serve some purpose. Suppose, for example, I negotiate a contract for my shop to be opened by a particular film star, and this is advertised widely. I will not be satisfied if the agency with whom I have made the contract sends either (a) someone with the same name as the film star, but with no other similar qualities; or (b) another film star, but not the one whose presence I have advertised. In such a case, the identity of the individual is of central importance to the contract. A misunderstanding on this matter should raise the possibility of the contract being void for mistake. On the other hand, there is no reason to allow a person to back out of a contract simply because they mistakenly thought the other party was wealthy, and therefore creditworthy.

The courts have been more willing to treat mistakes of identity as operative where the contract has been made through the post, or *via* an agent, rather than in person. In *Boulton v Jones* (1857), for example, the defendant had sent an order to one 'Brocklehurst' with whom he had dealt regularly. Brocklehurst had, however, just transferred the business to his foreman, who fulfilled the order. The defendant resisted a claim for payment by the foreman on the basis that he had a 'set-off' against Brocklehurst, arising out their previous dealings. The court accepted that the existence of this set-off made the identity of the other party of crucial importance to the defendant, and the contract was set aside.

This result may appear a little harsh to the plaintiff in *Boulton v Jones* who, while aware of the defendant's mistake, was not trying to take any unfair advantage. This was not the case, however, in *Cundy v Lindsay* (1878). A fraudulent individual named Blenkarn placed large orders for handkerchiefs with the plaintiffs. Blenkarn was trading from Wood Street, and the plaintiffs thought that they were dealing with a reputable firm by the name of Blenkiron & Co, which also had its business in Wood Street. Blenkarn deliberately contributed to this mistake by the manner in which he signed his order. The goods were supplied, and sold on to the defendant, who was an innocent third party. The House of Lords confirmed that there was no contract between the plaintiffs and Blenkarn. As Lord Cairns put it:

> Of him [Blenkarn], they [the plaintiffs] knew nothing, and of him they never thought. With him they never intended to deal. Their minds never for an instant of time rested upon him, and as between him and them there was no consensus of mind which could lead to any agreement or any contract whatever.

As will be noted, this introduces a rather more subjective element, concerned with the fact of agreement, than is usually the case in this area. Even from an objective point of view, however, the fact that the plaintiffs had addressed the orders, and other correspondence, to 'Messrs Blenkiron', indicated that they had been under a misapprehension about whom they were dealing with, and had not intended to contract with Blenkarn. The consequences of the decision, however, were serious for the innocent defendants, who had to return the handkerchiefs (for which they had paid) to the plaintiffs, and were left to seek compensation from the fraudulent Blenkarn.

10.5.2 Need for intended party to exist

For the mistake as to identity to be operative, the mistaken party must be able to show who it was that was the intended contracting party. Thus, in *King's Norton Metal Company v Edridge, Merrett & Co* (1897), although once again a contract was induced by a fraudulent person (Wallis), who was pretending to be a firm called 'Hallam & Co', the contract was upheld. This was because 'Hallam & Co' was a pure invention, created by Wallis. There was no genuine firm of that name with whom the plaintiffs could have thought they were dealing. The mistake was therefore not one of identity, but of attributes. The plaintiffs thought that they were dealing with a firm, though in fact they were dealing with a private individual, Wallis.

10.5.3 Contracts *inter praesentes*

It becomes much harder to argue for mistake where the contract is made in person or *inter praesentes*. The courts are reluctant to accept that you did not intend to contract with the person who is standing in front of you, even though you may have been under a misapprehension as to their attributes, or qualities.

In *Phillips v Brooks* (1919), a person went into a jeweller's shop. He selected various valuable items, including a ring. As he was writing a cheque in payment, he said 'You see who I am, I am Sir George Bullough', giving an address in St James Square. The plaintiff checked this information in a directory, and then allowed the man to take the ring with him. The cheque was dishonoured, and the man turned out not to be Sir George at all. He had in the meantime, however, passed the ring to the defendants, who had taken it in all innocence. The court held that the contract was with the person in the shop. The plaintiff had failed to establish that the identity of the person was a crucial element in the contract.

This approach was confirmed in *Lewis v Averay* (1972) in which the fraudulent party pretended to be a famous television actor, and on that basis induced the plaintiff to part with his car in return for a worthless cheque. In support of his claim, the fraud produced a 'pass' from Pinewood Film Studios which carried his photograph and an official stamp. By the time the cheque was dishonoured, and the plaintiff had discovered the fraud, the car had been sold to the defendant, who had bought it in good faith, innocent of any deception. The perpetrator of the fraud having disappeared from the scene, the plaintiff sued the defendant in the tort of conversion for recovery of the car, or its value plus damages. It was held that the contract, while probably voidable for misrepresentation, was not void for mistake, so that the innocent third party who was now in possession of the car was entitled to retain it. Looking at the outward appearances of the transaction, it was simply a contract under which the plaintiff sold the car to the fraudulent purchaser. The identity of the purchaser was not an important factor. Since the plaintiff had not managed to avoid the contract before the car had been sold to an innocent third party, the contract had to stand.

10.5.4 A conflicting decision

It is difficult, however, to reconcile with these two cases the decision in *Ingram v Little* (1961). Here, the contract was, as in *Lewis v Averay* (1972), for the sale of a car. It was owned by three women who lived together. A man calling himself

Hutchinson answered their advertisement. He offered a sum which was acceptable to the women, but then produced a cheque book. The woman who was conducting the negotiations at that point indicated that in no circumstances would they accept payment by cheque. The man then gave a full name and an address. One of the other women then left the house to visit the post office and consult a telephone directory, which confirmed that a person of that name lived at the address given. They then allowed him to take the car in exchange for the cheque. The man was not, however, Mr Hutchinson, and the cheque proved worthless. The women brought an action to recover the car from an innocent third party purchaser. The Court of Appeal confirmed the view of the trial judge that they should succeed. The response to the offer of a cheque, and the procedure of checking in the directory, indicated that the identity of the other contracting party was of the utmost importance, and the contract was therefore void for mistake.

10.5.5 Principle clear: problems of application

The principle applied is the same in all three of the cases just discussed, that is, the mistake must relate to identity, rather than attributes. It is difficult to see, however, that there really was that much difference in the situation in *Ingram v Little* (1961) to justify applying the principle differently from the way in which it was applied in *Phillips v Brooks* (1919) and *Lewis v Averay* (1972). Indeed, the decision was not unanimous, since Lord Devlin dissented. In the course of his judgment, he expressed the view that it was unfortunate that the rules relating to mistake meant that if it was operative at common law, and the contract was void, it often meant that, as in *Ingram v Little*, one of two innocent parties had to suffer, and there was no good basis for choosing between them. He suggested that it would be better to have some system whereby the losses could be apportioned in such a case. This suggestion, which would be likely to produce a fairer result in many cases, has not, however, been taken up.

It will be easier for a plaintiff to convince a court that the identity of the other party is important, if the plaintiff has sought the person out. If you advertise goods to the general public, it may be difficult then to suggest that you really wanted to contract with one person in particular. If, however, you have gone to that person's place of business, specifically to enter into a contract, then the argument that the identity of the other party was important is likely to be much more convincing. This may be illustrated by *Hardman v Booth* (1863). The plaintiff had approached a firm, Thomas Gandell & Sons. They dealt with Edward Gandell, a member of the family who they thought was acting for the firm, though in fact he was acting on his own account. He intercepted goods sent by the plaintiffs and sold them to the defendant. It was held that the plaintiffs never intended to deal with Edward, but only with the firm, and the contract was therefore void for mistake.

It may also be possible to rebut the presumption where the fraudulent party is deemed to have been contracted with on the basis that he or she was an agent for someone else, rather than contracting in her own right. This situation was considered in *Lake v Simmons* (1927). A woman went to a jeweller's shop, and represented that she was the wife of VB. She asked to be allowed to take two pearl necklaces, because VB was planning to purchase one for her, and he wished to see them on approval. She was allowed by the plaintiff to take the necklaces. In fact, she was not VB's wife, though she was living with him. Having received the necklaces she absconded. The issue in the case was whether the plaintiff could recover from his insurance company. The decision turned primarily on the terms of the insurance policy, and whether in giving the necklaces to the woman the plaintiff could be said to have 'entrusted them to a customer'. If that were the case, the insurance company would not be liable. The House of Lords held that since the transaction was entered in the plaintiff's books as being with VB, the woman was not the 'customer' and the plaintiff could recover under his insurance policy. Viscount Haldane also suggested, however, that the plaintiff was only dealing with the woman as wife of VB. Since the plaintiff was 'entirely deceived as to the identity of the person' with whom he was dealing, there was no *consensus ad idem*, and therefore no contract. Identity was significant here, since if the woman was simply VB's agent her own creditworthiness was irrelevant, whereas if she were contracting on her own behalf the plaintiff might well have been more reluctant to allow her to take goods without paying for them.

The argument based on agency will not apply, however, if the 'agent' is a mere 'conduit' for the performance of a transaction. This was the view taken in *Citibank NA v Brown Shipley* (1991), where a rogue obtained foreign currency from Bank A by inducing Bank B to issue a draft on a genuine account. The draft was collected by the rogue, or his associate, from Bank B and presented to Bank A. Bank A rang Bank B to check that the draft was genuine, and having been assured that it was, delivered the foreign currency to the rogue. It was held that in this case the identity of the rogue was irrelevant to the transactions as between the two banks. It had not been established that it was 'fundamental' to them that the person who collected the draft from Bank B and presented it to Bank A 'was a particular person about whom they were mistaken, as opposed to a person whose attributes did not include authority from their customer [that is, the holder of the genuine account against which the draft was drawn] as they believed'. An action against Bank A for conversion of the draft therefore failed.

10.6 Mistake in equity

As we have seen, the common law rules for identifying an operative mistake are very restrictive. The courts have allowed a more flexible approach under equity. The main limitation on equity, however, is that the courts will not allow it to be used to defeat the position of a *bona fide* purchaser of goods, who is not aware of any 'mistake'. Thus, where goods have been supplied under a contract induced by a mistake, but have then been sold on to an innocent third party, the original owner will only be able to recover them from the third party if a mistake which the common law will recognise as operative can be shown to have existed. If the goods are still in the hands of the original 'purchaser', however, or if the contract is of a type which has not led to third party involvement, the courts may well be prepared to allow equitable remedies to be applied.

In *Solle v Butcher* (1950), there had been a mistake as to whether the rent payable in relation to a particular property was subject to control under the Rent Restriction Acts. This was held not to be sufficiently serious to render the contract void. But, as Lord Denning put it:

> A contract is also liable in equity to be set aside if the parties were under a common misapprehension either as to facts or as to their relative and respective rights, provided that the misapprehension was fundamental, and that the party seeking to set it aside was not himself at fault.

This makes it clear that it is not every mistake which will give rise to equitable relief. It must be 'fundamental' – but this seems to be wide enough to include serious mistakes as to the quality or value of the subject matter of the contract.

The difference between a mistake which will give rise to the possibility of rescission in equity as opposed to one which will render a contract void at common law was considered by Evans LJ in *William Sindall plc v Cambridgeshire County Council* (1994). His conclusion was that there must be:

> ... a category of mistake which is 'fundamental', so as to permit the equitable remedy of rescission, which is wider than the kind of 'serious and radical' mistake which means that the contract is void and of no effect in law.

In trying to distinguish between them, he suggested that:

> The difference may be that the common law rule is limited to mistakes with regard to the subject matter of the contract, whilst equity can have regard to a wider and perhaps unlimited category of 'fundamental' mistake.

In the case before him, the mistake related to the existence of a sewer running across a piece of land sold for development. There was no mistake about the subject matter, which was the piece of land. The mistake as to the existence of the sewer could have been sufficiently serious to give rise to a right of rescission, but on the facts it was not. The additional cost raised by the existence of the sewer was no more than £20,000, which on a contract where the sale price was over £5 million could not be said to be 'fundamental'.

Even in equity, the mistake must be made at the time of contract. In *Amalgamated Investment and Property Co v John Walker & Sons* (1976), a property was listed as a building of special interest by the Department of the Environment.

This placed serious restrictions on the ways in which it could be used, and reduced its value by £1.5 million. This is clearly a mistake of the kind which might allow equitable relief, but unfortunately the 'listing' of the building had taken place two days after the contract for its sale had been concluded. The mistake was not operative at the time of the contract, and so there could be no relief on this basis either under common law or in equity.

10.7 Forms of equitable relief

Once it is established that equity will take account of the mistake, what remedies are available? There are basically three: refusal of specific performance; rescission on terms; and rectification.

10.7.1 Refusal of specific performance

As we will see in Chapter 15, the order of specific performance is a discretionary remedy. In deciding whether to order it, the court can take into account any hardship which might be caused by so doing. For example, the buyer of a painting which, between contract and performance, is discovered not to be by Constable, as had been thought, may well be able to resist specific performance (though there may still be a liability to pay compensatory damages). Thus, in *Malins v Freeman* (1837), where a buyer at an auction mistakenly bid for one lot, thinking that it was another, this mutual mistake was held to be sufficient to allow the buyer not to be made to go through with the contract. In contrast, in *Tamplin v James* (1880), where the defendant bid for an inn and shop, incorrectly thinking that a garden was included, the contract was enforced. The mistake as to the *extent* of the property was distinguishable from a case where the mistake was as to the *identity* of the property.

10.7.2 Rescission on terms

If the contract has been performed, but on the basis of a mistake which is operative in equity, the court may order the contract to be rescinded. It may at the same time, however, impose conditions on the grant of rescission, in order to ensure justice as between the parties. Thus, in *Solle v Butcher* (see 10.6 above), the lease was rescinded, but on condition that the tenant could remain, provided that he paid rent at the maximum which the landlord could have asked for under the rent control legislation. Similarly, in *Grist v Bailey* (1967), a house was sold for £850 on the basis that it had a sitting tenant. In fact, the tenant had died, which increased the value of the house to £2,250. The contract was not void at law, but could be rescinded in equity, provided that the vendor gave the purchaser the opportunity of buying for a 'proper vacant possession price'.

Rescission on terms is therefore a very powerful remedy, in that, effectively, it allows the court to substitute what it considers to be a just and fair arrangement for the contract as made by the parties. This degree of judicial intervention is unusual in contract law, and has the potential for giving rise to great uncertainty. It will often be hard to predict on precisely what conditions a court may be prepared to grant rescission. It may also, of course, in appropriate cases be prepared to grant rescission without imposing conditions.

10.7.3 Rectification

Where an agreement is contained in a document which contains an inaccuracy, in the form of either an error, or an omission, the equitable remedy of rectification may be granted. It is clearly available where both parties miss the error (that is, a common mistake), or if one party knows of the other's mistake (that is, a unilateral mistake). Thus, in *Roberts v Leicestershire County Council* (1961), a construction contract which contained a completion date which was a year later than the contractors believed it to be, was rectified, because there was clear evidence that representatives of the other party were well aware of the basis on which the contractors were undertaking the project. The position was similar in *Templiss Properties Ltd v Hyams* (1999), which concerned a lease where the intention had been that the rent should be exclusive of business rates whereas it was expressed to be inclusive of such rates. Although in this case the tenant's solicitors where not aware of the mistake, it was shown that the tenant himself was aware, and so rectification was ordered. If the mistake is simply a mutual mistake, however, the courts will not grant rectification. A sufficiently serious mistake of this kind will allow the contract to be rescinded, of course, but rectification will not be available (*Riverlate Properties Ltd v Paul* (1975)).

It follows from this that if an oral agreement, though based on a mistake, is accurately reproduced in a subsequent document, rectification is not appropriate, and will not be granted. In *Rose v Pim* (1953), for example, the plaintiff had been asked by a third party to supply 'horsebeans described as feveroles'. The plaintiffs entered into a contract with the defendants for the purchase of 'horsebeans'. Both plaintiffs and defendants thought that 'horsebeans' was just another name for 'feveroles'. In fact, feveroles are a higher quality horsebean. The defendants supplied ordinary horsebeans, but these were unacceptable to the third party, who wanted feveroles. The plaintiffs sought to have their written contract with the defendants rectified to refer to feveroles. They would then be able to succeed in an action for supply of goods of the wrong description. The Court of Appeal held, however, that this was not possible:

> Their agreement as expressed both orally and in writing, was for 'horsebeans'. That is all the sellers committed themselves to supply, and all they should be bound to.

Although there was a misapprehension underlying the contract, a 'common mistake', in fact, this was not a reason for providing the remedy of rectification.

10.7.4 Bars to rescission or rectification

Because these remedies are equitable, they may be lost by virtue of:

* lapse of time;

* the intervention of third party rights; or, in the case of rescission;

* the impossibility of reversing the contract – for example, where it concerns goods which have been consumed.

If this is the case, then the plaintiff will have to argue for common law mistake in order to obtain any remedy.

10.8 Contracts signed under a mistake

The courts are not inclined to be sympathetic towards people who put their names to contracts without reading or understanding them. In general, then, a person will be taken to have notice of, and to be bound by, all the provisions of a contract which has been signed, whether they have been read or not (*L'Estrange v Graucob* (1934) (see 8.3 above)). There are some exceptional circumstances, however, where the courts will allow a plea of *non est factum* – 'it is not my deed'. The mistake must be such that the document as a whole is 'radically different' from what the person thought they were signing. Moreover, the person must not have been 'careless' in signing the document. These principles are derived from the House of Lords' decision in *Gallie v Lee* (1971) (also reported as *Saunders v Anglia Building Society*), which is further discussed in 10.8.2 below.

10.8.1 Availability of the plea

The result of these principles, and in particular the second one, is that the doctrine will rarely be available to literate adults, of full capacity. The courts will, however, make the remedy available to those who are tricked into signing the contract. And it may also operate to protect those who from 'defective education, illness, or innate incapacity' (as Lord Reid put it in *Gallie v Lee* (1971)), fail to understand what they are signing.

A recent (fairly rare) example of the successful use of the plea is to be found in *Lloyd's Bank plc v Waterhouse* (1990). Here, the defendant, who was illiterate, signed a guarantee regarding his son's future liabilities to the plaintiffs. The father thought that this guarantee related solely to the son's purchase of a farm, whereas in fact it covered all the son's liabilities. The trial judge found that this did not amount to a fundamental difference, and that the defendant had been careless in not having the document read to him. He gave judgment for the plaintiff. The defendant appealed.

The majority of the Court of Appeal regarded the mistake as to the extent of the guarantee as being sufficient to support the plea of *non est factum*. The evidence showed that the father would not have signed it if he had known its true nature, even though he was aware of the financial value of the guarantee. As to carelessness, although the bank was unaware of the defendant's illiteracy, and there was no suggestion of impropriety on their part, the defendant had clearly taken steps (by asking questions of the bank's officials) to ascertain his liability. The plea of *non est factum* was made out.

10.8.2 Nature of the mistake

At one time, the difference in the extent of the guarantee in the above case would not have been regarded as sufficient, as it was thought that the document had to be of a different 'character' for the defence to be available. That test was rejected, however, in *Gallie v Lee* (1971), in favour of the more broadly based question of whether the document was 'radically' or 'fundamentally' different. In this case, an elderly widow had been tricked by her nephew into signing an assignment of the lease of her house to a third party. She thought she was signing a deed of gift to her nephew. The reason why she had failed to read the document was that she had broken her reading glasses. The House of Lords regarded this as an acceptable reason for failing to read the document, and held that it did not amount to 'carelessness'. The widow failed, however, on the first test, relating to the nature of the document. Although it involved a different transaction from what she thought, the purpose of the assignment was, albeit indirectly, to provide financial assistance to her nephew. This is what she had wished to achieve by the deed of gift. The document was not, therefore, sufficiently different for the plea to succeed.

If the plea is successful, then the transaction is void and unenforceable.

MISTAKE

A mistake may 'nullify' or 'negative' an agreement. Mistakes may be categorised as 'common', 'mutual', and 'unilateral'.

Common mistake

The clearest example of a common mistake is *res extincta* (*Galloway v Galloway* (1914); s 6 of the SGA 1979). Note, also, *Couturier v Hastie* (1856) as an example of 'commercial' rather than physical perishing.

- Subject matter never existed

  This will not render the contract void, if the existence has been *warranted* (*McRae v Commonwealth Disposals Commission* (1951)).

- Impossibility of performance

  This may take the form or physical (*Sheikh Bros v Ochsner* (1957)), legal (*Cooper v Phibbs* (1867)) or commercial (*Griffith v Brymer* (1903)) impossibility.

- Mistake as to quality

  The leading authority is *Bell v Lever Bros* (1931), which suggests little scope for this. But note *Associated Japanese Bank Ltd v Credit du Nord SA* (1988) which identifies some cases where such a mistake may be operative.

- Effect of an operative common mistake

  The effect is to render the contract void *ab initio*, and require the parties to be restored to their original position. This will override even third party rights.

Mutual mistake

In the case of mutual mistake, the parties are, unknowingly, at cross-purposes (*Raffles v Wichelhaus* (1864)). The approach is primarily objective (*Smith v Hughes* (1871)). The effect of such a mistake is to lead to a finding that there never was a contract.

Unilateral mistake

In the case of unilateral mistake, one party is aware that the other party has made a mistake as to some *term of the contract* (*Smith v Hughes* (1871)). The contract will be rendered void, if the mistake is serious.

- Mistake as to identity

  The courts will allow this to avoid a contract where it is shown that the identity was of fundamental importance, and relates to the person's *identity*, rather than *attributes*. This is easier where the parties are contracting at a distance (for example, *Cundy v Lindsay* (1878)), rather than *inter praesentes*, provided that there is a genuine confusion between two distinct people (*King's Norton Metal Company v Edridge, Merrett & Co* (1897)).

- Contracts *inter praesentes*

  The courts are reluctant to find an operative mistake as to identity (*Phillips v Brooks* (1919); *Lewis v Averay* (1972)), but will do so in appropriate circumstances (*Ingram v Little* (1961); *Hardman v Booth* (1863)).

Mistake in equity

Where a mistake is not operative at common law, but still relates to an important aspect of the contract, equitable remedies may be available (*Solle v Butcher* (1950)).

Forms of equitable relief

Forms of equitable relief are:

- refusal of specific performance (*Malins v Freeman* (1837)) (cf *Tamplin v James* (1880));

- rescission on terms (*Solle v Butcher* (1950); *Grist v Bailey* (1967));

- rectification of a document (*Roberts v Leicestershire County Council* (1961)).

Bars to rescission or rectification

These remedies may be lost by lapse of time, intervention of third party rights, or, in relation to rescission, the impossibility of restitution.

Contracts signed under a mistake

The plea of *non est factum* will only be allowed where the document signed is 'radically different' from that which the person thought they were signing, and the signer has not been 'careless' (*Gallie v Lee* (1971)).

CHAPTER 11

DURESS AND UNDUE INFLUENCE

11.1   Introduction

This chapter is concerned with situations in which an agreement which appears to be valid on its face is challenged because it is alleged that it is the product of improper pressure of some kind. This may take the form of physical coercion or threats, economic pressure, or psychological influence. The problem with the last two categories lies in establishing the boundaries of acceptable behaviour of this kind, because both may be argued to have a legitimate place within business dealings. If impropriety is established under any of the heads, the resulting contract is rendered voidable. The courts may be regarded as intervening either because there is no true agreement between the parties, or simply because it is unacceptable on grounds of public policy that agreements of this kind should be enforced. The latter argument is probably the one which best represents the approach of the modern courts to this issue.

11.2   Duress by physical threats or coercion

Although it is possible that a person could be physically forced to sign a contract, by someone holding their arm and moving it, the most obvious form of duress is where a contract is brought about as a result of a threat of physical injury. A fairly modern example is to be found in *Barton v Armstrong* (1975), where the managing director of a company was threatened with death if he did not arrange for his company to make a payment to, and buy shares from, the defendant. The Privy Council held that the contract was voidable for duress.

The threat need not be of serious physical violence – any illegality in the form of a crime or tort against the person (such as false imprisonment) will apparently be sufficient.

Threats in relation to goods were at one time held not to amount to duress sufficient to avoid an agreement (*Skeate v Beale* (1840)). It must be doubted, however, whether this doctrine, which was in any case apparently subject to the exception that money paid under duress of goods could be recovered (*Astley v Reynolds* (1731)), has survived the modern development of the concept of 'economic duress', which is dealt with in the next section.

The cases on duress are full of references to the plaintiff's will being 'overborne'. In many cases, this will be an inaccurate description of what has happened. The plaintiff has not been forced to act as an automaton. The decision to make the contract has been taken as a matter of choice. It is simply that the threat which has led to that choice is regarded by the courts as illegitimate, and justifies allowing the party threatened to escape from the consequent contract. The fact that this is the basis of the modern doctrine is illustrated by the fact that it was by no means certain in *Barton v Armstrong* (1975) that the threats which were made were the sole reason for the managing director's decision. The approach of the majority of the Privy Council appears in the opinion of Lord Cross. He noted that, in relation to misrepresentation, there is no need to prove that the false statement was the sole reason for entering into the contract (see 9.2.4 above). He then commented that:

> Their Lordships think that the same rule should apply in cases of duress and that if Armstrong's threats were 'a' reason for Barton's executing the deed he is entitled to relief even though he might well have entered into the contract if Armstrong had uttered no threats to influence him to do so ...

If this is the case, then it clearly is inappropriate to talk of the will of the person subject to the threats being 'overborne'. The duress simply becomes a wrongful act of a similar kind to a misrepresentation, which, if it has influenced the other party's decision to make a contract, provides a basis for that contract being voidable. As Lord Cross also makes clear, there is not even any need for it to be proved that the threats were the major element in the decision, 'for in this field the court does not allow an examination into the relative importance of contributory causes'.

11.3 Economic duress

The first recognition of economic duress is probably to be found in the *obiter* statements of Kerr J in *The Siboen and The Sibotre* (1976). The case concerned a renegotiation of charters of two vessels, under the threat that otherwise the charterers would go out of business. It was recognised that this could in some circumstances have amounted to duress sufficient to render the agreement voidable. On the facts, however, the other party had not agreed to the renegotiation under duress, but simply as a result of ordinary commercial pressures. In *North Ocean Shipping Company v Hyundai Construction* (1979), the devaluation of the dollar led to a demand for an increase in the price payable under a ship construction contract. Mocatta J held that this did amount to duress, but that the right to rescind had been lost through lapse of time. These two cases, therefore, recognised the possibility of duress based on improper commercial pressure, but did not in fact apply it to the facts before them. The difficulty with this test is the requirement that the pressure should be 'improper'. In commercial dealings, 'threats' may often be made as a means of encouraging the other party to contract – for example, 'If you don't agree to this contract we will take all our other business elsewhere', or 'we will not give you any discount on orders in the future', or 'we will provide these goods to your main competitor at a substantial discount'. All of these threats may have the effect of 'encouraging' the other party to contract, but they are unlikely to be regarded as 'improper'.

They are simply part of the rough and tumble of business life. Where, then, is the line to be drawn? It is suggested that, at the very least, the threat should involve the commission of a tort, or a breach of contract. In other words, a threat to do an act which is, in the broadest sense, unlawful. Thus the threat to encourage others not to fulfil their contracts with the victim (that is, the tort of 'inducing breach of contract'), or the threat to break other agreements which the threatener has with the victim, might give rise to the possibility of a plea of 'economic duress'. This test is satisfied in virtually all the cases where economic duress has been held to have occurred. There is one recent decision of the Court of Appeal, however, *CTN Cash and Carry v Gallaher* (1994), which contains *obiter* statements to the effect that a threat to commit an entirely lawful act may nevertheless constitute duress. This case is discussed further below at 11.3.4.

11.3.1 Industrial action

The cases which have subsequently developed and applied the concept of economic duress have often been concerned with industrial action. A trade union threatens to encourage its members to break their contracts with a particular employer, unless the employer agrees to act in a certain way. To carry out the threatened action would (subject to the applicability of any protective trade union legislation) amount to the tort of inducement of breach of contract. This may well be regarded as going beyond legitimate pressure, and thus amount to duress. For example, in *Universe Tankships Inc v International Transport Workers Federation* (1983), the union 'blacked' a ship owned by the plaintiffs, by instructing its members not to deal with it, and therefore preventing it from leaving port. In order to escape from this, the owners, *inter alia*, made a payment to the union's welfare fund. They later brought an action to recover this as a payment made under duress. It was held that the threatened industrial action was unlawful under English law, and the payment was recoverable. Subsequent changes in English employment law, extending the scope of unlawful industrial action, have had the effect of extending the scope of economic duress. This is shown by *Dimskal Shipping Co SA v International Transport Workers' Federation* (1991), which also confirmed that the question whether the actions of a party amount to economic duress must be judged by English law, not the law of the country where the actions took place. The ITF had, through industrial action, persuaded the respondents to agree to contracts involving the payment of large sums of money in respect of back pay to its crew. This was to bring the respondents' terms of employment in line with those approved by the ITF. The respondents sought to have these contracts, which were expressed to be governed by English law, avoided for duress. The judge at first instance refused, since the actions of the ITF were legal where they took place (in Sweden). The Court of Appeal overturned this judgment, and the ITF appealed to the House of Lords which held, with Lord Templeman dissenting, that the issue of what amounted to duress had to be determined by

English rather than Swedish law. Since the actions of the ITF would have been unlawful under English employment law, the respondents were entitled to avoid the contracts made as a result of them.

11.3.2 Breach of contract

Where the unlawful action threatened is simply a breach of contract, rather than a tort, which may well be the case outside the industrial context, it may be more difficult to identify the boundaries of legitimate pressure. Some assistance is provided by the opinion of Lord Scarman in the Privy Council case of *Pao On v Lau Yiu Long* (1980). In this case, the plaintiff had threatened not to proceed with a contract for the sale of shares, unless the other side agreed to a renegotiation of certain subsidiary arrangements. The defendant agreed, but when the plaintiff later tried to enforce these arrangements, claimed that they had been extracted by duress, and were therefore voidable. Lord Scarman identified the following factors as being relevant to whether a person acted voluntarily, or not, and therefore under duress:

- did the person alleged to have been coerced protest at the time?;
- did that person have an alternative course open, such as an adequate legal remedy?;
- was the person independently advised?;
- did the person take steps to avoid the contract, after entering into it?

On the facts of the case, the claim for duress failed, because the defendant had had an alternative course open. That is, he had an adequate legal remedy in an action for specific performance in relation to the original agreement. Lord Scarman referred to this test again in *Universe Tankships v ITF* (1983) where he referred to the victim having 'no practical choice but to submit to the duress'.

11.3.3 No alternative to compliance

A clear example of a person being faced with no alternative but to apply, in a case not concerned with industrial action, is to be found in *Atlas Express v Kafco* (1989). The defendants, Kafco, were a small manufacturing company who had a very valuable contract with Woolworths, a store with branches throughout the country. Kafco employed Atlas, a national firm of carriers, to make deliveries to Woolworths. Atlas found that they had, through their own miscalculation of the quantities of Kafco's goods which could be carried on their lorries at one time, entered into the contract on uneconomic terms. They told Kafco that they must agree to an increase in the charge for carriage, or else Atlas would not make the deliveries. Kafco could not risk being in breach of their contract with Woolworths, and so agreed to the increased charge, under protest. When Atlas brought an action to recover the increased charges, Kafco resisted on the grounds of duress. The court accepted the argument that losing the contract with Woolworths, or being sued by them, would have been so disastrous for Kafco that they had no real alternative but to go along with Atlas's suggestion. An action for damages against Atlas for breach of the original contract would not have been able to provide compensation sufficient to counteract the effects of the destruction of their business relationship with Woolworths. Kafco were not obliged to pay the additional carriage costs.

A major test for the illegitimacy of the threat of economic pressure, which turns it into duress, thus seems to be that the action threatened leaves the person threatened with no realistic alternative to compliance.

11.3.4 Must the threat be of an unlawful act?

The examples of duress so far considered have all involved an act which is in some respects a breach of law. It involves a crime, or a tort, or a breach of contract. Is this a necessary characteristic for duress, and in particular economic duress, to be operative? In *CTN Cash and Carry v Gallaher* (1994), the threat was to withdraw credit from the other party, and to insist on cash for goods supplied. The circumstances in which this occurred were that the plaintiffs had ordered from the defendants cigarettes to the value of £17,000. These had, as a result of the defendants' mistake, been delivered to the wrong warehouse, in a different town. It was arranged that the defendants would collect them and transport them to the right warehouse. Before this could be done, however, there was a burglary at the warehouse to which the cigarettes had been wrongly delivered, and they were stolen. The defendants believed, mistakenly as a matter of law, that the cigarettes were at the plaintiffs' risk when they were stolen. They therefore insisted that the plaintiffs should pay for them, backing this up with the threat to withdraw credit. The plaintiffs reluctantly paid, but then brought an action to recover the £17,000 on the basis that it had been paid under duress. The Court of Appeal found that, on the facts, there was no economic duress, partly because the 'threat' was issued in good faith. Although the defendants might have been regarded as abusing their position as the monopoly supplier of certain very popular brands of cigarettes, they were in this case genuinely under the impression that their claim for payment was legitimate. Moreover, as Steyn LJ commented:

> ... an extension [of the categories of duress] capable of covering the present case, involving 'lawful act duress' in a commercial context in pursuit of a *bona fide* claim, would be a radical one with far-reaching implications. It would introduce a substantial and undesirable element of uncertainty in the commercial bargaining process.

The court did not accept, however, that the fact that what was threatened was perfectly lawful, and would not have involved the supplier in any breach of contract, was in itself fatal to a claim. It thought that it was possible, in appropriate circumstances, for a threat to commit an entirely lawful act to amount to duress. In coming to this conclusion, it noted with approval the opinion of Professor Birks expressed in *An Introduction to the Law of Restitution*, 1989, p 177, to the effect that it ought not to be the case that 'those who devise outrageous but technically lawful means of compulsion must always escape restitution'. The Court of Appeal's statements on this issue are, of course, *obiter*, but they indicate a possible further extension of the concept of economic duress. Whether it is a desirable or necessary extension is open to doubt. The problems of drawing the line between legitimate pressure, and economic duress, will become even more difficult if a requirement of 'unlawfulness' is rejected. The arguments for and against such a development in the law are very similar to those which apply in relation to whether the courts should adopt a general principle that 'unconscionable' agreements are unenforceable. This is discussed below at 11.11.

11.4   Remedies for duress

The remedy that the victim of duress will be seeking is to escape from the agreement that has resulted from the duress – in other words rescission. As has been noted in relation to mistake and misrepresentation (see 10.7.4 and 9.3.1 above), however, rescission is an equitable remedy, and therefore may be lost through:

* lapse of time (see *North Ocean Shipping v Hyundai Construction* (1978) (above, 11.3));

* impossibility of restitution; or

* the intervention of third party rights.

11.5   Undue influence: the concept

Duress is essentially a common law concept. Alongside it must be placed the equitable doctrine of 'undue influence'. This operates to release parties from contracts that they have entered into, not as a result of improper threats, but as a result of being 'influenced' by the other party, whether intentionally or not.

The difficulty here, as with duress, is to find the limits of legitimate persuasion. If it were impermissible to seek to persuade, cajole, or otherwise encourage, people to enter agreements, then sales representatives would all be out of a job. 'Influence' in itself is perfectly acceptable: it is only when it becomes 'undue' that the law will intervene. How, then, do the courts decide when influence has overstepped the limits of acceptability, and become 'undue'? The basic test in English law is that it is only where there is some relationship between the parties (either continuing, or in relation to a particular transaction) which leads to an inequality between them that the law will intervene. The starting point for the law's analysis is therefore not the substance of the transaction, but the process by which it came about. Was this the result of a person who was in a position to influence the other party abusing that relationship in some way? An initial task is therefore to identify which relationships will give rise to this inequality. Once they have been identified, then further questions will arise as to the precise scope of the doctrine.

The whole area of undue influence has recently been given a thorough re-examination by the House of Lords in *Barclays Bank plc v O'Brien* (1993). In the leading speech, Lord Browne-Wilkinson confirmed the analysis of the Court of Appeal in *Bank of Credit and Commerce International ('BCCI') v Aboody* (1988), that there are two main categories of undue influence, the second of which must be divided into two further separate sub-categories. The categories are:

- actual undue influence; and

- presumed undue influence;
  which may be divided into:
  (i) relationships (such as solicitor/client) which will always give rise to a presumption of influence;
  (ii) relationships which may, *de facto*, be such that influence should be presumed.

These three categories will now be considered in turn.

11.6 Actual undue influence

In relation to actual undue influence, the plaintiff must prove, on the balance of probabilities, that in relation to a particular transaction, the defendant used undue influence. There is no need here for there to be a previous history of such influence. It can operate for the first time in connection with the transaction which is disputed. A recent example of this type of influence is to be found in *BCCI v Aboody* (1989). Mrs Aboody was 20 years younger than her husband. She had married him when she was 17. For many years, she signed documents relating to her husband's business, of which she was nominally a director, without reading them, or questioning her husband about them. On the occasion which gave rise to the litigation, she had signed a number of guarantees, and charges relating to the matrimonial home, in order to support loans by the bank to the business. She had taken no independent advice, though the bank's solicitor had at one meeting attempted to encourage her to take legal advice. During that meeting, Mr Aboody, in a state of some agitation, came into the room, and through arguing with the solicitor managed to reduce his wife to tears. It was held that, although Mr Aboody had not acted with any improper motive, he had unduly influenced his wife. He had concealed relevant matters from her, and his bullying manner had led her to sign without giving proper detached consideration to her own interests, simply because she wanted peace.

The Court of Appeal in this case, following *dicta* of Lord Scarman in *National Westminster Bank plc v Morgan* (1985), held that Mrs Aboody's claim to set aside the transaction nevertheless failed, because it was not to her 'manifest disadvantage'. The loans which she was guaranteeing had, in fact, given the company a reasonably good chance of surviving, in which case the potential benefits to Mrs Aboody would have been substantial. The risks involved did not, therefore, clearly outweigh the benefits. The House of Lords, in *CIBC Mortgages plc v Pitt* (1993), has now indicated, however, that 'manifest disadvantage' is not a requirement in cases of actual, as opposed to presumed, undue influence. If similar facts were to recur, therefore, a person in the position of Mrs Aboody would be likely to succeed in having the transactions set aside. 'Manifest disadvantage' may, however, be relevant in considering the effect of undue influence exercised by a third party to the transaction (see 11.9.8 below).

11.7 Presumed undue influence: recognised relationships

There are certain relationships which will be presumed to give rise to undue influence. Here, there is no need for the party seeking to escape from a contract to prove that the particular transaction was affected by such influence. The burden of proof will be on the other party to show that no such influence in fact operated in this case. This could be done by showing, for example, that the allegedly influenced party only acted after receiving independent legal advice.

The relationships which fall into this category include parent/child, doctor/patient, solicitor/client, religious adviser/disciple (*Goldsworthy v Brickell* (1987)). It does not include husband/wife (*Midland Bank plc v Shephard* (1988)). The relationships are ones where a person has placed trust and confidence in another, and so is liable to act on their suggestions without seeking independent advice. Other relationships (other than husband/wife) which have these characteristics could be added to the list in the future.

An example of this category of undue influence is *Allcard v Skinner* (1887). The plaintiff had entered a religious order of St Mary at the Cross, and had taken vows of poverty, chastity, and obedience. The defendant was the lady superior of the order. Over a period of eight years during which she was a member of the order, the plaintiff gave property to the value of £7,000 to the defendant, most of which was spent on the purposes of the order. It was held that the property was *prima facie* recoverable as having been given under the undue influence of membership of the order, which required obedience to the defendant. This was so, even though no direct pressure had been placed on the plaintiff. The influence was presumed from the relationship itself. The plaintiff's action to recover her property did not succeed, however, as she did not initiate her action until some six years after she had left the order. This lapse of time was held to operate as a bar on recovery.

For there to be recovery under this heading, the transaction which the plaintiff seeks to undo must have been to his or her 'manifest disadvantage' (*National Westminster Bank plc v Morgan* (1985)). This requirement is discussed further in the next section (11.8.1 below).

11.8 Presumed undue influence: other relationships

Even where a relationship does not fall into one of the categories listed in the previous section, it may in fact have developed in a way which indicates that one person is in a 'dominant' position over the other. The dominated person will be likely in such a situation to act on the advice, recommendation, or orders, of the other, without seeking any independent advice, and without properly considering the consequences of his or her actions. If that is so, then the courts will presume that *any* disadvantageous transaction entered into at the instigation of the dominant party will be affected by undue influence, unless the contrary is shown. A number of cases in this area concern the relationship of the dominant husband and the subservient wife, but the presumption does not only arise in this context, as is shown by *Lloyd's Bank Ltd v Bundy* (1975).

Mr Bundy was an elderly farmer. He had provided a guarantee and a charge over his house to support the debts of his son's business. He was visited by his son and the assistant manager of the bank. The assistant manager told Mr Bundy that the bank could not continue to support the son's business without further security. Mr Bundy then, without seeking any other advice, increased the guarantee and charge to £11,000. When the bank, in enforcing the charge, subsequently sought possession of the house, Mr Bundy pleaded undue influence. It was held that the existence of long standing relations between the Bundy family and the bank was important. Although the visit when the charge was increased was the first occasion when this particular assistant manager had met Mr Bundy, he was, as Sir Eric Sachs put it in the Court of Appeal, 'the last of a relevant chain of those who over the years had earned or inherited' Mr Bundy's trust and confidence. The relationship between Mr Bundy and the bank was therefore one which gave rise to a presumption of undue influence. This was not rebutted, and Mr Bundy was not bound by the charge over his house.

Although the period of time over which a relationship has developed is clearly relevant to deciding whether there should be a presumption of undue influence, it need not be all that long. In *Goldsworth v Brickell* (1987), for example, where the relationship existed between an elderly farmer and his neighbour, it had only been for a few months that the plaintiff had been relying on the defendant. Nevertheless, it was held that the relationship involved sufficient trust and confidence for the undue influence to be presumed.

In *Credit Lyonnais Bank Nederland NV v Burch* (1997), it was held that a relationship of presumed undue influence could arise between an employer and a junior employee. The employee had acted as babysitter for the employer, and had visited his family at weekends and on holidays abroad. She had agreed to her house being used as collateral for the employer's business overdraft. It was held by Millett LJ in the Court of Appeal that a presumption of undue influence between two people in a relationship which was 'easily capable of developing into a relationship of trust and confidence' could be established by the 'nature of the transaction' which had been entered into. If 'the transaction is so extravagantly improvident that it is virtually inexplicable on any other basis', then 'the inference will be readily drawn'. This use of the substance of the transaction as an element in establishing a presumption of undue influence is unusual. The other cases in this area operate on the basis of establishing the presumption from the way in which the relationship has developed, before looking at the position in relation to the transaction under consideration. As will be seen in the next paragraph, the disadvantageous nature of the transaction has generally been used as a basis for deciding whether or not relief should be granted, once a presumption of influence has been made. Millett LJ's approach was not specifically followed by the other members of the Court of Appeal, though Swinton Thomas LJ stated in general terms that he agreed with Millett LJ's reasons for his decision. The case may, therefore, indicate a further development in the way in which a presumption of undue influence is held to arise.

11.8.1 Requirement of 'manifest disadvantage'

As noted in the previous section, it is a requirement in relation to either type of presumed influence that the transaction which is to be set aside is to the 'manifest disadvantage' of the plaintiff. Not every transaction which is entered into by parties who are in a relationship of presumed influence will therefore be vulnerable. This principle derives from the case of *National Westminster Bank plc v Morgan* (1985). Here, Mrs Morgan had agreed to a legal charge over the matrimonial home as part of an attempt to re-finance debts which had arisen from her husband's business. She had been visited at home by the Bank Manager and had thereupon signed the charge. Lord Scarman, with whom the rest of House agreed, held that her attempt to have the charge set aside for undue influence failed for two reasons. First, the bank manager's visit was very short (only about 15 minutes in total), and there was no history of reliance as in *Lloyd's Bank v Bundy* (1975). Secondly, for the presumption to arise, the transaction had to be to the 'manifest disadvantage' of Mrs Morgan. This was not the case here. The charge 'meant for her the rescue of her home on the terms sought by her: a short term loan at a commercial rate of interest'. Thus, although any transaction which puts a person's home at risk must in one sense be regarded as 'disadvantageous', this cannot be sufficient on its own to render a contract voidable. If it were, every mortgage agreement would have to be so regarded. In looking for disadvantage, it is necessary to consider the context in which the transaction took place. If it is clear, as it seemed to be in *Morgan*, that the risks involved were, as far as the plaintiff was concerned, worth running in order to obtain the potential benefits of the transaction, and there is no other indication of unfairness, then the courts will be quite prepared to enforce it. This approach has recently been confirmed by the Court of Appeal in *Royal Bank of Scotland v Etridge (No 2)* (1998).

As has been noted above, some of Lord Scarman's comments in *Morgan* were interpreted by the Court of Appeal in *BCCI v Aboody* (1989) as applying the requirement of manifest disadvantage to situations of actual, rather than presumed, influence. This interpretation was firmly rejected by the House of Lords in *CIBC Mortgages plc v Pitt* (1993).

11.9 Undue influence and third parties

It is not uncommon for a wife to be persuaded by her husband to enter into a contract with a bank or other creditor, under which she will put property which she partly or wholly owns at risk, in order to secure her husband's personal or business debts. In such a situation, if the husband's actions amount to undue influence, does this affect the wife's transaction with the creditor? The husband is not a party to that transaction, and so the standard answer under the doctrine of privity would be 'no'. Nevertheless, in some situations of this kind (not necessarily involving husband and wife), the courts have been prepared to find that the transaction with the creditor can be set aside.

11.9.1 Agency

In some cases, for example, *Kings North Trust v Bell* (1986), this was done by treating the debtor (that is, the husband) as agent for the creditor in getting the other person (that is, his wife) to sign the agreement. If that is the case, then the creditor, as principal, would be infected with any wrongful acts of the debtor, as agent, in obtaining the agreement. A similar analysis was adopted, though not applied on the facts, in *Coldunell Ltd v Gallon* (1986) (which concerned a son taking advantage of his elderly parents). As was pointed out, however, by Scott LJ in the Court of Appeal in *Barclays Bank v O'Brien* (1992), the analysis of such cases in terms of agency is likely to be 'highly artificial'.

11.9.2 Special equity

Another possible analysis, which was preferred by Scott LJ, was to treat married women as being able to take advantage of a 'special equity'. This consists of a recognition by the courts that many wives are still in a position where the husband exercises considerable influence in relation to business decisions taken for the family. In such situations, there is therefore an obligation on the creditor, where the wife is entering a transaction which puts her home at risk, to ensure that the she is given full information, and is recommended to seek independent advice.

11.9.3 The current analysis

The House of Lords, however, in *Barclays Bank v O'Brien* (1993), was not inclined to adopt either of the analyses identified by Scott LJ. The facts of the case were as follows. Mr O'Brien persuaded his wife to sign a guarantee in relation to an overdraft facility provided by a bank, using the jointly owned matrimonial home as security. He had told her that the security was limited to £60,000 whereas in fact it was for £130,000. The employee of the bank who presented the documents for the wife's signature failed to follow a superior's instructions to explain the transaction, and to suggest that the wife took independent legal advice if she had any doubts about it. The papers were presented to the wife, open at the place for signature, and she did not read them before signing. When the bank tried to enforce the security, Mrs O'Brien claimed that she was only bound, at most, up to the £60,000 which her husband had told her was the limit of the liability.

It was found by the Court of Appeal, and not disputed in the House of Lords, that Mrs O'Brien was an intelligent and independent minded woman, who had not been unduly influenced by her husband. The case, therefore, turned on her husband's misrepresentation of the extent of the liability, and whether this affected the bank. Although the case is therefore not strictly one which is concerned with undue influence, it was accepted in both the Court of Appeal and the House of Lords, that the same principles should apply irrespective of whether the wife was claiming that it was her husband's undue influence, or his misrepresentation, which had led her to enter into the transaction.

Lord Browne-Wilkinson, who gave the only substantive speech in the House of Lords, found that the law in this area had been built on a rather obscure Privy Council decision, *Turnbull v Duval* (1902). The case concerned the setting-aside of a wife's guarantee of her husband's debts. But, close examination of the case showed no clear evidence of improper pressure from the husband. Moreover, although the case had been used to support the 'agency' analysis in later decisions, the Privy Council did not actually refer to this concept. Lord Lindley had simply stated that the creditors 'had left everything to [the husband] and must abide by the consequences'. The precise basis for the holding in favour of the wife was therefore not at all clear. Building on this uncertain foundation, the law had subsequently developed 'in an artificial way, giving rise to artificial distinctions and conflicting decisions'. As a result, he sought to 'restate the law in a form which is principled, reflects the current requirements of society and provides as much certainty as possible'.

11.9.4 The doctrine of notice

The basis on which he felt able to do this was by a proper application of the doctrine of 'notice', which he felt lies at the heart of equity. Where, for example, it is necessary to decide between the conflicting rights of two innocent parties, the issue may well be determined by asking whether the holder of the later right had actual or constructive notice of the former right. Looking first at the position of wives, Lord Browne-Wilkinson felt that the fact that many wives place confidence and trust in their husbands in relation to their financial affairs, and that the informality of business dealings between spouses raises a substantial risk of misrepresentation, meant that creditors should in certain circumstances be put on inquiry. These circumstances arose where:

(a)   the transaction is on its face not to the financial advantage of the wife; and

(b)   there is substantial risk in transactions of that kind that, in procuring the wife to act as surety, the husband has committed a legal or equitable wrong that entitles the wife to set aside the transaction.

The creditor who ignores the risk, and does not take steps to ensure that the wife is acting with fully informed agreement and consent, will be deemed to have constructive notice of the wife's rights, as against her husband, to set aside the transaction on the basis of misrepresentation or undue influence.

11.9.5 Relationships covered

Turning to the broader application of these principles, Lord Browne-Wilkinson saw no reason to confine them to wives. The special position of wives is not based on that status as such, but because of the emotional and sexual ties that arise from the marriage relationship. Such ties exist between all cohabitees, both heterosexual and homosexual, whether married or not. Moreover, the principles will also apply to any situation where the creditor is aware that the surety places trust and confidence in the debtor (as in *Avon Finance Co Ltd v Bridger* (1985) – son and elderly parents). The difference here is that whereas with cohabitees the risk of undue influence or misrepresentation can be inferred, as indicated above, from the combination of the relationship and the nature of the transaction, as regards other relationships it would need to be shown that the creditor had actual knowledge of the surety's reliance on, and trust in, the debtor.

11.9.6 Application of doctrine of notice

Summarising the position in the context of cohabitees, where one cohabitee has entered into an obligation to stand surety for the other, and the creditor is aware that they are cohabitees, Lord Browne-Wilkinson outlined the factors which will lead to the obligation being unenforceable, as follows:

• there must be undue influence, misrepresentation, or some other legal wrong by the principal debtor;

- the creditor will have constructive notice of such a wrong, and the surety's right to set aside the transaction, unless the creditor has taken reasonable steps to be satisfied that the surety entered into the obligation freely and in knowledge of the true facts;

- the creditor will normally be regarded as taking such steps by (a) warning the surety (not in the presence of the principal debtor) of the amount of the potential liability, and the risks involved; and (b) advising the surety to take independent legal advice.

Applying these guidelines to the facts of the case, Lord Browne-Wilkinson concluded that Mrs O'Brien, having been misled by her husband, and not having received proper advice from the bank, was entitled to set aside the legal charge on the matrimonial home.

11.9.7 Application of the doctrine of notice to actual undue influence

Barclays Bank v O'Brien (1993) was, as we have seen, dealt with not as a case of undue influence, but of misrepresentation. On the same day as it gave its opinion on this case, the House of Lords also ruled on another husband and wife case, which was agreed to have involved actual undue influence (*CIBC Mortgages plc v Pitt* (1993)). Mrs Pitt sought to set aside a mortgage over the matrimonial home granted by the plaintiffs, on the basis that she had been induced to agree to it by the undue influence of her husband. She was unaware of the amount of the mortgage (which was £150,000), though she was aware that her husband was borrowing money to finance share dealings. The trial judge found that Mr Pitt had not been acting as the creditor's agent, but that he had exercised actual undue influence over Mrs Pitt in persuading her to sign the mortgage. Moreover, the judge ruled that the mortgage agreement was to Mrs Pitt's manifest disadvantage. Nevertheless, he rejected Mrs Pitt's claim, because he held that the 'special equity' applying to wives only operated where the wife was standing surety, and not to a situation where there was a joint advance to both husband and wife by way of a loan. The Court of Appeal rejected Mrs Pitt's appeal, on the basis that the transaction was not to her manifest disadvantage. Mrs Pitt appealed to the House of Lords.

Lord Browne-Wilkinson again gave the leading speech. He, of course, applied the same approach as had been taken in *Barclays Bank v O'Brien* in relation to the effect of Mr Pitt's behaviour on the contractual relationship between Mrs Pitt and the creditor, that is, an approach based on notice. Before considering this, however, Lord Browne-Wilkinson ruled that the requirement of 'manifest disadvantage' did not apply to cases of actual undue influence. Mrs Pitt would, therefore, have been able to set aside the transaction as against Mr Pitt. As far as the creditor was concerned, however, it had no direct knowledge of the influence Mr Pitt had exercised. Should it be regarded as having constructive notice? The House of Lords thought not. To the creditor, it appeared to be a straightforward mortgage transaction:

There was nothing to indicate to the [creditor] that this was anything other than normal advance to a husband and wife for their joint benefit.

The situation of a joint advance could be distinguished from one involving a surety, because in the latter case:

> ... there is not only the possibility of undue influence having been exercised but there is also the increased risk of it having in fact been exercised because, at least on its face, the guarantee by a wife of her husband's debts is not for her financial benefit. It is the combination of these two factors that puts the creditor on inquiry.

11.9.8 Relevance of 'manifest disadvantage'

We see then, that the emphasis in these cases is now on actual, or constructive, notice. Note, however, that the concept of 'manifest disadvantage', which is central to cases of presumed undue influence, still has a minor role to play in cases of actual undue influence. It will not be relevant in two party situations, so that the party exercising the influence cannot claim to be able to enforce the agreement simply because it is not disadvantageous. Nor will it be relevant in the three-party situation, if the creditor has actual knowledge of the undue influence. If, however, in such a situation, the creditor does not have actual knowledge, then the fact that the transaction is, or is not, to the other party's disadvantage, will be relevant in deciding whether or not the creditor should be regarded as having constructive notice of the influence.

11.9.9 Consequences for creditors

The House of Lords' decision in *Barclays Bank v O'Brien* (1993) places a burden on creditors to ensure that they do give proper advice to a surety in any situation where there is a risk of undue influence. In terms of contractual principle, the case opens another fairly broad exception to the doctrine of privity, in that the actions of a third party are allowed to affect the relationship between creditor and surety. It should be noted, however, that if the bank's own procedures had been followed by its employees in this case, the requirements laid down by the House of Lords would have been fulfilled. It does not seem, then, that the House of Lords' approach will place unreasonable burdens on creditors, particularly those large organisations which will have standard procedures for dealing with such situations. The safest approach will be to ensure that any private individual standing as surety is advised along the lines suggested by the House of Lords.

Cases subsequent to *Barclays Bank v O'Brien* (1993), however, indicate that the courts may be prepared to accept something less than this. The whole area has been reviewed and summarised by the Court of Appeal in *Royal Bank of Scotland v Etridge (No 2)* (1998), which is discussed below at 11.9.10. First, however, some of the intervening cases will be noted, to indicate how the legal principles have developed.

In both *Massey v Midland Bank plc* (1995) and *Banco Exterior Internacional v Mann* (1995), the Court of Appeal took the view that a creditor who reasonably believed that a wife had been advised by a solicitor was protected against any impropriety on the part of her husband as regards undue influence or misrepresentation. Although the creditor might be put on notice by the relationship between the parties, and the nature of the transaction, it was entitled to assume that a solicitor would fulfil properly the professional duty to advise the wife properly. Furthermore, in *Halifax Mortgage Services Ltd v Stepsky* (1996), it was held that where the same solicitor acted for both the creditor and the debtor in relation to the mortgage of a house, the creditor could not be taken to have notice of the fact that the debtor had falsely stated the purpose for which the loan would be used, even though the solicitor was aware of this. At first instance, this was said to follow from the solicitor's general duty of client confidentiality: in the Court of Appeal the decision was based on the more specific provision contained in s 199(1) of the Law of Property Act 1925.

Two subsequent Court of Appeal decisions in this area, however, both decided in the summer of 1996, demonstrated two contrasting approaches to the obligation of the creditor in relation to third party impropriety. The first case, *Credit Lyonnais Bank Nederland NV v Burch* (1997), heard in June 1996 involved a relationship of presumed undue influence between an employer, the owner of a business, and a junior employee. The employee put up her own house (valued at £100,000) as collateral for the business's bank overdraft facility of £270,000. The bank's solicitors wrote to her on several occasions and told her that she should take separate legal advice before entering into the transaction, emphasising that the document she was being asked to sign was unlimited as regards amount and time. The employee wrote a letter (though this may well have been under the employer's direction) to the solicitors acknowledging their letters, and the contents of them, and confirming that she was aware of the implications of the transaction. When the business failed, and the bank tried to enforce the agreement against the employee, she pleaded undue influence. It was held by the Court of Appeal that the bank was precluded from enforcing the agreement. It was not enough in the circumstances for the bank, *via* its solicitors, to have stated that the employee's commitment was unlimited, and to have encouraged her to take legal advice. The transaction was so disadvantageous to the employee, that the bank should not have proceeded until the employee had had explained to her the full extent of the business's borrowings, and its overdraft limit. Nor should it have done so until the employee had actually received independent legal advice. The court was quite clear that this agreement was unconscionable, and could not be allowed to stand.

The second case, heard by a different Court of Appeal in July 1996, was less protective of the person unduly influenced. In *Banco Exterior Internacional SA v*

Thomas (1997), a woman, D, who was in difficult financial circumstances, was a close personal friend of M, who ran a second hand car business. M persuaded D to use her house as security for the debts of his business vis à vis the plaintiff bank, up to a value of £75,000. In exchange, he apparently agreed to pay D a regular income. D was, in effect, putting her capital at risk, in exchange for this income. The bank did not know of this aspect of the arrangement. It told D that she should take independent legal advice, and she consulted a solicitor nominated by the bank. In order to complete the arrangements concerning the charge over her house, the deeds needed to be received by the bank. These were held by a solicitor who had acted for D in the past. When D sought the deeds, and explained the arrangement she was entering into with M, this solicitor strongly advised her against it. He also telephoned the bank, told them of the advice that he had given D, and suggested that they should not continue with the arrangement. When M's business failed, the bank sought to enforce the charge against D's property. D died before the action came to trial, and it was continued against her executors. The trial judge held that D had been unduly influenced by M. He found against the bank on the basis that it was put on notice of this undue influence by the solicitor's phone call. He therefore held that the guarantee could not be enforced in relation to M's liabilities incurred after that date. The Court of Appeal disagreed. It was not sure, in the first place, whether any presumption of undue influence arose. Even if it did, all the bank needed to do to rebut it was to ensure that D received independent legal advice. This it had done. It was not obliged to make further inquiries into the affairs of D and M. To do so would have been an 'unwarrantable impertinence'. Nor did the phone call from D's solicitor put the bank on notice. It merely showed that D had been advised against the transaction, but, despite that advice, had decided to proceed. She was entitled to reject the solicitor's advice, and it was not for the bank to refuse to allow her to enter into the arrangement. The bank was therefore entitled to enforce the charge.

The reason for the difference in approach between this case and *Burch's* case seems to lie in two factors. One is that, in *Thomas*, there was little, if any, inequality in the relationship between the parties, whereas in *Burch* the parties were employer/employee. Secondly, the agreement in *Burch* was viewed as much more unequivocally disadvantageous to the guarantor. The general trend of cases in this area is better represented, however, by *Thomas* in that there has tended to be a reluctance to extend the effect of *O'Brien* in any way which might be seen as imposing unreasonable burdens on banks and other creditors. Provided that they take reasonable steps to insure that independent advice has been sought, then the courts will be reluctant to intervene.

A final issue was left unresolved in *Thomas*. There was in that case no legal transaction to which M, the alleged influencer, was a party. He was not a party to the guarantee, nor did he sign the charge. Sir Richard Scott VC thought that this should make no difference to the application of the principles in this area. Roch LJ, however, preferred to reserve the question for later decision, and

Potter LJ expressed no view. As Sir Richard Scott pointed out, however, provided that the creditor has actual or constructive notice of misrepresentation or undue influence, there seems little justification for making a difference in outcome dependent on whether or not the debtor happens to be a party to the transaction between the surety and the creditor.

11.9.10 Legal advice: *Royal Bank of Scotland v Etridge (No 2)* (1998)

In *Royal Bank of Scotland v Etridge (No 2)* (1998), the Court of Appeal reviewed the case law which has followed *Barclays Bank v O'Brien*, and summarised the principles which have been developed. One particular area which it focussed on was the issue of the extent to which the fact that the person providing the security (commonly the wife) has received legal advice will protect the bank. It noted that transactions using a matrimonial home as security for business loans are so commonplace and the 'efficient funding of small businesses so dependent on [their] validity' that there was a need for a set of principles which do not depend on fine distinctions, for example, as to the instructions given to solicitors. It found that the following principles had been established by the case law (they are stated by the Court in terms of the wife being the provider of security, but they are clearly capable of more general application):

(1) Where the wife deals with the bank through a solicitor, whether acting for her alone or for her and her husband, the bank is not ordinarily put on inquiry. The bank is entitled to assume that the solicitor has given proper professional advice to the wife, and taken account of any potential conflicts of interest.

(2) Where the wife does not approach the bank through a solicitor, it is normally sufficient for the bank to urge her to take independent legal advice.

(3) When giving advice to the wife the solicitor is acting exclusively as her solicitor. Whoever introduces the solicitor to the wife, the bank is entitled to expect the solicitor to regard himself as owing a duty to the wife alone when giving her advice. If instructed by the bank to advise the wife, the solicitor still acts as her solicitor and not the bank's solicitor when he interviews her.

(4) It follows from (3) above that the bank is not fixed with imputed notice of what the solicitor learns in the course of advising the wife (even if he is also the bank's solicitor).

(5) The bank is entitled to rely on the fact that the solicitor undertook the task of advising the wife as showing that he considered himself to be sufficiently independent for that purpose (even if the bank knows that that he is also the husband's solicitor).

(6) The bank is not concerned to question the sufficiency of the advice given, and is not put on inquiry by the fact that the solicitor was asked only to explain the transaction and ensure that the wife understood it and not to see that she was sufficiently independent of here husband. Nor is the bank put on inquiry by the fact that the confirmation provided by the solicitor is similarly limited.

As will be seen, these principles provide a fair degree of protection for the bank, as long as the wife has actually received legal advice. The court, as indicated by the comments noted above, was also clearly keen not to put unnecessary barriers in the way of, and thereby discourage, the provision of funding which enables many small businesses to survive, to the benefit of both husband and wife. It is perhaps significant that, in relation to all six cases which it was considering, it was decided in favour of the lender, and against the provider of the security.

Of course, if inadequate legal advice has been given, while the application of the above principles may not preclude the bank from enforcing its security, the solicitor may be in breach of the duty of care owed to the provider of the security, who may therefore be able to take action against the solicitor. The Court of Appeal in *Etridge* emphasised the fact that the solicitor must take care to ensure that the person concerned fully understands the extent of the liability involved, and should be prepared to negotiate on his or her behalf with the bank. If the transaction is one which no competent solicitor could advise a person to enter (as may well have been the case in *Credit Lyonnais Bank Nederland v Burch*), then the solicitor must make this clear. Indeed, in such a situation, it will be much more difficult for a bank to avoid being fixed with constructive notice, despite the operation of the principles outlined above.

11.10 Remedies for undue influence

The primary remedy for undue influence in cases such as those discussed in the previous section is the refusal of the courts to enforce the agreement against the person influenced. In other words, that person will often be in the position of defendant, and will use the alleged influence to escape from obligations.

In some cases, however, rescission may be sought (as in *Allcard v Skinner* (1887) (see 11.7 above)), and the usual limitations on this equitable remedy (such as lapse of time, involvement of third party rights, and impossibility of restitution) will apply.

Where rescission is ordered, the whole transaction will be set aside. In *TSB Bank plc v Camfield* (1995), the creditor tried to argue that, even if it had constructive notice of the debtor's misrepresentation of the extent of the transaction to his wife, the wife had been prepared to undertake some risk. In this case, she had been willing to go ahead with a transaction which put the matrimonial home at risk to the extent of £15,000, whereas in fact liability was unlimited. The bank argued that she should still be liable for £15,000. The Court of Appeal rejected this. The test was, what would the wife have done, had she known the truth? The answer was clearly that she would not have entered into the transaction at all. Therefore, the right result was for the whole transaction to be rescinded.

A slightly different situation arose in *Dunbar Bank plc v Nadeem* (1998). Here, the wife had not previously had any legal interest in the matrimonial home, which was held by her husband on a long lease. As part of a loan transaction, using the home as security, however, she acquired a beneficial interest in half of the property. When the husband defaulted on the loan repayments, the bank sought to enforce its charge over the property. The wife claimed undue influence. The trial judge held in her favour, but also ruled that simply setting aside the charge would leave her unjustly enriched, as she would have acquired an interest in the property without having to contribute to the purchase. He therefore made the rescission of the charge conditional on her repaying to the bank one half of the loan plus interest. The Court of Appeal held that this was not the correct approach. In fact, the Court of Appeal decided that the transaction should not be set aside at all, because it was not manifestly disadvantageous to the wife, and the husband had not taken any unfair advantage of her. But, if there had been undue influence, it suggested (though of course this was *obiter*) that the correct approach would have been for the wife give up her interest in the property (which would then have reverted to her husband). She would be released from any personal liability on the loans made to her husband, but would not have acquired any unfair benefit. Of course, this would mean that she would still not have been able to resist the bank's claim for possession of the property, which was her main objective.

11.10.1 Change in value of property

Where restitution is ordered, however, but the value of property has changed, it may be difficult to find the just result as to who should get what. This problem arose in *Cheese v Thomas* (1994). C, the plaintiff, and his great-nephew, T, the defendant, had bought a house for £83,000, C contributing £43,000, and T providing £40,000, by means of a mortgage for that amount. The house was in T's name, and C accepted that it would belong to T exclusively after C's death, but, in the meantime, it was agreed that C was to be entitled to have sole use of the house for the rest of his life. C became worried that T was not keeping up the mortgage repayments, and sought to withdraw from the arrangement. The trial judge ruled that the agreement could be set aside for undue influence. The issue before the Court of Appeal was the amount of money that C should receive, since the house had been sold for £55,400, that is, a loss of over £27,500. Should he recover his full £43,000, or only, as the judge held, the appropriate proportion of the selling price? The Court of Appeal upheld the judge's view.

The basic principle in applying a restitutionary remedy was that the parties were to be restored as closely as possible to the position they were in before the transaction was entered into. In general, if a plaintiff was able to return to the defendant property which had been transferred under the transaction, it did not matter that the property had meanwhile fallen in value. This case was different, however. The plaintiff had paid the defendant £43,000 not outright, but as part of a purchase price of a house in which both would have rights. Each had contributed a sum of money to buying a house in which each was to have an interest. In that situation, the appropriate course was for the loss on the value of the house to be shared. This was even more so where, as the judge had held, the personal conduct of the defendant was not open to criticism, in that he had acted as an 'innocent fiduciary', rather than in any morally reprehensible way.

This case was clearly a difficult one in which to do justice between the parties. It is not entirely convincing, however, on the need to depart from the basic principle of full restitution of cash paid for property, which would be the normal rule. It is not clear why the fact that the parties both had a continuing interest in the property should make such a difference. If the property had increased in value, would the plaintiff have been entitled to a share in that profit? The logical answer must be 'yes'.

11.11 Unconscionability

Does the approach of the courts to the issues of duress and undue influence simply reflect a general reluctance to enforce transactions which are so unfair as to be regarded as 'unconscionable'? Is this the underlying principle in these cases?

In *Lloyd's Bank Ltd v Bundy* (1974), Lord Denning based his decision in favour of Mr Bundy on a broader principle than that adopted by the other members of the Court of Appeal. He identified this as 'inequality of bargaining power'. By virtue of this, he claimed:

> English law gives relief to one who, without independent advice, enters into a contract on terms which are very unfair or transfers property for a consideration which is grossly inadequate, when his bargaining power is grievously impaired by his own needs or desires, or by his own ignorance or infirmity, coupled with undue influences or pressure brought to bear on him by or for the benefit of the other.

As will be seen, this puts the emphasis on the nature of the transaction, and its substantive fairness, and probably comes as close as any English judge has done to recognising a general principle of 'unconscionability'. Lord Denning's approach has not been followed, however, and indeed was specifically disapproved by Lord Scarman in *National Westminster Bank v Morgan* (1985), who felt that the fact that Parliament had intervened to deal with many situations of unequal bargaining power (for example, by the Consumer Credit

Act 1974 and the Supply of Goods and Services Act 1982) meant that the courts should be reluctant to assume the burden of formulating further restrictions. The closest that the courts have come in the plethora of cases which have followed *Barclays Bank v O'Brien* to recognising 'unconscionability' as a ground for intervention is in *Credit Lyonnais v Burch* (1997) (see 11.9.9 above). Though this case and, in particular, the judgment of Millett LJ can be seen as giving some support to an approach similar to that taken by Lord Denning in *Lloyd's Bank v Bundy*, the case can also be fitted within the orthodox general principles applying in this area, and it has not led to any significant change of direction in later cases.

The English law relating to both duress and undue influence is still, therefore, primarily concerned with procedural rather than substantive fairness. Unconscionability would require it to focus more directly on the nature of the contract itself, rather than the events which led to it being formed. As we have seen, the requirement of 'manifest disadvantage' does have a role to play in cases of presumed undue influence, but it is subsidiary to the issue of whether there was influence in the first place. If there was no such influence, it does not matter how disadvantageous the contract is, the courts will still allow it to stand.

DURESS AND UNDUE INFLUENCE

Duress by physical threats or coercion

A contract which results from threats of physical violence (*Barton v Armstrong* (1975)), or the commission of any crime or tort against a person, will be voidable.

Economic duress

The concept of economic duress involves 'improper' commercial pressure. First recognised in *The Siboen and The Sibotre* (1976), and *North Ocean Shipping Company v Hyundai Construction* (1979). Applied in *Universe Tankships Inc v International Transport Workers Federation* (1983).

'Impropriety' normally requires the threat of an unlawful act, in the form of a tort, or breach of contract. Further tests are set out by Lord Scarman in *Pao On v Lau Yiu Long* (1980), viz was there a protest at the time? Was there an alternative course of action? Was the person independently advised? Did the person seek to avoid the contract?

'No alternative to compliance' is one of Lord Scarman's tests – it means that the person must have 'no practical choice but to submit to the duress'. See, for example, *Atlas Express v Kafco* (1989), where non-compliance would have led to the collapse of the defendant's business. *CTN Cash and Carry v Gallaher* (1994) suggests that, in some cases, a *lawful* act may constitute duress.

Remedies for duress

Where duress is not being used as a defence to a claim for damages or specific performance, the remedy sought will be rescission. This is subject to the usual restrictions of lapse of time, impossibility of restitution, or the intervention of third party rights.

Undue influence

Undue influence is an equitable concept, which divides into actual and presumed undue influence. The presumption may arise from a standard, or a particular, relationship.

Actual undue influence

The plaintiff must prove that a particular transaction was affected by undue influence. An example is *BCCI v Aboody* (1989) – a husband intimidating his much younger wife.

Presumed undue influence: recognised relationships

The burden of proof will be on the defendant to disprove the influence. Relationships covered include parent/child, doctor/patient, solicitor/client, religious adviser/disciple, but not husband/wife (*Midland Bank plc v Shephard* (1988)). Examples include *Allcard v Skinner* (1887).

Recovery requires that the transaction is to the 'manifest disadvantage' of the person influenced (*National Westminster Bank plc v Morgan* (1985)).

Presumed undue influence: other relationships

Once it is shown that a person is in a 'dominant' position, *any* disadvantageous transaction will be presumed to have been affected by undue influence. This has been applied between bank manager and client (*Lloyd's Bank Ltd v Bundy* (1975)), neighbouring farmers (*Goldsworthy v Brickell* (1987)), and may also arise between husband and wife (*Barclays Bank plc v O'Brien* (1993) – though no such influence existed in that case).

The presumption will not arise unless the agreement is manifestly disadvantageous. Thus a short-term loan taken out to rescue the husband's business is not manifestly disadvantageous to the wife, even if it uses the matrimonial home as security (*National Westminster Bank plc v Morgan* (1985)).

Undue influence and third parties

Undue influence in the case of third parties should generally be dealt with by the doctrine of notice (*Barclays Bank plc v O'Brien* (1993)). If a surety has been affected by undue influence (or misrepresentation) by a third party (for example, her husband), the creditor will only be affected if he or she had actual or constructive notice.

Constructive notice will arise from knowledge of the relationship between the parties (for example, cohabitees), and the nature of the transaction (is it disadvantageous?).

The creditor will be protected by advising the surety of the risks involved, and the need to take independent advice. The creditor is entitled to assume that a solicitor will give proper advice (*Royal Bank of Scotland v Etridge (No 2)* (1998).

The same principle of notice applies to actual undue influence by a third party (*CIBC Mortgages plc v Pitt* (1993)).

Remedies for undue influence

The primary remedy for undue influence is the refusal to enforce.

Rescission may sometimes be sought, subject to the usual limitations (time, third parties, impossibility of restitution). Note the sharing of losses in *Cheese v Thomas* (1993).

Unconscionability

Note Lord Denning's attempt in *Lloyd's Bank Ltd v Bundy* (1974) to identify an underlying 'unconscionability' principle based on inequality of bargaining power, which has been rejected by the House of Lords (*National Westminster Bank v Morgan* (1985)).

Currently, the English approach concentrates more on procedural rather than substantive fairness, and therefore does not amount to a restriction on 'unconscionable' transactions as such.

CHAPTER 12

ILLEGALITY

12.1 Introduction

This chapter, like the previous one, is concerned with situations where the courts will intervene to prevent the enforcement of an agreement which on its face has all the characteristics of a binding contract. The general heading is that of 'illegality', but it is important to note that this extends far beyond agreements that involve a criminal element. An important area, for example, is agreements which involve an unacceptable restraint on trade (see 12.9 below) such as a restriction on where a person may work. The linking factor between this type of contract, and an agreement to commit a crime, is that both are considered contrary to 'public policy'. This concept permeates the whole area under discussion in this chapter, though at times it is a concept the boundaries of which it is difficult to define.

We start by looking at contracts which involve the commission of a legal wrong.

12.2 Contracts having a criminal element

There are two aspects to contracts which have a criminal element, namely:

*   contracts which constitute a criminal offence;

*   contracts which are *performed* in a way which contravenes a statute.

12.2.1 Contracts which constitute a criminal offence

In some circumstances, the making of the contract itself will be a criminal act. The most obvious example is an agreement to commit a crime, such as murder, or theft. If A asks B to kill C for a payment of £5,000, and B agrees, then their agreement has all the characteristics of a binding contract, in the form of offer, acceptance and consideration. It also amounts to the criminal offence of conspiracy to murder (under the Criminal Law Act 1977), and so will be unenforceable. Any agreement to commit any crime will be treated in the same way.

Certain contracts are made illegal by statute. Under the Obscene Publications Act 1959, for example, it is illegal to sell an 'obscene article'. Here (unlike conspiracy), the offence is only committed by one party, that is, the seller, but nevertheless the contract is illegal and will be unenforceable by either party.

12.2.2 Performance is contrary to statute

Performance which contravenes a statute involves contracts which are *prima facie* legal, and which are concerned with the achievement of an objective which is legal, but which contravene a statute by the way in which they are performed. In *Re Mahmoud and Ispahani* (1921), for example, the contract was to sell linseed oil. It was a statutory requirement that both seller and buyer should be licensed. The seller was licensed, but the buyer was not. It was held that the contract was unenforceable for illegality. In *Hughes v Asset Managers plc* (1995), however, the Court of Appeal upheld share transactions which had been conducted by unlicensed agents. Although the Prevention of Fraud (Investments) Act 1958 imposed sanctions on those who engaged in such trading without a licence, it did not expressly, or by implication, prohibit the making of the contracts themselves. The policy of the Act could be achieved simply by penalising those who traded without a licence.

The principles which should govern this area were considered by Devlin J in *St John Shipping Corpn v Joseph Rank* (1957), which concerned a shipping contract where performance had involved overloading the ship, contrary to the Merchant Shipping Regulations. He said it was necessary to ask:

- does the statute prohibit contracts *as such*, or only penalise certain behaviour?;

- if the answer to the first question is that it prohibits contracts, does this contract belong to the class which the statute is intended to prohibit?

In answering the first question, he suggested that it was helpful, though not conclusive, to ask whether the object of the statute was to protect the public. If so, then the contract was likely to be illegal. If on the other hand, the purpose was to protect the revenue (as, for example, in a requirement that those who sell television sets pass the names of the purchasers to the Post Office), then it would be likely to be legal. This test is difficult to apply, as was shown by the case itself, where despite the fact that the Merchant Shipping Regulations are clearly not designed simply to protect the revenue, the contract was held to be enforceable. It seems to have carried some weight with the Court of Appeal, however, in its decision in *Skilton v Sullivan* (1994). In this case, the plaintiff entered into a contract with the defendant for the sale of koi carp. The defendant paid a deposit. Subsequently, the plaintiff issued an invoice, which described the fish as 'trout'. The defendant alleged that the plaintiff was trying to avoid paying VAT, since trout were zero-rated and koi carp were not. Thus, he argued, the contract was illegal and could not be enforced against him. The Court of Appeal considered that the plaintiff's purpose was probably to defer the payment of VAT, rather than to avoid it altogether: nevertheless, this was still an illegal purpose. The court also considered, however, that the plaintiff had formed this dishonest intention after the contract had been entered into. It was therefore not necessary for the plaintiff to rely on his unlawful act in order to establish the defendant's liability. This was the main basis for the decision, but the court also relied on the principle that illegality which has the object of protecting the revenue is less likely to render a contract unenforceable than where the object is the protection of the public.

12.2.3 Relevance of knowledge

In *Archbolds v Spanglett* (1961), it was suggested that the knowledge of the parties might be important, so that if both parties know that the contract can only be performed in a way that will involve the breach of the statute, then it will be illegal. The case concerned a contract for the carriage of goods. The defendants agreed to transport a quantity of whisky from London to Leeds for the plaintiffs. The plaintiffs were unaware that the defendants held a licence which only entitled them to carry their own goods. Pearce LJ, holding on the facts that the plaintiffs could, nevertheless enforce the contract, stated that:

> ... if both parties know that though *ex facie* legal [a contract] can only be performed by illegality, or is intended to be performed illegally, the law will not help the plaintiffs in any way that is a direct or indirect enforcement of rights under the contract ...

This presumably means that if both parties are aware that a time limit stated as part of a contract of carriage can only be met by a vehicle exceeding the speed limit, the contract will be illegal and unenforceable. This test is not conclusive either, however, as is shown by *Ailion v Spiekermann* (1976). The contract was for the assignment of a lease, for which a premium was to be paid. This was illegal under the Rent Act 1968, and both parties were aware of this. Nevertheless, the court ordered specific performance of the contract of assignment (though without the illegal premium).

In *Anderson Ltd v Daniel* (1924), both the issue of the protection of the public, and the knowledge of the parties were considered relevant. The contract was for the sale of artificial manure, made up of sweepings of various fertilisers from the holds of ships. Regulations required that the seller should specify the contents of the fertiliser, and the proportions of each chemical it contained. This was impractical as far as sweepings were concerned. The Court of Appeal held the contract for sale unenforceable by the seller, because the statute was intended to protect purchasers. As Scrutton LJ put it:

> When the policy of the Act in question is to protect the general public or a class of persons by requiring that a contract shall be accompanied by certain formalities or conditions, the contract and its performance without these formalities or conditions is illegal, and cannot be sued upon by the person liable to the penalties.

This seems to suggest that the answer might have been different if the purchaser had sued, rather than the seller.

To sum up, the overriding questions are:

- does the statute prohibit contracts? In deciding this, it may be helpful to consider if it is intended to protect the public, or a class of the public;

- is this particular contract illegal? Here, it may be relevant to look at the knowledge of the parties, and the guilt or innocence of the party suing.

The second issue inevitably overlaps with the more general issue of the enforceability of illegal contracts, which is considered further below, at 12.14–12.15.

12.3   Contract to commit a tort

A contract to commit an intentional tort, such as assault or fraud, will be illegal in the same way as a contract to commit a crime. On the other hand, a contract which involves the unintentional commission of a tort will not generally be illegal. If, for example, there is a contract for the sale of property which belongs to a third party, but which both the buyer and seller believes to belong to the seller, this will involve the tort of conversion, but the contract itself will not be illegal.

12.4   Contract to indemnify

The parties may wish to make a type of insurance contract, whereby if one of them commits a crime or tort, the other will pay the amount of any fine or damages imposed, or otherwise provide compensation. Is such an agreement enforceable?

12.4.1 Criminal liability

It will generally be illegal to attempt to insure against criminal liability. There appears to be an exception, however, as regards strict liability offences (that is, where the prosecution does not need to prove any 'guilty mind' on the part of the defendant in order to obtain a conviction). Provided the court is satisfied that the defendant is morally innocent, then it seems the contract will be upheld. In *Osman v J Ralph Moss Ltd* (1970), the plaintiff was suing his insurance brokers who had negligently failed to keep him informed that his car insurance was no longer valid (because of the collapse of the insurance company). As a result, the plaintiff had been fined £25 for driving without insurance (an offence of strict, or absolute, liability). The Court of Appeal held that he could recover the amount of the fine from the defendants. Sachs LJ stated that:

> Where the person fined was under an absolute liability, it appears that such fine can be recovered in circumstances such as the present as damages unless it is

shown that there was on the part of the person fined a degree of *mens rea* or of culpable negligence in the matter which resulted in the fine.

The burden of proof was on the defendants to prove circumstances which rendered the fine irrecoverable.

12.4.2 Civil liability

A contract to indemnify will be illegal as regards torts which are committed deliberately, such as deceit, or an intentional libel (*WH Smith & Sons v Clinton* (1909)). It is regarded as perfectly acceptable, however, to have such an arrangement as regards the tort of negligence, or where a tort is committed innocently (such as an unintentional libel) (*Daily Mirror Newspapers Ltd v Exclusive News Agency* (1937)).

Where civil liability arises out of a crime, a contract which would provide compensation may be unenforceable. Thus, in *Gray v Barr* (1971), Barr who had been cleared of manslaughter by the criminal courts was sued in tort by the widow of his victim. He admitted liability, but claimed that he was covered by his Prudential 'Hearth and Home' insurance policy, which covered sums he became liable to pay as damages in respect of injury caused by accidents. The Court of Appeal held (in effect ignoring the verdict in the criminal court) that Barr's actions did amount to the criminal offence of manslaughter, and that he therefore could not recover under the insurance policy.

A similar refusal to allow reliance on an insurance contract was shown in *Geismar v Sun Alliance* (1978), where the plaintiff was seeking compensation for the loss of goods which had been brought into the country without the required import duty having been paid. There was nothing illegal about the insurance contract itself, which provided standard protection against loss by, *inter alia*, theft. The court held, however, that to allow the plaintiff to recover under the policy in relation to the smuggled goods, would be assisting him to derive a profit from a deliberate breach of the law. In arriving at this decision, it was relevant that the failure to pay import duty rendered the goods liable to forfeiture at any time by the customs and excise, and that the breach was deliberate. It was not suggested that the same approach would be taken in relation to unintentional importation or innocent possession of uncustomed goods.

Different considerations apparently apply, however, where the crime is one of strict liability, or in relation to 'motor manslaughter' (causing death by dangerous driving) (*Tinline v White Cross Insurance* (1921)). The rules in the motoring area are affected by the need to uphold the effectiveness of the system of compulsory insurance, so that the victims, and families of victims, of road accidents receive proper compensation. The exception in relation to motor manslaughter will not, however, apply if the offence was deliberate (*Gardner v Moore* (1984)).

12.5 Contracts contrary to public policy

The following sections concern contracts which are considered 'illegal', but not in the sense that they amount to, or are linked to, the commission of a crime or a tort. Rather, they have been held to be contrary to public policy, and for that reason void, and unenforceable. The categories of public policy appear to be closed, so that the courts will not apply this approach to a type of contract to which it has not been applied previously. This rule exists for reasons of certainty, and because public policy claims need to be kept within limits.

12.6 Contracts concerning marriage

The courts regard it as being in the interests of society to preserve the status of marriage. Certain types of contract which are regarded as threatening to the institution of marriage are therefore treated as illegal.

12.6.1 Future separation

A contract between spouses agreeing to separate at some point in the future is invalid if it is made either before the marriage or during cohabitation. In *Brodie v Brodie* (1917), Mr Brodie only agreed to marry the woman who was carrying his child if a written agreement to separate was drawn up. This, *inter alia*, precluded the woman from bringing legal proceedings against him. The agreement was held to be contrary to public policy, and so could not be enforced. The woman was free to take legal action.

This rule does not apply, of course, to an agreement which does not relate to the distant future, but is made in anticipation of immediate separation. Nor does it affect arrangements made by spouses who have been separated, and are then reconciled (*Harrison v Harrison* (1910)).

12.6.2 Restraint of marriage

A contract by someone which imposes liability on them if they marry is void. Thus, a promise by A that, if he marries, he will pay a sum of money to C is unenforceable (*Baker v White* (1690)). Similarly, a promise by A to make a payment if he marries anyone else other than B will also be unenforceable (*Lowe v Peers* (1768)).

12.6.3 Marriage brokage

Marriage brokage concerns a contract whereby A promises to procure a marriage for B. The rule is not limited to contracts to procure marriage with a particular person. Thus, in *Hermann v Charlesworth* (1905), Miss H entered into an agreement under which, if the defendant introduced her to someone whom she married, Miss H would pay the defendant £250. She paid a deposit which, after several unsuccessful introductions, she sought to recover. The Court of Appeal held that the contract was illegal, as being contrary to public policy. It is difficult to see, however, why such contracts are any more harmful than those between 'dating' or 'introduction' agencies and their clients, which have never been regarded as contrary to public policy. Such contracts do not, of course, depend on marriage between those introduced.

12.7 Contracts promoting sexual immorality

Contracts promoting sexual immorality will include any contracts for sex outside marriage, and would presumably cover otherwise lawful homosexual, as well as heterosexual activities. Such activities, while not constituting criminal offences, or civil wrongs, may still be regarded as immoral, and contracts which involve them will be treated as contrary to public policy.

The rule is not limited to contracts which directly concern sexual activity, as is shown by *Pearce v Brooks* (1866). Here, there was a contract under which the plaintiffs supplied the defendant with an ornamental brougham (a type of carriage), which was to be paid for by instalments. After one instalment had been paid, the brougham was returned in a damaged condition. The plaintiffs sued for £15 compensation which was payable under the agreement if the brougham was returned. The defendant, however, was a prostitute, and there was evidence that she intended to use the brougham to attract customers. Moreover, it seems that at least one partner in the plaintiffs' firm was aware of this. On this basis, the court held that this would be an illegal contract, so that the plaintiffs would be unable to recover either under the contract, or for the damage.

The knowledge of the plaintiffs was relevant here, but not every contract with a known prostitute will be illegal. In *Appleton v Campbell* (1826), the action was for the recovery of board and lodging in relation to a room rented from the plaintiff. The court held that the plaintiff could not recover if he knew that the defendant was a prostitute, *and* that she was using the room to entertain her clients. But:

> ... if the defendant had her lodgings there, and received her visitors elsewhere, the plaintiff may recover, although she be a woman of the town, because persons of that description must have a place to lay their heads.

There are thus two factors which are necessary for the contract to be unenforceable:

* knowledge that the other party is a prostitute; and

* knowledge that what was supplied under the contract is to be used for the purposes of prostitution.

The same approach will presumably apply to other 'immoral' contracts. The extent to which the other contracts are likely to be treated as 'immoral', however, must now be considered in the light of the recent decision in *Armhouse Lee Ltd v Chappell* (1996). In this case, the publishers of a magazine sought to recover payment for advertisements which had been placed by the defendants. The defendants resisted the claim on the basis that the content of the advertisements was illegal or immoral, since they related to telephone 'sex-lines', offering pre-recorded messages, live conversations, and sex dating. The trial judge found for the plaintiffs. On appeal, the Court of Appeal considered a range of ways in which the advertisements could be said to be illegal, including prostitution, obscenity, and conspiracy to corrupt public morals. All were rejected. In addition, the court refused to find that 'public policy' required the contracts to be treated as unenforceable. There was no evidence that any 'generally accepted moral code condemned these telephone sex lines'. Moreover, 'it was undesirable in such a case, involving an area regarded as the province of the criminal law, for individual judges exercising a civil jurisdiction to impose their own moral attitudes'. The decision of the trial judge was therefore upheld, and the contracts were enforceable by the plaintiffs. This case suggests that it is unlikely that there will be any significant extension of the range of contracts which will be struck down on the basis of sexual 'immorality'. In the light of the Court of Appeal's comments and decision, it would seem likely that illegality will only operate to prevent the enforcement of a contract where the behaviour concerned amounts to, or involves, a criminal offence.

12.8   Contracts to oust the jurisdiction of the court

The courts are very jealous of any attempt in a contract or other agreement to try to take away their powers to oversee the agreement, interpret it, and decide on its validity. They will hold any such agreement to be void as being contrary to public policy. For example, in *Baker v Jones* (1954), the rules of the British Amateur Weightlifters' Association provided that the association's central council was to be 'the sole interpreter of the rules', and that the council's decision was to be final. It was held that although it was perfectly in order to give a tribunal or council the power to make final decisions on questions of fact, the same could not be done as regards questions of law. These provisions in the rules were to that extent contrary to public policy, and void.

There are two exceptions to this general approach, which should be noted. First, in commercial matters the procedure whereby parties may submit a dispute for arbitration, on questions of both fact and law, has been approved by the courts (*Scott v Avery* (1855)), and legislation (the Arbitration Act 1996). Secondly, a clause in an agreement arrived at on the separation of husband and wife under which the wife, in return for a promise of maintenance, agrees not to apply to the courts, is void to the extent that the wife is still free to apply, but is enforceable as regards the husband's promise to pay (s 34 of the Matrimonial Causes Act 1973).

12.9 Contracts in restraint of trade: the general principles

Contracts 'in restraint of trade' are those which unfairly restrict competition, or unreasonably restrict people's ability to work. Such agreements are thought to be contrary to public policy, and therefore liable to be treated as unenforceable.

Two aspects of this topic are not discussed in any detail: first, the provisions of Art 81 of the Treaty of the European Communities which applies to restraints which have an affect on cross-border trade within the European Union; secondly, the legislative regime contained in the Competition Act 1998, which applies similar controls over anti-competitive trade or practices within the United Kingdom. Both of these areas are beyond the scope of this book, and are usually dealt with in courses on competition law, rather than contract law.

12.9.1 *Prima facie* void

Contractual provisions which attempt to restrict the ways in which one of the parties may do business, or earn a living, are *prima facie* void (*Nordenfelt v Maxim Nordenfelt* (1894)). This rule is now well established, though at times the common law has treated such provisions as *prima facie* valid. The current presumption of unenforceability can, however, be rebutted, as is outlined in the following sections.

12.10 Contracts relating to employment or the sale of a business

Examples of the kind of restraint we are dealing with would be a restriction on a sales representative from soliciting the customers of a former employer, or a restriction on the vendor of a business from setting up in competition to the purchaser. For such restraints to be valid, there are three requirements which must be fulfilled:

- there must be a valid interest to protect;

- the restraint must be no more extensive than is reasonable to protect that interest;

- the restraint must not be contrary to the public interest.

12.10.1 Must have a valid interest

Looking at the first of these requirements, an employer will have a legitimate interest in restricting the activities of a departing employee, where that employee has either acquired trade secrets, or has gained influence over the employer's customers, either because they rely on the employee's skill and judgment, or because they have dealt exclusively with that employee.

Examples from the cases include a hairdresser (*Marion White Ltd v Francis* (1972)), a sales representative (*T Lucas & Co v Mitchell* (1974)), and a tailor (*Attwood v Lamont* (1920)). Similarly, the purchaser of a business may well have paid a substantial amount for 'goodwill', that is, the existing trade which has been built up by the vendor. In that context, the purchaser has a legitimate interest in preventing the vendor from setting up a business which will attract all the old customers.

The courts have been prepared to recognise that the categories of interest are not closed. For example, in *Greig v Insole* (1978), which concerned restrictions placed on professional cricketers by the cricketing authorities, Slade J recognised that there might be a public interest that the game of cricket should be properly organised and administered. On the facts, however, the restraint was in any case unreasonable. In *Eastham v Newcastle United* (1964), however, Wilberforce J was unable to find a legitimate interest in relation to restrictions on freedom of transfer for professional footballers. It seems then that although in theory the categories of interest are open, the courts are likely to be very cautious in finding new interests.

12.10.2 Restraint must be reasonable

The reasonableness or otherwise of the restraint must be looked at in the context of the interest which is being protected. There are three main factors to consider:

- the geographical area covered;
- the length of time involved; and
- the scope of the activities covered.

For example, if a business is sold in one town, a restriction preventing the opening of a similar business anywhere in the country would be unlikely to be regarded as reasonable. In *Mason v Provident Clothing* (1913), a canvasser who had been employed to sell clothes in Islington, was restrained from entering into similar business within 25 miles of London. This was held to be too wide.

As regards time, this will again depend on the type of contract. In many employment cases, a restraint of one or two years at most will be all that is reasonable. In *Fitch v Dewes* (1921), however, a lifelong restraint on a solicitor's managing clerk was upheld. The justification was that the business was one to which clients were likely to return over a long period.

The type of activity restrained must also be related to the interest being protected. A clause restraining someone who had been employed as a chiropodist from working as a hairdresser would be unlikely to be regarded as reasonable.

At one time, the approach of the courts was to take clauses literally in assessing their reasonableness. Thus, if no area were specified, the restriction would be taken to be worldwide. The cases of *Littlewoods v Harris* (1978) and *Clarke v Newland* (1991), have suggested a different approach, requiring the restraint to be limited by the 'factual matrix' within which it was imposed. In *Littlewoods v Harris* (1978), an employee who had been employed solely in connection with the plaintiffs' mail-order business was made subject to a restraint which, on its face, covered all aspects of the plaintiffs' wide ranging business activities. The Court of Appeal, however, held that the relevant clause should be interpreted as being intended only to apply to the mail-order business in the UK. On that basis, it was reasonable. Similarly, in *Clarke v Newland* (1991), a broad agreement by a doctor 'not to practise' was held to mean 'practise as a general medical practitioner' (rather than, for example, in a hospital) since that was the role in which the defendant had previously been employed.

12.10.3 Public interest

There is some controversy as to whether the public interest part of the rules concerning enforceable restraints of trade does in fact exist. If it does, then it means that, even if a restraint satisfies the other conditions (that is, of legitimate interest, and reasonableness), it may still be struck down as being contrary to the public interest. This might be the case, for example, in relation to a restraint on the work of a leading artist, playwright, doctor or scientist, whose work might well be for the public benefit. The principle was stated in *Wyatt v Kreglinger and Fernau* (1933). The plaintiff's pension was made contingent upon his not taking any part in the wool trade. The Court of Appeal held that this stipulation was void, irrespective of whether it was reasonable as between the parties, because it was contrary to the public interest. This was followed in the similar case of *Bull v Pitney Bowes* (1967). It seems difficult, however, to find later authorities that have applied the principle, though Lord Denning supported it in relation to a solicitor in *Oswald Hickson Collier v Carter Ruck* (1984). In subsequent cases, such as *Deacons v Bridge* (1984) and *Kerr v Morris* (1986), the courts have refused to apply the principle to the circumstances before them, while not denying its existence.

12.10.4 Effect of breach of contract

As regards employment contracts, restraints will be unenforceable if the contract has been terminated following a repudiatory breach by the employer. This does not mean, however, that a restrictive contained in a contract which purports to make it enforceable after a repudiatory breach is therefore automatically unreasonable: *Rock Refrigeration Ltd v Jones* (1997). Thus, if the employee simply resigns, the restraint will be enforceable, provided it is otherwise reasonable according to the tests outlined above.

12.11 Contracts of exclusive dealing

It was confirmed by the House of Lords in *Esso Petroleum v Harpers Garage* (1968) that a contract in which one party agrees to take all supplies of a particular product from one source (sometimes known as a 'solus agreement'), could amount to an unreasonable restraint on trade. Such arrangements are particularly common in relation to the supply of petrol, and in relation to the supply of beer, etc, to public houses (see, for example, *Courage Ltd v Crehan* (1999)). 'Solus agreements' may well in some case fall foul of Art 81 of the EC Treaty, but they may also be ruled unlawful at common law. *Esso Petroleum and Harpers Garage* in fact concerned two solus agreements in relation to two garages run by the defendant. In respect of both, there was an agreement to take all supplies of petrol from Esso, and to keep the garage open at all reasonable hours. In relation to garage A, the agreement was to last for four years and five months. In relation to garage B, the agreement was to last for 21 years, and was linked to a mortgage over the premises held by Esso, which was also irredeemable for 21 years. The defendants started to sell cut price petrol of other brands. Esso sought an injunction to prevent them doing this. The defence was based on 'restraint of trade'.

The House of Lords held that contracts of this type could be regarded as being in restraint of trade. As with the categories looked at above, the question was then whether the restraint was reasonable as between the parties, and reasonable in the public interest. In relation to garage A, the five year restraint was reasonable. The 21 years in relation to garage B, however, was unreasonable, particularly as it was linked to a mortgage.

The *Esso* case gives no indication of what period greater than five years, but less than 21 years, might have been considered reasonable. In the later case of *Alec Lobb (Garages) Ltd v Total Oil (Great Britain) Ltd* (1985), however, a 21 year restraint was held to be reasonable because it was terminable after seven or 14 years.

In *Shell v Lostock Garage* (1977), the Court of Appeal had to address the issue of the point in time at which a restraint should be judged. A solus agreement requiring L to take supplies of petrol exclusively from S had originally been entered into in 1955, for a period of 20 years. In 1966, however, it had been varied to become in effect a permanent arrangement, but terminable by 12 months' notice. In 1975, at the time of an intense petrol price war, S began to supply petrol at heavily subsidised rates to garages in the same locality as L. L was not included in these arrangements, and was unable to compete without making heavy losses. It therefore sought to obtain supplies of petrol elsewhere. Part of its argument was that the restraint of trade had become unreasonable, by virtue of the S's discriminatory action in response to the price war. The majority of the Court of Appeal (Lord Denning dissenting) disagreed. They felt that the reasonableness of a restraint had to be judged at the time it was made, not in the light of later circumstances. Ormrod LJ though that any other approach would create considerable difficulties:

> It would introduce into the law an unprecedented discretion in the court to suspend for a time a term in a contract; the repercussions of this are quite unforeseeable and unmanageable. For example, it would at once alter the approach of the courts to covenants in restraint of trade generally, because, if the restraint could be temporarily suspended when it was operating oppressively, many more covenants would pass the normal test at the time they were entered into. Moreover, neither party will be able to know when a covenant is or is not enforceable, or if temporarily unenforceable, when it becomes enforceable again.

The agreement here, at least in the form which it had taken since 1966, was a reasonable one, and could not be struck down as being in restraint of trade. The conclusion is, therefore, that agreements have to be judged at the time they were made, and not in the context of subsequent developments.

12.11.1 Restraints on songwriters, and other entertainers

A particular area of difficulty has arisen in relation to contracts entered into by songwriters, or pop musicians, with music publishers or recording companies. These often require the artists to commit themselves to the one company for a lengthy period of time, with no necessary obligation on the company to promote, or even publish, the artists' work. The validity of this kind of 'exclusive dealing' agreement was considered in *Schroeder Music Publishing Co Ltd v Macaulay* (1974). The plaintiff was a young and unknown songwriter who entered into a standard form agreement with music publishers (the defendants). The copyright in all the plaintiff's compositions for the next five years was assigned to the defendants, with an automatic extension for a further five years if royalties exceeded £5,000. The defendants could terminate the agreement on one month's notice, but there was no similar power for the plaintiff. The defendants were under no obligation to publish any of the plaintiff's work. The plaintiff sought a declaration that the agreement was in restraint of trade, and void. The House of Lords held that, where there was unequal bargaining power, a standard form agreement has to be looked at to see if, *inter alia*, the restrictions it contains only go so far as is reasonably necessary to protect legitimate interests. In this case, the contract was in unreasonable restraint of trade, because, whereas the plaintiff was totally committed to the defendants, the defendants were not obliged to publish anything.

This decision was applied in the similar case of *Clifford Davis v WEA Records* (1975). In *Panayiotou v Sony Music Entertainment (UK) Ltd* (1994), on the other hand, a recording contract which was probably in restraint of trade when entered in to had been renegotiated after the performer concerned (George Michael) had become famous. His subsequent attempt to challenge the renegotiated agreement failed, because, although it contained some unfavourable conditions, the performer had received full legal advice. Moreover, the renegotiated agreement was part of a settlement of the dispute of the original contract. In this context, public policy favoured giving effect to the settlement, and therefore the revised contract. In any case, the recording company had a legitimate interest to protect, in that they wished to sell as many records as possible, and the restrictions on the performer were not unreasonable as a means of protecting that interest.

12.12 Trade associations

A group of manufacturers or producers may make an agreement between themselves to protect their interests. Such agreements may fall foul of legislative provisions relating to competition under domestic or European law, but they are also subject to the control of the common law and may be struck down as being in restraint of trade. The relevant principles were considered in *English Hop Growers v Dering* (1928). The defendant, in common with other hop-growers, had agreed to deliver all crops produced by him to a central selling agency. The object of the agreement was to protect the producers at a time when it was feared that there might be a glut of hops on the market. The defendant sought to escape from the agreement on the basis that it was in restraint of trade. Adopting a similar approach to the other areas which we have considered, the majority of the Court of Appeal asked whether the restriction was reasonable to protect a legitimate interest. It was held that the restraint was not in this case an unreasonable one and the agreement was upheld. This perhaps reflects the fact that the agreement here had been reached between parties bargaining at arms length. If such an agreement affects third parties, the court will be more likely to intervene, as in *Kores v Kolok* (1959). This concerned an agreement between two companies that neither would, without the consent of the other, employ any person who had been employed by the other company within the past five years. The agreement was intended to protect trade secrets, since they were both working on similar products involving chemical processes. In addition, at the time it was thought that their factories would be adjacent, though this turned out not to be the case. One of the companies brought an action to restrain the other from employing a particular former employee. It seems clear that there was in this case a legitimate interest to protect, but the Court of Appeal held that the restraint was too wide. It had the potential to cover an unskilled labourer, as much as the chief chemist. On that basis, it was unreasonable.

Note that this type of agreement would now be regulated by the legislation on restrictive trade practices mentioned above at 12.9.

12.13 Effects of illegality: enforcement

If a contract is found to be void for illegality, then this will, in general, mean that specific performance will be refused. This is so, even if neither party has pleaded illegality: *Birkett v Acorn Business Machines* (1999). The reason is that, if there is no contract, the court cannot order it to be performed. They may, however, in some circumstances, be prepared to award damages. This may be done by allowing the action to be framed in tort, as for example in *Saunders v Edwards* (1987) where the plaintiff who had been party to an illegal overvaluation of furniture (for the purpose of avoiding stamp duty) in a contract for the sale of a flat was nevertheless allowed to sue for deceit on the basis of the defendant's fraudulent misrepresentation that the flat included a roof garden. The court took account of the 'relative moral culpability' of the two parties, and this question of the 'guilt' or 'innocence' has always been relevant. During the 1980s, it was transformed by a number of decisions (for example, *Thackwell v Barclays Bank* (1987); *Howard v Shirlstar Container Transport* (1990)) into a rather vague test of whether enforcement would offend the 'public conscience'. The House of Lords in *Tinsley v Milligan* (1993) rejected this, and reasserted a test based on whether the plaintiff needs to rely on the illegality to found the claim. In this case, T and M had both supplied the money for the purchase of a house. It was, however, put into the name of T alone, in order to facilitate the making by M of false claims to social security payments. When the parties fell out, M claimed a share of the property on the basis of a resulting trust. It was argued for T that M could not succeed because the original arrangement had been entered into in order to further an illegal purpose. The trial judge and Court of Appeal found for M. The House of Lords also held by a majority of three to two, that M should succeed. In doing so, the majority rejected the approach taken by the Court of Appeal that the issue should be decided by considering whether 'the public conscience would be affronted by recognising rights created by illegal transactions'. This was too 'imponderable'. The proper test to be applied was whether the plaintiff needed to rely on the illegality in order to support her claim. In this case, the presumption of a resulting trust was raised simply by the fact that M had contributed to the purchase price of the house. It was T who had to raise the illegality in order to try to rebut that presumption. Therefore, M should succeed. A similar approach was taken in *Inntrepreneur Pub Co (CPC) Ltd v Price* (1998) where it was held that the plaintiff could rely on a rent review clause in a lease, even though the lease itself might be illegal because it involved a 'solus agreement' relating to the supply of beer. (Cf the approach taken to the recovery of property in cases such as *Bowmakers v Barnet Instruments* (1945) (see 12.15.4 below).)

12.14 Effects of illegality: recovery of money or property

The general principle which applies in the area of recovery of money or property is expressed in the Latin maxim *in pari delicto potior est conditio defendentis*.

This maxim, which is generally referred to in the abbreviated form '*in pari delicto*', roughly translates as, 'where there is equal fault, the defendant is in the stronger position'.

Thus, where money or other property has been transferred under an illegal contract, which is regarded as void, the court will not in general assist the plaintiff to recover it.

12.14.1 General rule: no recovery

An example of the application of the rule of no recovery is to be found in the case of *Parkinson v College of Ambulance* (1925). Colonel Parkinson was approached by a third party who told him that if he made a contribution to the College (a charity), it would be able to obtain a knighthood for him. Parkinson made a contribution of £3,000, but no knighthood was forthcoming. He brought an action to recover his money. It was held that the contract was illegal, and that Parkinson could not sustain his action without disclosing this, and his own complicity. The donation was on its face a gift, and therefore irrecoverable. It could only be explained as being part of a contract by disclosing the consideration alleged to have been given for it, that is the promise of the knighthood. The plaintiff's action could only have any force as being for breach of this contract, but since the contract was illegal, the action had to fail.

12.15 Exceptions to the general rule

The courts have developed and recognised a number of exceptions to this rule, and there are therefore several situations where recovery of money or property will be allowed despite the illegality.

12.15.1 Illegal purpose not yet carried out

If the contract is still executory, the plaintiff should have the chance to have a change of mind or heart, resile from the contract, and recover property transferred. Thus, in *Taylor v Bowers* (1876), the plaintiff had made a fictitious assignment of his goods to A as part of a scheme to defraud his creditors. Meetings of the creditors had been held, but no composition agreement had been reached. A had in the meantime parted with the goods to the defendant (who knew of the fraudulent scheme). The Court of Appeal held that because no creditors had actually been defrauded, the illegal purpose had not been carried out, and the plaintiff could recover his goods from the defendant. This approach was applied by the Court of Appeal in *Tribe v Tribe* (1995), where shares had been transferred by father to son as a means of keeping assets out of the hands of landlords who were expected to be seeking substantial contributions towards repairs on property rented by the father. The transfer had been put in the form of a sale, but the son had never paid any money for the shares. In the event, no demands were made by the landlords, and the Court of Appeal, applying *Taylor v Bowers* and *Tinsley v Milligan* (1993) (see 12.13 above), allowed the father to recover the shares. He had withdrawn from the transaction before any part of the illegal purpose had been carried into effect, and was in those circumstances allowed to use the explanation of what had been planned as a basis for undoing the apparent sale of the shares to his son.

This exception will not operate, however, where there has been substantial performance of the contract, as in *Kearley v Thomson* (1890). The plaintiff had paid money to the defendants, a firm of solicitors, in return for their agreement not to appear at the public examination of a bankrupt friend of the plaintiff, nor to oppose the order for his discharge. After the first part of the agreement had been carried out, the plaintiff changed his mind and tried to recover his money. The Court of Appeal refused to allow him to do so, because there had been 'a partial carrying into effect of an illegal purpose in a substantial manner'.

Note, also, that the withdrawal must be genuine. If the purpose of the contract is simply frustrated by the refusal of the other party to play his or her part, this exception will not apply (*Bigos v Bousted* (1951)).

12.15.2 Oppression

In the case of oppression, if the plaintiff was in a weak bargaining position, so that there was virtually no choice about entering into the agreement, recovery may be possible. Thus, in *Atkinson v Denby* (1862), a creditor refused to accept a composition agreement unless he was paid £50, so gaining an advantage over the other creditors. The debtor paid, but later brought an action to recover the money. It was held that the debtor could recover. Although the agreement was an illegal contract, the element of oppression meant that an exception to the general rule was justified.

The rationale of this exception is that the parties while both *in delicto* are not in fact *in pari delicto*, that is, they are not *equally* at fault. As Cockburn CJ put it in *Atkinson v Denby*:

> It is true that both are *in delicto*, because the act is a fraud upon the other creditors, but it is not *par delictum*, because the one has the power to dictate, the other no alternative but to submit.

12.15.3 Fraud

If one party entered into the contract as a result of the other's fraudulent misrepresentation that it was lawful, recovery will be allowed (*Hughes v Liverpool Victoria Legal Friendly Society* (1916)). Again, the parties are not regarded as being equally at fault.

12.15.4 No reliance on the illegal transaction

If the plaintiff can establish a right to possession of the property without relying on the illegal contract, then recovery will be allowed. In *Bowmakers v Barnet Instruments* (1945), for example, the defendant agreed to buy some machine tools on hire purchase terms from the plaintiffs. These agreements may well have been illegal, being in contravention of certain statutory regulations. There were three agreements. The defendants sold the machines which were the subject of two of the agreements, but kept the others. They refused to return them, or pay the hire. The plaintiffs' action to recover damages for conversion in relation to all the machines succeeded. The Court of Appeal held that they could establish their rights over the goods without needing to rely on the illegal contracts. The defendants' rights as bailees had been brought to an end by their actions, and so the plaintiffs could rely on their basic rights of ownership to found their action.

The decision in this case is not uncontroversial (see, for example, Treitel, *Law of Contract*, 9th edn, 1995, Sweet & Maxwell, pp 458–59), and is arguably inconsistent with *Taylor v Chester* (1869) where a person who had pledged a £50 bank note as security for a debauch in a brothel (an illegal contract) was held unable to recover it. Note, however, that the House of Lords adopted a similar line of argument in *Tinsley v Milligan* (1993) (see 12.13 above). The principle thus seems to be well established, though the basis of its application to the precise facts of *Bowmakers v Barnet Instruments* (1945) may be more difficult to justify, particularly in relation to the machines retained by the defendants.

12.15.5 Class-protecting statutes

In some situations, the purpose for which a statute makes an agreement illegal, is to protect a particular class. For example, the provisions forbidding the taking of illegal premiums under the Rent Acts, are designed to protect tenants. A member of that class may be able to recover property transferred under the agreement, notwithstanding the illegality. Many statutes of this kind now contain specific provisions for recovery (for example, s 125 of the Rent Act 1977; s 132 of the Financial Services Act 1986). Where they do not, however, the courts will apply the common law rule, and allow recovery as in *Kiriri Cotton Co Ltd v Dewani* (1960), which was a Privy Council decision concerning the payment of a premium by a tenant, which was illegal under Ugandan law. The underlying principle again seems to be that in this situation the parties are not equally at fault.

12.16 Severance

It is likely to be the case in many illegal contracts that it is only part of the arrangement which is illegal. To what extent can the contract be split into its constituent parts, with the legal section being valid, and the illegal section unenforceable? There are two aspects to this, namely, severance of the consideration, and severance of promises. Suppose, for example, A agrees to pay B £1,000 if B will fraudulently obtain a valuable painting and frame it. The first part of this contract, involving the fraud, is illegal, but the second part, for the framing, is *prima facie* a perfectly legal arrangement. If B does what is required, and then sues for the £1,000, the issue of the severance of the consideration will arise. B's consideration for the promise to pay the £1,000 consists of both an illegal and a legal act. Can the two be separated? In other words, can B recover the £1,000 simply for framing the picture? If the action is by A, however, in relation to B's failure to frame the picture, the question concerns the separation of the promises. These two issues will now be considered in turn.

12.16.1 Severance of consideration

For severance of consideration to be allowed, the lawful part of the consideration must be more important than the unlawful part. For example, in a contract for employment, the employee's consideration for the payment of wages may be made up of performing the required work (legal), and a promise not to compete after leaving the employment (possibly illegal (see 12.10 above)). Nevertheless, even if the restraint on future employment is too wide, the employee will be allowed to sue for wages. The consideration can be severed here, because the performance of the work is the major part of the consideration, and the restraint is subsidiary.

Note that the approach will in general be 'all or nothing'. Thus, in the example of the painting, given in the previous section, B would either be able to claim the full £1,000, or nothing at all (which would be the more likely outcome). This may not apply, however, if it is possible to assign a precise value to different parts of the contract. This occurred in *Ailion v Spiekermann* (1976) (see 12.2.3 above), where the contract to pay the illegal premium could be severed, because a precise amount could be assigned to the illegal part of the agreement. (Cf, also, *Carney v Herbert* (1985).)

12.16.2 Severance of promises

The attempt to sever promises occurs most frequently in relation to restraint of trade cases, where the wish is to 'edit out' from a list of restrictions those which make the restraint too wide, but to leave the rest in force. There have traditionally been two elements to the courts' approach, namely, the 'Blue Pencil Test', and the requirement that the nature of the contract must be retained.

12.16.3 The Blue Pencil Test

The Blue Pencil Test means that severance must be possible simply by cutting out the offending words. The court will not become involved in re-drafting the contract. Thus, in *Mason v Provident Clothing Co* (1913) (see 12.10.2 above), the court refused to substitute the phrase 'in Islington', for 'within 25 miles of London'. In *Goldsoll v Goldman* (1915), on the other hand, a covenant in the sale of a jewellery business contained a restriction on dealing in 'real or imitation jewellery' in any of a long list of countries. This was too wide both as regards scope (the business was only concerned with imitation jewellery) and geographical area (the business was limited to the UK). Both restrictions could be narrowed, however, by simple deletions, of the words 'real or', and the list of countries other than the UK, and this the court agreed to do.

Note that the strict application of this test requires that the clause as edited still makes sense, but see 12.16.5 below, on the current approach.

12.16.4 Nature of the contract must be retained

The requirement that the nature of the contract must be retained seems to derive from *Attwood v Lamont* (1920), but is quite difficult to apply. In *Attwood v Lamont*, the plaintiff owned a general outfitters. The defendant was employed in the tailoring department as a tailor and cutter. He found that his contract of employment bound him, after leaving his employment, not to be concerned in the trade or business of a tailor, dressmaker, general draper, milliner, hatter, haberdasher, gentlemen's, ladies', or children's outfitter. It was suggested that the clause could be made reasonable by cutting out all the trades except 'tailor'. The Court of Appeal refused to do this, treating the covenant as an entirety, intended to cover all aspects of the plaintiff's business. To sever it would be to affect its nature.

It is very difficult to reconcile this decision with the earlier decision in *Goldsoll v Goldman* (1915) (see 12.16.3 above), or the later decision in *Putsman v Taylor* (1927). In the latter case, the employee worked as a tailor at one branch, but the restriction covered all three branches owned by his employer. The court agreed to sever the names of the branches where the employee had not worked.

Despite this difficulty, the principle stated in *Attwood v Lamont* has not been overturned, and we must still accept that there is, alongside the Blue Pencil Test, a further requirement that the nature of the contract is not altered. How this principle will be applied, however, is very unpredictable.

12.16.5 The current approach

It may well be that the tests outlined in the previous two sections will not nowadays be applied so strictly by the courts. In *Lucas & Co Ltd v Mitchell* (1972), for example, the deletion left the phrase 'any such goods' in the contract. It was necessary to look at the deleted clause in order to see what 'such goods' meant, but the deletion was nevertheless allowed to stand. Moreover, the approach taken to the interpretation of restraint clauses in *Littlewoods v Harris* and *Clarke v Newland* (see 12.10.2 above) may mean that the severance of provisions may not be so necessary. As we have seen, the courts in these cases rejected the view that widely phrased restrictions should be given their literal meaning. Instead, they had to be interpreted within the factual context in which they had been put forward. Such an interpretation is likely to lead to the restraint, as redefined, being regarded as reasonable, thus obviating the need to consider severance.

ILLEGALITY

Introduction

'Illegality' covers all contracts which are considered to be contrary to 'public policy'.

Contracts which constitute a criminal offence

Contracts which constitute a criminal offence may be conspiracies (for example, agreement to murder), or statutory offences (for example, the Obscene Publications Act 1959).

Performance contrary to statute

If the manner of performance is unlawful (*Re Mahmoud and Ispahani* (1921)), it is relevant whether the statute prohibits contracts as such (*St John Shipping Corpn v Joseph Rank* (1957)). Knowledge of the parties is also important (*Archbolds v Spanglett* (1961)).

Contract to commit a tort

A contract to commit an intentional tort will be illegal.

Contract to indemnify

Validity of an indemnity contract depends on the type of liability:

- Criminal liability insurance is illegal, except as regards strict liability offences (*Osman v J Ralph Moss Ltd* (1970)).

- Civil liability indemnity is illegal with regard to intentional torts (*WH Smith & Sons v Clinton* (1909)), but possible as regards negligent or innocent liability (*Daily Mirror Newspapers Ltd v Exclusive News Agency* (1937)).

  Where civil liability arises out of a crime, indemnity will be illegal (*Gray v Barr* (1971)), except in relation to strict liability offences, and (non-deliberate) motor manslaughter (*Tinline v White Cross Insurance* (1921)).

Contracts contrary to public policy

'Public policy' covers a finite group of situations (outlined below), not involving crime or tort, which the courts have categorised as being contrary to public policy and therefore void.

Contracts concerning marriage

Contracts which threaten the institution of marriage will be contrary to public policy. This includes:

- future separation (*Brodie v Brodie* (1917));
- restraint of marriage (*Baker v White* (1690));
- marriage brokage (*Hermann v Charlesworth* (1905)).

Contracts promoting sexual immorality

Contracts promoting sexual immorality are unenforceable if related directly to immoral activities, or if goods or services are to be used for immoral purposes and both parties are aware of this (*Pearce v Brooks* (1866); *Appleton v Campbell* (1826)). But, cf *Armhouse Lee Ltd v Chappell* (1996).

Contracts to oust the jurisdiction of the court

Contracts made to oust the jurisdiction of the court cannot generally prevent the court's intervening (*Baker v Jones* (1954)), but there are exceptions with regard to arbitration, and separation agreements (the Arbitration Act 1996 and the Matrimonial Causes Act 1973).

Contracts in restraint of trade

Contracts in restraint of trade are *prima facie* void (*Nordenfelt v Maxim Nordenfelt* (1894)), but the presumption may be rebutted in relation to:

Employment and sale of business – restraint must:

- protect a valid interest (for example, trade secrets, business 'goodwill');
- be reasonable in its extent – as to area, time, and scope (*Mason v Provident Clothing* (1913); *cf Littlewoods v Harris* (1978));
- not be contrary to the public interest (*Wyatt v Kreglinger and Fernau* (1933)).

With regard to exclusive dealing, see *Esso Petroleum v Harpers Garage* (1968). Agreement must reasonable, judged at the time it was made (*Shell v Lostock*

Garage (1977)). Exclusive contracts for entertainers may also be found to be illegal, if too one-sided (*Schroeder v Macaulay* (1974)).

With regard to trade associations, agreements between producers may be reasonable (*English Hop Growers v Dering* (1928)), provided they do not act as a restriction on third parties (*Kores v Kolok* (1959)).

Effects of illegality

With regard to illegality, enforcement will generally not be allowed, and compensation will only be recoverable if the plaintiff is morally innocent, and does not need to rely on the illegality (*Saunders v Edwards* (1987) – action based on tort; *Tinsley v Milligan* (1993) – property rights).

Recovery of money or property. Generally dealt with by the principle of *in pari delicto*, which means no recovery (*Parkinson v College of Ambulance* (1925)). Exceptions include:

- illegal purpose which is not carried out (*Taylor v Bowers* (1876));

- oppression or fraud (*Atkinson v Denby* (1862); *Hughes v Liverpool Victoria Friendly Society* (1916));

- no reliance on illegal transaction (*Bowmakers v Barnet Instruments* (1945));

- class protecting statutes.

Severance

Consideration may be severed if the illegality constitutes only a minor part of it, or it is possible to assign value to the legal and illegal aspects (*Ailion v Spiekermann* (1976)).

Promises may be severed by applying:

- the Blue Pencil Test (*Goldsoll v Goldman* (1915));

- requirement that the nature of the contract is unchanged (*Attwood v Lamont* (1920)).

But note the current more relaxed approach to interpretation (*Littlewoods v Harris* (1978); *Clarke v Newland* (1991)).

CHAPTER 13

FRUSTRATION

13.1 The nature of the doctrine

The topic to be dealt with in this chapter, the doctrine of frustration, has links with preceding chapters, and with the one that follows. Frustration can, from one point of view, be looked at as something which vitiates a contract, in much the same way as mistake, or illegality. Whereas, however, these vitiating factors relate to things which happen, or states of affairs which exist, at or before the time when the contract is made, frustration deals with events which occur subsequent to the contract coming into existence. On the other hand, since frustration has the characteristics of an event which discharges parties from their obligations under a contract, it also has links with the topics of performance and breach (see Chapter 12).

The situation that the doctrine of frustration is concerned with is where a contract, as a result of some event outside the control of the parties, becomes impossible to perform, at least in the way originally intended. What are the rights and liabilities of the parties?

13.1.1 Original rule

In *Paradine v Jane* (1647), the court took the line that obligations were not discharged by a frustrating event, and that a party who failed to perform as a result of such an event would still be in breach of contract. The justification for this harsh approach was that the parties could, if they wished, have provided for the eventuality within the contract itself.

13.1.2 Subsequent mitigation

This approach, however, proved too strict, and potentially unjust, even for the 19th century courts, who were in many respects strong supporters of the concept of 'freedom of contract', taking the view that it was not for the court to interfere to remedy perceived injustice resulting from a freely negotiated bargain. The modern law has developed from the decision in *Taylor v Caldwell* (1863). This contract involved the letting of a music hall for the purposes of concerts, and other events. After the agreement, but before the first concert, the hall was destroyed by fire. It was held that, since performance was impossible, this event excused the parties from any further obligations under the contract. Blackburn J justified this approach on the basis that, where the parties must have known from the beginning that the contract was dependent on the continued existence of a particular thing, the contract must be construed:

> ... as subject to an implied condition that the parties shall be excused in case,
> before breach, performance becomes impossible from the perishing of the thing
> without the fault of the contractor.

The doctrine at this stage, then, is based on the existence of an implied term. This enabled the decision to be squared with the prevailing approach to freedom of contract, but it is in reality something of a fiction, and modern courts have preferred to base the doctrine simply on the need to avoid the injustice of imposing impossible obligations in the absence of fault.

13.2   Frustrating events

The types of event which will be regarded as frustrating a contract are those which render performance impossible, or at least, 'radically different' (Lord Radcliffe in *Davis Contractors Ltd v Fareham UDC* (1956)), from what had been contracted for. Unfortunately, neither 'impossibility' nor 'radical difference' has a self-evident meaning in this context. Both require interpretation in their application. There is, however, guidance to be obtained from looking at the cases. Although the categories can never be closed, it is possible to identify certain occurrences which have been recognised by the courts as amounting to frustration of the contract.

13.2.1   Destruction of the subject matter

In the same way that the destruction of the subject matter prior to the formation of a contract will render it void for mistake (see 8.6 above), destruction at a later stage will fall within the doctrine of frustration (*Taylor v Caldwell* (1863)). Complete destruction is not necessary. In *Taylor v Caldwell* itself, the contract related to the use of the Hall and Gardens, but it was only the Hall which was destroyed. The contract nevertheless become impossible as regards a major element (use of the Hall), and was therefore frustrated. In other words, if what is destroyed is fundamental to the performance of the obligations under the contract, then the doctrine will operate (cf s 7 of the Sale of Goods Act 1979; see 13.5 below).

It seems that complete physical destruction may not be necessary if the subject matter has been affected in a way which renders it useless. In *Asfar v Blundell* (1896), for example, a cargo of dates was being carried on a boat which sank in the Thames. The cargo was recovered, but the dates were found to be in a state of fermentation, and contaminated with sewage. The judge found that they 'had been so deteriorated that they had become something was not merchantable as dates'. On that basis, there was a total loss of the dates.

13.2.2   Personal services – supervening incapacity

If a contract envisages performance by a particular individual, as in a contract to paint a portrait, and no substitute is likely to be satisfactory, then the contract will generally be frustrated by the incapacity of the person concerned. Thus, in *Condor v Barron Knights* (1966), the drummer with a pop group was taken ill. Medical opinion was that he would only be fit to work three or four nights a week, whereas the group had engagements for seven nights a week. It was held that his contract of employment was discharged by frustration. The drummer was incapable of performing his contract in the way intended. In many cases, of course, the identity of the person who is to perform the contract will not be significant. Suppose, for example, a garage agrees to service a car on a particular day, but on that day, as a result of illness, it is short-staffed, and cannot carry out the service. This is more likely to be treated as a breach of contract than frustration. The contract is simply to carry out the service, and the car-owner is unlikely to be concerned about the identity of the particular individual who performs the contract, as long as they are competent. (Cf the cases on mistaken identity, discussed at 10.5.1 above.)

13.2.3 Non-occurrence of an event

If the parties reach an agreement which is dependent on a particular event taking place, then the cancellation of that event may well lead to the contract being frustrated. This situation arose in relation to a number of contracts surrounding the coronation of Edward VII, which was postponed owing to the King's illness.

In *Krell v Henry* (1903), the defendant had made a contract for the use of certain rooms owned by the plaintiff for the purpose of watching the coronation procession. It was held that the postponement of the procession frustrated the contract. Although literal performance was possible, in that the room could have been made available to the defendant at the appropriate time, and the defendant could have sat in it and looked out of the window, in the absence of the procession it had no point, and the whole purpose of the contract had vanished.

By contrast in another 'coronation case', *Herne Bay Steamboat Co v Hutton* (1903), the contract was not frustrated. Here, the contract was that the plaintiff's boat should be 'at the disposal of' the defendant on the 25 June to take passengers from Herne Bay for the purpose of watching the naval review, which the King was to conduct, and for a day's cruise round the fleet. The King's illness led to the review being cancelled. In this case, however, the Court of Appeal held that the contract was not frustrated. The distinction from *Krell v Henry* must be that the contract was still regarded as having some purpose. The fleet was still in place (as Stirling LJ pointed out), and so the tour of it could go ahead, even if the review by the King had been cancelled. The effect on the contract was not sufficiently fundamental to lead to it being regarded as frustrated.

13.2.4   Government intervention

If a contract is made, and there is then a declaration of war, which turns one of the parties into an enemy alien, then the contract will be frustrated. Similarly, the requisitioning of property for use by the government can have a similar effect (*Metropolitan Water Board v Dick Kerr* (1918)). In this case, a contract for the construction of a reservoir was frustrated by an order by the Minister of Munitions, during the First World War, that the defendant should cease work, and disperse and sell the plant.

Here, as is the case in relation to the non-occurrence of an event, it must be clear that the interference radically or fundamentally alters the contract. In *FA Tamplin v Anglo-American Petroleum* (1916), a ship which was subject to a five-year charter was requisitioned for use as a troopship. It was held by the House of Lords that the charter was not frustrated, since judging it at the time of the requisition, the interference was not sufficiently serious. There might have been many months during which the ship would have been available for commercial purposes before the expiry of the contract.

Similarly, the fact that the contract has been rendered more difficult, or more expensive, does not frustrate it. The closure of the Suez Canal in 1956 forced the sellers of goods to ship them *via* the Cape of Good Hope, extending the time for delivery by about four weeks. The House of Lords in *Tsakiroglou & Co v Noblee and Thorl* (1962) held that this was not frustration. The route for shipment had not been specified in the contract, nor was any precise delivery date agreed. The fact that the re-routing would cost more was regarded as irrelevant.

The government intervention need not relate to war or international relations. In *Gamerco SA v ICM/Fair Warning Agency* (1995), the Spanish government's closure of a stadium for safety reasons was held to frustrate a contract to hold a pop concert there.

An unsuccessful attempt was made in *Amalgamated Investment v John Walker* (1976) to base frustration on a different type of government interference, namely the 'listing' of a building as being of architectural and historic interest, and therefore subject to strict planning conditions. Despite the fact that this was estimated as reducing the market value of the building to £200,000 (the contract price was £1,700,000), the Court of Appeal held that the contract was not frustrated. It was not part of the contract that the building should not be listed, and the change in the market value of the property could not in itself amount to frustration. The decision presumably leaves open the possibility that if the non-listing of a building was a crucial element in the contract, then frustration could follow from such a listing.

Such an outcome is perhaps less likely in the light of the Court of Appeal's later decision in *Bormarin AB v IMB Investments* (1999). In this case, a contract for the purchase of the share capital of two companies had been set up with the main purpose of enabling the purchaser to be able to set off losses against gains, as was at that time allowed by tax law. Subsequently, the law changed, so that such losses could no longer be set-off. The seller sought to enforce the agreement but, at first instance, it was held that the contract had been frustrated by the change in the law. On appeal, however, the Court of Appeal ruled that frustration could not be used where, as a result of a change in the law, a bargain turned out to be less advantageous than had been hoped.

13.2.5 Supervening illegality

If, after a contract has been made, its purpose becomes illegal, then this will be regarded as a frustrating event. In *Denny, Mott and Dickson v James Fraser* (1944), there was an agreement for the sale of timber over a number of years. It provided that the buyer should let a timber yard to the seller, and give him an option to purchase it. In 1939, further dealings in timber were made illegal. The House of Lords held that not only the trading contract, but also the option on the timber yard, was frustrated. The main object of the contract was trading in timber, and once this was frustrated, the whole agreement was radically altered.

13.2.6 Other frustrating events

Other types of event which have been held to lead to frustration are strikes (*The Nema* (1981) – time charter affected so that only two out of the anticipated six or seven would be able to be made); and the effects of war (*Finelvet AG v Vinava Shipping Co Ltd* (1983) – ship trapped by continuing Gulf War between Iran and Iraq). Note that, in the former case, it was the extent of the effect of the strike that was important, and in the latter that it was made clear that the outbreak of war did not necessarily frustrate a contract on which it had a bearing. This again emphasises the point that, whatever the frustrating event (and the categories are never likely to be closed), it is the *effect* of that event on the contract, and what the parties have agreed, that is the most important consideration, and not the nature of the event itself. Only if it vitally and fundamentally changes the conditions of the contract, and makes performance radically different from what the parties had agreed, will frustration take place.

13.3   Limitations on the doctrine

The general limitations on the availability of a plea of frustration, in terms of the seriousness of the event, and its effect on what the parties have agreed, have been discussed above. In this section, three more specific limitations are noted.

13.3.1 Self-induced frustration

If it is the behaviour of one of the parties which, while not amounting to a breach of contract, has brought about the circumstances which are alleged to frustrate the contract, this will be regarded as 'self-induced frustration', and will not discharge the contract. This is an obvious restriction, but it may not always be easy to determine what type of behaviour should fall within its scope. An example of the application of this restriction is *Maritime National Fish v Ocean Trawlers* (1935). The appellants chartered a trawler from the respondents. The trawler was fitted with an 'otter' trawl, which it was illegal to use without a licence, as both parties were aware. The appellants applied for five licences to operate otter trawls, but were only granted three. They decided to use these for boats other than the one chartered from the respondents. They claimed that this contract was therefore frustrated, since the trawler could not legally be used. The Privy Council held that the appellants were not discharged. It was their own election to use the licences with the other boats which had led to the illegality of using the appellants' trawler.

This decision seems fair where it is the case, as it was here, that the party exercising the choice could have done so without breaking any contract (since the trawlers to which the licences were assigned all belonged to the appellants). It may not be so fair, however, if a person is put in a position where there is no choice but to break one of two contracts. Nevertheless, when this situation arose in *The Super Servant Two* (1990), the Court of Appeal applied the concept of self-induced frustration strictly. The parties had made a contract for the transportation of a drilling rig, which, as they both knew, could only be carried out by one of two vessels owned by the defendants, namely, *Super Servant One* and *Super Servant Two*. The defendants, intending to use *Super Servant Two*, allocated *Super Servant One* to other contracts. *Super Servant Two* then sank. The defendants claimed that the contract was frustrated, but the plaintiffs alleged that the impossibility of performance arose from the defendants' own acts, and that they should not therefore be discharged from performance. The Court of Appeal agreed that, even though the defendants were neither negligent, nor in breach of contract, in the way in which they had allocated the vessels, they were still liable under the contract with the plaintiffs. Bingham LJ felt that it was:

> ... inconsistent with the doctrine of frustration as previously understood on high authority that its application should depend on any decision, however reasonable and commercial, of the party seeking to rely on it.

It seems then that any exercise of choice by one of the parties, which contributes to a situation where the contract becomes impossible, or radically different, will prevent the doctrine of frustration from applying.

13.3.2 Events foreseen and provided for

One way in which the parties can avoid the situation discussed in the previous section, and its perceived unfairness, is by including specific provision in the contract to deal with that situation. Indeed, in *Super Servant Two* (1990), it was held that the defendants could take advantage of a specific *force majeure* clause, even though the contract was not frustrated as far as the common law was concerned. A *force majeure* clause is one which the parties have inserted to cover various eventualities outside their control, which may effect the contract. It will provide the way in which losses are to be distributed in such circumstances. The existence of such a clause, covering the facts that have arisen, will generally prevent the contract from being frustrated. It will not inevitably do so, however, as is shown by *Jackson v Union Marine Insurance Co Ltd* (1874). A ship was chartered in November 1871, to proceed with all possible dispatch, 'damages and accidents of navigation excepted' from Liverpool to Newport and there to load a cargo for carriage to San Francisco. She sailed on 2 January but, before reaching Newport, ran aground off the Welsh coast. On 15 February, the charterers abandoned the charter and found another ship. On 18 February, the ship got off, but repairs were not finished until August. The shipowner brought an action against the charterers for failure to load. It was held by the Exchequer Chamber that the exception in the contract absolved the shipowner from liability in the event of delay, but did not give him the right to sue if the delay was bad enough to frustrate the contract. This was the situation here, and so the shipowner's action failed.

A similar conclusion was reached in *Metropolitan Water Board v Dick Kerr* (1918) (see 13.2.4 above) where the contract contained a provision for extension of the time for performance in the event of delays 'howsoever caused'. It was held by the House of Lords that this provision was only meant to deal with temporary delays, and did not:

> ... cover the case in which the interruption is of such a character and duration that it vitally and fundamentally changes the conditions of the contract, and could not possibly have been in the contemplation of the parties to the contract when it was made.

13.3.3 Land

A contract for the sale of land can apparently be frustrated. This must have been assumed to be the case in *Amalgamated Investment v John Walker* (see 13.2.4 above), since otherwise there would have been no need to consider whether the listing of a building could have such an effect. In practice, the purchaser of land will virtually always insure it from the point of exchange of contracts, and so the issue of frustration will be unlikely to arise.

In relation to leases, at one time it seemed as though frustration was not possible. Although it is clear that the doctrine of frustration can apply to contracts to use property on the basis of a licence, as in *Taylor v Caldwell* (1863) and *Krell v Henry* (1903) (see 13.1.2 and 13.2.3 above), this was not necessarily the case with a lease, which involves the tenant taking an interest in the land itself. The issue was raised in *Cricklewood Property Investment Trust v Leighton's Investment Trusts Ltd* (1945). This concerned a building lease, which was expressed to last for 99 years, from May 1936. Following the outbreak of the Second World War in 1939, legislation was passed prohibiting building. The tenant claimed that the lease was frustrated. Two members of the House of Lords expressed the view that a lease could never be frustrated, while two others thought that it could if, for example, the land was washed into the sea, or became subject to a permanent ban on building. The fifth member of the panel refused to express a view on this issue, but agreed with the decision that on the facts there was in any case no frustration, because there were still 90 years left on the lease once the wartime restrictions were lifted.

The matter did not arise for decision again until 1981, and the case of *National Carriers Ltd v Panalpina (Northern) Ltd* (1981). This contract concerned a 10 year lease of a warehouse. After five years, the local authority closed the street, preventing access, because of problems with another (listed) building in the street. The closure was likely to last for about 18 months. There would, therefore, have been some three years of the lease to run after the street re-opened. The tenants, however, stopped paying rent, on the basis that the contract had been frustrated. The House of Lords took the view (Lord Russell dissenting) that there was no reason in logic or law why a lease should not be frustrated in a situation where no substantial use of a kind permitted by the lease and contemplated by the parties, remained possible for the lessee. Thus, even where the land itself remained available, rather than slipping into the sea, or being covered by sand, the lease could be frustrated, if its purpose had been frustrated. On the facts of the case, however, the interruption to the availability of the premises was not sufficient to amount to frustration, and the landlords' action for the rent therefore succeeded.

13.4 Effects of the doctrine: common law

The effects of a frustrating event are dealt with both by common law rules, and the provisions of the Law Reform (Frustrated Contracts) Act (LR(FC)A) 1943. This section deals with the common law, and the next one (13.5) with the Act.

13.4.1 Automatic termination

The first point to note is that the common law regards the frustrating event as automatically bringing the contract to an end. It is not a situation such as that which arises in relation to mistake, misrepresentation, or breach of contract, where one party can decide, notwithstanding what has happened, that the contract should continue. The application of this rule can be seen in *Hirji Mulji v Cheong Yeong Steamship* (1926). By a charterparty entered into in November 1916, shipowners agreed that their ship, the *Singaporean*, should be placed at the charterers' disposal on 17 March 1917, for 10 months. Shortly before this date, the ship was requisitioned by the government. The shipowners thought the ship would soon be released, and asked the charterers if they would still be willing to take up the charter when this happened. The charterers said that they would. In fact, the ship was not released until February 1919, at which point the charterers refused to accept it. The shipowners argued that the charterers had affirmed the contract after the frustrating event, and were therefore still bound. The House of Lords held that affirmation was not possible. The frustrating event automatically brought the contract to an end, and discharged both the shipowners and the charterers from their obligations.

13.4.2 Future obligations only discharged

It is important to note that frustration, unlike an operative common law mistake, does not render a contract void *ab initio*. Its effect is to bring the contract to an end prematurely, but all existing obligations at the time of the contract remain unaffected, as far as the common law is concerned. If money has been paid, or property transferred, then it cannot generally be recovered, and if valuable services have been provided, compensation cannot be claimed.

Thus, in *Krell v Henry* (1903) (see 13.2.3 above), the hirer of the room had paid a deposit, which was irrecoverable. On the other hand, the obligation to pay the balance did not, under the terms of the contract, arise until after the date on which the coronation procession was cancelled. This, therefore, was also irrecoverable. By contrast, in *Chandler v Webster* (1904), another case on the hiring of a room to view the coronation, under the terms of the contract the obligation to pay arose before the frustrating event occurred. In this case, it was held that not only could money paid not be recovered, but the obligation to pay money due before the event was cancelled remained. Because frustration only discharged the contract from the point when the event occurred, the court refused to regard this as a case where there was a total failure of consideration, which might have justified recovery in quasi-contract (for which see Chapter 16).

13.4.3 Total failure of consideration

This aspect of *Chandler v Webster* (1904) was, however, overruled by the House of Lords in *Fibrosa Spolka Ackyjna v Fairbairn Lawson Combe Barbour Ltd* (1942), where it was held that a frustrated contract could in some situations lead to a claim for recovery of money paid, on the basis of a total failure of consideration. An English company (the respondents) had made a contract to supply machinery to a Polish company (the appellants). The appellants had paid £1,000 towards this contract. It was then frustrated by the German invasion of Poland in 1939. The appellants sought to recover the £1,000. The House of Lords held that, since they had received nothing at all under the contract, there had been a total failure of consideration, and recovery was therefore possible.

This decision is probably an improvement on *Chandler v Webster*, but it still leaves two areas of difficulty, and potential injustice. First, it can only apply where the failure of consideration is total. If the other party has provided something, no matter how little, no recovery will be possible. Secondly, it takes no account of the fact that the party who has received the money may well have incurred expenses in relation to the contract, and so will end up out of pocket if the entire sum has to be refunded. Both of these difficulties are addressed by the LR(FC)A 1943 (see 13.5 below).

This Act also attempts to tackle another limitation of the common law, which is exemplified by *Appleby v Myers* (1867). In this case, the contract was for the erection of machinery on the defendant's premises. Payment was to be made on completion of the work. When the work was nearly finished, the whole premises, including the machinery, were destroyed by fire. The contract was undoubtedly frustrated, but the question was whether the plaintiffs could recover any compensation for the work that they had done. The answer was no. The obligation to pay had not arisen at the time the contract was frustrated, and therefore the plaintiffs were entitled to nothing.

The injustices caused by the application of these common law rules led to the reform contained in the LR(FC)A 1943.

13.5 Effects of frustration: the Law Reform (Frustrated Contracts) Act 1943

Before considering the provisions of s 1(2) and s 1(3), which contain the most significant provisions of the LR(FC)A 1943, it must be noted that not all contracts are within its scope. Section 2(5) indicates that the Act does not apply to, for example, charterparties, contracts of insurance, or contracts for the sale of specific goods. Note that some, but not all, contracts in the latter category are governed by s 7 of the Sale of Goods Act 1979, which provides that:

> ... where there is an agreement to sell specific goods, and subsequently the goods, without any fault on the part of the seller or buyer, perish before the risk passes to the buyer, the agreement is thereby avoided.

An 'agreement to sell' is a contract under which ownership (described as 'property') has not yet passed to the buyer. This concept, and the rules relating to passing of 'risk', are discussed further in Chapter 18.

In relation to these contracts, the common law rules on the effects of frustration will apply.

Section 2(3) states that:

> Where any contract to which this Act applies contains any provision which, upon the true construction of the contract, is intended to have effect in the event of circumstances arising which operate, or would but for the said provision operate, to frustrate the contract, or is intended to have effect whether such circumstances arise or not, the court shall give effect to the said provision and shall only give effect to the foregoing section of this Act to such extent, if any, as appears to the court to be consistent with the said provision.

This makes it clear that the parties may reach their own agreement as to what the effects of frustration are going to be. In this situation, again, the LR(FC)A 1943 will have no application.

13.5.1 Section 1(2): money paid or payable prior to frustration

Section 1(2) of the LR(FC)A 1943 deals with the *Chandler v Webster*, or *Fibrosa*, type of situation, that is, where money has been paid, or is owed under the contract, before the frustrating event takes place. It states that:

> All sums paid or payable to any party in pursuance of the contract before the time when the parties were so discharged [that is, by frustration] ... shall, in the case of sums so paid, be recoverable from his as money received by him for the use of the party by whom the sums were paid, and, in the case of sums so payable, cease to be so payable.

In other words, in such a situation, money paid is recoverable, and money owed ceases to be payable. To that extent the section adopts and extends the *Fibrosa* decision, in that the rule now applies even where there is not a total failure of consideration. Subject to the provisions of s 1(3) (see 13.5.2 below) concerning the conferring of valuable benefits, there can be recovery of sums paid even where there has been partial performance by the other side.

There is, however, a proviso to s 1(2) which is designed to limit the injustice in the *Fibrosa* decision (see 13.4.3 above), that is, that, even where there is a total failure of consideration, the other party may have incurred expenses in getting ready to perform. The section accordingly provides that if the party to whom sums were paid or payable:

> ... incurred expenses before the time of discharge in, or for the purposes of, the performance of the contract, the court may, if it considers it just to do so having regard to all the circumstances of the case, allow him to retain or, as the case may be, recover the whole of the sums paid or payable, not being an amount in excess of the expenses so incurred.

It is important to note two limitations on this attempt to spread the losses of frustration between the parties. First, the recovery of expenses can only take place where there was an obligation to pay some money prior to the frustrating event. If the contract provided for the entire payment to become due only on completion of the contract, then there will be no scope for the recovery of expenses under s 1(2). Secondly, even if some money was paid or payable, it is possible that the expenses will exceed this amount, and so will not be fully recoverable. For example, if on a contract worth £5,000 a deposit of £500 has been paid, but the other party has incurred expenses of £750, the maximum that can be retained under s 1(2) is £500. The remaining £250 is irrecoverable, unless s 1(3) (see 13.5.2 below) can be brought into play.

Finally, even if expenses have been occurred which could be compensated by money paid or payable, this cannot be claimed as of right. It is entirely at the court's discretion to decide whether or not there should be any recovery of expenses, depending on its view as to whether this would be just in all the circumstances. In *Gamerco SA v ICM/Fair Warning Agency* (1995), the court confirmed that the use of a broad discretion, rather than any other particular formula (for example, sharing losses equally) was the correct approach to the application of the proviso under s 1(2). The plaintiffs were claiming the repayment of $412,500 paid in connection with a pop concert which could not take place because the government had, on safety grounds, closed the stadium at which it was to be held. The defendants wished to retain an amount to cover their expenses. On the facts, there were considerable difficulties in calculating the defendants' expenses, but the judge estimated that they might have amounted to $50,000. In all the circumstances, and taking account of the other party's loss (around $450,000), the judge concluded that justice would be done if the money paid by the plaintiffs (that is, the $412,500) was returned without deduction. The decision emphasises the very broad power which the court has in relation to the proviso to s 1(2).

13.5.2 Section 1(3): compensation for a 'valuable benefit'

Section 1(3) of the LR(FC)A 1943, provides that, where a party to a contract has obtained a 'valuable benefit' (other than money) before the time of discharge, the other party can obtain compensation for having provided this. Suppose, then, that A has contracted to hire B's hall for a series of 10 concerts, with the entire fee to be payable at the end of the contract. If after one concert, the hall is destroyed by fire, under the common law, B would not be able to recover anything from A. By virtue of s 1(3), however, B would be entitled to seek compensation from A in relation to the use of the hall for the one concert that took place. As with s 1(2), recovery is not available as of right, but is in the discretion of the court, which can award what it considers just in all the circumstances, up to the value of the benefit to the party obtaining it. In particular, the court is directed to take into account any expenses incurred by the party obtaining the benefit, and the effect, in relation to the benefit, of the circumstances which frustrated the contract.

This provision would seem at first sight to provide a more satisfactory outcome to the case of *Appleby v Myers* (1867) (see 13.4.3 above), in that it might allow the supplier of the machinery to recover compensation for the work that had been done. This depends, however, on whether the 'valuable benefit' has to be judged before or after the frustrating event has occurred. If it is the former, then some compensation may be possible; if it is the latter, then the other party may well argue that no benefit has in the end been received, since the machinery was not completed, and was in any case destroyed by the fire.

These issues were considered in some detail by Goff J, as he then was, in the only reported case on the LR(FC)A 1943, *BP Exploration v Hunt* (1982). The case concerned oil concessions which had been frustrated by expropriation by the

Libyan government. Goff J started by stating that the underlying principle of the Act was not the apportionment of losses, but the prevention of the 'unjust enrichment' of one party to a frustrated contract at the expense of the other. Applying this approach to s 1(3) he came to the conclusion that 'benefit' means the 'end product' of what the plaintiff has provided, not the value of the work that has been done. Thus, he concluded:

> ... where a contract is frustrated by a fire which destroys a building on which work has been done, the award will be nil.

In other words, he adopted the second of the approaches outlined in the previous paragraph as regards the assessment of the benefit. This is not accepted as the correct analysis by all commentators. Treitel, for example, argues that although the Act makes reference to the relevance of the effect of the frustrating circumstances, this should be interpreted as applying to the assessment of the 'just sum' to be awarded, rather than the valuation of the benefit itself (*Law of Contract*, 10th edn, Sweet & Maxwell, p 853). Goff J's judgment, however, was approved by the Court of Appeal and the House of Lords, and must be taken to represent the current law on this issue. As a result, it is clear that in a case such as *Appleby v Myers* (1867), the answer given by the LR(FC)A 1943 is the same as that under the common law, and that no compensation will be recoverable for the work that has been done, because, once the frustrating event has occurred, it is of no value to the other party.

FRUSTRATION

Nature of the doctrine

A frustrating event is one which, without any fault on either party, prevents performance of the contract. It was originally not thought to discharge obligations (*Paradine v Jane* (1647)) but, since *Taylor v Caldwell* (1863), it has been accepted that this is its effect.

Frustrating events

Anything which renders performance impossible, or at least 'radically different' (*Davis Contractors Ltd v Fareham UDC* (1956)), can be a frustrating event. Thus, it includes destruction of the subject matter (*Taylor v Caldwell* (1863)); personal incapacity (*Condor v Barron Knights* (1966)); non-occurrence of an event (*Krell v Henry* (1903)); government intervention (*Metropolitan Water Board v Dick Kerr* (1918)); supervening illegality (*Denny Mott and Dickson v James Fraser* (1944)); industrial action (*The Nema* (1981)); or the effects of war (*Finelvet AG v Vinava Shipping Co Ltd* (1983)).

Limitations on the doctrine

The contract must not still have some surviving purpose (*Herne Bay Steam Boat Co v Hutton* (1903)). Nor is it enough that the contract is made more difficult or more expensive to perform (*Tsakiroglou & Co v Noblee and Thorl* (1962)).

- Self-induced frustration

  If the impossibility results from a choice exercised by one party, then the contract will not be frustrated (*Maritime National Fish v Ocean Trawlers* (1935)). This is so even if the party had in the end no choice but fail to perform one contract or another (*The Super Servant Two* (1990)).

- Events foreseen and provided for

  Parties may include a clause dealing with the consequences of frustration. The courts will generally give effect to this, provided that the clause was truly intended to cover the circumstances which have occurred (*Jackson v Union Marine Insurance Co Ltd* (1874)).

Land

It seems that contracts for the sale of land can be frustrated (*Amalgamated Investment v John Walker* (1976)). It is also possible, though unlikely, for a lease to be frustrated (*National Carriers Ltd v Panalpina (Northern) Ltd* (1981)).

Effect of frustration: common law

The contract is automatically terminated (*Hirji Mulji v Cheong Yeong Steamship* (1926)). Only future obligations are discharged, those which arose prior to the event still survive (*Chandler v Webster* (1904)). Recovery of money paid will be allowed, however, if there has been a total failure of consideration (*Fibrosa Spolka Ackyjna v Fairbairn Lawson Combe Barbour Ltd* (1942)). There can be no recovery, however, for work done before the frustrating event but for which payment was not yet due (*Appleby v Myers* (1867)).

Effects of frustration: Law Reform (Frustrated Contracts) Act 1943

Note that the LR(FC)A 1943 does not apply to all contracts, for example, charterparties, insurance, or the sale of specific goods. Nor does it apply where the parties have included their own provision for the consequences of frustration.

- Section 1(2): money paid or payable prior to frustration

  This will be recoverable, cease to be payable, subject to a deduction for expenses incurred by the other party. This is subject to the courts' view as to what is just in all the circumstances. This is a very broad discretion: *Gamerco v ICM/Fair Warning Agency* (1995).

- Section 1(3): compensation for a valuable benefit

  If a party has obtained a valuable benefit, the other party can obtain compensation, to the extent that the court considers just in all the circumstances. The benefit must survive the frustrating event, however, otherwise there can be no recovery (*BP Exploration v Hunt* (1982)).

CHAPTER 14

PERFORMANCE AND BREACH

14.1 Introduction

This chapter is concerned with ways in which a contract may be discharged, so that the parties no longer have any obligations under it. We have already discussed one way in which this can happen in the previous chapter, under the doctrine of frustration. Contracts may also be discharged by express agreement. If both parties decide that neither of them wishes to carry on with a contract which contains continuing obligations, or in relation to which some parts are still executory, they may agree to bring it to an end early. The only problems which arise here are where the executory obligations are all on one side, so that the party who has completed performance receives no consideration for promising not to enforce the other party's obligations. This issue has already been dealt with in Chapter 3, in connection with the doctrine of consideration, and in particular the concept of promissory estoppel (see 3.8–3.10 above), and so is not discussed further here. The focus in this chapter is on discharge by performance or by breach: discharge in this context meaning that all further obligations of either or both of the parties are at an end.

14.2 Discharge by performance

Once the parties have done all that they are bound to do under a contract, all 'primary' obligations will cease. (There may, of course, be some continuing 'secondary' obligations, such as the obligation to pay compensation if goods turn out to be defective at some point after sale and delivery.) The problem that concerns us here is what constitutes satisfactory performance. If there is some minor defect, does this negative discharge by performance?

14.2.1 Performance must be precise and exact

The general rule is that performance must be precise and exact, and the courts have at times applied this very strictly. Consider, for example, two cases under the Sale of Goods Act 1893. In *Re Moore and Landauer* (1921), the defendants agreed to buy from the plaintiffs 3,000 tins of canned fruit. The fruit was to be packed in cases of 30 tins. When the goods were delivered a substantial part of the consignment was packed in cases of 24 tins. It was held that this did not constitute satisfactory performance, and the defendants were entitled to reject the whole consignment. Similarly, in *Arcos Ltd v Ronaasen* (1933), the buyer had ordered timber staves for the purpose of making barrels. The contract description said that they should be ½" thick. Most of the consignment consisted of staves which were in fact 9/16" thick. They were still perfectly usable for making barrels. Nevertheless, it was held that this did not constitute satisfactory performance, and the buyer was entitled to reject all the staves. In other words, in both these cases, the seller had not performed satisfactorily, and so had not discharged his obligations under the contract.

Both of these cases turned in part on the interpretation of s 13 of the Sale of Goods Act 1893, which implied an obligation to supply goods which match their contract description. The same provision is now contained in s 13 of the Sale of Goods Act 1979. In recent years, the courts have been a little more flexible in the application of this section (see 18.5.2 below), and s 15A now prevents a business purchaser from unreasonably rejecting goods which are only slightly different from the contract description. The principle that each party is entitled to expect the other to perform to the letter of their agreement remains, however. This was confirmed by the Privy Council in *Union Eagle Ltd v Golden Achievement Ltd* (1997). This concerned a contract for the sale of a flat. Time for performance had been made 'of the essence', and under the contract the purchase price was to tendered by 5 pm on a particular day. In fact, it was tendered at 5.10 pm. The Privy Council confirmed that this entitled the seller to repudiate the agreement and retain the deposit that had been paid. The interests of certainty meant that the court should in this type of situation strictly enforce what the parties had agreed.

14.2.2 Partial provision of services

In the sale of goods cases, a failure to meet the terms of the contract prevented the seller from claiming any compensation, even in relation to any goods supplied which did match the contract description. The same approach is applied to the provision of services. Here, a person may have done a certain amount of work towards a contract, and the question is whether there is any right to claim payment under the contract for what has been done, if it does not amount to complete performance. The starting point for the consideration of this issue is *Cutter v Powell* (1795). The defendant agreed to pay Cutter 30 guineas provided that he served as second mate on a voyage from Jamaica to Liverpool. The voyage began on 2 August. Cutter died on 20 September, when the ship was 19 days short of Liverpool. Cutter's widow brought an action to recover a proportion of the 30 guineas. This failed. The contract was interpreted as being an 'entire' contract for a lump sum, and nothing was payable until it was completed. Thus, even though the defendant had had the benefit of Cutter's labour for a substantial part of the voyage, no compensation for this was recoverable. One reason for this rather harsh decision seems to have been that the 30 guineas was about four times the normal wage for such a voyage. The court therefore looked on it as something of a gamble. Cutter had agreed to take the chance of a larger lump sum at the end of the voyage, rather than to take wages paid on a weekly basis. This element of the decision was not picked up in later cases, however, and *Cutter v Powell* was taken to lay down a general rule that in 'entire' contracts (that is, where various obligations are to be performed in return for a lump sum) nothing is payable until the contract has been fully completed.

14.2.3 Divisible contracts or obligations

One way to mitigate this rule, which has the potential to operate very harshly, is to find that the contract is not entire, but divisible into sections, with the completion of each section giving rise to a right to some payment. Thus, if Cutter had been engaged at a certain rate per week, instead of for a lump sum for the whole voyage, his widow would probably have been able to recover for the time he had actually served.

This will also apply if there are concurrent but independent obligations. In *Bolton v Mahadeva* (1972), there was a contract to (a) install a central heating system, and (b) supply a bathroom suite. The central heating system turned out to be defective, and there was no obligation to pay for this, but the supply of the bathroom suite was severable, and an appropriate proportion of the contract price was recoverable in relation to this obligation.

14.2.4 Non-performance due to other party

If one party prevents the other from completing the obligations under an entire contract, the party who has partly performed will be able to recover on a *quantum meruit* basis for the work already done. Thus, in *Planché v Colburn* (1831) (discussed further at 16.3.1 below), the plaintiff recovered £50 towards the work which he had done in writing a book for a series which had then been cancelled by the defendants. The contract price had been £100, but the plaintiff had not completed the book at the time that the defendants brought the contract to an end. A plaintiff in this situation may also be able to recover damages for consequential losses.

14.2.5 Acceptance of partial performance

If a party accepts partial performance, this may be sufficient in certain circumstances to discharge the other party's further obligations under the contract, and moreover allow that party to sue on a *quantum meruit* for the work already done. For example, suppose that goods are to be transported from London to Hull, and the van breaks down en route. If the recipient of the goods agrees to take delivery at Doncaster, the carrier will be able to sue for a proportion of the carriage. In *Christy v Row* (1808), this rule was said to be based on a fresh agreement involving an implied promise to pay for the benefit received. In this case, there was a contract of carriage in relation to seven keels of coal, to be taken from Shields to Hamburgh. Seven keels were delivered at Gluckstadt by arrangement with the consignee. It was held that the carrier was entitled to recover freight at the contract rate of £20 per keel.

This exception will not apply, however, if the party effectively has no option but to accept the performance. In *Sumpter v Hedges* (1898), the plaintiff, a builder, contracted to build two houses and stables on the defendant's land, for £565. The plaintiff did work to the value of £333, and then abandoned the contract, because he had no money. The defendant finished the buildings himself, using building materials left by the plaintiff. The plaintiff brought an action to recover the value of the work he had done on the buildings. Although it might appear that the defendant had accepted the performance, the Court of Appeal held that the plaintiff could not recover. As Collins LJ pointed out, although in some circumstances an agreement to pay might be inferred from the acceptance of a benefit, nevertheless:

> ... in order that that may be done, the circumstances must be such as to give an option to the defendant to take or not take the benefit of the work done.

It would not be reasonable to expect the defendant to keep on his land a building which was in an incomplete state, and would constitute a nuisance.

14.2.6 Substantial performance

The principle of 'substantial performance' has the potential to constitute a more general exception. It is based on the idea that where there is only a minor variation from the terms of the contract, the other party cannot claim to be discharged, but must rely on an action for damages for breach. The origins of it can be traced to *Boone v Eyre* (1779), a case concerning the sale of a plantation, together with its slaves. It was suggested by Lord Mansfield CJ that the fact the seller could not establish ownership of every single slave stated to be included in the contract would not prevent him from recovering payment from the buyer under the agreement. The principle is, however, stated most clearly in *Dakin v Lee* (1916), and *Hoenig v Isaacs* (1952).

In *Dakin v Lee*, the contract was for the repair of a house. The work was not done in accordance with the contract. In particular, the concrete underpinning was only half the contract depth; the columns to support a bay window were of 4 in diameter solid iron, instead of 5 in diameter hollow; and the joists over the bay window were not cleated at the angles or bolted to caps and to each other. The official referee found that the plaintiffs had not performed the contract, and therefore could not claim for any payment in respect of it. The Court of Appeal noted that there was a distinction between failing to complete (as in *Sumpter v Hedges* (1898) (see 14.2.5 above), and completing badly. Here, the contract had been performed, though badly performed, and the plaintiff could recover for the work done, less deductions for the fact that it did not conform to the contract requirements.

Similarly, in *Hoenig v Isaacs* (1952), there were found to be defects (which would cost £55 to repair) in work done in redecorating a flat. The total contract price was £750. It was held that there was substantial performance, and that the plaintiff could recover the contract price, less the cost of repairs.

The Court of Appeal refused to apply this, however, in *Bolton v Mahadeva* (1972), as regards the obligation to install a central heating system. The system as fitted gave out much less heat than it should have done, and caused fumes in one of the rooms. Although the complete system had been fitted, it did not fulfil its primary function of heating the house, and so the installer was not allowed to recover. The doctrine of substantial performance appears to be infrequently used, and may not be of great significance in practice. That it is still available, however, was confirmed by the Court of Appeal in *Young v Thames Properties Ltd* (1999). The court expressed the view that the question of whether there had been substantial performance was one of fact and degree, and, therefore, essentially an issue for the trial judge. On the facts, which concerned the construction of a car park, the judge had been entitled to conclude that the various defects which had been identified did not prevent a finding that there had been substantial performance.

14.3   Tender of performance

Being ready to perform a contract ('tender of performance') is generally treated as equivalent to performance, in the sense that if it is rejected, then it will lead to a discharge of the tenderer's liabilities. Thus, as of s 27 of the SGA 1979, puts it, where the expectation is that goods will be paid for on delivery:

> ... the seller must be ready and willing to give possession of the goods to the buyer in exchange for the price and the buyer must be ready and willing to pay the price in exchange for the possession of the goods.

14.3.1   Definition of tender

What amounts to satisfactory 'tender', so as to bring the above principle into play? This will largely depend on the terms of the contract, but something of the approach of the courts can be seen from *Startup v Macdonald* (1843). The plaintiff agreed to sell 10 tons of oil to the defendant. Delivery was to be 'within the last 14 days of March'. Delivery was in fact tendered at 8.30 pm on the 31 March, which was a Saturday. The defendant refused to accept or pay for the goods. It was held that provided that the seller had actually found the other party, and that there was time to examine the goods to check compliance with the contract, this was a satisfactory tender.

From this, it will be seen that the requirements are that the tender should meet the strict terms of the contract, and that it should be brought to the attention of the other party in time for any rights which might arise on tender to be exercised.

14.3.2 Tender of money

If a debtor tenders payment, and this is not accepted, this does not cancel the obligation to pay. The debtor, however, is not obliged to attempt to pay again, but can wait until the creditor calls for payment.

The exact amount must be tendered. There is no legal obligation to give change, though of course in the majority of situations the creditor will be quite happy to do so.

There are particular statutory rules as to the maximum amounts of particular types of coin which will constitute 'legal tender' (s 2 of the Coinage Act 1971).

14.3.3 Time

Is the time for performance important? Is time, as the courts put it, 'of the essence'? The common law said that it was, unless the parties had expressed a contrary intention. Equity took the opposite view, so that time was not of the essence unless the parties had specifically made it so. The equitable rule was given precedence in s 21 of the Law of Property Act 1925, so that where under equity time is not of the essence, contractual provisions dealing with time should be interpreted in the same way at common law. Note also that s 10(1) of the SGA 1979 states that:

> Unless a different intention appears from the terms of the contract, stipulations as to time of payment are not of the essence of a contract of sale.

The reference to the intention of the parties which appears in this section is of general application, as was confirmed by the House of Lords in *United Scientific Holdings Ltd v Burnley Borough Council* (1978). Refusing to be bound by the position as regards the common law and equitable rules prior to 1873, the House preferred to look at the nature of the contract itself. The dispute concerned the operation of a rent review close within a 99 year lease. The House held that time was not of the essence as far as the activation of the review machinery was concerned, so that the landlord was able to put it in motion even though he had just missed the 10-year deadline specified in the lease itself.

Where time is not initially of the essence, it seems that it may become so by one party giving notice. This is what happened in *Rickards v Oppenheim* (1950), the facts of which are given in Chapter 3 (see 3.7.2 above). This possibility appears to arise as soon as the contractual date for performance has passed. This was the view taken by the Court of Appeal in *Behzadi v Shaftesbury Hotels Ltd* (1991), which was a contract for the land. The court held that if the contract contained a specific date for performance, even though this was not of the essence, there was nevertheless a breach of contract as soon as that date had passed, and the party not in breach was entitled to serve a notice immediately making time of the essence. As Purchas LJ put it:

> I see no reason for the imposition of any further period of delay after the breach of contract has been established by non-performance in accordance with its terms before it is open to a party to serve such a notice. The important matter is that the notice must in all the circumstances of the case give a reasonable opportunity for the other party to perform his part of the contract.

Only after that period had expired would the party who has issued the notice be entitled to treat the contract as repudiated by the other side's failure to perform. Cf, however, *British and Commonwealth Holdings plc v Quadrex Holdings Inc* (1989) which seemed to suggest that there must be an unreasonable delay before the right to give notice making time of the essence arises. Since both these cases are Court of Appeal decisions, the latter one, that is, *Behzadi v Shaftesbury*, must be taken to prevail, pending a ruling by the House of Lords.

14.4 Discharge by breach

A breach of contract will have a range of consequences. It may entitle the innocent party to seek an order for performance of the contract, to claim damages, or to repudiate the contract. It is the last of these consequences that we are concerned with in this chapter (the other two are discussed in Chapter 15), since repudiation of the contract will also entail the discharge of future obligations.

14.4.1 Effect of repudiatory breach

There have at various times been suggestions that a breach of contract, if sufficiently serious, might bring a contract to an end automatically, irrespective of the wishes of the parties. See, for example, Lord Denning's judgment in *Harbutt's Plasticine v Wayne Tank and Pump* (1970), or, in the employment law context, *Hill v CA Parsons* (1972) and *Sanders v Neale* (1974). The current view, however, is that a breach only ever has the effect of allowing the innocent party the choice of whether to terminate the agreement, or allow it to continue. This was confirmed in the employment area by the Court of Appeal in *Gunton v London Borough of Richmond upon Thames* (1980), and more generally by the House of Lords in *Photo Productions v Securicor* (1980) (see 8.4.3 above). In all cases, therefore, the innocent party will have the possibility of electing to either treat the contract as repudiated, or to affirm it (and possibly claim damages).

Repudiation is not the same thing as 'rescission', though the courts do not always distinguish between them, and in certain circumstances the effects are the same. In a simple sale of goods transaction, for example, if there is a repudiatory breach in relation to the quality of the goods, the effect will be that the buyer will return the goods, and can reclaim the price. This is exactly the same as if there had been rescission for misrepresentation. There are differences, however. First, there will always be a right to claim damages for a repudiatory breach, whereas rescission (for example, in relation to a totally innocent misrepresentation) may be a remedy in itself. Secondly, although in a simple transaction the effects may be the same, in a complex, or continuing contract, whereas rescission requires the whole transaction to be undone, repudiation may leave certain obligations which have arisen prior to the breach intact.

As Lord Wilberforce explained in *Johnson v Agnew* (1979), where there is reference to 'rescission' for breach of contract:

> ... this so called 'rescission' is quite different from rescission *ab initio*, such as may arise for example in cases of mistake, fraud or lack of consent. In those cases, the contract is treated in law as never having come into existence ... In the case of repudiatory breach, the contract has come into existence but has been put to an end or discharged. Whatever contrary indications may be disinterred from old authorities, it is now quite clear, under the general law of contract, that acceptance of a repudiatory breach does not bring about 'rescission *ab initio*'.

This meant that, if there had been a repudiatory breach, and the plaintiff had been granted an order of specific performance, but such performance became impossible, a court had the power to discharge the order and award damages for the original breach.

14.4.2 Nature of repudiatory breach

What types of breach of contract will give rise to the right to treat the agreement as repudiated? There are a number of ways of approaching this issue. It could be said that this is a matter for the parties to determine, and that they should agree in their contract whether a particular type of breach is to be repudiatory or not. Secondly, it could be argued that the issue can only be determined when the consequences of an actual breach are known. Thirdly, it might be thought best to have specific legal rules which state that particular contractual obligations fall into one category or the other. English law, as we shall see, uses a mixture of all three approaches. It will be convenient, however, to start with the third, and look at a situation where a statute determines the consequences of particular breaches.

14.4.3 Sale of Goods Act 1979: implied conditions and warranties

The implied terms under the SGA 1979 are labelled as being either 'conditions' or 'warranties'. The consequences of this are spelt out in s 11(3), which indicates that a 'condition' is a stipulation the breach of which may give rise to a right to treat the contract as repudiated, whereas a breach of 'warranty' may give rise to a claim for damages, but not to a right to reject the goods.

The SGA 1979 thus uses the terminology of condition and warranty to distinguish between repudiatory and other breaches. Only if the term broken is a condition will the breach be repudiatory. The question then arises as to which terms are conditions and which are warranties? As far as the implied terms under the SGA 1979 are concerned, the Act itself provides the answer, by labelling them as one or the other. In relation to other provisions in a sale of goods contract, however, the question is, as s 11(3) makes clear, one of the 'construction of the contract'. This is the position in relation to most other contracts, as well, and so we need to consider this next.

Before doing so, however, it is important to note that both 'condition' and 'warranty' are at times used in other senses than the ones under consideration here. 'Condition' is used for example in relation to a 'condition precedent' or 'condition subsequent', or generally to mean the provisions of a contract, as in 'terms and conditions'. 'Warranty' on the other hand can mean simply a 'promise' or a 'guarantee'. Care is needed, therefore, in looking at discussions of contractual terms, particularly by judges, in order to be sure that the meaning which is being attached to a particular word is clear.

14.4.4 Categorisation of terms: the courts' approach

Where a term is not labelled by statute, the courts themselves have to decide whether it is a condition, breach of which will be repudiatory, or a warranty, breach of which will only give rise to a right to damages. The main factor will be the importance of the term in the context of the contract. Is it of major significance in relation to the purpose of the contract, or is its role only minor?

The approach of the courts can be seen in the contrasting cases of *Bettini v Gye* (1876) and *Poussard v Spiers* (1876). Both cases concerned singers. In *Poussard v Spiers* (1876), the singer was contracted to play a part in an operetta. She was unable, as a result of illness, to be present at the start of the run, and arrived a week late. By this time, a substitute had been employed, and her failure to appear was treated as a repudiatory breach. In *Bettini v Gye* (1876), the singer was required to be present for rehearsals six days before the start of the performance. Again, as a result of illness, he was delayed, and arrived three days late. On this occasion, the court treated the failure to appear for the rehearsals as a breach which was not repudiatory. As Blackburn J said, the classification of terms 'depends on the true construction of the contract as a whole'. In *Poussard v Spiers,* the failure to meet the obligation to be present for a performance was treated as much more serious than Bettini's failure to meet the obligation to be present for a rehearsal. The former breach had a much more significant impact on the main purpose of the contract than the latter.

In some cases, the courts will not look so much to the interpretation of the individual contract, but to the expectations of parties who regularly include clauses of a particular type in their agreements. In *Bunge Corporation v Tradax Export SA* (1981), it was stated that time clauses in mercantile contracts should usually be treated as conditions. As Lord Wilberforce explained, to treat such terms as 'innominate' would be commercially 'most undesirable':

> It would expose the parties, after a breach of one, two, three, seven and other numbers of days, to an argument whether this delay would have left the seller time to provide the goods. It would make it, at the time, at least difficult, and sometimes impossible, for the supplier to know whether he could do so. It would fatally remove from a vital provision in the contract that certainty which is the most indispensable quality of mercantile contracts, and lead to a large increase in arbitrations.

Applying this approach to the facts, a four day delay in giving notice of the readiness of a vessel to receive a cargo was a breach of a condition in the shipment contract, entitling the sellers to treat the contract as repudiated.

A similar approach to a clause relating to time was taken by the Privy Council in *Union Eagle Ltd v Golden Achievement Ltd* (1997), as noted above at 14.2.1.

14.4.5 Categorisation of terms: labelling by the parties

One way in which the courts may be able to determine the parties' intentions as regards the effect of breaking particular terms, is where these have been labelled. If they have gone through the contract and referred to certain terms as conditions, and the rest as warranties, then it may be presumed that this was intended to have the same significance as the labels used in the SGA 1979. The use of labels will not be conclusive, however, as is shown by *Schuler AG v Wickman Tools Sales Ltd* (1973). The defendants were under an obligation to make weekly visits to six named firms, over a period of four and a half years, in connection with a contract under which they were given the sole selling rights of the plaintiffs' panel presses. This obligation was referred to as a 'condition', and none of the other 19 clauses in the contract was described in this way. This would seem to suggest that the parties intended that any breach of it would be repudiatory. The majority of the House of Lords refused to interpret it in this way, however. Noting that the contract required in total some 1,400 visits to be made, and that it was likely that in a few cases a visit would be impossible, Lord Reid pointed out that:

> ... if Schuler's contention is right failure to make even one visit entitles them to terminate the contract, however blameless Wickman might be. This is so unreasonable that it must make me search for some other possible meaning of the contract.

This the House found by treating a breach of the visits clause as being a 'material breach' sufficient to bring into play other termination procedures under another clause.

The decision in *Schuler v Wickman* does not mean that the parties' own labelling of terms is to be ignored, simply that it is not conclusive of the issue. In subsequent cases, the courts have shown themselves to be willing to give effect to clearly stated provisions as to the consequences of a breach. In *Awilco A/S v Fulvia spA di Navigazione, The Chikuma* (1981), for example, in discussing a clause giving a right to withdraw a ship for late payment of hire, Lord Bridge said that where parties bargaining at arm's length use 'common form' clauses, it is very important that their meaning and legal effect should be certain:

> The ideal at which the courts should aim, in construing such clauses, is to produce a result such that in any given situation both parties seeking legal advice as to their rights and obligations can expect the same clear and confident answer from their advisers and neither will be tempted to embark on long and expensive litigation in the belief that victory depends on winning the sympathy of the court.

Similarly, in *Lombard North Central plc v Butterworth* (1987), the Court of Appeal upheld the parties own express provisions as to the consequences of breach of terms as to payment in a contract of hire, even though they were not happy about the justice of the overall result.

14.4.6 Consequences of categorisation

The categorisation of terms as either conditions or warranties, implies that the actual consequence of a particular breach is not a relevant factor. Once a term is a 'condition', any breach of it will be repudiatory, no matter that it can be easily remedied, or has on this occasion caused no substantial loss to the other party. Similarly, whatever the consequences of a breach of warranty, and however great the losses it causes, it will never give rise to the right to treat the contract as repudiated. This approach is therefore rigid, and may appear to cause injustice in some cases, but it has the merit of certainty, in that the parties can be aware in advance what the legal consequences of any particular breach will be (cf the comments of Lord Bridge in *The Chikuma* (see 14.4.5 above).

14.4.7 Intermediate terms

There are times when the categorisation of terms in the way outlined in the previous sections does not work, and at least since 1962, the courts have recognised that it is necessary to have an intermediate category. The leading case is *Hong Kong Fir Shipping Co v Kawasaki Kisen Kaisha* (1962), though some would argue that earlier decisions were in fact based on the same considerations. The term that was under consideration in *Hong Kong Fir* was that of 'seaworthiness', which appeared in a time charter of a ship. Diplock LJ admitted that some terms may be classifiable as conditions or warranties, but felt that there are many contractual undertakings of a more complex nature which cannot be classified in that way. The obligation as to seaworthiness, for example, could be broken in any number of ways. For example, the failure to have the correct number of lifejackets on board could render a ship 'unseaworthy' just as much as a major defect in the hull. In such a case, it was not possible to determine beforehand the consequences of a breach, in terms of whether it would be repudiatory or not. Rather, what a judge had to do was to:

> ... look at the events which had occurred as a result of the breach at the time when the charterers purported to rescind the charterparty and to decide whether the occurrence of those events deprived the charterers of substantially the whole benefit which it was the intention of the parties as expressed in the charterparty that the charterers should obtain from the further performance of their own contractual undertakings.

So, on this analysis, the focus is not on the parties' intentions at the time of the contract, but on the effect of the actual breach which has occurred: that is, the second of the approaches outlined at the start of this section (see 14.4.2 above). If the breach is so serious as to strike fundamentally at the purpose of the contract, then it will be treated as repudiatory, in the same way as if it was a breach of condition; if it is less serious it will give rise only to a remedy in damages, like a warranty.

14.4.8 Effects of *Hong Kong Fir*

It has never been doubted since the decision in *Hong Kong Fir* that there are three categories of term, namely conditions, warranties, and 'innominate' or intermediate terms. An approach based on the consequences of breach has even been adopted, perhaps somewhat surprisingly, in relation to sale of goods contracts (*Cehave NV v Bremer Handelgesellschaft mbH (The Hansa Nord)* (1975)). Lord Denning, in this case, was concerned with the definition of 'merchantable quality' (now 'satisfactory quality' – see 18.5.3 below) under the SGA 1893, the obligation to supply goods of such quality being a term labelled as a 'condition' by the statute itself. In determining whether the goods are 'merchantable', however, Lord Denning suggested that:

> In these circumstances, I should have thought a fair way of testing merchantability would be to ask a commercial man: was the breach such that the buyer should be able to reject the goods?

In other words, the consequences of breach are to be used to determine merchantability, and therefore, indirectly, whether or not a breach of condition has occurred. On the facts, since the goods, though damaged, had been used for its intended purpose as animal feed, there was not a breach which should have entitled the buyer to reject, and the goods were thus 'merchantable'. This ingenious incorporation of a *Hong Kong Fir* approach into the area of the statutorily labelled implied terms has, however, probably been superseded by the much more specific statutory definitions of quality to be found in the current SGA 1979 (see Chapter 18 at 18.5.3 below). In other areas, however, the attraction of the flexibility of Diplock LJ's analysis in *Hong Kong Fir* has frequently bowed to considerations of the desirability of commercial certainty, spelt out in the quotation from Lord Bridge in *The Chikuma* (1981) (see 14.4.5 above). Thus, in *The Mihalis Angelos* (1970), the obligation of being 'expected ready to load' at a particular time, a clause which clearly could be broken with varying degrees of seriousness, was treated as a condition, irrespective of the consequences of the particular breach. And as we have seen (see 14.4.4 above), a similar view was taken of time clauses in mercantile contracts in *Bunge Corporation v Tradax SA* (1981). It will continue to be important, therefore, to ask the question 'is this a condition or a warranty', before considering the consequences of the breach of contract. The answer to that question may render such consideration unnecessary.

14.5 Some special types of breach

There are two particular situations which call for some special consideration. The first is where the contract is to be performed in instalments, and the breach relates to only a small proportion of those instalments. The second is where the consequences of the breach do not affect the possibilities of the physical performance of the contract, but its commercial viability.

14.5.1 Instalment contracts

In a contract which is to be performed by instalments, will the breach of one of them ever amount to a repudiatory breach? If so, then the contract can been brought to an end as soon as that one breach has occurred, and there will be no further obligations as regards the rest of the instalments. On the other hand, if the innocent party allows the contract to continue, that may well amount to affirmation of the contract, so that the breach could not subsequently be relied on as being repudiatory.

The resolution of these issues may, of course, be determined by what the parties have themselves agreed in the contract. This is confirmed by s 31(2) of the SGA 1979, which states that in cases of defective delivery, or a refusal to accept delivery:

> ... it is a question in each case depending on the terms of the contract and the circumstances of the case whether the breach of contract is a repudiation of the whole contract or whether it is a severable breach giving rise to a claim in compensation but not to a right to treat the whole contract as repudiated.

An example of the application of this is to be seen in *Maple Flock Co Ltd v Universal Furniture Products (Wembley) Ltd* (1934). The sellers had contracted to sell 100 tons of rag flock to the buyers. Out of the first 20 loads delivered, one, the 16th, was defective. The Court of Appeal held that this was not a repudiatory breach, since it related only to one instalment, and therefore only one and a half tons out of the whole contract. In contrast, in *RA Munro & Co Ltd v Meyer* (1930), 1,500 tons of meat and bone meal were to be delivered in 12 instalments of 125 tons. After 768 tons had been delivered, it was discovered that all were adulterated, and did not match the contract description. It was held that this was sufficient to amount to a repudiatory breach.

The proportion of the instalments involved in the breach is not the only issue, however, as is shown by the House of Lords' decision in *Mersey Steel and Iron Co v Naylor, Benzon & Co* (1884). The contract was for the sale of 5,000 tons of steel, to be delivered at the rate of 1,000 tons per month, with payment within three days of receipt of the shipping documents. The sellers delivered only part of the first instalment, but delivered the second complete. Shortly before payment was due the sellers were the subject of petition for winding-up, and as a result the buyers (acting on inaccurate legal advice) withheld payment. The sellers sought to treat this as repudiatory breach. The House of Lords noted that the buyers had indicated a continuing willingness to pay as soon as any legal difficulties had been resolved, and therefore held that this was not a repudiatory breach. The context was important in determining the effect of a breach in relation to one instalment.

As well as illustrating the courts' approach to instalment contracts, this case shows that the intention of the party in breach, and the reasons for the breach, may be important factors in determining whether it is repudiatory. The fact that the buyers had no intention to repudiate, but were acting under a *bona fide* mistake of law, was a very relevant consideration.

14.5.2 Commercial destruction

In most cases of repudiatory breach, there is some act or omission which means that the obligations under the contract have only partially been fulfilled. Goods do not match their description, or are supplied in insufficient quality; services are not supplied, or do not meet contractual standards; money owed is paid late or not at all. In all these situations the innocent party is being deprived of the benefit of the contract. It is possible, however, for a party to complete his or her major obligations, but for the consequences of some minor breach to be such that, although it does not affect the practical possibility of continuing with the contract, commercially it would be unreasonable to do so. This is exemplified by *Aerial Advertising Co v Batchelors Peas* (1938). The contract was for the towing of an advertising banner on daily flights by an aeroplane. The pilot was supposed to clear his flight plan each day, but on one occasion he failed to do so. He flew over Salford, and saw a large crowd assembled in the main square. He flew close to it displaying the sign 'Eat Batchelors' Peas'.

Unfortunately, the date was 11 November, and the crowd had assembled to keep the traditional two minutes silence on Armistice Day. The actions of the pilot led to much criticism of Batchelors. The judge held that it was 'commercially wholly unreasonable to carry on with the contract' and that, in the circumstances, the consequences of the breach (that is, the failure to clear the flight plan) meant that Batchelors were entitled to treat the contract as repudiated.

14.6   Anticipatory breach

While there are obligations still to be performed, one party may indicate in advance that he or she intends to break the contract. This is known as an 'anticipatory breach', and will generally give the other party the right to treat the contract as repudiated, and to sue at once for damages. For example, in *Hochster v De La Tour* (1853), the defendant engaged the plaintiff on 12 April to enter his service as a courier, and accompany him on foreign tour. This employment was to start on 1 June. On 11 May, the defendant wrote to the plaintiff to inform him that his services would no longer be required. It was held that the plaintiff was entitled to bring an action for damages immediately, without waiting for 1 June.

The reason for allowing this type of action, rather than making the plaintiff wait until performance is due, was given by Cockburn CJ in *Frost v Knight* (1872). He held that it involves a breach of a right to have the contract kept open as a subsisting and effective contract. It, of course, also has the practical benefit of enabling the innocent party to obtain compensation for any damage speedily.

As will be seen in the next section, however, the innocent party does not have to accept the anticipatory breach as repudiating the contract. He or she may wait until performance is due, and then seek damages for non-performance at that stage. It has even been held in one case that the innocent party can legitimately incur expenses towards his or her own performance even after a clear indication of an intention to break the contract has been given by the other side. These may then be claimed as damages once the contract date for performance has passed (*White and Carter (Councils) v McGregor* (1961)).

14.7   Effect of breach: right of election

In relation to all repudiatory breaches, the innocent party has the right to elect to treat the contract as discharged, and claim for damages, or to affirm the contract, notwithstanding the breach. The latter course will prevent the contract from being discharged, but damages may still be recovered.

14.7.1 Need for communication

Where the innocent party elects to treat the breach as repudiatory, this decision will normally only be effective if communicated to the other party. That this is not, however, universally necessary is shown by the House of Lords' decision in *Vitol SA v Norelf Ltd* (1996). V and N had entered into a contract on 11 February 1991 for the purchase of a cargo of propane. On 8 March, V sent a telex to N repudiating the contract. This was subsequently agreed to amount to an anticipatory breach which, if accepted by N would bring the contract to an end immediately. N did not communicate with V but, on 12 March, started to try to find an alternative buyer and, on 15 March, sold the cargo to X. V challenged the arbitrator's decision that these actions by N amounted to an acceptance of the anticipatory breach. Phillips J upheld the decision of the arbitrator. The Court of Appeal, however, reversed this decision. Since the differing consequences following from acceptance of repudiation on the one hand, or affirmation of the contract on the other, were immediate and serious it was essential that the choice of repudiation should be clear and unequivocal. It needed to be manifested by word or deed. As Nourse LJ put it:

> A choice, however resolute, which gains no expression outside the bosom of the chooser cannot be clear and unequivocal in the sense that the law requires. Silence and inaction, being in the generality of cases equally consistent with an affirmation of the contract, cannot constitute acceptance of a repudiation.

What if the innocent party has failed to perform his or her obligations under the contract, as had happened here? Is this sufficient to indicate acceptance of repudiation? The Court of Appeal thought not. The failure to perform was equally consistent with a misunderstanding by the innocent party of his or her rights under the contract, indecision, or even inadvertence. The House of Lords, however, rejected the view of the Court of Appeal and restored the decision of the arbitrator and the judge at first instance. Lord Steyn set out three principles which apply to acceptance of a repudiatory breach:

- Where a party has repudiated a contract the aggrieved party has an election whether to accept the repudiation or affirm the contract.
- An act of acceptance of a repudiation requires no particular form: a communication does not have to be couched in the language of acceptance. It is sufficient that the communication or conduct clearly and unequivocally conveys to the repudiating party that the aggrieved party is treating the contract as at an end.
- The aggrieved party need not personally, or by an agent, notify the repudiating party of his election to treat the contract as at an end. It is sufficient that the fact of the election comes to the repudiating party's attention, for example notification by an unauthorised broker or other intermediary may be sufficient.

In applying these principles to the case, Lord Steyn noted that the specific issue before the House was 'whether non-performance of an obligation is ever *as a matter of law* capable of constituting acceptance' (emphasis added). Their Lordships answered this question in the affirmative, stating that whether there is acceptance in a particular case 'all depends on the particular contractual relationship and the particular circumstances of the case'. These were issues of fact, which the arbitrator was in the best position to decide. Lord Steyn was quite prepared to accept, however, the seller's (N's) failure to take the next step which would have been required if the contract was to continue, that is submitting the bill of lading to the buyer (V), could be found to amount to an unequivocal notification to V of N's acceptance of V's repudiation. The arbitrator was entitled to come to that conclusion on the facts, and his decision should be restored.

Despite this decision, which opens up the possibility of acceptance by inaction, the safest course for a party who intends to accept a repudiatory breach is to do so specifically, by communicating this to the other party. This will remove any danger that the behaviour of the party not in breach will be deemed 'equivocal', and therefore not sufficient to constitute a valid acceptance.

14.7.2 Risks of acceptance

There are, of course, dangers in treating an action by the other party as repudiatory, if it turns out to be viewed otherwise by the court. The party purporting to accept a repudiatory breach may well take action (as was the case in *Vitol v Norelf*) which itself involves a breach of obligations under the contract. If this turns out not to be justified by what the other party has done, then the party who thought they were acting in response to a repudiatory breach, may find the tables turned, and that they themselves are now liable to damages for their own breach of the contract. In *Federal Commerce and Navigation v Molena Alpha* (1979), which concerned the operation of three time charterparties, the charterers deducted various amounts from the hire which they paid to the owners. The owners objected and issued instructions to the masters of the vessels concerned to, *inter alia*, withdraw all authority to the charterers or their agents to sign bills of lading. This action was held to amount to a repudiatory breach which entitled the charterers to terminate the charterparties.

In *Woodar v Wimpey* (1980), the majority of the House of Lords seemed to take the view that this consequence would not necessarily follow if the party purporting to accept the repudiation was acting as a result of a mistake made in good faith as to his or her rights. Most commentators regard this aspect of the *Woodar v Wimpey* decision as dubious, and prefer to follow the bulk of authorities which suggest that an unjustified failure to meet contractual obligations is itself a repudiatory breach, even if it is a response to action from the other party which is mistakenly thought to be repudiatory.

14.7.3 Risks of affirmation

An election to affirm the contract carries risks as well, as is shown by *Avery v Bowden* (1855). The plaintiff chartered his ship to the defendant. The ship was to sail to Odessa, and there to take a cargo from the defendant's agent, which was to be loaded within a certain number of days. The vessel reached Odessa, but the agent was unable to supply a cargo. The ship remained at Odessa, with the master continuing to demand a cargo. Before the period specified in the contract had elapsed war broke out between England and Russia, and the performance of the contract became legally impossible. The plaintiff sued for breach. It was held, however, that even if the original action of the agent constituted a repudiatory breach, the contract had been affirmed by the fact that the ship remained at Odessa awaiting a cargo. The contract was then frustrated, and it was too late at that stage for the plaintiff to claim for breach.

Similarly, in *Fercometal Sarl v Mediterranean Shipping Co SA* (1988), it was held that a party which had affirmed a contract following an anticipatory breach could not subsequently rely on that breach to justify its own failure to fulfil its obligations under the contract.

PERFORMANCE AND BREACH

Discharge by performance

Parties will be released from primary obligations once they have completed all that they were bound to do by the contract.

*   Performance must generally be precise and exact

    (*Re Moore and Landauer* (1921); *Arcos v Ronaasen* (1933)).

*   Partial provision of services

    If the contract or obligation is 'entire', performance must be complete to discharge (*Cutter v Powell* (1795)).

*   Divisible contracts or obligations

    Compensation can be recovered for partial performance.

*   Non-performance due to promisee

    Promisor will be able to claim *quantum meruit* (*Planché v Colburn* (1831)).

*   Acceptance of partial performance

    May have the effect of discharging further obligations, and allow recovery on a *quantum meruit* (*Christy v Row* (1808)). This will not apply where the acceptor has no real choice (*Sumpter v Hedges* (1898)).

*   Substantial performance

    Minor defects in performance will not necessarily prevent discharge (*Dakin v Lee* (1916); *Hoenig v Isaacs* (1952)). The distinction is made between failure to complete, and completing badly.

Tender of performance

Generally, this is treated as equivalent to performance (cf s 27 of the SGA 1979). Satisfactory tender will depend on the terms of the contract, and the overall context (*Startup v Macdonald* (1843)). Note: there are special rules regarding the tender of money.

*   Time of performance

    Time is not generally 'of the essence' unless the contract makes it so (cf s 41 of the Law of Property Act 1925; s 10 of the SGA 1979). Time may become of the essence by giving notice (*Rickards v Oppenheim* (1950)).

Discharge by breach

Only 'repudiatory' breaches will lead to discharge. The effect is not automatic, but depends on the acceptance of the breach as repudiatory by the innocent party (*Gunton v London Borough of Richmond upon Thames* (1980)). Whether breach is repudiatory depends on either the classification of terms, or the effects of the breach.

- Classification of terms

  The SGA 1979 classifies implied terms into 'conditions' and 'warranties'. Breach of condition is repudiatory; breach of warranty allows only damages to be recovered. This classification is also used by the courts, based largely on the significance of the term (cf *Bettini v Gye* (1876) with *Poussard v Spiers* (1876)).

- Labelling of terms by the parties

  This may be indicative of their intentions, but is not conclusive (*Schuler AG v Wickman Tools Sales Ltd* (1973)). Parties bargaining on equal terms, however, should normally be taken to have intended the consequences of what they have stated in the contract (*The Chikuma* (1981); *Lombard North Central plc v Butterworth* (1987)).

- Intermediate terms

  This category was recognised in *Hong Kong Fir Shipping Co v Kawasaki Kisen Kaisha* (1962). Whether the breach is repudiatory will depend on its consequences – does it deprive the other party of 'substantially the whole benefit' of the contract. The approach has the advantage of flexibility, but reduces certainty.

- Instalment contracts

  The effect of the breach will largely depend on its extent – cf *Maple Flock Co Ltd v Universal Furniture Products (Wembley) Ltd* (1934) with *RA Munro & Co Ltd v Meyer* (1930).

Anticipatory breach

An advance indication of an intention to break a contract may in itself be treated as a repudiatory breach (*Hochster v De La Tour* (1853)). However, it does not have to be accepted as such (*White and Carter (Councils) v McGregor* (1961)).

Right of election

An innocent party may accept a repudiatory breach, or affirm the contract, cf *Vitol SA v Norelf Ltd* (1995). Treatment of the breach as repudiatory, if not justified, may itself be a breach of contract (*FCN v Molena Alpha* (1979)).

Affirmation will prevent future reliance on the breach if, for example, the contract is frustrated (*Avery v Bowden* (1855)), or as a justification for the other party's failure to perform (*Fercometal Sarl v Mediterranean Shipping Co SA* (1988)).

CHAPTER 15

REMEDIES

15.1 Introduction

At various points during the earlier chapters, remedies of one kind or another have been considered. Rescission for mistake, and damages for misrepresentation were discussed in Chapter 8, for example, and repudiation as a result of breach was dealt with in Chapter 12. Here, we are considering more generally the award of damages for breach of contract, and the order of specific performance to compel a party to go through with an agreement. Some reference to injunctions will also be necessary. In general, the common law aims to put the parties into the position they would have been in had the contract been performed by ordering one party to pay money to the other. Where one of the parties has performed its side of the bargain, and is awaiting payment from the other party, this can be achieved by the 'action for an agreed sum', or in sale of goods contracts the 'action for the price' (see 18.9.3). In other words, the party who has promised to pay for goods or services which have been transferred or performed by the other party, can be required to make good that promise. This was, for example, the form of action taken by Mrs Carlill to compel the Carbolic Smoke Ball Co to pay her the £100 (see 2.3.5). In other situations, the normal requirement will be for the payment of compensatory damages. An order to perform part of the contract, other than paying money that is owed, is unusual.

We start, therefore, by considering the remedy of 'damages', and will then look at specific performance and injunctions.

15.2 Damages: purpose

The basic principle of contractual damages is that of *restitutio in integrum*, or full restitution. In other words, the innocent party is to be put into the position he or she would have been in had the contract been performed satisfactorily (*Robinson v Harman* (1848)). The main objective of contract damages is therefore compensation, not punishment. Although, of course, in some situations, a party thinking about breaking an agreement may be deterred by the prospect of having to pay damages, or a party who has broken an agreement may suffer considerably from having to pay compensation, nevertheless these consequences are not the purpose of the award. This is shown by the fact that if the party not in breach has suffered no quantifiable loss, only nominal damages will be awarded. If, for example, there is a failure to deliver goods, and the buyer is able to obtain an alternative supply without problem, and at a price which is the same or lower than the contract price, no substantial damages will be recoverable (see s 51(3) of the Sale of Goods Act (SGA) 1979).

It should be noted at this point that a possible exception to the solely compensatory nature of contract damages has been opened up by the *obiter* suggestions of the Court of Appeal in *Attorney General v Blake* (1998) that they might also be used to require a defendant to disgorge a benefit acquired by breaking a contract, even where there is no corresponding loss to the claimant. This is discussed below at 15.3.3.

15.3 Damages: measure

Within the general principle of compensation, there are three basic methods by which damages may be calculated. These are conveniently labelled as 'expectation', 'reliance', and 'restitution'. Some consideration also needs to be given to consequential losses, and non-pecuniary losses.

15.3.1 Expectation interest

This is the approach which most clearly relates to putting the innocent party into the position he or she would have been in had the contract been performed. It is concerned with fulfilling the expectations of that party as to the benefits that would have flowed from the successful completion of the contract. In particular, where the innocent party, as will commonly be the case, was expecting to make a profit as a result of the contract, that will generally be recoverable (subject to the rules of remoteness, mitigation, etc, dealt with below at 15.4), as well as any other consequential losses flowing from the breach. Suppose, for example, A has a piece of machinery that needs repair, and he engages B to carry out the work. A tells B that the work must be done on 1 November, because A has an order for which he needs the machine on 2 November, and which he will lose if it is unavailable. If B, in breach of contract, fails to carry out the work, A will probably be able to claim the lost profit on the 2 November contract. If B had performed the contract properly, A would have made the profit, and therefore it should be recoverable.

Even if the profit was not certain to be made, there may be a partial recovery, on the basis that the plaintiff has lost the chance to make it. In *Chaplin v Hicks* (1911), for example, the breach of contract prevented the plaintiff from taking part in an audition. She was allowed to recover a proportion of what she might have gained had she been successful in the audition. Similarly, in *Simpson v London and North Western Ry Co* (1876), the defendant failed to deliver some specimens to a trade fair by the specified date. The plaintiff was allowed to recover compensation for the loss of sales he might have made had the specimens arrived on time. In these cases, it should be noted that the plaintiff may do better than would have been the case if the contract had not been broken. Ms Chaplin might not have been selected at the audition, and Mr

Simpson might not have made any sales. The court may be said in fact to be placing a monetary value on what is essentially a non-pecuniary loss – that is, the loss of a chance. Alternatively, it might be said that in this situation the compensatory aspects of contract damages are tinged with a punitive element, in that the defendant is made to pay in order to show that his or her behaviour fell below an acceptable level.

The problem of finding the appropriate award to meet the plaintiff's expectations can also arise in connection with the situation (usually occurring in construction contracts) where the cost of providing the plaintiff with exactly what was bargained for may be out of all proportion to the benefit which he or she would thereby obtain. This is discussed below at 15.3.4, in connection with the House of Lords' decision in *Ruxley Electronics and Construction Ltd v Forsyth* (1995).

15.3.2 Reliance interest

In some situations, it may not be easy for the plaintiff to estimate the profits that would have been made. Here it may prove more sensible to abandon the attempt, and instead to seek recovery of the expenditure which has been incurred in anticipation of the contract. An example of this type of situation is *Anglia Television v Reed* (1971). Reed was an actor who was under contract to play a leading role in a television film. At a late stage, Reed withdrew, and the project was unable to go ahead. In suing Reed for breach of contract, Anglia did not seek their lost profits. It would have been very difficult to estimate exactly what these would have been, given the uncertainties of the entertainment industry. Instead, they sought, and were awarded, compensation for all the expenses incurred towards setting up the film. This included expenditure incurred *before* the contract with Reed was entered into, provided that these fell within the rule of remoteness (see 15.4 below).

The decision as to whether to seek expectation or reliance damages will generally lie with the plaintiff (as was made clear in *Anglia v Reed*). There have been examples, however, of the court deciding that reliance is the appropriate measure. This was the case in *McRae v Commonwealth Disposals Commission* (1951) (see 10.3.1 above), in relation to the contract to salvage a non-existent ship. In some situations, on the other hand, the court may say that the reliance measure should not be available. This will be the case, for instance, where the difficulty in identifying profits results primarily from the fact that the plaintiff has made a bad bargain. Thus, in *C and P Haulage v Middleton* (1983), some of the plaintiff's costs were in fact reduced as a result of the breach, and the plaintiff's loss of equipment (which had to be handed over to the defendant) was an integral part of the original contract. In that situation, the plaintiff was only allowed to sue for the expectation interest. The burden of proving that the bargain was 'bad' in this sense falls, however, on the defendant (*CCC Films v Impact Quadrant Films* (1984)). The plaintiff does not have to prove that sufficient would have been made on the contract to cover the expenses incurred.

15.3.3 Restitution

'Restitution' in relation to contract damages generally refers to the return of money paid, such restitutionary damages, being largely a corollary of repudiatory breach. There is, however, another meaning to 'restitution', as discussed in Chapter 16, which refers to the rectification of a situation which has led to the 'unjust enrichment' of a party. Contract damages have not traditionally been awarded on this measure, and the idea was specifically rejected by the Court of Appeal in *Surrey CC v Bredero Homes Ltd* (1993). The recent Court of Appeal decision in *Attorney General v Blake* (1998) has, however re-opened this possibility. The case is discussed below. Looking first, however, at the restitution following repudiatory breach. If such a breach has been accepted, and the plaintiff has returned any benefits received, or is willing to do so, then he or she will also be entitled to claim the restitution of anything which has been given to the defendant. The easiest example is the situation of defective goods. The buyer returns the goods, and expects the refund of the price. In many situations, and in particular in relation to consumer contracts, that may be all that can be recovered by way of damages. The buyer may not have been expecting to make a profit out of the use or resale of the goods, and there may be no other losses resulting from the breach.

Restitution also has a more general role to play in relation to contracts which are void, or rescinded (for example, for mistake or misrepresentation), or where no contract has ever come into existence (see 16.3.3 below). These situations are not ones which arise on breach, and so are not discussed further here.

We must now consider the alternative type of 'restitutionary damages', as discussed by the Court of Appeal in *Attorney General v Blake* (1998). The case concerned the notorious spy George Blake, who had been a member of the British secret services. He was convicted in 1961 of spying for Russia and sentenced to a total of 42 years' imprisonment. In 1966, he escaped and fled to Moscow where he continues to live. While there, he wrote his autobiography, which was published in 1990. The book included descriptions of his life as a member of the secret services. He was to be paid £50,000 on the signing of the contract, £50,000 on the delivery of the manuscript and £50,000 on publication. At the time of the legal action, £90,000 remained payable by the publishers. The Attorney General brought an action to prevent Blake receiving any further benefit from the book. The Court of Appeal held that the Attorney General could succeed in that in his role as guardian of the public interest, he could obtain an injunction to prevent a person benefiting from criminal activity (the disclosures made by Blake in the book amounting to offences under the Official Secrets Act 1989). But, the court in addition considered the situation as regards contract law. Blake was in breach of contract, since when he joined the secret service he undertook a lifelong contractual obligation not to disclose anything about his work. The problem was to establish any loss for which compensation could be awarded to the Crown. If no such loss existed, then the damages could only be nominal. The Court of Appeal, however, felt that, although the Attorney General declined to argue the point, this was a situation where an exception to the general compensatory rule might be made. It suggested that the law was 'now sufficiently mature to recognise a restitutionary claim for profits made from a breach of contract in appropriate circumstances'. What are the 'appropriate circumstances'? The Court of Appeal suggested two. First, in relation to 'skimped performance':

> This is where the defendant fails to provide the full extent of the services which he has contracted to provide and for which he has charged the plaintiff.

The example given is of a fire service which did not provide the contracted number of firemen, horses, or length of hosepipe (as in the American case of *City of New Orleans v Firemen's Charitable Association* (1891)). The fire service had saved expenses, but had not failed to put out any fires. Nevertheless, it would be just to allow the other contracting party to recover damages based on the amount which the fire service had saved by this defective performance.

The second situation in which the court suggested that restitutionary damages might be appropriate is where the defendant has obtained a profit 'by doing the very thing which he contracted not to do'. This was exactly Blake's situation. He had promised not to disclose information about his work, but this was precisely what he had done in writing and publishing the book. It is clear that, had the Attorney General pursued this issue, the court would have been prepared to award damages for breach of contract on this basis. It is difficult to reconcile this with *Surrey CC v Bredero Homes Ltd* (1993), however, where a developer deliberately built more houses on a piece of land than it was entitled to under its contract with the local authority from which the land was acquired, and the Court of Appeal held that the damages would only be nominal because the local authority had suffered no loss. The court in *Blake* referred to the *Bredero* case, but regarded it as allowing restitutionary damages to be available in exceptional cases.

If the judgment in *Blake* is developed in later cases, it has the potential to amount to a very significant additional area of contract damages. Although the Court of Appeal clearly saw its use as being limited to two specific areas, once the principle of allowing restitutionary damages has been accepted, it may well prove difficult to keep it within narrow bounds.

15.3.4 Consequential losses

There are some losses which flow from the breach, but which cannot be put into the category of 'expenses' (that is, reliance) or thwarted expectations. Provided the causal link can be established, and they are not too remote (see 15.4 below), then they will be recoverable. If there is a contract for the purchase of a piece of machinery, for example, and it is defective, then the expectation interest may allow the recovery of lost profits that would have been gained by using the machine. If, however, the defect causes the machine to explode, which results in damage to the buyer's premises, this consequential loss can also be recovered. In general, the court will allow the recovery of the 'cost of cure' – that is, the expense of repairs and refurbishment to put the premises back into the position they were in prior to the explosion. This is subject to the limitation that if the cost of cure is significantly greater than the reduction in value of the property concerned, then the court may refuse to allow it (*Watts v Morrow* (1991) – cost of repairing house £34,000; diminution in value £15,000). This limitation does not, however, normally apply to the situation where the 'cure' relates to the plaintiff providing something which was specifically promised in the contract. Thus, in *Radford v De Froberville* (1978), the plaintiff was allowed to recover for the cost of building a brick wall, because this is what had been contracted for, even though a cheaper fence would have served the purpose (which was simply to mark a boundary). Even in this type of situation, however, if the cost of cure is substantially higher than the value of any resulting benefit to the plaintiff, the courts may refuse to award it, as is shown by *Ruxley Electronics and Construction Ltd v Forsyth* (1995). This case was not actually concerned with a consequential loss, simply with defective performance of the contract, but it illustrates the issue with which we are concerned.

The defendant entered into a contract for the construction of a swimming pool and building to enclose it, at a cost of £70,000. The depth of this pool at one end was to be 7 ft 6 in. After the work was completed, the depth of the pool was discovered to be only 6 ft 9 in. The plaintiff sought to recover payment for the installation of the pool. The defendant counterclaimed that the pool did not meet its specification, and sought compensation for this. It was not possible for the pool to be adapted, and the only way to produce a pool with a depth of 7ft 6in would have been by total reconstruction. This would have cost over £20,000. The trial judge found that the pool was entirely suitable for the purpose for which the defendant wished to use it, and held that the measure of damages should be the difference in value between the pool as supplied, and a pool which met the contract specification. He assessed this difference as nil, but awarded the defendant £2,500 for 'loss of amenity'. The defendant appealed, and the Court of Appeal held that he was entitled to have a pool which met the contract specification. It awarded him damages of over £20,000 to meet the cost of reconstruction. The plaintiff appealed. The House of Lords restored the trial judge's decision. It held that in building contracts there are two principal measures of damages, namely, the difference in value, and the cost of reinstatement. Where it would be unreasonable to award the cost of reinstatement, because, for example, the expense would be totally out of proportion to the benefit to be obtained, then the court should award the difference in value. As Lord Jauncey put it:

> Damages are designed to compensate for an established loss and not to provide a gratuitous benefit to the aggrieved party.

Given that the defendant had a perfectly serviceable swimming pool, 'were he to receive the cost of building a new one and retain the existing one he would have recovered not compensation for loss but a very substantial gratuitous benefit'. The appropriate measure here was therefore the difference in value, which (given the judge's finding) meant that only nominal damages were recoverable under this head. The House of Lords was, however, prepared to allow the judge's award of £2,500 for loss of amenity to stand.

The House of Lords' decision in this case appears quite sensible on the facts. Nevertheless, it leaves open the problem that an unscrupulous contractor can apparently now play fast and loose with the contract specifications in a construction contract, provided that the final product is fit for the purposes for which the other party wishes to use it. If it is so fit, then the cost of reconstruction to meet the contract specification is likely to be considered unreasonable, and there may well be little or no difference in the market value of the building. The innocent party is effectively left without a remedy, despite the fact that what has been provided is not what he or she wanted. Comparison can be made with the position as regards sales of goods, where the purchaser may still have a remedy, even if goods are 'fit for their purpose', if they do not match the contract description. By virtue of s 13 of the SGA 1979, the purchaser will generally be able to reject such goods. The person who contracts for the construction of a building now seems to be in a much weaker position. Much will depend on just how far the courts are prepared to go. Suppose, for example, I contract for a house to be built with a special warm air heating system which has to be built into the walls during construction. The builder constructs a house with a conventional gas-fired central heating system, and radiators. The house is perfectly fit to be lived in, and its value is not significantly different from the house with a warm air system (indeed, it may have a higher market value). Am I really to be left without any effective remedy against the builder? The principles applied by the House of Lords in *Ruxley Electronics v Forsyth* would seem to suggest so. This is a situation which could be dealt with by the restitutionary approach suggested in *Attorney General v Blake* (1998) (see 15.3.3 above). The constructors of the swimming pool had delivered a 'skimped performance' and the *Blake* approach would have allowed the court to award to the plaintiff the money that had been saved in not building the swimming pool to the contract specification.

15.3.5 Supervening events

The issue of the measure of damages when supervening events have increased the plaintiff's loss was considered by the Court of Appeal in *Beoco Ltd v Alfa Laval* (1994). The first defendants had installed a heat exchanger at the plaintiffs' works. A leak was discovered, and a repair attempted by the second defendants. The plaintiffs put the heat exchanger back in use without carrying out proper tests. In fact, the defects in the exchanger were more extensive than had been realised, and shortly afterwards it exploded. The plaintiffs sought to recover from the first defendants an amount relating to the loss of profits they would have suffered as a result of the need to further repair or replace the exchanger had it not exploded. Their action was based on the defendants' breach of contract in their initially having supplied a defective exchanger. The Court of Appeal held that the measure of damages for hypothetical losses should be the same in contract as in tort (for which, see *The Carslogie* (1952)). Thus, where a supervening event causes greater damage than the original breach of contract, the plaintiff cannot recover losses which would have been suffered had the event not occurred. Since the explosion was caused by the negligence of the plaintiffs' employees, they could not recover the lost profits which they might otherwise have suffered as a result of the first defendants' breach of contract. This conclusion is out of line with the normal approach to the assessment of contractual damages, which requires the issues to be looked at in the light of the parties knowledge *at the time of the contract*. This is the way in which the question of 'remoteness' (see 15.4.1 below) is dealt with. Taking account of later events, as in this case, means that they may well have the effect of reducing the defendants' liability. If, however, the event does not occur until after the damages have been assessed, then this will not apply. Thus, if, in this case the explosion had not occurred until after trial, the plaintiffs would probably have been able to claim the lost profits they were seeking. This runs the risk of making the assessment of damages dependent on rather arbitrary factors, such as when exactly a particular event occurs.

A different approach to a particular type of supervening event was taken by the House of Lords in *South Australia Asset Management Corpn v York Montague Ltd* (1996). This was concerned with cases where there has been a negligent over-valuation of a property which has been used as security of a loan. The question at issue is to what extent should the negligent valuer be liable for the fact that the property has reduced in value because of a fall in the market. Suppose, for example, that the property is valued at £15m when its true value is £10m. The lender lends £12m. When the borrower defaults, the property is sold but, because of a fall in market values, only realises £5m. Should the valuer be liable for the full loss which the lender has suffered (that is, £7m) or only the difference between the valuation and the actual value at the time of the contract (£5m)? The House of Lords took the view that the valuer should only be liable for those losses which are properly attributable to having given wrong information. It held that the lender's loss in this situation is having less security for the loan than was thought. The correct measure of damages is therefore the difference between the actual and true valuations – in the example given above, £5m. The decision, which reversed the judgment of the Court of Appeal, is not uncontroversial. There is some strength in the Court of Appeal's view that, if the valuer had given correct information, the lender would not have entered into the transaction at all, and that therefore the full losses should be recoverable. The House of Lords has, however, settled this issue for the time being.

15.3.6 Non-pecuniary losses

Contract damages are primarily concerned with economic losses of one kind or another, which are more or less quantifiable in money terms. In some situations, however, non-pecuniary losses will be caused. If, for example, a defective product results in personal injury to the purchaser, there is no reason why damages should not be recovered in relation to the pain and suffering so caused. Of course, third parties who are injured will have to rely on tortious remedies at common law or under the Consumer Protection Act 1987.

A more difficult question arises in relation to mental distress, anguish, or annoyance caused by a breach of contract. The courts have tended to be wary of awarding compensation under this heading. In *Addis v Gramophone Company Ltd* (1909), the House of Lords refused to uphold an award which had been made in relation to the 'harsh and humiliating' way in which the plaintiff had been dismissed from his job in breach of contract. This line was followed in a more recent dismissal case, *Bliss v South East Thames RHA* (1988), where a surgeon had sued the health authority by which he was employed. The authority had, following a dispute between the surgeon and a colleague, required him to undergo a psychiatric examination. The surgeon refused, and was suspended. The surgeon treated this as a repudiatory breach, and sued for breach of contract. He succeeded at first instance, and was awarded £2,000 for mental distress. The Court of Appeal held, however, that it was bound by *Addis v Gramophone*, and held that it was not possible to recover damages for mental distress in an action for wrongful dismissal.

In coming to this conclusion, it disapproved the decision in *Cox v Phillips Industries Ltd* (1976) where damages were recovered for distress and anxiety resulting from a demotion. Some doubts about *Addis v Gramophone* were raised by the decision of the House of Lords in *Malik v BCCI* (1997) the facts of which have been given at 7.5.7. The House took the view that where there was a breach of the implied term of trust and confidence in an employment contract, *Addis* should not be regarded as precluding an award of damages for loss of reputation or difficulty in obtaining future employment. The House were not, however, dealing with the manner of dismissal in this case, and were not concerned with 'injury to feelings'. The Court of Appeal has subsequently confirmed, in *Johnson v Unisys Ltd* (1999), that *Addis* should not be regarded as having been overruled in *Malik v BCCI*. Damages for distress and injury to feelings resulting from the manner of a dismissal are still unavailable.

On the other hand, it has been held that where one of the purposes of the contract is to provide pleasure and enjoyment, damages for distress and disappointment caused by a breach may be recovered. Thus, in *Jarvis v Swan's Tours* (1973), such damages were awarded in relation to breach of contract in the provision of a holiday which had promised to provide 'a great time'. A similar approach can be seen in *Jackson v Horizon Holidays* (1975) (see 5.4 above). Where, however, the contract is a purely commercial one, damages for anguish and vexation will not be allowed. Thus, in *Hayes v James and Charles Dodd* (1990), the plaintiffs were suing their solicitors for breach of contract. The solicitors had given an assurance that a right of way existed in relation to access to a property which the plaintiffs were purchasing for their business. This turned out to be untrue, and the plaintiffs' business failed as a result. The trial judge awarded damages of £1,500 to each plaintiff for anguish and vexation. The Court of Appeal, however, applied the same approach as in *Bliss v South East Thames RHA*. This meant that, as Staughton LJ held:

> ... damages for mental distress in contract are, as a matter of policy, limited to certain classes of case. I would broadly follow the classification by Dillon LJ in *Bliss v South East Thames RHA*: '... where the contract which has been broken was itself a contract to provide peace of mind or freedom from distress.' It may be that the class is somewhat wider than that. But it should not, in my judgment, include any case where the object of the contract was not comfort or pleasure, or the relief of discomfort, but simply carrying on a commercial activity with a view to profit.

Subsequent cases have taken a similar line. Thus, in *Alexander v Rolls Royce Motor Cars Ltd* (1996), the Court of Appeal refused to award damages for disappointment, loss of enjoyment or distress resulting from a breach of a contract to repair the plaintiff's motor car. Similarly, in *Farley v Skinner* (2000), the claimant was seeking damages from a surveyor who had inspected and reported on a house which the claimant had then bought. The surveyor had failed to mention that the house was near an aircraft navigation beacon, so that the use and enjoyment of the property was affected by aircraft noise (particularly at weekends). The Court of Appeal held that no damages were available under this heading. The contract was not one where the object was 'to provide pleasure, relaxation, peace of mind or freedom from molestation' so as to bring it into the exceptional category where damages for non-physical distress and annoyance can be awarded.

15.4 Limitations on recovery

There are two main limitations on the amount of damages which can be recovered for a breach of contract, namely, the rule of remoteness and the requirement of mitigation. The issue of contributory negligence will also be considered at 15.4.7 below.

15.4.1 The rule of remoteness

At various points in this chapter, it has been mentioned that the award of damages under a particular head will be subject to the rule of remoteness. This is a rule which basically prevents consequential losses extending too far, and placing unreasonable burdens on the defendant. It should also be recalled that in Chapter 9 (see 9.3.2 above) it was noted that in relation to the tort of deceit, and the remedy for negligent misrepresentation under s 2(1) of the Misrepresentation Act 1967, all consequential losses are recoverable, without limitation. This is exceptional, however, and in general, in both tort and contract, damages are only recoverable in relation to losses which are not too remote.

The type of recovery the rule is designed to prevent is as follows. Suppose that a contract for the hire of a car is broken, because the one supplied is unfit for its purpose and breaks down. The hirer may as a result fail to arrive at a sale where she would have been able to buy a valuable painting which she could have resold for a £100,000 profit. Should the hire company be liable for the £100,000? English law will normally regard this loss as too remote from the breach to be recoverable.

15.4.2 The rule in *Hadley v Baxendale*

In contract, the starting point for the rule of remoteness is *Hadley v Baxendale* (1854). In this case, there was delay in the transport of a broken mill-shaft which resulted in considerable losses for the mill-owner, because no spare shaft was available. The court stated the rule as being that the defendant will only be liable for losses:

> ... either arising naturally, that is, according to the usual course of things, from such breach of contract itself, or such as may reasonably be supposed to have been in the contemplation of both parties at the time they made the contract as the probable result of the breach of it.

Applying this to the facts of the case, the court held that in most cases of a breach of this kind, no such losses would have followed, so that it could not be said that the losses followed naturally from the breach. Nor were the defendants aware, at the time of the contract, of the circumstances which meant that the mill would not be able to function at all without this particular shaft. Therefore, the losses were not recoverable.

15.4.3 Relevance of knowledge

There are two aspects of this test which should be noted. First, it is clear that remoteness rule has to be assessed on the basis of the parties' knowledge at the time the contract is made. The reason for this is that awareness of a particular risk may affect the terms of the contract. If, to use the example given above, the firm hiring a car is aware that the customer is using it to attend a sale in order to buy a rare painting, the firm may want to:

- increase the price;

- insert an exclusion clause;

- seek insurance of the risk; or

- refuse to enter into the contract at all.

Knowledge which the defendant acquired after the formation of the contract is therefore irrelevant to the rule of remoteness.

15.4.4 'Reasonable contemplation' test

Secondly, the rule as stated in *Hadley v Baxendale* (1854) appears to have two parts, the first relating to the natural consequences of breach, and the second to the contemplation of the parties. As interpreted in the later cases of *Victoria Laundry (Windsor) Ltd v Newman Industries* (1949), and *The Heron II* (1969), however, the two limbs are really just aspects of one general principle. The situation must be looked at through the eyes of the reasonable defendant, who will be presumed to have in contemplation the normal types of loss which would follow from the breach. As regards anything more unusual, it will have to be established that the defendant had sufficient actual knowledge to be aware of the risk. The test is thus, simply, what can this defendant, bearing in mind his or her state of knowledge, be reasonably presumed to have expected to be the consequence of the breach of contract which occurred.

In *Victoria Laundry (Windsor) v Newman*, the breach of contract was a lengthy delay in the delivery of a boiler which the plaintiffs (as the defendants were aware) wished to use in their laundry and dyeing business. The Court of Appeal held that the plaintiffs could recover from lost profits at a level reasonably to be anticipated from a business of this type. They could not recover, however, in relation to some particularly lucrative dyeing contracts with the Ministry of Defence, of which the defendants were unaware.

15.4.5 Degree of risk

In *The Heron II* (1969), the plaintiffs lost money when the ship they had chartered to carry a cargo of sugar deviated from its route and arrived late at the port of destination. The sugar was sold immediately, as had always been the plaintiffs' intention, but the market price had fallen significantly as compared with the date on which the ship should have arrived. The issue was whether the shipowners were liable for this loss, since they were not specifically aware of the charterers' intentions in relation to the sale of the cargo. The House of Lords therefore had to consider the degree of risk that had to be contemplated before a loss was not too remote. It is a difficult concept to pin down, and there is no clear, single phrase, which is used to express it. The House agreed, however, that the test in contract was distinguishable from that in tort, which is based on 'reasonable foreseeability'. The contract test is stricter than that, and depends on the loss being contemplated as 'not unlikely', or 'liable to result'. Lord Reid put it this way:

> The crucial question is whether, on the information available to the defendant when the contract was made, he should, or the reasonable man in his position would, have realised that such loss was sufficiently likely to result from the breach of contract to make it proper to hold that the loss flowed naturally from the breach or that loss of that kind should have been within his contemplation.

Applying this approach, it was held that the sellers should have known that it was not unlikely that the sugar would be sold as soon as it arrived at its destination. They must also have been aware that the price of sugar fluctuates, and that there was a risk that a delay would mean that the plaintiffs would suffer a loss on the sale.

It seems that it is the *type* of loss, rather than the precise way in which it occurs, or its extent, which must be contemplated. In *Parsons (Livestock) Ltd v Uttley Ingham & Co Ltd* (1978), the defective installation of a hopper used for storing pig food led to the death of a large number of the plaintiff's pigs, as a result of the food going mouldy. The defendants were held liable for this loss, because some harm to the pigs was within the reasonable contemplation of the parties as something which would result from a defective installation, even though the particular disease was not. As Lord Scarman put it:

> While, on [the judge's] finding, nobody at the time of contract could have expected E coli to ensue from eating mouldy nuts, he is clearly, and as a matter of common sense, rightly, saying that people would contemplate ... the serious possibility of injury and even death among the pigs.

Where a particular unusual aspect of the plaintiff's activity has increased the loss caused by the defendant's breach, the defendant will only be liable if he had actual knowledge. Thus, in *Balfour Beatty Construction (Scotland) Ltd v Scottish Power plc* (1994), the House of Lords held that a supplier of electricity who was in breach of contract because of an interruption in the supply was not liable for the full losses suffered by the plaintiff. The interruption had occurred while the plaintiff was in the middle of a construction project which required a 'continuous pour' of concrete. The break in supply meant that the work which had been done was worthless, and had to be demolished. There was no evidence, however, that the defendants were aware of the need for a continuous pour, and there was no presumption that a supplier of a commodity should be taken to be aware of all the techniques involved in the other party's business.

15.4.6 Mitigation

Once a breach of contract has occurred, the plaintiff is not entitled to sit back and do nothing while losses accumulate. There is an obligation to take reasonable steps to mitigate losses, which was laid down by the House of Lords in *British Westinghouse Electric and Manufacturing Company v Underground Electric Railways Co of London* (1912). Viscount Haldane, LC, explained that this obligation:

> ... imposes on a plaintiff the duty of taking all reasonable steps to mitigate the loss consequent on the breach, and debars him from claiming any part of the damage which is due to his neglect to take such steps.

Furthermore:

> ... this ... principle does not impose on the plaintiff an obligation to take any step which a reasonable and prudent man would not ordinarily take in the course of his business. But when in the course of his business he has taken action arising out of the transaction, which action has diminished his loss, the effect in actual diminution of the loss he has suffered may be taken into account even though there was no duty on him to act.

In other words, the court will look at what the plaintiff's actual losses are, rather than what they might hypothetically have been had the plaintiff not acted, even though the plaintiff's actions in reducing the loss have gone beyond what might reasonably have been required. If the plaintiff has done nothing, however, the court will consider what steps might reasonably have been taken to reduce the losses. The plaintiff will be debarred from claiming any part of the damage which is due to a failure to take such steps. So, if the seller fails to deliver in a sale of goods contract, the buyer will be expected to go into the market and attempt to obtain equivalent goods. If such are available at, or below, the market price, then only nominal damages will be recoverable. If the buyer fails to enter the market until the price has risen, or pays over the odds, these increased losses will not be recoverable. Similarly, a reasonable offer of performance following a breach should not be spurned. In *Payzu Ltd v Saunders* (1919), the plaintiffs had failed to make prompt payment for an instalment of goods. The defendants had, in breach of contract, then refused to deliver unless the plaintiffs agreed to pay cash with each order. It was held that the plaintiffs should have accepted this offer, which would have reduced their loss (since the market value of the goods in question was rising above the contract price).

Mitigation only requires the plaintiff to act 'reasonably' in all the circumstances. In *Wroth v Tyler* (1974), the plaintiff's lack of resources was considered a reasonable ground for a failure to go into the market and make an alternative purchase.

The principle of mitigation raises particular problems in cases of anticipatory breach. If the plaintiff accepts the breach, and the contract terminates immediately, then the normal rules will apply. If, however, the plaintiff does not accept the breach, but elects to wait for the other party to perform, it seems that there is not at that stage any duty to reduce losses. In *White and Carter (Councils) v McGregor* (1962), the defendants had contracted to buy advertising space on litter bins owned by the plaintiffs. This contract was wrongfully cancelled by the defendants before any work had been done. The plaintiffs refused to accept this anticipatory breach, and went ahead with the production and display of the advertisements. They then sued for the full sum due under the contract. The House of Lords held that there is no obligation on the plaintiff in such a situation to mitigate the losses, and full recovery is possible. The decision has been regarded as harsh on the defendant, and has been widely criticised, but it still stands as the leading authority on this issue.

15.4.7 Contributory negligence

In tort, it is well established that the damages recoverable may be reduced by the plaintiff's own, contributory, negligence (the Law Reform (Contributory Negligence) Act 1945). Does the same principle apply in contract? The issue was considered by the Court of Appeal in *Forsikringsaktieselskapet Vesta v Butcher* (1988), which stated, *obiter*, that the 1945 Act did apply where there was concurrent liability in tort and contract (that is, where the breach of contract consisted of negligent performance, in a situation where there was also a tortious duty of care). Where, on the other hand, the breach of contract is based on strict liability, there is no scope for contributory negligence, and the 1945 Act is irrelevant. This was confirmed by the Court of Appeal in *Barclays Bank plc v Fairclough Building Ltd* (1994), which concerned a breach of strict obligations arising under a building contract. The judge had held that the plaintiffs had failed to supervise the work properly, and therefore reduced the damages. The Court of Appeal reversed this decision. Where contractual liability was strict, it was inappropriate to apportion losses, even if the defendant might also be said to have been negligent. Simon Brown LJ explained his reasons for coming to this conclusion in this way:

> The very imposition of a strict liability upon the defendant is to my mind inconsistent with an apportionment of the loss. And not least because of the absurdities that the contrary approach carries in its wake. Assume a defendant, clearly liable under a strict contractual duty. Is his position to be improved by demonstrating that besides breaching that duty he was in addition negligent?

Where, however, the contractual liability is based on 'negligence', but there is no concurrent tortious duty, there is no clear authority. There is some suggestion from the case of *De Meza and Stuart v Apple Van Straten* (1974) that the Act does apply in such a case, but this was not supported by *dicta* in *Vesta v Butcher*. And although losses were apportioned in *Tenant Radiant Heat Ltd v Warrington Development Corporation* (1988), this was on the basis of one side having broken the contract, and the other being independently liable in tort. The area is thus in some confusion, and a clear ruling from the House of Lords would be helpful.

One issue which has been considered by the House of Lords is the way in which contributory negligence should be dealt with in cases of over-valuation of property. The general rule for calculating damages in such cases has been established in *South Australia Asset Management Corpn v York Montague Ltd* (1996), discussed above, at 15.3.5. The issue in *Platform Home Loans Ltd v Oyston Shipways Ltd* (1999) was, first, whether contributory negligence applied where the claimant's 'negligence' is different from the defendant's negligence; and, secondly, if it does, to what sum any reduction should be applied. On the first question, the Court of Appeal held that the fact that the lender had an imprudent lending policy could operate as contributory negligence to reduce damages, even though this had nothing to do with the defendant's negligent over-valuation of the property. The analogy was used of the seat belt cases in tort; not wearing a seat belt will not contribute to the negligence of the driver, but it can be used as a reason for reducing the claimant's damages. The House of Lords upheld the Court of Appeal on this issue. It disagreed, however, on the second, that this, the way in which the reduction should be calculated. The Court of Appeal had held that the percentage reduction suggested by the trial judge should be applied to the lender's loss as established by the *South Australia Asset Management Corporation* approach. This limited the loss to the difference between the over-valuation and the true valuation at the time of the contract. Thus, in this case, the difference in the valuations was £500,000 and the judge had found the lender's 20% contributorily negligent. The Court of Appeal therefore awarded damages of £400,000. The House of Lords, however, held that the reduction should be applied to the lender's full loss, which had been increased by the fall in market values. In this case, the property had been resold for only £435,000, and the trial judge had found that the lender's full loss was £611,748. It was to this figure that the 20% reduction should be applied. Only if the resulting amount was higher than the figure arrived at on the *South Australia Asset Management Corporation* calculation should it be capped at that level. In this case, the 20% reduction produced a figure of £489,398. Since this was below the figure of £500,000, the lender was entitled to recover this amount, rather than the £400,000 awarded by the Court of Appeal.

15.5 Liquidated damages and penalty clauses

The parties to a contract may decide to include provision as to the compensation which is to be paid in the event of a breach. This is known as a 'liquidated damages' clause, and is generally a perfectly acceptable arrangement, to which the courts will happily give effect. The limitation on this is that the sum specified in the contract must be a 'genuine pre-estimate' of the plaintiff's loss, and not a 'penalty'. If it is the latter, then it will be unenforceable. This distinction was insisted upon by the House of Lords in *Dunlop Pneumatic Tyre Co Ltd v New Garage and Motor Co Ltd* (1915). In this case, a sum of £5 was stated to be payable 'by way of liquidated damages and not as a penalty' in relation to a wide range of breaches of contract. The House of Lords held that, despite the parties' own statement, a sum payable could constitute a penalty not only if it was excessive in comparison to the loss, but also if it was payable on the occurrence of a range of events, which would be likely to produce a range of different losses. That was the case here, but nevertheless the House felt that on balance the £5 should not be regarded as a penalty.

15.5.1 Application of the principles

The principles in this area are clear enough. The difficulty comes in applying them to particular provisions. The area was reconsidered by the Privy Council in *Philips Hong Kong Ltd v Attorney General of Hong Kong* (1993). The case concerned a claim by Philips that they were not liable to pay the Hong Kong government liquidated damages for delay to completion of contract works, because these amounted to a penalty. The Court of Appeal of Hong Kong allowed an appeal from a first instance decision upholding Philips' claim. Philips appealed to the Privy Council. The Privy Council stated that in deciding whether a clause was a penalty clause, or a genuine pre-estimate of damages, the court was not helped by the use in argument of unlikely hypothetical examples of situations where the sums payable under the liquidated damages clause would be wholly out of proportion to any loss. Although the clause must be judged objectively, at the date the contract was made, what happened subsequently could provide valuable evidence of what could reasonably be expected to be the loss at the time the contract was made. The appeal was dismissed. In reaching its conclusions, the Privy Council accepted Lord Dunedin's statement in *Dunlop Pneumatic Tyre Co Ltd v New Garage and Motor Co* (1915) that:

> The question whether a sum stipulated is penalty or liquidated damages is a question of construction to be decided upon the terms and inherent circumstances of each particular contract, judged of as at the time of the contract not at the time of the breach ...

Nevertheless, it was felt that what had actually happened might provide a better guide than hypothetical examples thought up by counsel. Furthermore, where the range of possible losses was broad, the better approach might be simply to say that the clause was not intended to apply to breaches where the liquidated damages would be totally out of proportion to the loss, rather than to strike the clause down in its entirety. The court was clearly influenced by the fact that this was a commercial contract where 'what the parties had agreed should normally be upheld'. The decision suggests a flexible, but to some extent unpredictable, approach to the effect of such clauses.

In *Duffen v Fra Bo SpA* (1998), the Court of Appeal considered a term in an agency contract which provided that on termination by the agent the principal should immediately pay the agent £100,000. This was stated in the contract to be 'liquidated damages' with the sum being 'agreed by the parties to be a reasonable pre-estimate of the loss and damage which the agent will suffer on termination of the agreement'. Nevertheless, the court held that it was a penalty clause, and unenforceable. It was not a genuine attempt to estimate the loss which the agent would suffer following breach by the principal, nor was it graduated in relation to the unexpired term of the agent's contract. Enforcing it would give the agent a substantial windfall which would be both 'extravagant and unconscionable'.

It should also be noted that a clause which imposes an obligation on a consumer to pay a 'disproportionately high sum' for failure to fulfill an obligation may well be unenforceable by virtue of the Unfair Terms in Consumer Contracts Regulations 1999 (see Sched 3, para 1(e)). These Regulations are discussed in more detail in Chapter 8 (see 8.12 above).

15.6 Specific performance

The remedy of specific performance involves the court in issuing an order directing one of the parties to a contract to carry out his or her obligations. The sanction for a failure to comply is that the person concerned will be in contempt of court, and liable to fines and imprisonment as a consequence. The remedy is, of course, an equitable one, developed by the chancery courts. As a result, unlike damages, it is discretionary. This means that a plaintiff is not entitled to the order simply as a result of proving that the other party is in breach of his or her obligations. Once this has been established, the court will then decide whether it is appropriate in this particular case that the order should be made. For example, as we saw in Chapter 10, one way in which the courts will allow a party to escape the consequences of a mistake concerning the terms of the contract is by refusing to order specific performance (see 10.7.1 above). Similarly, the order may not be granted if the plaintiff has taken advantage of the defendant, for example, because he or she was drunk (*Malins v Freeman* (1837)).

Although this discretionary element inevitably attaches a degree of uncertainty to the remedy, in fact, the courts have developed a number of rules about its use, which mean that, in many cases, it will be fairly easy to determine whether or not the order is likely to be granted. The rest of this section looks at these.

15.6.1 Adequacy of damages

One of the reasons why the remedy of specific performance developed is that, in certain situations, damages will be an inadequate remedy. If no pecuniary loss can be established, or it is impossible to quantify, this would mean that there would be no effective sanction for a breach of contract, in the absence of the order for specific performance. In *Harnett v Yielding* (1805), for example, Lord Redesdale said:

> Unquestionably, the original foundation of these decrees was simply this, that damages would not give the party the compensation to which he was entitled; that is, it would not put him in a situation as beneficial to him as if the agreement were specifically performed.

Thus, as Kindersley VC explains in *Falcke v Gray* (1859), the Courts of Equity would not allow an injustice to stand, but intervened to order performance of the obligations. Now, of course, the remedy is available in all courts, and the question to be asked is, when will damages not be regarded as an adequate remedy?

If there is a contract for the sale of goods in which there is an active market, then it is very unlikely that an order for specific performance will be granted. The party not in breach can buy or sell in the market, and be compensated by way of damages for any financial loss resulting from a difference between the contract and market prices. If, on the other hand, what is being sold is a valuable antique, or some other item which is not generally available, specific performance may well be the appropriate remedy. This distinction is supported by s 52 of the SGA 1979, which allows for specific performance in relation to 'specific' or 'ascertained' goods, but not 'generic' goods (see 18.2.3–18.2.7 below for discussion of these categories).

Similarly, it is normally the case that the order will be available to enforce contracts for the sale of land, since every piece of land is regarded as unique. In *Behnke v Bede Shipping Co Ltd* (1927), a 'unique' ship was held to be capable of being subject to an order for specific performance, but in *The Stena Nautica* (1982) the decision went the other way.

The Court of Appeal accepted that as a matter of law a ship could, in appropriate circumstances, be the subject of an order for specific performance. On the facts, however, it was felt that the judge had been wrong to make such an order, relating to the plaintiffs' option to purchase a vessel. A factor that had apparently weighed heavily with the judge was that the ship concerned was a sister ship of other vessels operated by the plaintiffs. On the other hand, he had made the order subject to another charter with a third party which was to operate for the next two years. The Court of Appeal found these two elements in the judge's decision to be inconsistent. As May LJ commented:

> If the sister ship point was relevant and indeed vital, in deciding whether the [plaintiffs] should be limited to their remedy in damages, it is I think somewhat surprising that the learned Judge went on in effect to deprive them of the use of the sister ship over the next two years, in imposing the condition that he did on the order for specific performance which he made.

Indeed, it is always like to raise a question as to whether such an order is necessary, on the basis that damages are inadequate, if it is made subject to a delay in its operation.

In some cases, it seems that if damages would only be nominal then the order may be made. Thus, in *Beswick v Beswick* (1968) (see 5.2.1 above), the fact that the deceased's estate suffered no direct loss from the failure of the nephew to pay his aunt meant that only nominal damages would be recoverable in an action by the estate. Justice clearly demanded, however, that the contract should be enforced, and so the order was granted. It will not always be the case that the fact that damages would be nominal will allow specific performance to be ordered. If that were so it would include all the cases of sale of goods where there is an available market offering a price more attractive than the contract one. There must be some other factor which will persuade the court to make the order, but it is difficult to predict what this will be, or to make a list of the appropriate circumstances.

15.6.2 Need for supervision

The court will be reluctant to order specific performance where it would have to supervise the parties over a period of time to ensure compliance. In *Ryan v Mutual Tontine Westminster Chambers Association* (1893), for example, the court refused to grant specific performance of a landlord's obligation to have a resident porter 'constantly in attendance'. It appears, however, to be only where the supervision would need to concern the detail of performance that this limitation applies. In *Wolverhampton Corporation v Emmons* (1901), for example, the contract concerned a building contract for some new houses, which would obviously take time to complete. The court was prepared to order specific performance because the obligations of the defendant were clearly defined by the building plans, and so there would be no need for detailed supervision while the work was being done.

A more recent example of the application of this principle is to be found in *Co-operative Insurance Society Ltd v Argyll Stores (Holdings) Ltd* (1998). In this case, the plaintiffs were seeking specific performance of a covenant in a lease of retailed premises to keep them open for business during particular hours. The defendants had closed the supermarket which had been run at the premises. The trial judge refused specific performance, but this ruling was overturned by the Court of Appeal. The House of Lords in its turn restored the ruling of the trial judge. It held that it was not usually appropriate to give an order of specific performance requiring someone to carry on a business. One of the main reasons for this was the prospect of the court having to make a series of orders over a period of time, backed up by the heavy handed remedy of contempt of court, in order to ensure compliance. This was not appropriate, not least in terms of likely cost to the parties and the resources of the judicial system. A one off award of damages would be much more satisfactory. The trial judge's decision should therefore be restored.

15.6.3 Personal services

The courts will be reluctant to grant an order for specific performance in relation to employment, or other contracts for personal services. The fact that the matter has come to court almost certainly shows that relations between the parties have broken down, and it would be undesirable to try to force them to work together. Where, however, it can be demonstrated that mutual trust and respect does still exist, then the order may be available. In *Hill v Parsons* (1972), for example, a dismissal had resulted from union pressure, rather than a dispute between employer and employee. This limitation on the general rule as regards personal services was also recognised in *Powell v Brent London Borough Council* (1987), where an injunction was granted. The problem in this case had arisen simply because the employer had appointed the employee after a procedure which did not comply with the requirements of its equal opportunities procedures. The subsequent dismissal of the employee was a result of this rather than any dissatisfaction with the employee's work. Of course, most disputes about employment will nowadays fall to be considered under the employment protection legislation, which specifically provides for 're-instatement' as one of the remedies for unfair dismissal.

15.6.4 Need for mutuality

A court will not order specific performance unless it would also be available against the party seeking it. Thus, a minor trying to enforce a contract for non-necessary goods would be likely to fail on the basis of this lack of mutuality. If, however, unenforceable obligations have in fact already been performed, the court may order the other side to go through with the contract. The time to assess the issue is as at the date of trial, rather than the date of contract (*Price v Strange* (1978)). In this case, the defendant had granted the plaintiff the continuation of an underlease of a flat, at an increased rent, in consideration for his agreeing to carry out certain internal and external repairs. The agreement started to operate, and the plaintiff carried out the interior repairs. At that point, the defendant purported to terminate the agreement. She then had the exterior repairs completed at her own expense. The plaintiff sought an order for specific performance, but the trial judge rejected this. His reason was that at the time of the contract the plaintiff's obligations to carry out the repairs would not have been specifically enforceable, so that there was a lack of mutuality. The Court of Appeal disagreed. By the time of the trial, all the repair work had been completed, and the plaintiff was not in danger of being forced to grant the underlease without being able to enforce the obligation to carry out the repairs. The court felt that the time of trial was the correct point at which to decide the issue, and therefore granted the order sought by the plaintiff.

15.6.5 Hardship

If the granting of an order, which on other grounds would seem to be available, will cause disproportionate hardship to the defendant, the court will refuse it. This is an aspect of the general 'equitable' nature of the remedy, which requires the court always to have in mind the need to achieve justice between the parties. In *Denne v Light* (1857), for example, specific performance of a contract for the sale of land would have left the defendant with a plot surrounded by land owned by others, and with no point of access. The order was not granted. Even straightforward financial hardship, if sufficiently severe, may be enough, particularly if it was unforeseeable at the time of contract. In *Patel v Ali* (1984), the defendant had become disabled, and relied greatly on a network of support from neighbours. This network would have been lost if she had been forced to move, and it would have been very expensive to have to pay for equivalent help. The order for specific performance was not granted.

15.6.6 Plaintiff must have acted equitably

Since specific performance is an equitable remedy the courts will apply the general equitable maxims that 'he who seeks equity must do equity', and 'he who comes to equity must come with clean hands'. In other words, the plaintiff will not be granted the remedy unless he or she, in the eyes of the court, has also acted equitably (*Walters v Morgan* (1861) – plaintiff taking advantage of defendant's ignorance as to the true value of property over which a mining lease had been granted). Thus, in *Shell v Lostock Garage* (1977) (see 7.5.6 above), the Court of Appeal refused to grant an injunction which would have in effect compelled the defendants to go through with a contract. The plaintiff's discriminatory pricing policy was regarded as unfair, and a basis for refusing the order.

15.7 Injunctions

In some situations, the courts will be prepared to grant an injunction restraining a person from acting in a way which will amount to a breach of contract. The injunction may be 'interlocutory', that is, temporary, pending a full trial, or permanent. One example of a situation where this may be a valuable remedy is in relation to restrictive covenants relating to the sale of a business, or competing employment (see 12.10 above). In any contract in which a party promises *not* to do something, there will be potential scope for the use of an injunction. An injunction, however, like the order for specific performance, is an equitable remedy, and thus subject to the discretion of the court.

The courts will not allow an injunction to be used as an indirect means of specifically enforcing a contract for which a direct order to perform would not be granted. Thus, in *Page One Records v Britton* (1968), the court refused an injunction which would have restrained a pop group from employing anyone as their manager other than the plaintiff, with whom they had fallen out. This was regarded as effectively forcing the group to employ the manager, and would amount to an indirect enforcement of a contract for personal services. Earlier decisions, however, had shown the courts being more willing to act in this area. In *Lumley v Wagner* (1852), for example, a singer had been restrained from singing in other theatres (cf *Lumley v Gye* (1853) (see 5.11 above)) and, in *Warner Bros v Nelson* (1937), the actress Bette Davis had been restrained from working in films or theatre for any other company. The court in this case felt that she was not being compelled to work for Warner Bros because she could have found employment other than as an actress, a conclusion which was technically correct, but practically very unrealistic! It may be that the *Page One* decision represents the more likely approach of a modern court to these issues.

REMEDIES

Damages

The purpose of damages is *restitutio in integrum*, not punishment. The plaintiff should be put in the position he or she would have been in had the contract been performed satisfactorily (*Robinson v Harman* (1848)).

The measure of damages

- Expectation interest

  This is the normal measure of damages. It can take into account lost profits. It will also cover the 'loss of a chance' (*Chaplin v Hicks* (1911)).

- Reliance interest

  This allows the plaintiff to recover lost expenses, instead of the expectation interest (*Anglia Television v Reed* (1971)). The choice of which remedy to seek normally lies with the plaintiff.

- Restitution

  This will be available if a repudiatory breach leads to the return, for example, of the goods and money exchanged under a sale of goods contract.

  'Restitutionary' damages based on the benefits acquired by the defendant, rather than the loss suffered by the claimant, may be appropriate in some cases: *Attorney General v Blake* (1998).

- Consequential losses

  Losses which flow from the breach may be recovered, as long as they are not too remote. The 'cost of cure' will generally be allowed, in place of 'diminution in value', unless the difference is significant (*Watts v Morrow* (1991)).

- Non-pecuniary losses

  Damages may be recovered for physical injuries, but not usually for injury to feelings (*Addis v Gramophone Company Ltd* (1909)). An exception exists, however, for contracts which have the provision of enjoyment as one of their purposes (*Jarvis v Swans Tours* (1975)).

Limitations on recovery

The rule of remoteness derives from *Hadley v Baxendale* (1854). As interpreted by *Victoria Laundry (Windsor) Ltd v Newman Industries* (1949) and *The Heron II* (1969), it limits recovery to those losses which were within the reasonable contemplation of the parties as not unlikely to result from the breach.

The plaintiff has an obligation to take reasonable steps to mitigate losses (*British Westinghouse Electric and Manufacturing Company v Underground Electric Railways Co of London* (1912)). Lack of resources may make it unreasonable to mitigate (*Wroth v Tyler* (1974)). Where there is an anticipatory breach which is not accepted, there is no obligation to mitigate prior to the date of performance (*White and Carter (Councils) v McGregor* (1962)).

The Law Reform (Contributory Negligence) Act 1945 probably applies only where there is concurrent liability in tort and contract (*Forsikringsaktieselskapet Vesta v Butcher* (1988)).

Liquidated damages and penalty clauses

Genuine pre-estimates of loss will be enforced; penalty clauses will not (*Dunlop Pneumatic Tyre Co Ltd v New Garage and Motor Co Ltd* (1915)). The clauses must be judged objectively as at the time the contract was made (*Philips Hong Kong Ltd v Attorney General of Hong Kong* (1993)), but subsequent events may provide valuable evidence or what could reasonably have been expected at that time.

Specific performance

Specific performance is an equitable remedy, available at the court's discretion. It may be awarded where damages provide an inadequate remedy (*Harnett v Yielding* (1805)). This will generally be the case in relation to land.

- Need for supervision

  The order will not generally be made if it would require detailed supervision to enforce (*Ryan v Mutual Tontine Westminster Chambers Association* (1893); *Co-operative Insurance Society Ltd v Argyll Stores (Holdings) Ltd* (1998)).

- Personal services

  The courts are reluctant to enforce contracts of service, unless it is clear that mutual trust and respect still exists between the parties (*Hill v Parsons* (1972)).

- Need for mutuality

  The order will not be available, unless the plaintiff would also be liable to it. Thus, a minor may have difficulty in obtaining the order in relation to a contract for non-necessary goods.

- Hardship

  If the order will cause disproportionate hardship, it will not be granted (*Denne v Light* (1857); *Patel v Ali* (1984)).

- Plaintiff must have acted equitably

  Walters v Morgan (1861).

Injunctions

Injunctions may be awarded where a party has promised not to do something. They must not, however, become an indirect method of enforcing a contract for which specific performance would not be available (*Page One Records v Britton* (1968)) (but cf *Lumley v Wagner* (1852), and *Warner Bros v Nelson* (1937)).

CHAPTER 16

QUASI-CONTRACT AND RESTITUTION

16.1   The nature of the concepts

The topics to be covered in this chapter have close links with those dealt with Chapter 15. We are concerned again with ways in which a person can seek compensation for losses, or, perhaps more accurately, avoid suffering a loss. In this case, however, we are dealing with situations where the standard contract remedies are unavailable because the parties are not in a contractual relationship. This will either be because their attempt to make a binding agreement has failed in some way (for example, it is void for mistake), or their negotiations have never succeeded in reaching the stage of a mutually acceptable contract. We are therefore concerned with situations which have some relationship to contract (hence, the label 'quasi-contract') but which strictly speaking fall outside its remit. This area can be regarded as part of a more general area of law, which has come to be known as 'restitution'. Its basis and limits have been most fully expounded by Goff and Jones in *The Law of Restitution*, 4th edn, 1993, Sweet & Maxwell. Central to this concept is the idea of 'unjust enrichment'. Restitution comprises a body of rules for recovery of money or property in order to prevent a person becoming 'unjustly enriched'. As Lord Wright put it in *Fibrosa Spolka Ackyjna v Fairbairn Lawson Combe Barbour* (1943):

> It is clear that any civilised system of law is bound to provide remedies for what has been called unjust enrichment, or unjust benefit, that is, to prevent a man from retaining the money of, or some benefit derived from, another which it is against his conscience he should keep.

It is English law's response to this requirement that we are concerned with in the rest of this chapter. There are two main topics to consider: the recovery of money, and the payment for work which has been done.

16.2   Recovery of money

The transfer of money outside a contractual relationship raises particular problems. Whereas, if I give you possession of my car in connection with a contract which turns out to be void I can maintain an action for the recovery of it relying on my continuing rights of ownership, with money the position is more complicated. There will not be any possibility of identifying the particular notes or coins which have been transferred, or of 'unmixing' funds from a bank account into which they have been paid. In other words, the money itself has become the property of the person to whom it has been transferred, and the most that is left is the obligation to repay an equivalent sum. There are four situations where the possibility of such recovery is clearly recognised: first, where there is a total failure of consideration; secondly, where the money was transferred under a mistake of fact; thirdly, where the money was transferred under a mistake of law; and fourthly, where money has been paid to a third party for the benefit of the defendant.

16.2.1 Total failure of consideration

One example of this situation has already been discussed in Chapter 13, in relation to the doctrine of frustration. As we saw there, the House of Lords in *Fibrosa Spolka Ackyjna v Fairbairn Lawson Combe Barbour Ltd* (1942) (see 13.4.3 above) accepted that, if a party who had paid money under a frustrated contract had received nothing in return, the money could be recovered. The rule is thus that the plaintiff must have received nothing of what had been contracted for or, rather, that the defendant has not performed any part of the contractual duties in respect of which payment is due (*per* Lord Goff in *Stocznia Gdanska SA v Latvian Shipping Co* (1998)). If there has been partial performance of any kind, then this remedy will not be available.

As we saw in the *Fibrosa* case itself, this rule has the potential to cause a certain amount of injustice, in that the defendant who has used the money to prepare for performance may lose out. It was in part for this reason that the procedure for a rather more equitable distribution of losses was introduced in the frustration area by the Law Reform (Frustrated Contracts) Act (LR(FC)A 1943 (see 13.5 above).

The action based on a total failure of consideration has also been used, not without controversy, in the sale of goods area. In *Rowland v Divall* (1923), the plaintiff car dealer had bought a car from the defendant. The car had previously been stolen, but neither party was aware of this at the time. The plaintiff resold the car to a third party, from whom it was reclaimed, some months later, by the true owner's insurance company. The plaintiff had to repay the purchase price to the third party, and then sought to recover what he had paid to the defendant. Despite the fact of the lapse of time, and the consequent reduction in the value of the car, which was demonstrated by the fact that the insurance company had in fact sold it back to the plaintiff at much less than the original contract price, the plaintiff was allowed to recover what he had paid to the defendant in full, on the basis of a total failure of consideration. The use that the plaintiff had made of the car was irrelevant. The essence of a sale of goods contract is not the use of the goods, but the transfer of ownership. Since this had never been transferred, because the car was stolen, the plaintiff was entitled to recover all his money.

In *Rowland v Divall*, the plaintiff as a dealer was primarily interested in the ability to resell the car. The same principle, however, applies to a private purchaser. In *Butterworth v Kingsway Motors* (1954), the plaintiff had bought a car which, unknown to him, was subject to a hire purchase agreement, and was reclaimed by the finance company nearly a year later. The plaintiff was allowed to recover the full purchase price from the defendant, notwithstanding the fact that the defendant was equally ignorant of the defect in title. The plaintiff thus had almost a year's free use of the car. This decision has been the subject of considerable criticism, but has not as yet been overruled.

In a contract to design and construct an object, and then to transfer it to the buyer, as opposed to simply a contract of sale, the failure to transfer ownership will not amount to a total failure of consideration. This was confirmed by the House of Lords in *Stocznia Gdanska SA v Latvian Shipping Co* (1998), applying *Hyundai Heavy Industries Co Ltd v Papadopoulos* (1980). The contract was for the construction and supply of a number of ships, and payments were made in instalments. The ships were never completed or transferred, but it was held by the House of Lords that the shipyard was entitled to resist a claim by the buyers for recovery of the instalment payments on the basis of a total failure of consideration.

In cases outside the sale of goods area, the fact that property has been used by the plaintiff, for example by his or her going into residence under a tenancy, may well prevent a claim based on a total failure of consideration (*Hunt v Silk* (1804)).

16.2.2 Mistake of fact

Money paid under a mistake of fact will be recoverable, provided that the mistake is as to a fact which, if true, would have legally (*Aiken v Short* (1856)), or morally (*Larner v LCC* (1949)), obliged the plaintiff to pay the money, or, at least, is sufficiently serious to justify the requirement of repayment. Where a contract is void as a result of being based on a common mistake of fact (such as a false belief in the existence of the subject matter), then recovery will certainly be possible. Other situations where recovery has been held to be possible include mistaken payments under insurance policies. Thus, in *Norwich Union Fire Insurance Society Ltd v Price Ltd* (1934), payment was made on the basis that cargo of fruit had been destroyed, whereas in fact it had been resold because it was becoming overripe. Recovery of the payment was allowed. Similarly, in *Kelly v Solari* (1841), payment was made on a life insurance policy as a result of the company failing to realise that the final premium had not been paid. Although it might be argued that this was something of which the company should have been aware, recovery of the payment was allowed.

Lord Goff has suggested (in *Barclays Bank Ltd v Simms and Cooke (Southern) Ltd* (1980)) that recovery under this head will not be possible if the payer intended the payee to benefit in any event; or there is good consideration from the payee (such as the discharge of a debt); or the payee has changed his or her position in good faith as a result of the payment. As far as payment to discharge an existing debt is concerned, it was confirmed by the Court of

Appeal in *Lloyds Bank Plc v Independent Insurance Co Ltd* (1998) that this would constitute a good defence to a claim for restitution based on a mistake of fact.

16.2.3 Mistake of law

Until 1998, it was accepted that it was not possible to reclaim money paid under a mistake of law. This was based on the maxim that 'ignorance of the law is no excuse' as applied in this situation in *Bilbie v Lumley* (1802). However, in *Kleinwort Benson Ltd v Lincoln City Council* (1998), the House of Lords overturned this rule, and held that in certain circumstances money paid under a mistake of law could be recovered. In coming to this conclusion, it was following developments which had taken place in other parts of the common law world, and recommendations for change from the Law Commission (in its Report No 227, *Restitution: Mistakes of Law and* Ultra Vires *Public Authority Receipts and Payments* (1994)).

The factual background to this decision were 'interest rate swap' agreements entered into by various local authorities during the 1980s as a means of raising money. The agreements involved the advance of a capital sum by the lending bank, coupled with an agreement for mutual payment of interest on a notional sum, one side paying at a fixed rate, the other at a market rate. A balancing of liabilities was to take place at various points. Clearly, the arrangement involved a prediction (almost a 'gamble') as to how market rates would change vis à vis the fixed rate. In *Hazell v Hammersmith and Fulham LBC* (1991), it was held by the House of Lords that agreements of this kind were *ultra vires* as regards the local authorities, and therefore unlawful and void. The question then arose as to whether the bank could recover the money that it had lent. The local authorities denied any liability to repay, on the basis that the money had been paid under a mistake of law, and was therefore irrecoverable.

The House of Lords in *Kleinwort Benson*, with Lord Goff delivering the main speech, held that it was time to recognise that there could be recovery of money paid under a mistake of law, where this would otherwise lead to the unjust enrichment of the recipient. The recipient's honest belief in his entitlement to the money would not in itself provide a defence. The fact that the recipient had changed his position in reliance on the payment might do so. The test is whether it would be unjust to allow the recipient to retain the benefit of the money paid.

The House also confirmed that this new principle would apply where the payments were made 'under a settled understanding of the law which is subsequently departed from by judicial decision'. Thus, the fact that at the time of the payment the law appeared to be clear provides no defence to an action for recovery if a court subsequently rules that the understanding amounted to an incorrect view of the law. Given that judicial decisions have a declaratory and retrospective effect (unlike statutes), there was no need to limit the principle in this way. The House in *Hazell* having ruled that interest swap agreements were *ultra vires* local authorities, all such agreements which had been entered into up until that time had therefore been made on the basis of a mistake of law. Finally, the House held that it was irrelevant to the application of the principle that the transaction concerned had been fully performed.

The decision in *Kleinwort Benson* is clearly a very significant addition to the law of restitution. The precise way in which it will operate in practice remains to be seen. The House of Lords was only concerned with the preliminary issue of whether an action for recovery based on mistake of law was possible, not with how this should apply to the particular transactions entered into by the local authorities. There has been one reported case where the principle has been applied: *Nurdin and Peacock plc v DB Ramsden & Co Ltd* (1999). This concerned over-payments made under a lease. After these had been made for some months, the plaintiffs discovered that they had been paying too much. Up until that point, the payments were made under a mistake of fact. The final payment, however, was made with full knowledge of the situation, but on the basis of incorrect legal advice to the effect that it would automatically be repayable if proceedings being taken against the defendant were successful. This was therefore made under a mistake of law. The court held that recovery for mistake of law did not depend on a belief on the part of the payer that there was a liability to make the payment. The final payment was recoverable as having been made on the basis of a mistake of law.

16.2.4 Payment to a third party

What is the position in respect of money which has been paid by the plaintiff to a third party, but which benefits the defendant? Can the plaintiff recover this money from the defendant? One major limitation on this is that the plaintiff must not have been acting purely as a volunteer, but under some constraint. A mother who decides, out of the goodness of her heart, to settle her son's debts, cannot then claim restitution from the son. This rule was applied in a commercial context in *Macclesfield Corporation v Great Central Railway* (1911), where the plaintiffs carried out repairs on a bridge which the defendants were legally obliged (but had refused) to maintain. The plaintiffs were regarded as acting purely as volunteers, and so could not recover from the defendants the money spent on the work. An example of a situation where recovery was allowed is *Exall v Partridge* (1799). The plaintiff in this case paid off arrears of rent owed by the defendant. The reason for doing this was to avoid the seizure by bailiffs of a carriage belonging to the plaintiff which had been left on the defendant's premises. The plaintiff was thus acting under a constraint, and not simply as a volunteer, and could recover his money.

A second limitation is that the *defendant* must have been under a legal obligation to pay the money. In *Exall v Partridge,* for example, the obligation on the defendant was to pay his rent. In *Metropolitan Police District Receiver v Croydon Corporation* (1956), however, the plaintiff failed to satisfy this requirement. A policeman had been injured and could not work, but the plaintiffs, the police authority, were obliged to continue to pay his wages. The policeman sued the defendants for negligence, and recovered compensation. This did not, however, contain any element for loss of wages, since the policeman was still being paid by the plaintiffs. The plaintiffs sought to recover the cost of the policeman's wages from the defendants. Their argument was that they had made payments to the policeman which were the responsibility of the defendants, since it was their negligence which had caused the policeman to be off work. Their payment of the policeman's wages was thus a benefit to the defendants. The court, however, took the view that the defendants had no legal obligation to pay the policeman's wages. Their only obligation was to compensate him for his losses. Since he had lost no wages, there was no legal obligation in this respect, and therefore the plaintiffs could not recover.

16.3   Recovery of compensation for a benefit

The plaintiff, rather than paying money to the defendant, may have done work, or provided some other benefit. Since, by definition, any compensation for such a benefit is not defined by any agreement between the parties (because we are concerned with the situation where there is no contract), the plaintiff will be seeking compensation on a *quantum meruit* basis. This means, the payment of an amount equivalent to the value of the benefit conferred. An analogy may be drawn with the remedy under s 1(3) of the LR(FC)A 1943, which empowers the court to award a sum that is just and reasonable in all the circumstances on the basis of the benefit received by the other party (see 13.5.2 above). There are three situations to consider, namely where a contract has been broken; where it is void; and where agreement is never reached.

16.3.1 Contract broken

A broken contract will not usually give rise to consideration of a *quantum meruit* remedy, but an example of how it can be appropriate can be seen in *Planché v Colburn* (1831). The plaintiff had been engaged to write a book on Costume and Ancient Armour. He carried out research, and did some of the writing. The defendants then abandoned the project. There were some further negotiations to try to renew the contract, but these failed, and the plaintiff then sued for breach of contract, and for a *quantum meruit*. The action for breach of contract would have been unlikely to succeed, because it appears that the original contract was 'entire' (see 14.2.2 above), with a specific sum payable on completion of the book. The court held that, nevertheless, the plaintiff could recover on a *quantum meruit* basis, and awarded him 50 guineas.

This type of action is likely to be unusual, but is clearly available in appropriate circumstances where a contract has come to an end, and the plaintiff would otherwise be without a remedy. It is difficult to see, however, that the defendant had received any benefit from the plaintiff's work, since a half-finished book was of no use to them. This also makes it difficult to fit this case within the general principle of 'unjust enrichment', since the defendants had not in fact been 'enriched'.

16.3.2 Contract void

We have seen that money paid under a void contract is recoverable. Equally, work which has been done may be compensated on a *quantum meruit* basis. In *Craven-Ellis v Canons Ltd* (1936), for example, the proper procedures were not followed in appointing the plaintiff as managing director. As a result, his appointment was a nullity. Before this was discovered, however, the plaintiff rendered services for the company in accordance with the agreement which he thought had been entered into. Since the company had benefited from this work, he was allowed to recover on a *quantum meruit* claim. This enabled him to claim reasonable remuneration for the work which he had done. Similarly, in *Mohammed v Alaga* (1999), the Court of Appeal held that a person who had provided translation services under an illegal, and therefore void, fee sharing agreement with a firm of solicitors could claim on a quantum meruit basis for the work actually done.

16.3.3 Agreement never reached

It is not uncommon in relation to complex contracts, such as those entered into in the building or engineering industries, for work to be done on a project prior to the formalisation of a contract. Although an 'agreement to agree' will not be enforced (*Courtney and Fairbairn v Tolaini Bros (Hotels) Ltd* (1975)), no particular problem arises with this as long a contract does materialise at some point. The Court of Appeal's decision in *Trentham Ltd v Archital Luxfer* (1993) (discussed above at 2.7.5) confirms that in such a situation the courts will be happy to allow the eventual contract to act retrospectively, and govern the work that has been done. Moreover, that decision has also relaxed to some extent the rules concerning formation, making it more likely that a binding contract will be found. Nevertheless, there will still be situations where no contract exists, and it becomes necessary to decide whether, and if so on what basis, compensation can be recovered for work that has been done. (The position as regards money paid will be governed by the rules discussed above at 16.2.)

16.3.4 Principles governing recovery

Two principles seem to govern this area. First, recovery will be allowed where the work has been requested by the defendant. Secondly, if the work has been done without a request, but has been 'freely accepted', it seems likely that the defendant will be expected to pay something for it. In *William Lacey (Hounslow)*

Ltd v Davis (1957), the plaintiffs had submitted the lowest tender for a building contract, and had been led to believe that they would be awarded it. At the defendant's request, they then prepared various plans and estimates. The defendants then decided not to proceed. The court argued by analogy from *Craven-Ellis v Canons* (1936) (see 16.3.2 above). If it was possible to recover in relation to work done on a void contract, Barry J thought that the same should be true of:

> ... work done which was to be paid for out of the proceeds of a contract which both parties erroneously believed was about to be made. In neither case was the work done gratuitously, and in both cases the party from whom the payment was sought requested the work and obtained the benefit of it.

The plaintiffs were therefore allowed to recover a reasonable sum for the work done.

This line was followed in *British Steel Corpn v Cleveland Bridge and Engineering Co Ltd* (1984). The project in this case was for the construction and delivery of a set of cast steel nodes. A 'letter of intent' was issued by the defendants, indicating that they intended to enter into the contract with the plaintiffs. The defendants then requested the plaintiffs to start work on the construction of the nodes. It proved impossible to reach agreement, however, on a number of major terms, including the price. Despite this, all the nodes were eventually constructed and delivered, though some were delivered late. The plaintiffs claimed for the value of the nodes. It was clear that there was no contract. On the other hand, the defendants had requested the work to be done, and had freely accepted the nodes when they were delivered. As a result, the plaintiffs were able to succeed in a restitutionary claim for the value of what had been supplied. It should be noted, however, that the defendants' counterclaim for compensation for late delivery failed. Since there was no contract, there could be no obligations concerning the date for delivery, and therefore there was no basis on which such a claim could succeed. This indicates that although the remedy of restitution does allow the courts to avoid unjust enrichment, it is not sufficiently flexible as yet to allow the courts to take into consideration all the circumstances, and distribute losses and benefits between the parties accordingly.

QUASI-CONTRACT AND RESTITUTION

Nature of the concepts

Quasi-contract and restitution provide remedies where money or property has changed hands, or benefits have been provided, but a contract has failed to come into existence, or has been avoided (for example, for mistake). It is based on principle that the law should provide remedies against 'unjust enrichment' (Lord Wright in *Fibrosa Spolka Ackyjna v Fairbairn Lawson Combe Barbour* (1943)).

Recovery of money

There are three bases for the recovery of money:

- Total failure of consideration

  This ground for recovery was recognised in the *Fibrosa* case. It has been applied in the Sale of Goods Act 1979 area, with controversial results (*Rowland v Divall* (1923); *Butterworth v Kingsway Motors* (1954)). Any partial performance will prevent a claim on this basis (*Hunt v Silk* (1804)).

- Mistake of fact

  There must be a mistake as to a fact which if true would have involved a legal or moral obligation to pay (*Aiken v Short* (1856); *Larner v LCC* (1949)), or at least is very serious. Contracts void for common mistake will fall within this. Note also its use in relation to insurance contracts – for example, *Kelly v Solari* (1841).

- Mistake of law

  Recognised for the first time in *Kleinwort Benson Ltd v Lincoln City Council* (1998). Applied in *Nurdin and Peacock plc v DB Ramsden & Co Ltd* (1999).

- Payment to a third party for the defendant's benefit

  The payment must be made under some constraint (*Macclesfield Corporation v Great Central Railway* (1911) – no constraint, therefore no recovery; *Exall v Partridge* (1799) – payment to protect plaintiff's property; recovery allowed). The *defendant* must have been legally bound to pay the money (*Metropolitan Police District Receiver v Croydon Corporation* (1956)).

Recovery of compensation for a benefit

This will involve a *quantum meruit* claim for work done.

- Contract broken

  A restitutionary remedy may be appropriate where there has been a breach of an entire contract towards which work has been done (*Planché v Colburn* (1831)).

- Contract void

  Work done on a contract which is void can be compensated for (*Craven-Ellis v Canons Ltd* (1936)).

- Agreement never reached

  The courts will not enforce an 'agreement to agree'(*Courtney & Fairbairn v Tolaini Bros (Hotels) Ltd* (1975)). Some recovery will be allowed, however, for work which has been done at the request of the defendant, or which has been freely accepted by the defendant (*William Lacey (Hounslow) Ltd v Davis* (1957)). See, also, *British Steel Corpn v Cleveland Bridge and Engineering Co Ltd* (1984) where work was done on the strength of a 'letter of intent' from the defendant.

CHAPTER 17

AGENCY

17.1 The concept of 'agency'

The concept of the agent is a useful one in the law of contract, but not all that easy to define. For our purposes, we may take it as referring to the situation where one person (the agent) has the power to bring another person (the principal) into a contractual relationship with a third party. (Throughout this chapter, the 'third party' will be used to refer to a person who deals with an agent.)

It is important to remember that to describe someone as an agent is to identify a *relationship* and not a *job*. Thus, although many agents will be appointed and described as such, many other 'agents' have this status simply from the responsibilities which arise out of their employment. The shop assistant who deals with customers is in that situation acting as agent for the owner of the shop. The company director who makes a contract on behalf of an incorporated company is equally acting as an agent. The company has a separate legal personality, but of course cannot itself physically make contracts. It has to act through human agents.

It quickly becomes apparent that the concept of agency is of vital importance in all areas of commercial activity. Without it, dealings would become cumbersome, expensive, and impractical.

17.1.1 Relevance of labels

Because the central core of agency is the relationship that it denotes, the labels used by the parties are of only minor significance. If a person is described as an 'agent' this many well indicate that he or she has authority to bind his or her principal, but it does not necessarily do so. The point was considered in *Lamb & Sons v Goring Brick Company* (1932). The GBC were manufacturers of bricks and other building materials. Lamb & Sons were builders' merchants. An agreement was made under which Lamb were appointed 'sole selling agents' of GBC's bricks and other materials. Following a change of ownership of GBC, it became important to establish the exact effect of this agreement. The Court of Appeal held that it did not create a relationship of agency. The arrangement was that GBC sold its bricks to Lamb, and that Lamb then sold them on to others. In a true agency relationship, Lamb, as agent, would simply have brought GBC into a contractual relationship with the purchasers, and would not themselves have bought and sold the bricks.

It was confirmed by the Court of Appeal in *AMB Imballagi Plastici SRL v Pacflex Ltd* (1999) that a similar arrangement, where the one party found potential customers, but the transactions involved sale by the supplier to the 'agent', and then sale by the 'agent' to the customer, did not fall within the scope of the Commercial Agents (Council Directive) Regulations 1993 (see 17.1.3 below).

17.1.2 Relationship to doctrine of privity

In some situations, agency operates as an exception to the doctrine of privity. This is particularly so where the agent contracts on behalf of an undisclosed principal. In other words, the third party thinks that he or she is contracting with the agent in person, whereas in fact there is a principal standing behind the agent, who will step in and take over the contract. This, as far as the third party is concerned, is an exception to the general principle that only those who are parties to a contract can have rights and liabilities under it. Moreover, the concept of agency can be used to circumvent the restrictions of privity. In *New Zealand Shipping Co v Satterthwaite* (1974), for example (see 5.9.2 above), the carriers were deemed to be the agents of the stevedores in order to create a contract between the stevedores and the owners, and thus give the stevedores the protection of an exclusion clause set out in the contract between the owners and the carriers.

17.1.3 Commercial agents

This chapter is concerned with the common law rules applying to agency. It should be noted, however, that a particular category of commercial agency is now governed additionally by Regulations deriving from a European Directive. These are the Commercial Agents (Council Directive) Regulations 1993. They apply to independent commercial agents who have continuing authority to negotiate the sale or purchase of goods. They do not apply to agents who are also employees, or company directors, or partners. Nor do they cover an agent engaged for a particular transaction. The details of these regulations are beyond the scope of this book (and of most contract courses). This chapter simply notes at the relevant points the areas where the provisions of the Regulations differ significantly from the common law rules. For a full discussion of the Regulations, reference should be made to a specialist agency or commercial law text (for example, Stone, *Law of Agency*, 1996, Cavendish Publishing).

17.2 Creation of agency

Agency can be created in a variety of ways. The three principal ones are express agreement; implied agreement; and operation of law. The agent may be appointed generally, to make contracts on behalf of the principal in a range of situations, or simply to act in connection with one particular project.

17.2.1 Express agreement

Subject to the limitations indicated by *Lamb & Sons v Goring Brick Company* (1932), there are no particular problems with this way of creating agency. No special formalities are required, and the agreement does not even need to constitute a contract. Even where the agent has the power to make agreements which have to be in writing (such as contracts for the sale of land), the appointment does not have to be in writing.

The one exception to this is where the agent is to have power to execute a deed, for example a conveyance of land. In that situation, the agency itself must be created by deed, generally known as a power of attorney.

17.2.2 Implied agreement

The courts here profess to be looking for the intentions of the parties, and if they think that they intended to create an agency relationship, then that will be given effect. As is usual in contract law, the intention will be determined by an objective consideration of what the parties have said or done. We have already noted one situation where the courts implied agency, that is, in *New Zealand Shipping Co v Satterthwaite* (1974). It may well be thought, however, that although the parties probably did intend that the stevedores should be able to take the benefit of the exclusion clause, it is much more dubious whether they intended to achieve this by means of the concept of agency. A similar pragmatic approach to the implication of agency may perhaps also be seen in *Heatons Transport (St Helens) Ltd v Transport and General Workers Union* (1972), where shop stewards were deemed to be agents of the union, and thus rendered the union responsible for their unlawful continuance of industrial action.

17.2.3 Operation of law

Agency can be imposed by law, irrespective of the intentions of the parties in three ways, that is, by statute, by necessity, or from cohabitation.

An example of agency created by statute is to be found in s 56(2) of the Consumer Credit Act 1974, which has the effect of making a dealer who negotiates with a customer to arrange a credit transaction, such as a hire purchase arrangement, the agent of the finance company for the purpose of such negotiations. (This reversed the common law position as stated in *Branwhite v Worcester Works Finance* (1969), which made the dealer the agent of the *customer*.)

Agency of necessity arises chiefly in relation to shipping contracts. Thus, if a cargo is in danger of perishing, the master of the ship will have the power to sell it, or even jettison it (*The Gratitudine* (1801)). Similarly, if the ship itself is in urgent need of repairs, the master may incur expenses towards this, or even sell the ship to raise the money to carry out the work (*Gunn v Roberts* (1874)). The Court of Appeal's decision in *The Choko Star* (1990) emphasised the exceptional nature of agency of necessity, and the fact that it would only arise where the 'agent' was unable to receive instructions from the 'principal'. Modern communications make it rare that such instructions will be unobtainable, and thus the scope for this type of agency seems greatly reduced.

Agency from cohabitation is presumed wherever a man and woman are living together in a household (not, for example, as managers of a hotel – *Debenham v Mellon* (1880)), whether or not they are married. It will entitle the woman to pledge the man's credit in order to purchase 'necessaries' (*cf* the position in relation to minors' contracts at 6.2 above). In *Miss Gray Ltd v Earl Cathcart* (1922), the presumption was said to be rebuttable by the issue of an express warning to traders; by the fact that the woman was already adequately supplied, or had a sufficient allowance, or had been specifically forbidden to pledge the man's credit; or if the order was extravagant. Given these limitations, the practical application of this type of agency seems very limited.

17.3 The powers of an agent

The power that an agent has to bind the principal depends on the agent's authority. There are three types of authority to be considered: express, implied, and ostensible.

17.3.1 Express authority

The limits of the agent's authority may well be expressly established by the agreement between the principal and agent. This may occur when the relationship is first established, or may change over time. The principal will generally be entitled at any time to alter the agent's authority, provided that this does not conflict with any contractual agreement between them. The third party will be bound by the limits of the agent's express authority, as long as he or she is aware of them. If the third party does not know of certain limitations, and contracts outside them, then issues of implied or ostensible authority, or ratification, may arise. This will also be the case if the agreement between principal and agent is silent, or unclear, as to the extent of the agent's authority.

17.3.2 Implied authority

Implied authority derives either from the type of work which the agent is doing, or the place where the agent is working. The first category will be referred to here as 'usual authority', that is, the authority 'usually' attaching to a particular job. The second category will be labelled 'customary' authority, in that it will arise out of the customs of a particular place of business.

A classic, though not unproblematic, example of usual authority is to be found in *Watteau v Fenwick* (1893). The defendant owned a beerhouse and employed a manager, who had authority to buy goods for the business. The manager was under express instructions, however, not to buy cigars, as these would be supplied by the defendant. The manager bought cigars on credit from the plaintiff. The plaintiff sued the defendant for the price of the cigars. It was held that, since the plaintiff was unaware of the express limitation, and since it was within the usual authority of a manager of a beerhouse to order goods of this type, the defendant was liable.

The decision may be contrasted with *Daun v Simmins* (1879) where it was held that the manager of a 'tied' public house would normally only have authority to buy spirits from a particular source. The supplier in this case could not rely on an implied usual authority in order to sue the principal.

The main issue here is therefore one of fact. What exactly is the usual authority of this particular type of agent, and was the third party aware of any express limits on it?

The controversial aspect of *Watteau v Fenwick* is that the third party was unaware that he was dealing with an agent, and it is not at all clear that the usual authority should be allowed to operate in the situation of an undisclosed principal (see *Rhodian River Shipping Co SA v Halla Maritime Corpn* (1984)).

Customary authority operates to authorise the agent to act according to the usages or customs of a particular place or market. Thus, in *Scott v Godfrey* (1901), a custom of the Stock Exchange allowed a stockbroker to act as agent for several principals at once in buying shares from one seller, thus bringing each principal into a separate contractual relationship with the seller.

17.3.3 Ostensible authority

Ostensible authority involves the principal having, by words or action, led the third party to believe that the agent has authority, when in fact the agent does not. It is also sometimes referred to as 'apparent authority' or 'agency by estoppel'.

The requirements for its existence were set out in *Rama Corporation Ltd v Proved Tin and General Investments Ltd* (1952). Slade J said that ostensible authority was a kind of estoppel, and that therefore what was needed was:

- a representation;
- a reliance on the representation; and
- an alteration of your position resulting from such reliance.

The precise nature of the representation required was expanded on by Diplock LJ in *Freeman and Lockyer v Buckhurst Properties (Mangal) Ltd* (1964) in the following passage:

> ... 'ostensible' authority ... is a legal relationship between the principal and the contractor created by a representation, *made by the principal to the contractor*, intended to be and in fact acted upon by the contractor, that the agent has authority to enter on behalf of the principal into a contract of a kind within the scope of the 'apparent' authority so as to render the principal liable to perform any obligations imposed upon him by such a contract. (Emphasis added.)

Moreover, the agent 'must not purport to make the agreement as principal himself'.

The 'representation' may come from conduct rather than a statement. In *Summers v Solomon* (1857), for example, it came from the conduct of the principal in allowing the agent to buy goods for his jewellery business. When the agent was dismissed, the ostensible authority created by this conduct survived, and a third party who was unaware of the termination of the agency was allowed to recover from the principal the price of jewellery with which the agent had absconded. Similarly, in *Lloyd v Grace, Smith & Co* (1912), the representation came from the fact that a firm of solicitors had allowed a clerk to carry out conveyancing work without supervision. The firm was liable when the clerk acted fraudulently in relation to the third party.

As the quotation by Diplock given above makes clear, the representation must emanate from the principal, not the agent. This was confirmed in *Armagas v Mundogas* (1986), where the agent, a chartering manager, falsely represented that he had authority for a particular transaction involving the sale and lease back of a ship. The third party could not enforce the transaction against the principal, since the principal had not made any representation of authority. This principle has, however, been weakened by subsequent Court of Appeal decisions (*City Trust v Levy* (1988), and *First Energy (UK) Ltd v Hungarian International Bank Ltd* (1993)) which suggest that authority to enter into a transaction can be distinguished from authority to communicate that the principal has given approval for such a transaction. The latter type of ostensible authority may exist even where the former does not. If this is so, the agent has only to claim that approval has been given in order to bind his or her principal to a contract with the third party.

The other two requirements for ostensible authority noted by Slade J are more easily dealt with. That of reliance simply means that the third party will not be able to plead ostensible authority if he or she was not aware of the representation, or did not actually believe that the agent had authority, or ought to have known that the agent's authority was limited (*Overbrooke Estates Ltd v Glencombe Properties* (1974)). The requirement of an 'alteration of position' will be satisfied in the context in which we are discussing agency by the fact that the third party has entered into a contract.

17.4 Ratification

Where an agent enters into an authorised contract, the principal may be happy to adopt it. This can be done by the process of ratification. For ratification to be available, however, the agent must purport to act on behalf of a principal, the principal must be in existence at the time of the contract, and the principal must have capacity.

17.4.1 Agent must purport to act for a principal

Ratification is not available where the principal is undisclosed. The third party must know that there is, or is supposed to be, a principal in the background. If the third party thinks that the agent is acting on his or her own account, no later ratification will be possible (*Keighley Maxted & Co v Durant* (1901)). In this case, the agent had made a contract at a higher price than that which his principal had authorised. The principal later purported to ratify this unauthorised act. The House of Lords held that he could not, because the agent had not disclosed to the third party that he was acting on behalf of someone else.

Provided, however, that the agent mentions the principal, it does not matter that the agent is in fact intending to act independently. In *Re Tiedemann and Ledermann Frères* (1899), the agent acted in the principal's name in relation to a sale which he in fact intended to be for his own benefit. The third party then tried to rescind the contract on the basis of the misrepresentation as to whom he was contracting with. The principal, however, ratified the contract, and this prevented the third party from rescinding it.

17.4.2 Principal must have been in existence

The issue of the existence of the principal arises mainly in relation to contracts made on behalf of new companies which are being formed. In *Kelner v Baxter* (1866), it was held that if the company was not in existence, that is, it had not been incorporated, at the time of the contract, it could not later ratify the agreement. The purported 'agents', the promoters of the company, were therefore personally liable. Such personal liability is now imposed by statute, by virtue of s 36C of the Companies Act 1985.

17.4.3 Principal must have capacity

There are in theory two aspects to the rule that the principal must have capacity. The first is that the principal must have capacity to make the transaction at the time of the contract. This has most obvious relevance to minors, who might want to ratify after reaching majority. It could also apply to contracts made outside the powers of a company. Both these situations have now been affected by statutory provisions, however, namely ss 1–3 of the Minors' Contracts Act 1987 (see 6.1 above), and s 36 of the Companies Act 1985, which means that this aspect of the rule is of little practical significance.

The second aspect is that the principal must have capacity at the time of ratification. This was applied in *Grover and Grover v Matthews* (1910). A contract of fire insurance was purported to be ratified after a fire had destroyed the property which was the subject of the insurance. It was held that this was ineffective, because at the time of the purported ratification the principal could not have made the contract himself (because the property no longer existed). 'Capacity' is thus being given a rather broader meaning than usual, to cover the issue as to whether the principal would have in practice been able to make the contract in question.

17.4.4 Effect of ratification

Ratification is retrospective in its effect, and the original contract must be treated as if it had been authorised from the start. This was confirmed by the Court of Appeal in *Presentaciones Musicales SA v Secunda* (1994). The implications of this rule are clear from the decision in *Bolton Partners v Lambert* (1889). Bolton Partners owned a factory, which Lambert offered to buy. This offer was accepted by the managing director, though in fact he had no authority to do this. On 13 January, there was a disagreement, and Lambert withdrew his offer. On 17 January, Bolton Partners started proceedings for breach of contract. On 28 January, the Board of Directors of Bolton Partners ratified the actions of the managing director. Lambert argued that this ratification came too late, but the Court of Appeal held that it had retrospectively validated the original contract, and that Lambert's attempt to withdraw was therefore ineffective.

Despite the considerable leeway granted by this decision it has subsequently been held that the ratification must take place within a reasonable time of the acceptance, and certainly before the contract has been performed (*Metropolitan Asylums Board Managers v Kingham & Sons* (1890)). Moreover, if the contract has been specifically stated to be 'subject to ratification', a withdrawal prior to ratification will be effective (*Watson v Davies* (1931)).

17.5 Duties of the agent

An agent has a duty to carry out instructions, to act with due care and skill, and to act personally rather than through another. In addition, the agent has various fiduciary duties.

17.5.1 Carry out instructions

An agent is obliged to do anything which the agreement creating the agency binds him or her to do. In *Fraser v Furman* (1967), an agent failed to take out an insurance policy on behalf of some employers, who, as a result, were liable to compensate an injured employee. The agent was held liable to re-imburse the employer.

An agent is also under a duty not to exceed the authority granted by the principal. We have already considered the issue of authority as it effects the third party. At this point, we are looking at the express and implied authority as between principal and agent. Express authority needs no discussion. Implied authority will arise from the relationship, and will include authority to take all actions necessarily incidental to the purposes for which the agent has been engaged. The authority as between principal and agent may not be identical with that between agent and third party, as is shown by the following quotation from *Waugh v Clifford* (1982). Note that 'implied authority' is here used to refer to the authority as between principal and agent. Brightman J said that if, in a defamation action, the defendant's solicitor offered £100,000 in settlement:

> It would in my view be officious on the part of the plaintiff's solicitor to demand to be satisfied as to the authority of the defendant's solicitor to make the offer. It is perfectly clear that the defendant's solicitor has *ostensible* authority to compromise the action on behalf of his client, notwithstanding the large sum involved ... But it does not follow that the defendant's solicitor would have *implied* authority to agree to damages on that scale without the agreement of his client. In the light of the solicitor's knowledge of his client's cash position it might be quite unreasonable and indeed grossly negligent for the solicitor to commit his client to such a burden without first inquiring if it were acceptable ... It follows in my view that a solicitor (or counsel) may in a particular case have ostensible authority vis à vis the opposing litigant where he has no implied authority vis à vis his client.

Thus, an agent may be able to bind the principal to a contract with the third party, but at the same time be in breach of the duty to carry out instructions.

17.5.2 Must act with due care and skill

The degree of care and skill required of an agent will depend on the circumstances. The agent must act with the skill which an agent in his or her position would normally possess. Thus, a solicitor or accountant must act with the skill to be expected of someone qualified in that profession. The standard is one of 'reasonable care' in that context.

If the agent is not acting for reward, then this duty will be applied less strictly.

17.5.3 Non-delegation

The agent is normally expected to act personally on behalf of the principal. Delegation of the agent's responsibilities will only be permissible where this has been authorised, expressly or impliedly, by the principal (*De Bussche v Alt* (1878)). Such delegation will not create any privity between the sub-agent and principal, unless this is specifically provided for. This was the case in *De Bussche v Alt*, so that the sub-agent was, unusually, held directly liable to the principal. Since the sub-agent had made a secret profit (see 17.5.5 below) from dealing with the principal's property, he was liable to account to the principal for this.

17.5.4 Fiduciary duties: conflict of interest

The agent must not put him or herself into a position where there is a conflict between the duties owed to the principal and the agent's own interests. In *Armstrong v Jackson* (1917), a stockbroker sold his own shares to a client. This was held to involve a conflict of interest:

> As vendor it is to his interest to sell his own shares at the highest price. As broker, it is his clear duty to the principal to buy at the lowest price and to give unbiased and independent advice ... as to the time when and the price at which shares shall be bought.

As a result, the principal was entitled to rescind the contract, and this was available irrespective of any of the normal bars to rescission for misrepresentation (see 9.3.1 above).

The agent will not be liable, however, if the principal is fully aware of the position. In *Harrods v Lemon* (1931), one department of the plaintiffs was acting as estate agents for the defendant, Mrs Lemon, and another department as surveyors for a person who was seeking to buy her house. There was a clear conflict of interest, but Mrs Lemon continued with the contract with full knowledge of the facts. Harrods were entitled to their commission.

17.5.5 Fiduciary duties: secret profits and bribes

An agent who makes a secret profit out of his or her position will be liable to account for this (that is, hand it over) to the principal (as in *De Bussche v Alt* (1878)).

Equally, the agent must not take a 'bribe', which was defined in *Industries and General Mortgage v Lewis* (1949) as involving:

- a payment made, or to be made, to the agent by the third party;
- knowledge by the third party that the agent is acting as an agent;

- failure by the third party to disclose the payment to the agent to the principal.

If these three conditions are satisfied, the payment will be treated as a bribe. There is no need to show any fraudulent intent on the part of anyone involved.

The effects of a bribe being given are that the agent may be dismissed, and the principal may sue the agent and the third party in tort for any loss caused by the bribe. Alternatively, the principal may recover the amount of the bribe from the agent, or from the third party, if not yet paid (*Mahesan v Malaysia Government Officers' Co-operative Housing Society Ltd* (1979)). Moreover, in *Attorney General for Hong Kong v Reid* (1994), the Privy Council held that a principal was able to 'trace' money given as a bribe into other property which may have been purchased with it, and to recover the full value of the relevant property at the time when the agent is compelled to disgorge the bribe. If the bribe is paid over, the principal is still entitled to set aside the transaction to which it related (*Logicrose Ltd v Southend United Football Club Ltd* (1988)).

17.5.6 Commercial agents

Commercial agents covered by the Commercial Agents (Council Directive) Regulations 1993 (see 17.1.3 above) are also under a general duty to act 'dutifully and in good faith', and to perform various specific duties, such as to supply the principal with 'all the necessary information available to him'.

17.6 Duties of the principal

The main duty of the principal is to pay the agent for the work that has been done. The agent's right to be paid will exist wherever this can be either expressly or impliedly taken to arise from their agreement. Where there is a written agreement, the courts will look at this very carefully in deciding whether the agent is entitled to payment. Thus, in *Taylor v Brewer* (1813), the agreement referred to the principal paying 'such remuneration ... as shall be deemed right'. It was held that this did not entitle the agent to reasonable remuneration, or indeed to any payment at all. It was entirely at the discretion of the principal. Similarly, in *John Meacock v Abrahams* (1956), the fact that the contract provided for payment in certain circumstances (which had not arisen) precluded the agent from claiming on a *quantum meruit* basis.

17.6.1 When is payment earned?

If it is decided that the agreement does allow for payment, when will it be earned? As would be expected, this will be when the agent has done what he or she has been employed to do. The difficulty arises, however, in deciding in some cases whether this has occurred. In one of the leading cases, for example, *Luxor (Eastbourne) Ltd v Cooper* (1941), a company wished to sell some cinemas, and Cooper agreed to try to provide a purchaser. He was to be paid 'on completion of the sale'. Cooper provided a willing purchaser, but the company withdrew from the sale. The House of Lords refused to imply a term that the principal would not unreasonably prevent the completion of the transaction. The clause referred to payment 'on completion'; since that had not occurred the agent was not entitled to his commission. The way around this is for the agent to insist that the commission should be earned by providing someone 'ready, willing and able' to purchase. This was held to be effective to entitle the agent to his commission in *Christie Owen and Davies v Rapacioli* (1974), and, more recently, in *FDP Savills Land and Property Ltd v Kibble* (1998).

Here again, the approach is to look very carefully at the wording of the agreement, and to apply it strictly.

17.6.2 Commercial agents

In relation to commercial agents falling within the Commercial Agents (Council Directive) Regulations 1993 (see 17.1.3 above) the principal has an obligation to act 'dutifully and in good faith'. The regulations also give the agent a more general right than exists under the common law to reasonable remuneration for work done, and a right to receive information on a range of issues relating to the agency, including the basis on which commission has been calculated.

17.7 Position of third party vis à vis the principal

Where the principal is 'disclosed', that is, the third party knows who the principal is, or at least is aware that the agent is acting for a principal, the basic rule is that the agent will drop out of the transaction. The third party will be able to sue the principal, and *vice versa*. Where the principal is undisclosed, however, the position is more complex.

17.7.1 Undisclosed principal

As has been noted above, the fact that an undisclosed principal is allowed to take over a contract from an agent runs counter to the general doctrine of privity. It means that the third party will find that he or she has rights against, and liabilities towards, a person with whom there was no intention to contract, and of whom the third party had no knowledge at the time of the contract. This rather unusual concept has been limited by two requirements: first, that the terms of the contract should be consistent with an agency relationship; secondly, that no personal considerations should militate against allowing the principal to take over the contract.

17.7.2 Consistency with contract

If an undisclosed principal is going to step in, this must be consistent with the terms of the contract. In *Humble v Hunter* (1848), for example, the alleged 'agent' who had entered into a charter of a boat, was described in the documentation as 'owner'. It was held that this designation was inconsistent with his acting as an agent, and so the court refused to allow an alleged undisclosed principal to take over the contract. In *Fred Drughorn Ltd v Rederiaktiebolaget Transatlantic* (1919), however, the description of a party as 'charterer' rather than 'owner' was held not to preclude an undisclosed principal from stepping into the agent's place.

17.7.3 Personal considerations

If the character of the person with whom he or she is contracting is an important consideration for the third party, an undisclosed principal may be prevented from suing on the contract. For example, in *Collins v Associated Greyhound Racecourses* (1930), the Court of Appeal held that the identity of the underwriters of shares in a new company was crucial, because the company needed to be sure that they were 'responsible persons'. If the underwriters failed then the company would be in financial difficulties. There was no scope in this situation for an undisclosed principal.

The concerns need not relate to financial solvency. In *Said v Butt* (1920), a person had arranged for someone else to buy him a ticket for the first night of a play, when he knew that the manager would not have sold him one. It was held that since at first nights the manager traditionally exercises control over the audience, the 'principal' should not be allowed to use the ticket acquired by his 'agent'. On the other hand, if the contract is not of a type to which personal considerations are relevant, the fact that there is personal animosity between the principal and third party will not be a bar to their being brought together by an agent, without the third party's knowledge. This was the case in *Dyster v Randall* (1926) which concerned the sale of a piece of land. The personal considerations were held to be immaterial to this contract.

17.7.4 Liability of principal

The third party will, of course, have rights against the principal (whether disclosed or undisclosed) in the same way as any other contracting party. Problems may arise, however, where payment to the third party is to be made *via* the agent. If the principal pays the agent, but the agent fails to pass this on, can the third party still sue the principal? In *Armstrong v Stokes* (1872), it was held that if the third party was unaware that the other party was dealing as agent, and the principal paid the agent in good faith while the third party was still giving credit to the agent, the third party could not then recover from the principal. This case suggests then that the third party cannot recover from the principal if the principal has paid the agent. The court, however, clearly limited its views to the facts before it, and did not express an opinion as to what the situation would be if:

• the principal was disclosed; or

• if the principal had a set-off against the agent.

The first situation was considered by the Court of Appeal in *Irvine v Watson* (1880) where it was held that even though a disclosed principal had paid the agent, the third party could still recover from the principal. The only exception would be where the third party had acted in such a way as to lead the principal to believe that the agent had paid the third party.

The second situation (that is, that of set-off by the principal against the agent) does not seem to have been judicially considered. The reverse situation, that is, a set-off between agent and third party was considered in *Cooke v Eshelby* (1887). The House of Lords held that the third party could not plead a set-off against the agent in an action by the principal, unless the principal had acted so as to induce the third party to believe that the agent was contracting as principal. By analogy, it would seem to follow that in an action by the third party against the principal, the principal would not be able to rely on a set-off against the agent.

17.8   Position of third party vis à vis the agent

The general rule, as has been stated above, is that the agent drops out, and has no liability under, or power to enforce, the contract between the principal and third party. In some situations, however, the third party may be able to sue the agent. The dominant issue is the intention of the parties. According to Brandon J in *The Swan* (1968), this is to be determined from:

• the nature of the contract;

• its terms;

• the surrounding circumstances.

The test is objective, based on:

> ... what two reasonable businessmen making a contract of that nature, in those terms, and in those surrounding circumstances, must be taken to have intended.

Relevant factors may include the way in which the agent has signed the contract. If the signature indicates that it is signed on behalf of someone else, then this will suggest the agent is not liable. Custom or trade usage may also suggest that the agent may have some liability or rights under the contract.

In *The Swan* itself, the relevant surrounding circumstances included the fact that the agent was also the owner of the boat, which was chartered to a company of which the agent was the major shareholder. The company, *via* the agent, ordered repair work to be done by the third party. It was held that since the repairers knew that the agent was also the owner, it was natural for them to assume that he would accept personal liability for the repairs.

17.8.1 Position where there is no principal

There are two situations to consider here. First, it may be that the agent is in fact the principal, and is just pretending to be an agent. In this situation, the agent will certainly be liable on any contract, and will also be able to enforce, unless the third party would thereby be prejudiced (for example, if there were personal considerations involved (cf above at 17.7.3)).

Secondly, the principal may not be in existence, for example, because it is a company which has not yet been formed. The position is now largely governed by statute, that is, s 36C(1) of the Companies Act 1985. This states:

> A contract which purports to be made by or on behalf of a company at a time when the company has not been formed has effect, subject to any agreement to the contrary, as one made with the person purporting to act for the company or as agent for it, and he is personally liable on the contract accordingly.

This is very clear as regards the agent's *liability*. It is not specific as to whether the agent would also be able to enforce against the third party. The Court of Appeal (in *Phonogram v Lane* (1981)) has, however, indicated a willingness to interpret the section broadly, in line with its purpose, and this suggests that the agent would be allowed to sue the third party in such a situation. Earlier authorities, such as *Newborne v Sensolid* (1954), which turned on narrow interpretations of the precise form of signature used, must now be regarded as of dubious authority.

17.8.2 Right of election

If the third party can sue either the principal or the agent, at what stage does a choice have to be made as to whom to pursue? Judgment cannot be enforced against both, but what if, for example, the principal is sued, but turns out to be unable to pay. Can the third party at that stage act against the agent?

The rules are not very clear, but s 3 of the Civil Liability (Contribution) Act 1978, has established that (contrary to the previous position) obtaining judgment against one party is not an automatic bar to suing the other. The test in all cases now seems to be whether the third party has 'elected' to sue one party or the other. The case of *Clarkson Booker Ltd v Andjel* (1964) said that this was a question of fact not law. What was required was a 'truly unequivocal act' taken with 'full knowledge of all the facts'. Clearly, a choice exercised at a time when the third party was unaware that the selected defendant was insolvent would not be taken with 'full knowledge'. Otherwise, however, the court seemed to feel that the institution of proceedings would raise a *prima facie* case of election. It is not an area, however, about which it is possible to state any propositions with any degree of certainty.

17.8.3 Collateral contract

It may be possible for the third party to take action against the agent on the basis of a collateral contract. This will be particularly appropriate as regards pre-contractual statements or promises which the agent may have made. An example is *Andrews v Hopkinson* (1957) where a dealer told the plaintiff that a car being bought on hire purchase terms was 'a good little bus. I would stake my life on it'. When the car later turned out to be seriously defective, the plaintiff was allowed to recover on the basis of a collateral contract.

17.8.4 Implied warranty of authority

The final way in which the agent may be liable to a third party is for breach of the implied warranty of authority. Any agent who purports to act as such, impliedly warrants that he or she has the required authority to enter into the contract. If this turns out to be untrue, the third party may sue. The remedy is less satisfactory than in an action for breach of contract, however, in that recovery will be limited to whatever the third party would have been able to obtain from the principal. If the principal is insolvent this may be very little.

The remedy exists, however, irrespective of whether the warranty is fraudulent, negligent, or innocent (*Collen v Wright* (1857)). It has even been held to be available where, unknown to the agent, the principal had become a certified lunatic, and therefore the agent's authority automatically terminated (*Yonge v Toynbee* (1910)).

In *Penn v Bristol & West Building Society* (1997), it was held by the Court of Appeal that a third party could sue on a breach of the warranty of authority even though the loss resulted from the third party contracting with someone other than the principal. A bank had lent money to a prospective purchaser of a house, relying on a solicitor's representation that he was acting for both the current owners (who were husband and wife). In fact, he had no authority to act for the wife. When the sale was subsequently, at the wife's instigation, declared null and void, it was held that the bank could recover from the solicitor its losses resulting from lending money to the purchaser, on the basis of the solicitor's breach of the implied warranty of authority.

17.9   Termination of agency

Agency may be brought to an end either by the act of the parties, or by operation of law.

17.9.1   Act of the parties

Where the agency was created by agreement, it will be determinable in the same way. A continuing agency may also be determined by giving such period of notice as is specified in any agreement, or failing that, reasonable notice. Finally, if either party acts in a way which is inconsistent with the continuation of the agency then it will be terminated – though of course this may well give rise to rights of action for breach of contract.

17.9.2   Operation of law

If an agency is for a particular transaction, the relationship will terminate when that transaction is completed. If it is for a specified period, it will cease at the end of that period.

Agency may also be terminated by subsequent events. These may be physical, as where, for example, the subject matter is destroyed, or the principal or agent dies, or becomes insane. Alternatively, they may be legal, as where the principal or agent becomes bankrupt, or the relationship becomes illegal (for example, if the principal becomes an enemy alien).

17.9.3   Effects of termination

As far as principal and agent are concerned, rights vested at the time of the termination will subsist, but no new rights can be created, at least once the agent has notice of the termination.

In relation to the third party, again rights accrued against either principal or agent will remain. New rights against the principal will only arise on the basis of ostensible authority. Otherwise, the agent will be liable, either directly on the contract, or for breach of the implied warranty of authority.

17.9.4   Commercial agents

In relation to commercial agents falling within the Commercial Agents (Council Directive) Regulations 1993 (see 17.1.3 above), there are special provisions as to termination provided by the regulations. These cover such matters as the minimum periods of notice which must be given, and the rights of the agent to compensation when an agreement is terminated. It was held in *Hackett v Advanced Medical Computer Systems Ltd* (1999) that no particular formality was required for giving notice under the Regulations.

AGENCY

Concept of agency

Agency depends on the type of relationship, not on labels (*Lamb & Sons v Goring Brick Co* (1932)). It can operate as an exception to, or a way around, the doctrine of privity (*New Zealand Shipping Co v Satterthwaite* (1974)).

Creation of agency

Creation of agency can be by express or implied agreement. No special formalities are required, unless the agent is to have power to execute a deed.

Agency can be created by operation of law as a result of a statutory provision (for example, s 56 of the Consumer Credit Act 1974), necessity (for example, *The Gratitudine* (1801); *The Choko Star* (1990)) or cohabitation. The presumption of agency from cohabitation is rebuttable (*Miss Gray Ltd v Earl Cathcart* (1922)).

The powers of an agent

The powers of an agent may be defined by express, implied, or ostensible authority.

Implied authority can be divided into 'usual' authority, based on the type of job (for example, *Watteau v Fenwick* (1893)), and 'customary' authority, based on the place of business (for example, *Scott v Godfrey* (1901)).

Ostensible authority requires a representation, reliance, and alteration of position (*Rama Corporation Ltd v Proved Tin and General Investment Ltd* (1952)). The representation may be by conduct (for example, *Summers v Solomon* (1857); *Lloyd v Grace, Smith & Co* (1912)), but must come from the principal, not the agent (*Armagas v Mundogas* (1986)).

Ratification

For ratification to be possible, the agent must purport to be acting for a principal (*Keighley Maxted & Co v Durant* (1901)), the principal must have been in existence (*Kelner v Baxter* (1866)), and the principal must have capacity both at the time of contract and at the time of ratification (*Grover and Grover v Matthews* (1910)).

Ratification is retrospective (*Bolton Partners v Lambert* (1889)). It must take place within a reasonable time, and before the contract has been performed (*Metropolitan Asylums Board Managers v Kingham & Sons* (1890)).

Duties of the agent

The agent must carry out instructions (*Fraser v Furman* (1967)). This will include things which are implied by, or incidental to, the main purpose of the agency (*Waugh v Clifford* (1982)). The agent must also act with due care and skill, and not delegate without authorisation (*De Bussche v Alt* (1878)).

The agent must not get into a position where the agent's interests conflict with those of the principal (*Armstrong v Jackson* (1917)). Nor must the agent take a secret profit, or bribe. The principal may recover either the bribe, or any loss suffered (*Mahesan v Malaysian Government Officers' Co-operative Housing Society Ltd* (1979)).

Duties of the principal

The main duty of the principal is to pay the agent. The existence of the right to payment (*Taylor v Brewer* (1813)), and the question when payment is earned (*Luxor (Eastbourne) Ltd v Cooper* (1941)), both depend on the terms of the agreement.

Position of third party vis à vis principal

Where the principal is disclosed the third party can sue, and be sued. Where undisclosed, the third party will only be liable if the terms of the contract are consistent with its being made by an agent (*Humble v Hunter* (1848)), and personal considerations are not important (*Collins v Associated Greyhound Racecourses* (1930); *Said v Butt* (1920)).

Where the principal has paid the agent, but this has not been passed on, an undisclosed principal may not be liable (*Armstrong v Stokes* (1872)), but a disclosed principal generally will be (*Irvine v Watson* (1880)).

Position of third party vis à vis agent

Normally, the agent drops out, but sometimes there may be personal liability. This depends on an objective view of whether in all the circumstances a reasonable businessperson would have expected the agent to be liable (*The Swan* (1968)).

If the agent is in fact the principal, he or she will be fully liable. If the principal is an unincorporated company, then the agent will again be liable by virtue of s 36C(1) of the Companies Act 1985, and will probably be able to sue as well (*Phonogram v Lane* (1981)).

If third party can sue either principal or agent, an election to sue one will preclude action against the other (*Clarkson Booker Ltd v Andjel* (1964)).

The agent may also be liable on a collateral contract (*Andrews v Hopkinson* (1957)), or for breach of the implied warranty of authority (*Collen v Wright* (1857); *Yonge v Toynbee* (1910)).

Termination of agency

Agency may be brought to an end by the agreement of the parties, notice, or by breach of the original agreement. It may also be terminated by operation of law, or the destruction of the subject matter, or the death or bankruptcy of either party.

Effects of termination are that rights vested at the time will subsist. No new rights can be created, other than by ostensible authority.

CHAPTER 18

SALE OF GOODS

18.1 Definition

Every contract for the sale of goods, be it for a packet of tea in a supermarket, or for goods worth many thousands of pounds between two large companies, is governed by the Sale of Goods Act (SGA) 1979. (Note, however, that international sales may be subject to different rules.) Throughout this chapter, unless otherwise stated, section numbers refer to the SGA 1979.

Section 2(1) of the SGA 1979 defines a contract for the sale of goods as a:

> ... contract by which the seller transfers or agrees to transfer the property in goods to the buyer for a money consideration, called the price.

Note that there must be at least partial money consideration. An exchange of goods is not within the scope of the SGA 1979. Nor does the Act cover other similar contracts which may transfer the possession or ownership of goods, such as hire, hire purchase, or contracts for work and materials. These types of contract are controlled by other statutes, principally the Consumer Credit Act 1974, and the Supply of Goods and Services Act 1982. If A engages B to build a wall, for example, the bricks which make up the wall will become A's property. The contract is for work and materials, however, and so is not governed by the SGA 1979. It will, however, be to some extent controlled by the Supply of Goods and Services Act 1982, for example, as regards implied terms as to the quality of the bricks.

There is an unresolved issue as to whether computer software comes within the definition of 'goods'. There is little doubt that if it is purchased on floppy disc or CD, then the disc will be regarded as goods, in the same way as a CD or tape containing music or a DVD or videocassette containing a film. If the disc does not operate correctly, there will be a potential for a claim under the SGA 1979. Where, however, the software is downloaded off the internet, or, in a commercial context, is loaded on to the buyer's computer system by the supplier of the program, then it is difficult to see that there is any sale of goods involved. That was the view, *obiter*, of Sir Iain Glidewell in the Court of Appeal in *St Alban's City and District Council v International Computers Ltd* (1996). In most situations where there is a problem with what has been supplied, the distinction will not matter, since terms similar to those contained in the SGA 1979 are likely to be implied by the courts. In some cases, however, it may be more important to be clear about whether the contract does fall within the scope of the 1979 Act. At the moment, there is no definitive ruling on the issue.

18.1.1 Agreements to sell

Section 2(5) distinguishes 'sales' from 'agreements to sell'. Whereas under a sale the property in the goods is transferred at the time of the contract, if this is to take place at some point in the future, the contract is an agreement to sell.

18.2 Passing of property

The SGA 1979 uses the phrase 'passing of property' to refer to what would in common parlance be called 'transfer of ownership'. It defines the moment when the buyer becomes the owner of the goods, and is very important to determine. If one party has been fraudulent, or the goods are destroyed, or cause damage to a third party, it will be vital in the determining of rights and liabilities to know whether property has passed.

Before looking at the rules relating to this, it is important to emphasise that 'property' and physical 'possession' are entirely distinct as far as the law is concerned. It is quite possible for goods to become the property of the seller while still remaining in the possession of the buyer, and *vice versa*. Equally, the question of payment does not determine the passing of property. A person may become the owner of goods before paying for them, or may pay, yet only become the owner at some later point.

The rules relating to the passing of property are to be found in ss 16–18 of the SGA 1979.

18.2.1 Goods must be ascertained

Section 16 requires that goods must be 'ascertained' before property can pass. If there is an order for 5,000 grade 3 widgets, for example, no property will be able to pass until the particular widgets which are to comprise the order are identified or 'ascertained'. This is subject to s 20A, under which in certain circumstances the property may pass in relation to unascertained goods forming part of an identifiable 'bulk'. Section 20A is discussed further above at 18.2.9.

18.2.2 Intention of the parties

Subject to s 16, the parties themselves are entirely free to decide when property is to pass. This is made clear by s 17. They are not, therefore, automatically bound by any of the following rules, set out in s 18. These apply only where the intention of the parties cannot be determined from the contract itself, the parties conduct, or the surrounding circumstances. If the parties wish to express their own intention as to when property should pass, however, this must be done before or in the contract. In *Dennant v Skinner* (1948), the plaintiff sold a car by auction. The buyer wanted to pay by cheque and take the car. The plaintiff was only prepared to agree if the buyer signed a document stating that property would not pass until the cheque was cleared. The buyer signed the document, took the car, and sold it to the defendant. The cheque was not met. It was held that the expression of intention came too late, and the rules in s 18 applied, which meant that property had passed to the buyer, and then to the defendant. The plaintiff could not recover his car, but was left with his remedy against the buyer.

18.2.3 Specific goods: deliverable state

Section 18, r 1 states that where there is an unconditional contract for the sale of specific goods in a deliverable state then property passes when the contract is made. Many shop sales will be of this kind, though it can also apply in other situations.

'Specific goods' are defined in s 61(1) as 'goods identified and agreed on at the time' of the contract. 'Deliverable state' is defined in s 61(5) as meaning that the goods 'are in such a state that the buyer would under the contract be bound to take delivery of them'.

18.2.4 Specific goods: not deliverable

Section 18, r 2 states that if specific goods are not in a deliverable state at the time of the contract, then property does not pass until the seller has put them into such a state, and the buyer has notice that this has been done. If goods are loose in a warehouse, for example, and need to be packaged for delivery, then this will delay the passing of property.

18.2.5 Specific goods: price not ascertained

Section 18, r 3 deals with specific goods in a deliverable state, but which need to be weighed, measured, etc by the seller to determine the price. It may be, for example, that the contract is for an entire stock of grain which is sitting in bags in the seller's warehouse. The price may have been fixed at so much per bag, but the parties may not know precisely how many bags there are. Property will not pass until the seller has counted them, and has given the buyer notice that this has been done.

18.2.6 Approval, or sale or return

Where goods are provided 'on approval', or on a 'sale or return' basis, s 18, r 4 governs the passing of property. This states that property will pass either when the buyer signifies approval or acceptance to the seller, or when the buyer does some other act 'adopting the transaction'. Using, or reselling, the goods, would clearly come into this category. Failing any action on the part of the buyer, property will pass on the expiry of any term fixed for the return of the goods, or else at the expiry of a reasonable time.

If the buyer decides to reject some or all of the goods, the notification to the seller must be clear, but does not need to spell out in detail precisely which goods are being rejected: *Atari Corp (UK) Ltd v Electronic Boutique Stores (UK) Ltd* (1998).

18.2.7 Unascertained or future goods

Where the contract is for the sale of unascertained or future goods by description, s 18, r 5 states that property will not pass until goods are 'unconditionally appropriated' to the contract. The meaning of 'ascertained' has been indicated above. Future goods are defined in s 61(1) as 'goods to be manufactured or acquired by the seller' after the making of the contract. The 'appropriation' may be done by either the seller or the buyer, but must be with the express or implied 'assent' of the other party, which can be given either before or after the appropriation. The appropriation must be unconditional. The fact that the seller has set aside goods in his or her warehouse, and has it in mind that these will be the ones to be supplied to the buyer, may well not satisfy r 5. Although there has clearly been an appropriation, it is not 'unconditional', in that the seller could later decide to send different goods matching the contract description to the buyer. Giving the goods to a carrier will often amount to unconditional appropriation, as is recognised by r 5(2), but will not necessarily do so. In *Healey v Howlett* (1917), the contract was for 20 boxes of mackerel. The seller handed over 170 boxes to the carrier, with instructions that 20 were to be delivered to the buyer, and the rest to other contractors. The mackerel deteriorated in transit, and was rejected by the buyer. It was held that property had not passed to the buyer on delivery to the carrier. There was no unconditional appropriation because no specific 20 boxes had been assigned to the buyer's contract until the point where the carrier was about to deliver.

Rule 5 contains special provision for goods which form part of an identified 'bulk' (for which see 18.2.8 below), out of which there is a contract to supply a specified quantity of unascertained goods. If the bulk is reduced to (or below) the amount due under the contract, and the buyer is the only one to whom goods are due, then the remaining goods are taken to be appropriated to the contract, and property in them passes to the buyer (r 5(3)). The same will apply in relation to a buyer who has several contracts relating to the same bulk, if the amount reduces to (or below) the total due under those contracts (r 5(4)).

18.2.8 Property in goods forming part of a bulk

Section 20A deals with the rights of a buyer in relation to a contract for the sale of a specified quantity of unascertained goods which form part of an identified 'bulk', and for which the buyer has paid all or part of the price. A 'bulk' is defined in s 61(1) as:

> ... a mass or collection of goods of the same kind which:
> (a) is contained in a defined space or area; and
> (b) is such that any goods in the bulk are interchangeable with any other goods therein of the same number or quantity.

The most obvious example is a quantity of loose (or bagged) goods, for example, grain, held in a particular warehouse. A buyer who makes a contract to buy a specified quantity of such goods from that warehouse, and pays for them, will fall within the scope of s 20A. Such a buyer will, as soon as the above conditions are met (or at a later time, if the parties so agree), become the owner of an undivided share in the bulk, proportionate to the amount of goods paid for. The buyer also becomes an 'owner in common' of the bulk. If there are several buyers, and the aggregate of their shares exceeds the whole of the bulk, each buyer's share will be reduced proportionately to make the aggregate equal to the bulk (s 20A(4)). Section 20B contains consequential provisions allowing co-owners to deal with, or take delivery of, parts of the bulk falling within their undivided share, and deeming the other co-owners to consent to this.

The effect of these provisions is to provide greater protection to the purchaser of goods from bulk where the seller becomes insolvent. Before their enactment, such a purchaser would probably be in no better position than any other unsecured creditor. By virtue of s 20A, however, the purchaser will have property rights over the goods, and thus will be able to take precedence over other creditors. (See 18.4 below, concerning reservation of title.)

18.2.9 Passing of risk

The risk of loss or damage to the goods will generally pass at the same time as the property in the goods, according to the rules just discussed (s 20). The parties may, however, agree to a different arrangement, if they so wish.

18.3 Transfer of title

The rules we have just been considering are concerned with the point in time at which property passes, and the buyer becomes the owner. This section is concerned with the question of who may pass a good title to the buyer, and in what circumstances. The basic rule is set out in s 21(1), and states that where the goods are sold by someone who is not the true owner, then the buyer will obtain no better title than the seller. This is often referred to as the *nemo dat* rule, this being shorthand for the Latin phrase, *nemo dat quod non habet* – no one may give what they do not have. It means, for example, that if goods are stolen, and then sold by the thief, the person who buys from the thief will be liable to re-imburse the true owner, either by returning the goods or paying compensation.

The law has long recognised however, that the innocent purchaser who buys in good faith needs some protection, and so there are various exceptions to the *nemo dat* rule.

18.3.1 Owner's conduct

If the owner has led the buyer to believe that the person has the right to sell, then the buyer will acquire a good title (s 21(1)). An agent might, for example, have obtained goods by fraud from his or her principal, and the principal might, before discovering the fraud, tell the buyer that the agent has the right to sell. The mere fact that the owner has allowed the seller to be in possession of the goods, however, is not enough to bring this exception into operation. A person who is in possession under a hire purchase agreement will not generally, therefore, be able to pass on a good title. Note, however, that there is special protection for the private purchasers of motor cars which are subject to hire purchase agreements, under ss 27–29 of the Hire Purchase Act 1965.

18.3.2 Sale by factor

Section 2 of the Factors Act 1889, provides an exception to the rule where a mercantile agent is in possession of goods, or documents of title, and is acting in the ordinary course of business. This is recognised by s 21(2)(a) of the SGA 1979.

18.3.3 Statutory or common law power

This exception, which appears in s 21(2)(b), covers sales of goods which have been pledged, or which are the subject of a court order.

18.3.4 Sale under a voidable title

The exception of a sale under a voidable title, which is contained in s 23, deals with the situation where the original owner has sold goods under a contract which is voidable. This might be because of misrepresentation on the part of the buyer. If the goods are sold on before the contract is avoided, the new buyer will acquire a good title. The original seller thus needs to move quickly as soon as any fraud is discovered. In *Car and Universal Finance Co Ltd v Caldwell* (1964), the owner had sold a car to N in return for a cheque, which was dishonoured. The owner at once informed the police and the Automobile Association. It was held that this was sufficient to avoid the contract, in the circumstances. Since the owner had acted before N had managed to resell the car, the innocent third party who had bought it had acquired no title, and could not rely on s 23. The owner could therefore recover the car.

18.3.5 Seller left in possession

Where the seller has retained possession of the goods after property has passed to the buyer, the seller may 'resell' the goods to another. If the second buyer is an innocent purchaser in good faith, and without notice of the previous sale, he or she will obtain a good title (s 24). There must, however, be actual delivery of the goods, or documents of title, in order for this exception to apply.

18.3.6 Buyer in possession

This is the converse situation to the previous one, and is dealt with by s 25, that is, the buyer has been allowed by the seller to take possession of the goods or documents of title before property has passed, and then resells. Provided again that there is actual delivery, the new purchaser who takes in good faith and without notice will obtain a good title. In *National Employers Mutual General Assurance v Jones* (1987), the Court of Appeal confirmed that the references to the 'seller' in s 25 were to be taken to refer to the true owner. Where the 'buyer in possession' had obtained the goods from someone other than the true owner, s 25 did not apply.

18.3.7 Market overt

The antiquated exception which used to exist in relation to sales in 'market overt' was repealed with effect from 3 January 1995.

18.4 Retention of title

A seller who is concerned that the buyer may become insolvent before paying for goods, may try to protect his or her position by inserting a clause into the contract whereby the property is not to pass until the seller has been paid. This is recognised by s 19, which refers to the reservation of the right of disposal. If effective, this will allow the seller to reclaim the goods themselves, rather than having to stand in line with the insolvent buyer's other creditors. Despite attempts to develop complicated *'Romalpa'* clauses (named after the case of *Aluminium Industrie Vaasen BV v Romalpa Aluminium Ltd* (1976)), the device really only works if the goods are still in the buyer's possession. If they have been mixed with other goods, or sold to a third party, the original owner will be unlikely to establish any proprietary claim over the mixed goods, or the proceeds of any resale, unless a charge has been registered. The third party will of course be protected by s 25 (see 18.3.6 above).

18.5 Implied terms

Various terms are implied into all sale of goods contracts by virtue of ss 12–15 of the SGA 1979. We saw in Chapter 14 (see 14.4.3 above) that these are labelled as 'conditions' or 'warranties'. The consequences of that labelling in terms of remedies is not discussed here in detail but the effect of s 15A should be noted (see 18.5.6 below).

18.5.1 Title

Section 12 is concerned with 'title' in the sense of the 'right to sell'. There is an implied condition in every sale of goods contract that the seller has this right 'at the time when property is to pass'. The condition will be broken if the goods belong to someone else, or if they cannot be sold without infringing another's rights, for example, in a trade mark (*Niblett v Confectioners' Materials* (1921)). Note, also, the effects of a breach of this condition as regards a 'total failure of consideration'. This issue, and the decision in *Rowland v Divall* (1923) has been discussed in Chapter 16 (see 16.2.1 above).

Section 12 also contains an implied warranty of quiet possession, and freedom from encumbrances.

18.5.2 Description

Section 13 says that where goods are sold by description there is an implied condition that they will match the description. The description may come from the seller or the buyer, and can apply to specific, as well as generic goods (*Varley v Whipp* (1900)). Section 13(3) makes it clear that selection by the buyer, as in a self-service shop, does not prevent the sale being by description. Virtually all sales will, as a result, be sales by description, unless the buyer indicates a particular article which he or she wishes to buy, without describing it in any way, and the article itself has no label or packaging containing a description. There must, however, be some reliance on the description by the buyer in order for s 13 to apply. *Harlingdon and Leinster Enterprises v Christopher Hull Fine Art Ltd* (1990) concerned the sale of a painting which turned out not to be by the artist to whom it was attributed in the catalogue. It was found as a matter of fact that the buyer had not relied on this attribution, and therefore this was not a sale by description.

It is important to distinguish statements as to *quality* from statements of *description*. To describe a car as 'new' is description; to say that it has 'good acceleration' is a statement of quality, and not within s 13. Statements in advertisements can, however, be regarded as part of the description, even if the goods have subsequently been inspected. In *Beale v Taylor* (1967), a car was advertised as a 1961 model. In fact, it was made of two halves welded together, only one of the halves dating from 1961. It was held that there was a breach of s 13.

Note that s 13 applies to private sales, as well as those in the course of a business.

18.5.3 Satisfactory quality

Where a sale of goods contract is made in the course of business, s 14(2) implies a term of 'satisfactory quality'. The scope of the phrase 'in the course of business', which also applies to the implied term under s 14(3) (18.5.4 below), was considered by the Court of Appeal in *Stevenson v Rogers* (1999). The case concerned the sale by a fisherman of his fishing boat. The court noted that the original wording of the relevant section in the Sale of Goods Act 1893 had limited liability to where the seller dealt 'in goods of that description'. This limitation had been removed, however, and did not appear in s 14 of the 1979 Act. The fact, therefore, that the fisherman was not regularly in the business of selling fishing boats did not prevent this being a sale 'in the course of business', so that the implied term under s 14(2) applied. In coming to this conclusion, the court held that the narrower interpretation of 'the course of a business' used by the Court of Appeal in *R and B Customs Brokers v UDT* (1988) in relation to the Unfair Contract Terms Act 1977 (see 8.5.3) should not be used in this context.

Where the requirement of 'satisfactory quality' applies, this means according to s 14(2A), that the goods must:

> ... meet the standard that a reasonable person would regard as satisfactory, taking account of any description of the goods, the price (if relevant) and all other relevant circumstances.

This test of satisfactory quality was substituted for the previous test of 'merchantable quality' by the Sale and Supply of Goods Act 1994. The previous case law on s 14(2) is therefore only of limited assistance in the interpretation of this section. Section 14(2B), however, indicates some of the factors which will be relevant in applying the new test. These include the state and condition of the goods, and in particular their:

(a)   fitness for all the purposes for which goods of the kind in question are commonly supplied;

(b)   appearance and finish;

(c)   freedom from minor defects;

(d)   safety; and

(e)   durability.

The test of 'merchantable quality' had centred on the issue now dealt with in (a) above. By virtue of the decision in *Aswan Engineering Establishment Co v Lupdine Ltd* (1986), however, goods which were fit for just *one* of the purposes for which they were commonly used would be merchantable. The new wording contained in (a) above means that the fitness of the goods for *all* such purposes will be relevant to the test of whether they are of satisfactory quality.

Defects which have been brought to the buyer's attention prior to the contract, or which should have been revealed by any inspection actually undertaken by the buyer, will not make the goods of unsatisfactory quality (s 14(2C)).

There seems no reason to doubt that the new test will, like the test of merchantability, include the containers in which the goods are supplied, and may also include instructions for use. If the goods are supplied in bulk, extraneous items which are concealed within them may render the goods unsatisfactory. In *Wilson v Rickett Cockerell Co* (1954), the presence of detonators in a bag of coal was held to make the coal unmerchantable.

The test does not relate to the particular use that the buyer has in mind (for which see s 14(3), below at 18.5.4) but to the general standard of the goods.

18.5.4 Fitness for a particular purpose

If the buyer wants the goods for a particular purpose, and the seller is aware of this, there will be an implied term in all sales in the course of a business, that the goods will be reasonably fit for that purpose (s 14(3)), unless:

> ... the circumstances show that the buyer does not rely, or that it is unreasonable for him to rely on the skill and judgment of the seller.

The section can apply even though the goods only have one purpose, in which case the seller will be taken to have notice of it (*Priest v Last* (1903)), but it will usually be more appropriate to use s 14(2) in such circumstances. Section 14(3) may need to be relied on, however, if there is something special about the circumstances in which the goods are to be used. In *Griffiths v Peter Conway* (1939), the plaintiff contracted dermatitis from wearing a Harris Tweed coat. This was brought about by the fact that the plaintiff had an unusually sensitive skin. On the facts, this was not something which the seller knew, and so the claim under s 14(3) failed. If the seller had been aware, however, then the action under this section would have been the appropriate one, despite the fact that the coat only had one 'purpose', that is, to be worn.

The same approach was used by the House of Lords in *Slater v Finning Ltd* (1996). A camshaft supplied by the defendants failed when used in an engine fitted to the plaintiffs' fishing boat. Replacement camshafts supplied by the defendant also failed. The plaintiffs sold the engine, with its latest replacement camshaft, and it was fitted to another fishing boat in which it was apparently used without problem. The judge found that the problem of the failure of the camshafts must have been caused by some unexplained idiosyncrasy of the plaintiffs' fishing boat. There was therefore no breach of the implied condition of fitness for purpose. This conclusion was confirmed by the House of Lords, which also made clear that where the problem arose from an abnormal or unusual situation not known to the seller, it was irrelevant for the purposes of s 14(3) whether or not this situation was known to the buyer.

A claim will not succeed under s 14(3) where the problems arise from the buyer's misunderstanding of instructions supplied with the goods (*Wormell v RHM Agriculture (East) Ltd* (1987)). This decision appears to accept, however, that defective instructions could lead to goods being found to be not fit for a particular purpose.

Once it is clear that the seller knew of the particular purpose, the burden is on the seller to show that there was no, or unreasonable, reliance. This is a hard test to satisfy, since the courts tend to favour the buyer, and have made it clear that partial reliance is sufficient to found an action (*Ashington Piggeries v Christopher Hill* (1972)).

18.5.5 Sale by sample

Where there is a sale by sample there is an implied condition, by virtue of s 15:

(a)   that the bulk will correspond with the sample in quality;

(b)   [repealed];

(c)   that the goods will be free from any defect, making their quality unsatisfactory, which would not be apparent on reasonable examination of the sample.

This section does not seem to have given rise to any serious difficulties in application.

18.5.6 Right to reject in non-consumer contracts

As we have seen in Chapter 14 (see 14.4.2 above), where there is a breach of condition, the other party will normally have the right to treat this as a repudiatory breach, and reject the goods. Section 15A, however, modifies this right in non-consumer contracts (unless the parties agree otherwise). Where the breach is of one of the implied conditions contained in ss 13, 14, or 15, and the buyer is not a consumer, the right to reject is removed if the breach is so slight that it would be unreasonable for the buyer to reject the goods. Minor deviations from the contract description, therefore, such as in *Re Moore and Landauer* (1921) or *Arcos v Ronaasen* (1933), will no longer in themselves enable the buyer to escape from the contract, even though the goods are still perfectly usable.

18.6   Exclusion of the implied terms

Exclusion of the implied terms under the SGA 1979 is governed by s 6 of the Unfair Contract Terms Act 1977. Liability for breach of s 12 (title) may never be excluded. Similarly, there can be no exclusion of liability under s 13 (description), s 14 (satisfactory quality, fitness for particular purpose) or s 15 (sample) in relation to a consumer contract. Where the buyer contracts other than as a consumer, however, liability for breach of these sections may be excluded, provided the clause satisfies the 'requirement of reasonableness' under s 11 (for discussion of which see 8.8 above).

A person contracts 'as a consumer' when he or she does not contract 'in the course of a business'. The narrow definition of 'course of a business' adopted in *R and B Customs Brokers v UDT* (1988) should be noted (the case is discussed in Chapter 8 (see 8.5.3 above)). This significantly reduces the situations in which exclusion of the implied terms will be permissible. As noted above (18.5.3), the Court of Appeal has adopted a narrower test of 'course of a business' in relation to the question of when the implied terms under s 14 of the SGA should be included in a contract: *Stevenson v Rogers* (1999).

18.7 Delivery

Payment and delivery are concurrent conditions, unless otherwise agreed (s 28). Delivery can include handing over the means of control, as well as physical transfer. In *Four Point Garage v Carter* (1985), it was held that delivery by the original seller (S) to a person who had bought from the original buyer (B) constituted delivery from S to B.

18.7.1 Place of delivery

Subject to anything contrary in the agreement, the buyer is obliged to collect the goods from the seller's premises, or wherever the goods are at the time of the contract (s 29(2)). In practice, this will often be varied by the contract, so that the seller arranges delivery to the buyer's premises.

18.7.2 Delivery of the wrong quantity

The rules relating to delivery of the wrong quantity are set out in s 30, and impose strict obligations on the seller. If less than the contract amount is delivered, the buyer may refuse delivery, or may accept what is offered, and pay for it at the contract rate. Somewhat more surprisingly, if *more* than the contract quantity is delivered, the buyer may again reject the whole consignment. The buyer may also, however, accept the whole amount, and pay for the excess at the contract rate, or accept the contract quantity, and reject the rest. The right to reject a delivery of the wrong quantity will, however, not be available to a non-consumer purchaser where the difference is so slight that such rejection would be unreasonable. The inference must be that the consumer purchaser is entitled to act unreasonably in rejecting on these grounds.

18.7.3 Instalments

The rules relating to instalments are set out in s 31. They follow the more general rules in this area discussed in Chapter 14 (see 14.5.1 above), and so are not discussed again here.

18.8 Acceptance

It is important to identify whether or not the buyer has accepted the goods, because this will determine whether the buyer can reject for breach of condition, or simply sue for damages (s 11(4)). Section 34 states that the buyer shall not be deemed to have accepted the goods until he or she has had a reasonable opportunity of examining them for the purpose of ascertaining whether they are in conformity with the contract, and in relation to a sale by sample, of comparing the bulk with the sample. Section 35, on the other hand, sets out certain circumstances in which the buyer will be deemed to have accepted. This will be the case where the buyer intimates to the seller that the goods are being accepted, or where the buyer does some act which is inconsistent with the seller's ownership, such as the consumption of the goods. The buyer will not be deemed to have accepted, however, simply because he has asked for, or agreed to their repair under an arrangement with the seller. This addition to the section, which was made by the Sale and Supply of Goods Act 1994, means that the buyer who receives defective goods will no longer run the risk of losing the right of rejection for breach of condition simply because the seller is allowed to make some attempt to put the defect right. The revised s 35 also provides that delivery of the goods to another, for example, under a sub-sale, will not in itself mean that the buyer is deemed to have accepted them. The previous rule had the potential to operate harshly where, for example, goods were resold without the first buyer having inspected them. The section continues to provide, however, that the buyer will be deemed to have accepted if he retains the goods beyond a reasonable time without telling the seller that he is rejecting them. In deciding whether such a time has passed, one of the questions to be asked is whether the buyer has had a reasonable opportunity to examine the goods. The rule relating to lapse of time was applied very strictly in *Bernstein v Pamsons Motors (Golders Green) Ltd* (1987). The buyer had purchased a car, which he had had for three weeks, and driven for 140 miles, when, without warning, it broke down, owing to a serious defect in the engine. The judge held that there was a breach of s 14(2), in that the car was not of merchantable quality (the predecessor of 'satisfactory quality'), but that the right to reject had been lost for lapse of time. This first instance decision has been regarded as very harsh, and is also not easy to reconcile with the Court of Appeal decision in *Rogers v Parish* (1987) in which the buyer of a car which had suffered from a series of defects from the point when it was purchased was allowed to reject it after it had been used for about six months, and driven for 5,500 miles. The point of distinction may be that the buyer in *Rogers v Parish* had from the start made it clear that the car would not be 'accepted' until all defects had been remedied.

18.8.1 Right of partial rejection

Where the buyer has a right to reject goods, acceptance of some of them does not amount to acceptance of all, and the buyer will, by virtue of s 35A, retain the right to reject those not accepted. Part of a delivery of goods may, for example, fail to match the contract description. The buyer is entitled to reject either the whole consignment, or simply those that are defective. The section does not, however, prevent the buyer accepting some of the *defective* goods, and rejecting the rest, if he chooses to do so.

18.9 Damages

The basic rules for the award of damages for breach of a sale of goods contract are the same as for any contract, as have been discussed in Chapter 13. The rule of remoteness, and the rules for recovery of consequential losses, apply in exactly the same way.

In relation to breaches of the implied terms as to the quality of the goods, s 53(3) states that, *'prima facie'*, the loss is the:

> ... difference in the value of the goods at the time of delivery to the buyer and the value they would have had if they had fulfilled the warranty.

In *Bence Graphics International Ltd v Fasson UK Ltd* (1998), however, the Court of Appeal confirmed that the *prima facie* position was not necessarily the correct one to apply. Section 53(2) states that the measure of damages is 'the estimated loss directly and naturally resulting, in the ordinary course of events' from the breach. Thus, if the 'difference in value' approach does not on the facts match the actual loss suffered by the buyer (as was the position in the case before it), the court should be prepared to depart from the *prima facie* rule and calculate the damages on a different basis.

The SGA also sets out particular rules relating to non-acceptance, or non-delivery, based on the 'available market' test.

18.9.1 Non-acceptance

If the buyer wrongfully refuses to accept and pay for goods, the seller's damages may be based on the 'available market' test (s 50(3)). This means that if there is an available market, then damages will be based on the difference between the contract price and the market price at the time of breach. If the market price is lower, then the seller will receive this difference as damages. If the market price is higher, however, then the seller will only be able to recover nominal damages.

If there is no available market, then the damages will be based on the lost profit on the particular transaction. But note that, if the goods have been resold, there may be no lost profit. In *Lazenby Garages v Wright* (1976), the buyer refused delivery of a second hand car. It was held that there was no 'available market' because each second hand car is unique. But, the seller had not lost anything on this transaction, because the car had been resold at a higher price, and it could not be shown that overall a sale had been lost by the buyer's rejection.

18.9.2 Non-delivery

Where the seller wrongfully fails to deliver, the available market test will again be used to assess the buyer's damages (s 51(3)). Here, of course, substantial damages will only be recoverable if the market price is higher than the contract price. The courts will, in applying the available market test, generally ignore any resale that has in fact been arranged. In *Williams Bros v Agius* (1914), the contract price was 16 shillings per ton, and the buyer's had arranged a resale at 19 shillings. The market price at the time of the seller's default was 23 shillings. The buyer was allowed to recover the full seven shillings per ton in damages.

The court may decide that if the contract was for one particular load, or cargo, that the available market test should not be applied, even though similar goods are available. In *Re Hall (R and H) and WH Pim's Arbitration* (1928), the contract price for a cargo of wheat was 51 shillings per quarter. The buyer had arranged a resale at 56 shillings. When the seller defaulted, similar goods were available at 53 shillings. Nevertheless, the court held that the resale of this particular cargo had been in the contemplation of the parties at the time of the contract, so the available market test should not be applied, and the buyer was awarded five shillings per quarter damages.

18.9.3 Action for the price

An alternative action for the seller when the buyer refuses to pay for goods is the action for the price, under s 49. This will be available where either property, or the date fixed for payment in the contract, has passed. If the seller has not delivered the goods, he or she must be able and prepared to do so.

18.10 Unpaid sellers' property rights

Sections 38–48 of the SGA 1979 provide the unpaid seller with certain rights over the goods. These are available even where the property in the goods has passed to the buyer. There are three rights, namely, lien, stoppage in transit and resale.

18.10.1 Lien

Lien arises, under s 41, when the seller remains in possession of the goods. He or she is entitled to retain them until paid where:

- no credit has been given to the buyer; or
- the credit term has expired; or
- the buyer has become in insolvent.

18.10.2 Stoppage in transit

This right enables the seller to recover the goods from a carrier, and retain them pending payment of the price (s 44). It arises only where the buyer has become insolvent. It is exercised by taking possession of the goods, or by giving notice to the carrier (s 46).

The right seems to be of little practical importance in modern law. Increasingly, sophisticated banking arrangements have probably rendered it largely unnecessary in relation to export sales, and as regards domestic sales the period of transit will generally be too short to enable the right to be exercised.

As we have seen (s 24; see 18.3.5 above), the seller who remains in possession can resell the goods and pass a good title to the second purchaser, whether or not property has passed. The seller will also pass a good title if he or she resells after exercising the rights of lien, or stoppage in transit (s 48(2)). But the seller will in all these cases almost certainly still be in breach of the contract with the original buyer, unless the following provisions of s 48 apply.

Where the goods are perishable, or the unpaid seller gives notice of an intention to resell and the buyer does not within a reasonable time pay or tender the price, the seller is entitled to resell the goods, and claim damages from the original buyer (s 48(3)).

Furthermore, if the seller has expressly reserved the right of resale in the event of the buyer's default, a resale by the unpaid seller will rescind the original contract. The seller may then also sue the original buyer for damages.

SALE OF GOODS

Definition

The definition of a sale of goods is contained in s 2(1). It excludes exchanges, hire purchase contracts, and contracts for work and materials. Note the distinction between 'sale' and 'agreement to sell' (s 2(5)).

Passing of property (ss 16–18)

Property passes according to the intentions of the parties (s 17), provided the goods are ascertained (s 16) (but note *Dennant v Skinner* (1948)). If no intention is expressed, the rules in s 18 apply. In respect of specific goods in a deliverable state, property passes on contract (r 1). In respect of specific goods, which are not deliverable, or which need weighing, etc to determine the price, property passes when the seller has done what is necessary, and has told the buyer (rr 2 and 3). In respect of sales on approval or sale or return, property passes with the buyer's accepting by words or conduct, or by the lapse of time (r 4). In respect of unascertained or future goods, property passes when goods are unconditionally appropriated to the contract (r 5 – note, also, *Healey v Howlett* (1917)). Special rules apply to purchases from a specific bulk. Risk will normally pass with property (s 20).

Transfer of title

The basic rule of transfer of title is *nemo dat* (s 21(1)). Exceptions exist in relation to indications from the conduct of the owner (s 21(1)); sale by a factor (s 21(2)(a)); sale under a statutory or common law power (s 21(2)(b)); sale under a voidable title (s 23); seller left in possession (s 24); buyer in possession (s 25).

Retention of title

The possibility of the seller retaining a right of disposal pending payment is acknowledged by s 19, but *Romalpa* clauses have had limited effect in protecting the seller once the buyer no longer possesses the goods in their original state.

Implied terms

The Act implies various terms into all sale of goods contracts:

- Title (s 12)

  Implied condition of 'right to sell' at the time when property is to pass. There is also an implied warranty of quiet possession and freedom from encumbrances.

- Description (s 13)

  Most sales will be 'by description'. There is an implied condition of compliance with the description. Note the distinction between description and quality, and that there must be reliance on the description by the buyer (*Harlingdon and Leinster Enterprises v Christopher Hull Fine Art Ltd* (1990)).

- Satisfactory quality (s 14(2))

  Where the sale is made in the course of a business (as defined in *Stevenson v Rogers* (1999), there is an implied condition of satisfactory quality (s 14(6)). It covers everything supplied (*Wilson v Rickett Cockerell Co* (1954)), but not defects revealed, or which should have been discovered, by the buyer's inspection (s 14(2)). The goods must be fit for all their common uses. Satisfactory quality can relate not only to functionality, but also appearance, safety and durability (s 14(2B)).

- Fitness for a particular purpose (s 14(3))

  This implied condition can apply where the goods have only one purpose (*Priest v Last* (1903)). Otherwise, the particular purpose must be made known to the seller (*Griffiths v Peter Conway* (1939)), and there must have been reasonable reliance on the seller's skill and judgment.

- Sale by sample (s 15)

  There is a an implied condition of correspondence with the sample in quality.

Exclusion of implied terms

The exclusion of implied terms is governed by s 6 of the Unfair Contract and Terms Act 1977. There can be no exclusion of s 12. Sections 13, 14, and 15 cannot be excluded from a consumer contract. In business contracts, these can be excluded, provided the term meets the requirement of reasonableness.

Delivery

Delivery and payment are concurrent conditions (s 28). There are strict rules about delivery of the wrong quantity (s 30). Instalment deliveries are dealt with by s 31.

Acceptance

Acceptance of the goods will deprive the buyer of the right to reject. The buyer should have a chance to examine the goods (s 34). The buyer will be deemed to have accepted where this is intimated to the seller, or the buyer does some act inconsistent with the seller's ownership (s 35). Acceptance will also arise from lapse of time – a strict test was applied in *Bernstein v Pamsons Motors (Golders Green) Ltd* (1987).

Damages

The normal contractual rules apply to damages, but in relation to non-delivery, and non-acceptance, the starting point is the 'available market' test (ss 50 and 51). The seller may also bring an action for the price (s 49).

Unpaid seller's property rights

The unpaid seller's property rights are the right of lien (s 41); stoppage in transit (s 44); and resale (s 48).

FURTHER READING

General

Adams, J and Brownsword, R, *Understanding Contract Law*, 2nd edn, 1994, Fontana

Atiyah, PS, *Essays on Contract*, 1986, Clarendon

Atiyah, PS, *The Rise and Fall of Freedom of Contract*, 1979, OUP

Beale, H and Dugdale, T, 'Contracts between businessmen: planning and the use of contractual remedies' (1975) 2 Br J of Law and Soc 45

Campbell, D and Harris, D, 'Flexibility in long term contractual relationships: the role of co-operation' (1993) 20 J of Law and Soc 166

Collins, H, *The Law of Contract*, 3rd edn, 1997, Butterworths

Fried, C, *Contract as Promise*, 1981, Harvard UP

Fuller, L and Perdue, W, 'The reliance interest in contract damages' (1936) 46 Yale LJ 52 and 373

Gilmore, G, *The Death of Contract*, 1974, Ohio State UP

Kronman, A and Posner, R, *Economics of Contract Law*, 1979, Little, Brown

Macaulay, S, 'Non-Contractual Relations in Business' (1963) 28 Am Sociological Rev 35

Macneil, IR, 'Contracts: adjustments of long term economic relations under classical, neo-classical and relational contract law' (1978) 72 Northwestern UL Rev 854

Posner, R, *Economic Analysis of Law*, 4th edn, 1992, Little, Brown

Smith, SA, 'Performance, punishment and the nature of contractual obligations' (1997) 60 MLR 360

Creation of the Contractual Obligation (Chapters 2–6)

Adams, J and Brownsword, R, 'Privity and the concept of the network contract' (1990) 10 Legal Studies 12

Adams, J, Beyleveld, D and Brownsword, R, 'Privity of contract – the benefits and the burdens of law reform' (1997) 60 MLR 238

Beatson, J, 'Reforming the law of contracts for the benefit of third parties: a second bite at the cherry' [1992] Current Legal Problems 1

Beyleveld, D and Brownsword, R, 'Privity, transitivity and rationality' (1991) 54 MLR 48

Gardner, S, 'Trashing with trollope: a deconstruction of the postal rules in contract' (1992) 12 OJLS 170

Halson, R, 'Sailors, sub-contractors and consideration' (1990) 106 LQR 183

Halson, R, 'The offensive limits of promissory estoppel' [1999] LMCLQ 256

Hamson, CJ, 'The reform of consideration' (1938) 54 LQR 233

Hedley, S, 'Keeping contract in its place: *Balfour v Balfour* and the enforceability of informal agreements' (1985) 5 OJLS 391

Hepple, B, 'Intention to create legal relations' (1970) 29 CLJ 122

Hird, NJ and Blair, A, 'Minding your own business – *Williams v Roffey* revisited' [1996] J of Business Law 254

Howarth, W, 'The meaning of objectivity in contract' (1984) 100 LQR 205

Law Commission, *Privity of Contract – Contracts for the Benefit of Third Parties,* Cm 3329, 1996

Lewis, R, 'Contracts between businessmen: reform of the law of firm offers' (1982) 9 Br J of Law and Soc 153

Luther, P, 'Campbell, Espinasse and the sailors: text and context in the common law' (1999) 19 Legal Studies 526

McKendrick, E, 'The battle of the forms and the law of restitution' (1988) 8 OJLS 197

Miller, CJ, '*Felthouse v Bindley* revisited' (1972) 35 MLR 489

O'Sullivan, J, 'In defence of *Foakes v Beer*' (1996) 55 CLJ 219

Simpson, AWB, 'Quackery and contract law: the case of the Carbolic Smoke Ball' [1985] J Leg St 345

Thompson, MP, 'Representation to expectation: estoppel as a cause of action' (1983) 42 CLJ 257

Unger, R, 'Intention to create legal relations, mutuality and consideration' (1956) 19 MLR 96

The Contents of the Contract (Chapters 7–8)

Adams, J and Brownsword, R, 'The Unfair Contract Terms Act: a decade of discretion' (1988) 104 LQR 94

Beale, H, 'Unfair contracts in Britain and Europe' [1989] Current Legal Problems 197

Bradgate, R, 'Unreasonable standard terms' (1997) 60 MLR 582

Collins, H, 'Good faith in European contract law' (1994) 14 OJLS 229

Coote, B, *Exception Clauses*, 1964, Sweet & Maxwell

Dean, M, 'Unfair contract terms: the European approach' (1993) 56 MLR 581

Kronman, A, 'Paternalism and the law of contract' (1983) Yale LJ 763

Law Commission, *Law of Contract: The Parol Evidence Rule*, No 154, Cmnd 9700, 1986

Macdonald, E, 'Exclusion clauses: the ambit of s 13(1) of the Unfair Contract Terms Act 1977' (1992) Legal Studies 277

Macdonald, E, 'Incorporation of contract terms by a consistent course of dealing' (1988) 8 Legal Studies 48

McMeel, G, 'The rise of commercial construction in contract law' [1998] LMCLQ 382

Phang, A, 'Implied terms in English law: some recent developments' [1993] J of Business Law 242

Phang, A, 'Implied terms revisited' [1990] J of Business Law 394

Reynolds, F, 'Unfair contract terms' (1994) 110 LQR 3

Spencer, J, 'Signature, consent and the rule in *L'Estrange v Graucob*' (1973) 32 CLJ 103

Yates, D, *Exclusion Clauses in Contracts*, 2nd edn, 1982, Sweet & Maxwell

Vitiating Factors (Chapters 9–12)

Allen, D, *Misrepresentation*, 1988, Sweet & Maxwell

Bennett, HN, 'Statements of fact and statements of belief in insurance contract law and general contract law' (1998) 61 MLR 886

Buckley, RA, 'Illegal transactions: chaos or discretion' (2000) Legal Studies 155

Cartwright, J, 'Damages for misrepresentation' [1987] Conv 423

Cartwright, J, '*Solle v Butcher* and the doctrine of mistake in contract' (1987) 103 LQR 584

Cartwright, J, *Unequal Bargaining*, 1991, OUP

Chen-Wishart, M, 'The *O'Brien* principle and substantive unfairness' (1997) 56 CLJ 60

Cretney, S, 'The little woman and the big bad bank' (1992) 108 LQR 534

Enman, SR, 'Doctrines of unconscionability in Canadian, English and Commonwealth contract law' (1987) 16 Anglo-Am LR 191

Fehlberg, B, 'The husband, the bank, the wife and her signature' (1994) 57 MLR 467

Grodecki, J, '*In pari delicto*' (1955) 71 LQR 254

Halson, R, 'Opportunism, economic duress and contractual modifications' (1991) 107 LQR 649

Kronman, A, 'Mistake, disclosure, information, and the law of contracts' (1978) 7 Legal Studies 1

Phang, A, 'Common mistake in English law: the proposed merger of common law and equity' (1989) Legal Studies 291

Smith, SA, 'Contracting under pressure: a theory of duress' (1997) 56 CLJ 343

Smith, SA, 'In defence of substantive fairness' (1996) 112 LQR 138

Tiplady, D, 'The limits of undue influence' (1985) 48 MLR 579

Tjio, H, '*O'Brien* and unconscionability' (1997) 113 LQR 10

Trebilcock, M, 'An economic approach to unconscionability', in Reiter, B and Swan, J (eds), *Studies in Contract Law*, 1980, Butterworths

Trebilcock, M, *The Common Law Doctrine of Restraint of Trade*, 1986, Sweet & Maxwell

Treitel, G, 'Mistake in contract' (1988) 104 LQR 501

Discharge and Remedies (Chapters 13–15)

Beale, H, 'Penalties in termination provisions' (1988) 104 LQR 355

Beale, H, *Remedies for Breach of Contract*, 1980, Sweet & Maxwell

Brownsword, R, 'Retrieving reasons, retrieving rationality? A new look at the right to withdraw for breach of contract' (1992) 5 J of Contract Law 83

Burrows, A, 'Specific performance at the cross roads' (1984) 4 Legal Studies 102

Burrows, A, *Remedies for Torts and Breach of Contract*, 2nd edn, 1994, Butterworths

Cartwright, J, 'Remoteness of damage in contract and tort: a reconsideration' (1996) 55 CLJ 488

Chandler, A, 'Self-induced frustration, forseeability and risk' (1990) NILQ 362

Harris, D, 'Incentives to perform, or break contracts' [1992] Current Legal Problems 29

Harris, D, 'Penalties and forfeiture: contractual remedies specified by the parties' [1990] LMCLQ 158

Harris, D, *Remedies in Tort and Contract*, 1988, Weidenfeld and Nicolson

Haycroft, A and Waksman, D, 'Restitution and frustration' [1984] J of Business Law 207

Hedley, S, 'Carriage by sea: frustration and *force majeure*' (1990) 49 CLJ 209

McKendrick, E (ed), *Force Majeure and the Frustration of Contract*, 1991, Lloyd's of London

McKendrick, E (ed), *Force Majeure*, 2nd edn, 1995, LLP Professional

Ogus, AI, *The Law of Damages*, 1973, Butterworths

Phang, A, 'Specific performance – exploring the roots of settled practice' (1998) 61 MLR 421

Poole, J, 'Damages for breach of contract – compensation and personal preferences: *Ruxley Electronics and Construction Ltd v Forsyth*' (1996) 59 MLR 272

Reynolds, F, 'Discharge of contract by breach' (1981) 97 LQR 541

Shea, A, 'Discharge from performance of contracts by failure of condition' (1979) 42 MLR 623

Smith, SA, 'Performance, punishment and the nature of contractual obligation' (1997) 60 MLR 360

Stewart, A and Carter, J, 'Frustration contracts and statutory adjustment: the case for a reappraisal' (1990) 49 CLJ 66

Trakman, L, 'Frustrated contracts and legal fictions' (1983) 46 MLR 39

Treitel, G, 'Damages on rescission for breach of contract' [1987] LMCLQ 143

Wightman, J, 'Negligent valuations and a drop in the property market: the limits of the expectation loss principle" (1998) 61 MLR 68

Yates, D, 'Drafting *force majeure* and related clauses' (1991) 3 J of Contract Law 186

INDEX

Index

Index

Index